"Denault does an amazing job with this biography, redefining the term *exhaustive research* in the process. After just a few pages into this book it was obvious Todd Denault had written an instant classic. I cannot recommend this book enough."   – www.hockeybookreviews.com

"While there are many sports books as anyone who delves into the subject will soon find out, *Jacques Plante* is a sports book like few others. Even those not enthusiastic about hockey will find this book hard to put down. It has the drama of a good mystery and the excitement of a thriller."
                                                        – *CM* magazine

THE
GREATEST
GAME

THE MONTREAL CANADIENS,

THE RED ARMY,

AND THE NIGHT THAT SAVED HOCKEY

TODD DENAULT

McClelland & Stewart

Library and Archives Canada Cataloguing in Publication

Denault, Todd
    The greatest game : the Montreal Canadiens, the Red Army, and the night that saved hockey / Todd Denault.

ISBN 978-0-7710-2634-8

1. Montreal Canadiens (Hockey team) – History. 2. HC CSKA Moscow – History. 3. Super Series (Hockey tournament) – History. I. Title.

GV847.7.D45 2010   796.962'66   C2010-901570-3

We acknowledge the financial support of the Government of Canada through the Book Publishing Industry Development Program and that of the Government of Ontario through the Ontario Media Development Corporation's Ontario Book Initiative. We further acknowledge the support of the Canada Council for the Arts and the Ontario Arts Council for our publishing program.

Published simultaneously in the United States of America by McClelland & Stewart Ltd., P.O. Box 1030, Plattsburgh, New York 12901

Library of Congress Control Number: 2010934189

Typeset in Baskerville by M&S, Toronto
Printed and bound in the United States of America

ANCIENT FOREST
FRIENDLY

This book is printed on acid-free paper that is 100% recycled, ancient-forest friendly (100% post-consumer waste).

McClelland & Stewart Ltd.
75 Sherbourne Street
Toronto, Ontario
M5A 2P9
www.mcclelland.com

1 2 3 4 5   14 13 12 11 10

To the memory of my grandfather Ted Denault, who from the comfort of his own living room never missed a Montreal Canadiens game on the television – right up until the very end, which came on the evening of December 31, 1975.

"In a display of skill and sportsmanship rarely seen here in recent times, the Montreal Canadiens and the Central Red Army demonstrated to millions of Canadians that their national game reaches an art form when discipline and hard work take priority over mayhem. In recapturing their primacy as Canada's foremost sporting aggregation, the Canadiens did an incalculable favour for the youth of the nation with their exemplary conduct. It came when hockey was at its nadir, beset on all sides for its avarice, violence, and poor quality."

TIM BURKE, Montreal *Gazette*, January 2, 1976

"The New Year's Eve game is etched in my memory forever."

DANNY GALLIVAN

CONTENTS

PROLOGUE

Montreal, Quebec, December 19, 1975. When it came to getting the best tickets for events at the Montreal Forum, Mike Boone was a seasoned veteran. The box office opened at half past nine each weekday morning and Boone knew how to time it perfectly so that he could be at the front of the line to score the best seats going for hot tickets such as concerts by Bob Dylan or the Rolling Stones.[1]

From his experience of lineups past, Boone figured that this Friday morning would be no different, especially since the weather was biting cold. When he stepped outside his door, the wind lashed at his face, proving that the forecast of −24 degrees Celsius had not factored in the wind chill. But when he arrived at the Forum an hour and a half before the box office opened, he was dismayed to find the longest lineup he'd ever seen.

In twelve days' time, the Montreal Canadiens, the most successful franchise in the NHL, would play host to their Russian counterparts, the Central Red Army, the pre-eminent team in the Soviet Union. This first-ever encounter between the teams would be the key game in what was being promoted as the "Super Series." The lengthening line of fans waiting in the freezing air that morning was testament to the anticipation the public held for this history-making matchup, to take place on New Year's Eve.

Despite the unbearable cold, the line stretched along the face of the Forum, down Ste-Catherine Street, then north along the eastern side of the building. Boone counted at least one hundred people in line ahead of him and settled in for the long wait.

For the past year, he had been employed by the *Montreal Star*, the largest English daily newspaper in the city. For Boone, it was a dream job. He spent most of his time at the paper covering college sports, with the occasional foray into baseball.[2]

As a writer in the sports department, Boone could have asked his sports editor, the legendary Red Fisher, for complimentary tickets or media passes for the upcoming game. Fisher had spent the last two decades writing about all sports but had gained fame as the foremost English-language chronicler of the Montreal Canadiens. Like many other aspiring sports journalists, Boone had grown up reading and idolizing Fisher. Though Boone worked alongside the venerable editor, he felt intimidated in his presence. In his first year with the *Star* he couldn't recall a single conversation between them. And so the thought of approaching him for tickets was out of the question.

Instead, Boone chose to stand outside, in the bitter morning cold, waiting in the longest line of his experience. As uncomfortable as it might be to wait, the possibility of missing the upcoming New Year's Eve game had never crossed Boone's mind.

At 9:30 Mike Boone reached the wicket. And even though the tickets he got were in the white section, in the far reaches of the Forum, Boone couldn't contain his excitement. He clutched his two tickets tightly, like a kid with the gift he's longed for on Christmas morning.

Billed as a mere exhibition game, this contest, it turned out, would be history in the making, an event marking the dawn of a new era in hockey.

On New Year's Eve Mike Boone climbed to the white section and took in the game, in the company of thousands of other enthralled spectators in the Forum. In the thirty-five years since then, he has never regretted that frigid morning standing in line, not for a second.

"With the exception of the birth of my daughter, the 3–3 tie was the greatest event I've ever seen in my life."[3]

PART ONE

THE HISTORY

"To this day I do not understand why the best Canadian professionals cannot meet the leading European selected teams from time to time at some interesting type of tournament. Both sides would win from such a meeting. The professionals would get acquainted with another school of hockey. The Europeans would learn much from the Canadians. The hockey fans would gain an attractive spectacle."

ANATOLI TARASOV, *Road to Olympus*, 1969

1.

A RUDE AWAKENING

Stockholm, Sweden, March 7, 1954. Canada is a country often divided by geographic, spiritual, and linguistic differences, and yet there is one sport that can bring everyone together. The first organized indoor hockey game on ice took place in Montreal on March 3, 1875, and by the dawn of the twentieth century, hockey was established as Canada's most popular sport.

The popularity of hockey soon expanded into other countries, particularly in Europe. At the 1920 Winter Olympics the first World Championship was contested, and Canada, represented by the Winnipeg Falcons, breezed to the gold medal, outscoring its opponents 27–1.[1]

The World Championships became an annual event in 1930, and Canada, represented by teams like the RCAF Flyers and the Edmonton Mercurys, emerged as hockey's dominant country, winning fifteen of the first eighteen championships in which it entered. In spite of their previous successes, the Canadian Amateur Hockey Association was unable to find a team that was willing to go overseas and represent the country at the 1954 World Championship in Stockholm. The issue was the ever increasing financial concerns. In addition to the travelling costs involved in such a venture, there was a growing resentment from within the association that the Canadian teams were not getting a fair shake overseas. In the days leading up to the tournament the Canadian teams would routinely play exhibition games throughout Europe. Wherever they played, the touring Canadians gathered tremendous crowds, but they received very little, if any, of the gate receipts. This left the touring Canadian team with no way of recouping their travel, meal, and accommodation expenses. As well, many of the Canadian teams had become increasingly frustrated with what was seen as a bias against the "Canadian" style of hockey, which in the view of many of their European opponents and officials was characterized by its aggressiveness, belligerence, and overt physicality.

Despite all of these issues and with many of the best Senior A teams declining the invitation, the Canadian Amateur Hockey Association found a willing team in the East York Lyndhursts. A Senior B amateur team located in suburban Toronto, the Lyndhursts were not up to the standards of some of Canada's previous entries, many of whom were former Allan Cup winners, which annually crowned the best team in Senior A hockey.

However, once the tournament began, none of this seemed to matter, as the Lyndhursts outscored their opponents 57–5, winning all six of their games with ease. In their seventh game, the Lyndhursts would be playing for the gold medal. Their opponents were participating in their first international tournament and like Canada had won all six of their games. For the very first time a Canadian team would play against a Soviet team in an encounter with serious political overtones.

In March 1954, the Cold War was less than a decade old and was already characterized by an uninterrupted state of political conflict, military tension, and economic rivalry that placed the Soviet Union (and its satellite countries) on one side and Canada (and much of the Western world, led by the United States) on the other side.

A unique characteristic of the Cold War was that the two sides never engaged in direct conflict but instead focused their attention on competition on every level. The two warring sides struggled for military superiority, raced each other to the moon, and fought for scientific and technical supremacy. In the quest for global authority, propaganda became a valuable tool in the conflict and the fields of sports and culture became important fronts, whether it was events like the Olympics or high-profile chess games. Hockey was not immune from this conflict and international matches took on an added importance, as "us vs. them" became a rallying cry for both sides.

The deciding game of the 1954 World Hockey Championship was contested in the afternoon. The combination of the warm spring weather and an outdoor facility normally reserved for football made the skating surface the worst it had been throughout the tournament. In among a crowd of sixteen thousand spectators sat a lone reporter from Canada representing Canadian Press.

As the Soviets skated out, he couldn't help but make note of their appearance. Their jerseys hung too long on their slender builds, their sticks were all homemade, and in a time when most players went bare-headed, the Soviet team sported bicycle helmets. For the Lyndhursts the Soviet team may as well have come from another planet. The Canadians were unfamiliar with many of the Soviet players and woefully unprepared for what was to come. The Russians, on the other hand, were not so ill prepared. In the days leading up to their encounter the Russians had closely studied the team from East Lyndhurst. They were alarmed by the loud noise of the puck careening off the boards as the Canadians shots let out a large thumping sound. Not possessing any hard shooters themselves, the Russians strategy was to take away the powerful shot from their Canadian adversaries.[2]

The game was barely a few minutes old when the differences between the two teams became apparent to all those in attendance. The Lyndhursts seemed nervous and played a tentative game, allowing the Soviets to take control, using a variety of quick passes, hard checking, and superior skating. The stunned Canadian squad was unable to mount any sort of counterattack.

"The Russians also took a leaf out of Canada's book by bodychecking fiercely and by racing to face the Canadians before they had time to start plays," reported Canadian Press. "The result was that the Canadian attacks were limited to stray sorties."[3]

"Their slowest skater was faster than our fastest skater," remembered Canadian forward Eric Unger, expressing just how outclassed the Lyndhursts were that day.[4]

"Their passes clicked while Canada's went astray," Canadian Press observed. "Their defense took competent charge of most East York attacks while the Canadians frequently left Goalie Don Lockhart unprotected in their headlong charges up the ice. The former Maritime netminder played brilliantly but the constant Russian pressure took a steady toll."[5] With their offensive thrusts going virtually unopposed, the Soviets ran up a 4–0 lead after the first period, extended it to 7–1 at the end of the second period, and protected their lead on their way to icing a 7–2 win and the country's first championship.

As the final buzzer echoed through the stadium, dozens of excited Russian officials, clad in long black coats, ran onto the ice and planted triumphant kisses on their jubilant players. The directors of the tournament then presented the players with their gold medals as the Soviet anthem played in the background. Standing on their own blue line the defeated Canadians could only watch as the Soviet flag was slowly hoisted in the air.

In a war where propaganda was a valuable tool, the victory was treated in the Soviet Union as a national triumph. The state-sponsored newspapers downplayed the Lyndhursts' amateur status, instead reiterating that the Soviets had defeated "Team Canada."

And while the Soviet Union celebrated, Canada found itself in the midst of a national crisis. Canada had slipped from its pedestal, and the sport had turned a corner.

Lionel Conacher, a sitting Member of Parliament and the man honoured as Canada's greatest athlete of the first half of the twentieth century, proclaimed the result "a catastrophe" for Canadian hockey.[6] "Canadian youngsters are brought up to believe that we have the best hockey players in the world," said Conacher, expressing in words the shame that spread through the Canadian hockey community. "Now they know only that the Russians beat us."[7]

Conn Smythe, the founder and then-managing director of the Toronto Maple Leafs, took it a step further, announcing on the night after the decisive game "that his team is prepared to go to Russia immediately . . . we're only interested in one thing – to keep the old flag flying."[8]

Smythe went on to boldly announce that once the NHL playoff season concluded in late April that the Leafs would be available to travel to Moscow to confront the champion Soviets.

In the end, the words of challenge did not amount to much. The Toronto Maple Leafs never did make the trek to Russia. In fact, it would be another twenty-one years before a team from the National Hockey League faced off against a team from the Soviet Union.

2.

THE FATHER OF RUSSIAN HOCKEY

Krefeld, West Germany, March 6, 1955. Yevgeny Babich was inconsolable.

Alone in his hotel room, he played out in his mind what had happened a few hours before at the Rheineland-Halle. After the euphoria of winning the World Championship gold medal the year before in 1954, a second-place finish was unacceptable. The top right-winger in all of the Soviet Union started breaking sticks, then throwing the remains outside the window to the street below. For good measure, he also took his skates and heaved them into the Krefeld night.[1]

In the year leading up to the 1955 World Championship much had changed, not the least of which was the renewed vigour and desire of Canada to recapture the gold medal.

"Russia's win last year stunned the Canadian sports world," the *Globe and Mail* proclaimed. "Nothing less than victory this year would have appeased those who felt the defeat reflected on Canada as the cradle of hockey."[2]

Suddenly, teams that only months before had refused to travel to the World Championship were now rapidly lining up for the chance to avenge last year's defeat of the East York Lyndhursts. The winners of the 1954 Allan Cup, British Columbia's Pentiction Vees, accepted the challenge and took on the responsibility of representing Canada at the 1955 World Championship. Led by the notorious Warwick brothers, Bill, Dick, and player/coach Grant, and supplemented with some imported talent, the Vees were undoubtedly the best senior team in Canada, as well as the toughest. Just as the Lyndhursts had done the year before, the Vees romped their way toward the gold-medal game, scoring sixty-one goals in eight games, while allowing a meagre six into their own net. In the gold-medal game they were matched against the only other undefeated team in the tournament: the defending champions from the Soviet Union.

In contrast to the year before, the 1955 World Championship garnered considerable interest, especially from the Canadian media. In the space of only one year the World Championships had gone from a mere afterthought in Canada to a test of the national identity. Led in goal by the seemingly impenetrable Ivan McLelland, the Vees were quickly able to assert their physical superiority and territorially dominate the overmatched Russian squad. The Canadians opened the scoring four minutes into the game and added a goal in the second period before putting the game away with three more goals in the third, resulting in a 5–0 win.

As the seconds ticked off the clock, the delirious Canadians that made up most of the crowd leapt over the boards to get a piece of the victorious players, who "jumped wildly about, hollering and singing. Meanwhile, the Russians grimly left the ice, their world crown gone."[3]

"Canadian superiority asserted itself," the *Globe and Mail* reported the next day, "as the Allan Cup champions erased a smudge on Canada's hockey reputation. The way the V's beat Russia was a triumph for the game as it is played in Canada . . . [4] The victory fully redeemed Canadian hockey honour."[5]

For the crestfallen Russians, and in particular for Yevgeny Babich, the defeat was a crushing blow.

"Babich could do anything," remembered Anatoli Tarasov, the head coach on his Soviet Elite League team, the Central Red Army. "He would wind up a beautiful attack, he could feed his partners sizzling passes and if need be, he could play defense." Yet for Tarasov, the fact that Babich was a highly skilled player represented only a small part of the equation. Of greater importance to his demanding coach was the undeniable fact that in his eyes Babich was a complete player, one who was willing to sacrifice his individual goals for the greater good of the team, a player who measured success not in goals and assists, but in championship gold.[6]

Anatoli Tarasov was that rarest of hockey coaches, a man who studied theory and taught tactics. An extremely complex man, he was part psychologist and part tyrant, and a strict believer in the principles of communism. He adored Canadian hockey, but his ego, along with his ambition, allowed him to believe that he could improve on it. In the process he created a different style of hockey, perfected and played the Soviet way.

Not only was he able to shape an international hockey superpower in his towering image, but he was able to do it in the relative seclusion of the Soviet Union. Because his country did not have an entrenched hockey tradition, he had the opportunity to try different types of tactics and training. He was free to experiment, to keep what he liked and discard what he didn't.[7] In the end he pioneered techniques, philosophies, and ideals that have since been adopted worldwide.

The conclusion of the Second World War saw the Soviet Union emerge as a superpower on the global stage. As an "iron curtain" descended throughout Europe, cutting off the East from the West, Russia began to look inward for ways to spread its Communist influence. The Soviet Union was swept up in a tidal wave of patriotism, which not only intensified the people's love of country but also renewed their belief in the virtues of the Communist system.

The Soviet Union, eager to establish superiority in all fields, became a leading cultural force as the Bolshoi Ballet, the Moscow Circus, and the Moscow Symphony Orchestra all became famous throughout the world. In part because of the ever-present need to increase military and defence funding, science and technology thrived. Crucial to this expansion was development in sports, which was seen by the ruling Communist Party as crucial for spreading both political philosophy and nation building on a world stage.[8]

In 1946, the Central Committee, the top policy-making body in the Soviet Union, decreed that sport was to be the "provision for the development of a mass physical culture movement in the country and for the rise in the level of sports mastery of Soviet athletes. The fulfillment of these objectives should secure the victory of Soviet athletes in the world championships in the most important sports in the near future." In short, the final goal was absolute: world sports supremacy.[9]

For the Soviets the ultimate display of sporting supremacy was the Olympic Games. And in the Winter Games, no sport was more important than hockey. The Soviets made it their mission to dominate the sport, and to do that they would have to wrest the title of hockey pre-eminence from the country that invented the game, Canada.

"Eight time zones away were the Rocket, Howe, Maple Leaf Gardens," wrote Ken Dryden and Roy MacGregor years later in their book, *Home Game*. "It seemed an impossible, unbridgeable distance between that game and this . . . their challenge was enormous."[10]

Before the war, hockey had been a game that was at best, played sporadically in the Soviet Union. It was the ice sport of bandy, a game very similar to field hockey, which had captivated the Russians for years. Played outdoors, with eleven players to a side, on an ice surface the size of a soccer field, bandy had long been the country's winter sport of choice.

The process of educating the Russian public about their new winter pastime, all the while converting bandy players to the unknown sport of ice hockey, quickly began. In anticipation of that fall's inaugural season of the Russian hockey league, a group of students from the Moscow Physical Training Institute gave a public demonstration of the sport in the early part of 1946. The league was made up of twelve teams, eight of them from military and police organizations, with each playing a seven-game schedule that first season, which lasted only one month. The fact that a majority of the league's players were young, professional, Communist ideologues helped set the template for the future Russian player: obedient, disciplined, and a believer in the greater good of the collective.

The league's leading scorer that initial season was Anatoli Tarasov, who starred for the Air Force team. The first championship team was the Moscow Dynamo, coached by the quiet and reserved Arkady Chernyshev. Coincidentally, both men would be among the most important names in Soviet hockey over the next quarter of a century.

In addition to being the leading scorer that first year, Tarasov coached the Air Force team. However, by the next season, Tarasov was behind the bench of the Central Red Army team after a dispute over player selection with Vasily Stalin, the son of the long-time Soviet dictator Joseph Stalin, who took a personal interest in the Air Force team.[11]

In retrospect, the move was a testament to Tarasov's obstinence and inflexibility, qualities that later proved to be invaluable in the development of Soviet hockey. Disagreeing with a Stalin in the Soviet Union of that era was considered to be unwise, at the very least.

Yet Tarasov was allowed to move on and he quickly built the Central Red Army team into the dominant force in the early years of the nascent Russian league, winning the championship in 1948, 1949, and 1950. Tarasov was soon established as his country's leading hockey voice. In 1950, he published his first book on the sport and introduced dryland training to supplement the more traditional hockey workouts of the day.

Not surprisingly, Tarasov's success did not go unnoticed, least of all by his old adversary, Vasily Stalin, who ordered three of the Red Army's best players to his Air Force team. The public was led to believe that the players had joined the Air Force team voluntarily, which had not been the case. However, there was no recourse available for the players or Tarasov. Such was the inherent power in being the son of the Soviet dictator. Bolstered by many of the league's best players, the Vasily Stalin–run Air Force team took the league championship in 1951, 1952, and 1953.

Vasily Stalin's dominant role in the Soviet league came to an end on March 5, 1953, with the death of his father. Without his father, Vasily's power and privilege soon disappeared. A little over a month later on April 28, 1953, he was arrested on a series of charges, including criminal negligence and denigrating the new Soviet leadership. He would spend the next decade in and out of penitentiaries before succumbing to the effects of chronic alcoholism on March 19, 1962.[12]

With Vasily Stalin out of the picture, Tarasov was elevated to his rightful post as the tsar of Soviet hockey. Assuming control, Tarasov's methods and teachings stood in stark contrast to his Canadian contemporaries. In Canada, a nation that stressed the rights of the individual, young players at the time were coached by various coaches, stressing different philosophies, and made their way up the ranks based on their natural ability. In the Soviet Union, where the rights of the collective were paramount, and with the support of the government, intermediary coaches taught the sport based solely on Tarasov's theories, resulting in a generation of young hockey players being well versed in Tarasov's way of playing the game.

Early on, Tarasov harboured some doubts about what lay in front of him. He had originally sought permission to travel to Canada to learn the game from its leading practitioners first-hand. However, a fateful conversation with friend and soccer coach Mikhail Tovarovsky set Tarasov on a different path. "There's nothing for you in Canada," Tovarovsky advised him. "Go your own way. Devise your own style of hockey."[13] At the time, not copying the Canadians seemed to be pure folly. However, in time, it would turn out to be a stroke of genius.

Tarasov became obsessed with hockey theory, spending every spare moment scouring available hockey texts and watching 8mm films of the Stanley Cup Finals.[14]

In preparing his ideal hockey player, Tarasov stressed the importance of an all-consuming physical excellence, which could only be achieved through a relentless schedule of weightlifting and strenuous dryland training. The end goal for Tarasov was to develop a set of players who not only were second to none in physical conditioning and skill but could also play the game without emotion. In essence, the Soviet player was expected to subjugate his individual desires and personality to those of the team.[15]

Tarasov's conditioning program was unorthodox. In one of his most famous strength-building exercises, he designed a thirteen-kilogram rubber belt that was worn by his players during practice. As a result Tarasov's players had enhanced leg, back, and upper body muscles, all the while improving their balance on skates. He also had his players run on the sand of various beaches to build up strength in their ankles.[16]

Tarasov stressed the beauty of the game to his charges and forbade anything remotely resembling rough play, feeling it tarnished him, his players, and their country. He believed that a roughhousing style of play was a sign of cowardice and that the end result, a period of time spent in the penalty box, made the whole team suffer. He later wrote that "courage means the ability to stay out of a fight."[17] Tarasov appreciated quiet courage from his players but above all wanted them to be efficient. Such opinions would have been considered blasphemy in Canadian hockey circles at the time.

"He viewed hockey as an art, with the coach as choreographer, the players as performers," Roy MacGregor later wrote. "The principles of dance and piano – endless practice, repeated movements, perfected technique – would create a base from which true artistry could grow."[18]

Interestingly, just as Tarasov was beginning to build the Soviet hockey system, a Canadian came forward with many of the same ideas. Published in 1951, Lloyd Percival's *The Hockey Handbook* was the first book to take a methodical approach toward hockey skills, team play, personal diet, and conditioning. In the book Percival laid out his training methods, which were designed to provide the skater with greater balance, agility, and lateral movement. Each of these would, in time, become hallmarks of the Soviet game.

In Canada, the book was ignored, if not roundly dismissed, by those involved in the sport. An NHL head coach at the time called the book "the product of a three-year-old mind." Tarasov, on the other hand, studied the book intensely, and upon meeting Percival told him that "your wonderful book . . . introduced us to the mysteries of Canadian hockey, I have read it like a schoolboy."[19]

Percival's book was so ignored by the Canadian hockey establishment that when the Soviets began to make their mark at the international hockey level they were praised by Canadian journalists for their novel approaches to physical conditioning. Of course, many of these approaches were first laid out in *The Hockey Handbook*.

As Russian hockey gained in popularity in the late fifties, Tarasov's methods became more widespread as various sports schools were formed throughout the Soviet Union. The move toward standardizing Tarasov's theories was also aided by the government. In 1956, special boarding schools designed for the athletically gifted were created by the Kremlin. Four years later saw the introduction of extended day schools that focused on sports development, with the students working in their chosen sport, both before and after regular school hours. Set up throughout the greater Soviet Union, these schools varied in their operation, but the main admission requirement was that prospective students demonstrate athletic prowess in an entrance examination. By 1970, the enrolment in these schools would pass the five million mark. These schools served as factories for those who would become the nation's future pre-eminent athletes and hockey players – with all of them learning under the Tarasov influence.[20]

It's impossible to overstate the role that the government played in the rise of the sport in the Soviet Union. It provided the funding for these various schools, outfitted a generation of young hockey players, built more rinks, and created the infrastructure that allowed Tarasov's teachings to be put into practice.

In addition to building up a national program from scratch, Tarasov set about re-establishing the supremacy of the Central Red Army in Russian league play. In 1955, the Red Army recaptured the league championship, and repeated the feat in 1956, going undefeated in the now 28-game schedule, scoring 207 goals, and allowing only 29 along the way. After finishing as the league's runner-up in 1957, Tarasov's charges would win the next four league championships in a row.

Aside from having Tarosov, the circuit's premier coach, the Red Army run at the top was aided by its virtual monopoly on the country's top talent. Since all able-bodied Russian men were required to serve a term in the military, the Red Army had a clear advantage over the other Russian league clubs. By joining the Red Army team, one's military career would then consist entirely of practising and playing hockey. And being on the Red Army team almost automatically made one a member of the Russian National Team, since Tarasov coached both.

After losing to Canada at the 1955 World Championship, the Soviets rebounded the following year by capturing their first Olympic gold medal in hockey, at the games in Cortina d'Ampezzo, Italy. This particular win helped to validate the Russians on the world stage as an emerging hockey power, and not as a one-time fluke, as many had hoped.

A little over two years later, a Soviet team including some, but not all, of the country's best players became the first hockey team to play in Canada. Named the Soviet Selects, they played seven exhibition games against various senior and junior squads. Their arrival generated a significant amount of attention from a curious media, a skeptical group of the Canadian hockey elite, and the ticket-buying public. For many Canadians, this was their first opportunity to see the Soviet brand of hockey.

"The tremendous interest aroused by the first visit of a Russian hockey team to this country was most pronounced," wrote the *Globe and Mail.* "For instance, never in Canada has there been such a contingent from press, radio, and television for a mere workout of an athletic group. [There were] more than 200 rinksiders at the closed to the public practice . . . On the ice, the 20 players under former standout player and now coach, Anatoli Tarasov, whipped through the strangest gymnastics ever seen on a Canadian rink."[21]

Searching for contrasts between the Soviet style of play and their own, the Canadian reporters observed that unlike the standard NHL drills, which included odd-man rushes on the goalie, skating around the rink, and taking undefended shots on goal, the visiting Soviets practised the art of stickhandling while skating on one leg and worked on their balance by carrying teammates on their shoulders. But most shocking to the Canadian observers was their devotion to playing soccer on an outdoor field as a way to prepare for an upcoming game.

Those watching also made note of the propensity of the Soviet visitors to rotate their men on and off the ice as part of a five-man unit, as opposed to the Canadian way of changing their forward and defensive units separately. Not only were the offensive lines and defensive pairings changed at different times, but in Canadian hockey they were also initially constructed in complete isolation of one another. Tarasov took the opposite tack. "We have every right to demand that all players [five not three] be equal in their playing skills and, first of all, in their speed," Tarasov informed an inquisitive media. "If one of the defenseman is a slow skater, then it is no longer a fivesome, but a foursome."[22]

Tarasov called his approach to the game the "creative" or "attacking" style of hockey, which was built on the qualities of speed, mobility, teamwork, and passing. For a curious group of reporters he openly contrasted this with the Canadian style, which he referred to as "power" hockey, which was predicated on the twin virtues of bodychecking and intimidation.[23]

Sitting in the crowd for the first game of the exhibition series, Lloyd Percival's observations bore out some of Tarasov's claims. While the game played out in front of him Percival took note of the number of passes each team made. The Russians attempted 298 passes to the Canadian squad's 179, completing 198 to Canada's 96. These results confirmed the belief that the Russians played more of a possession game than Canada, who preferred to dump and chase the puck. Percival also noted that while the Canadian defencemen mainly passed the puck to a stationary target, the Russians followed a Tarasov rule that passes should always be made toward a teammate going at a faster speed than the puck holder.[24]

Despite the passing advantage, the Russians lost 7–2 to the Whitby Dunlops in the series kickoff at Maple Leaf Gardens. After the game, an NHL executive approached Tarasov and suggested that the Soviets make use of a Canadian coach who would help them take their game to the next level. A decade before Tarasov might have considered the offer, but his recent successes had given him the strength of confidence. Tarasov politely declined the offer and reflected later that a Canadian coach would not be familiar with the Soviet athlete, his background, and his psychological and physical makeup. In many ways, he was striving to preserve the purity of the Russian game as he had envisioned it.

In truth, on that first trip to Canada, Tarasov was taken aback by the lack of respect he received from much of the Canadian hockey elite, especially those from the NHL. "It had been my dream to see professional players," he remembered years later, the sting of rejection still all too fresh. "You [the Canadians] came to my practices and I went to yours, but there was a difference. You watched for five or ten minutes, and laughed at me and my players. Then everyone left. I sat through your practices bewitched. I've never written so much so fast. It pleased me that you laughed at us. Either you were too smug and didn't care, or you didn't understand what kind of hockey we were playing."[25]

Tarasov never forgot the slight and was able to harness it as motivation for his ultimate goal, an encounter between his Soviet team and the professionals of the NHL: his best versus Canada's best. But that would be many years in the future.

After the loss to the Dunlops on the opening night of the series, the touring Russians tied a Windsor team 5–5 and lost to the Kitchener-Waterloo Dutchmen 4–2 before reeling off a five-game winning streak to close the series.

The last game of the series was held before a sold-out crowd in Ottawa against the Ottawa-Hull Junior Canadiens, who had bolstered their lineup by adding five top-level junior players from the Toronto Marlboros. Standing behind the Junior Canadiens' bench that evening was a young NHL executive named Sam Pollock. Pollock, who moonlighted as the coach of the team, was an integral part of the Montreal Canadiens' front office. He had entered the Ottawa arena full of confidence. As soon as the puck was dropped, however, it didn't take long for all of his bluster to disappear. Despite the added skill, the touring Soviets pummelled the stunned Junior Canadiens 10–1.

"I'm simply amazed," Pollock told the reporters after the game. "Everything they did wrong before they do right now. They've learned to backcheck and forecheck, they don't pass blindly and their shooting is uncanny. And their goalie stops everything."[26]

It was during this tour that Tarasov and the Russian brain trust attended their first NHL game, between Toronto and Chicago, with the Leafs edging the Black Hawks 2–1. Pavel Korotkov, like Tarasov, a coach in the Russian league, observed that "the skills shown in this game were highly developed, much superior to ours. But we are catching up. Already we are equal or superior in many phases." The watching Soviets noted that while their own players were faster skaters on an individual basis, the pace of an NHL game was faster than their own. They also felt that their own goaltending was inferior when compared to their NHL compatriots.[27]

In retrospect, the first Russian tour of Canada was invaluable to the Soviets. For the first time Tarasov and company were able to observe for themselves what was considered the hockey ideal. For Tarasov, the NHL was the benchmark against which he would judge the progress of the Soviet system. It would remain that way until these adversaries finally squared off, but that was still far off in the distance.

On the other side, the first Russian tour of Canada was nothing more than a temporary curiosity, taken with all the seriousness of a circus exhibition by those in positions of power and influence in Canadian hockey.

"After all, what could they teach us," wrote Ken Dryden and Roy MacGregor decades later in their book, *Home Game,* reflecting the prevailing attitude of the day. "We were better. It was through this optic that we saw everything. We shot harder and more often; we rushed the puck solo in great end-to-end dashes; we bodychecked. If they passed more, shot and bodychecked less, it could only mean that they passed too much, shot and bodychecked too little. Because we were better. What interested Canadians about the Soviets was beating them, that's all, and that was getting harder."[28]

In 1957, for the first time, Russia hosted the World Championship. The majority of the games were held in the recently built Luzhniki Palace of Sports, the Soviet Union's first indoor ice hockey facility. However, the final game of the championship was moved outdoors to the Luzhnicki Stadium, where Sweden and the Soviets would play in front of a record crowd of fifty thousand. The two teams would play to a tie, giving the Swedes the gold medal while the disappointed host country had to settle for a silver medal.

In the following two World Championships Russia once again finished second best, this time to Canada, first to the Whitby Dunlops in 1958 and then to the Belleville McFarlands in 1959. Both teams, however, were augmented with outsiders, in the form of numerous former NHL players.

A decade before, Canada had been able to breeze to victory by sending over any team. Now, their best senior teams were being forced to add professionals to hold off the Soviet threat. Years later, looking back at 1958, Wren Blair, the manager of the Dunlops, admitted that he needed the professionals if Canada wanted to finish in first place.[29]

The 1960 Winter Olympics saw the Americans capture the gold medal on home ice, much to the shock of both Canada and the Soviet Union, who claimed the silver and bronze medal, respectively. The next year the Trail Smoke Eaters captured Canada's nineteenth World Championship as the Russians once again had to settle for bronze.

As the Soviet Union approached the end of their first decade on the international hockey scene, they could look back on those years as an unprecedented success. They had won a World Championship in 1954 and an Olympic Gold Medal in 1956, and also taken home four silver medals and two bronzes. In each of the eight championships they had participated in they had finished in the medals, an accomplishment that was only matched by Canada. Furthermore, they had tested themselves against the best junior teams from Canada, on Canadian soil, and emerged with a winning record. In less than a decade, they had become the biggest threat to Canada's supremacy on the international hockey stage.

3.

THE GODFATHER
AND THE GOALTENDER

In 1964, when Sam Pollock became the general manager of the Montreal Canadiens, there were those who questioned whether he was capable of doing the job, especially when considering the unprecedented success of his famed predecessor, Frank Selke. After all, Selke had transformed the Canadiens into the NHL's most successful team in his eighteen years at the helm.

In time, however, Pollock would prove to be every bit the equal of Selke, and maybe his superior, as he shepherded the organization through the turbulent waters of NHL expansion, rival leagues, salary escalation and the entry draft, and in the process constructed a dynasty to rival Selke's. He accomplished this by becoming both the hardest worker and the smartest operator in hockey.

As a boy growing up in Depression-era Montreal, Sam Pollock had long dreamt of becoming a baseball player, spending his summers hanging around the city's numerous sandlots. The son of an English immigrant haberdasher, he left school after the tenth grade to join his father in the garment business. Despite his father's disdain for all sports, Sam acquired his first pair of ice skates at the age of twelve. Four years later he showed up at a tryout camp that was being run by the Montreal Royals hockey team. The head coach of the team immediately took one look at the short, slightly rotund Pollock and told him to go home.[1]

Disappointed but realistic, Pollock turned his attention to organizing teams in different sports throughout the city. Despite possessing a full-time job at a railway agency, Pollock channelled his prodigious energy and quickly became well known as a key figure on the Montreal sporting scene.

Red Fisher, the famed sportswriter, remembers the first time he crossed paths with Sam Pollock.

"I knew him when he was a teenager, and even then he was developing a mystique for winning. He was only 17 when he managed a fastball team comprised largely of Montreal Canadiens players. Goaltender Bill Durnan was his pitcher, the best in Canada. Doug Harvey was his third baseman. Toe Blake and Elmer Lach were on the team. So was Ken Reardon. They were among hockey's grandest names, but teenager Pollock was in charge."[2]

A few years later, the twenty-year-old Pollock's acumen for organizing various teams throughout the city brought him to the attention of Wilf Cude, a former goaltender for the Canadiens, who was now managing and coaching one of their top farm teams, the Montreal Junior Canadiens. Unable to offer him any money, Cude entrusted the eager Pollock with the task of unearthing the best young players in the city, on a voluntary basis. At the end of that first year, Cude resigned and was replaced by Frank Currie, who retained Pollock in his scouting role. When he received an offer to coach Edmonton in the Western League, the outgoing Currie suggested to Frank Selke Sr., who had just been named the Canadiens' general manager, that Pollock would be an ideal choice to take over his managerial and coaching duties with the Junior Canadiens.

However, when Selke offered the job to him, Pollock hesitated. Taking the job with the Canadiens would mean a pay cut for Pollock, who was earning a higher salary with his full-time job at the railway agency. It was only after the practical Pollock had negotiated a leave of absence from his other employer that he felt able to take up the offer of employment in the Canadiens front office in 1947.[3]

Pollock would soon become Selke's most trusted lieutenant and play an integral role in the junior system that the Canadiens were constructing. Pollock began by coaching and managing the Junior Canadiens. Routinely working seventeen hours a day, he also supervised the Canadiens-sponsored Peterborough junior team as well.[4] Three years later he was named the team's director of player personnel.

Over the next fourteen years in the job, he would continually travel through Ontario and Quebec, scouting and evaluating future prospects, while also overseeing the Canadiens' existing junior and minor-league squads. Wherever he went, success seemed to follow. Two of his teams, the 1950 Montreal Junior Canadiens and the 1958 Ottawa-Hull Junior Canadiens, captured the Memorial Cup. In 1962, he helped guide the Ottawa-Hull Junior Canadiens to the Eastern Professional League title and two years later managed the Omaha Knights to the Central Hockey League crown.[5]

Despite his high profile within the organization, Pollock doesn't appear in any Canadiens team photo from this era. Nor is his name engraved on the Stanley Cup for the six Montreal championship teams of the fifties that he had a hand in assembling.

Pollock was an intensely private individual who actively sought the shadows and shunned attention. A calculating man, he pondered every word he spoke and every move he made, always careful to only reveal what he wanted you to know. During the course of a game, with the fans' attention drawn down toward the ice, he would silently slip behind all of them, famously watching the Canadiens play from section 66 in the Montreal Forum – the highest part of the building.[6]

So when the Canadiens ownership tapped him to replace the retiring Selke on May 15, 1964, as the team's next general manager, his appointment was met with a degree of skepticism from many in the media who were not only unfamiliar with Pollock but doubted the ability of anyone following in the immense footsteps of his predecessor, Frank Selke.

"What kind of person is Sam Pollock? A tyrant? A genius?" asked a curious Louis Chantigny in *La Patrie*. "He is not a man of long speeches and grand declarations. In official meetings and press conferences, where Frank Selke is in the spotlight, Sam Pollock stands at a distance, in a corner where he attracts no attention. He is an enigmatic personality who exercises power in the shadows, behind the scenes."[7]

To those at the Montreal Forum who watched him at work on a daily basis, Pollock's ascension to the organization's top job was seen as a natural progression. "Each year, under Selke's careful grooming, Pollock has assumed more responsibility in the Canadiens scheme of things," wrote Red Burnett in the *Toronto Star*. "You might say his career was patterned after Frank Selke, the man he will succeed."[8]

By the time Pollock became the general manager, there was no person in the organization more knowledgeable about its inner workings, a fact readily acknowledged by Selke's own son, Frank Jr., when he heard of Pollock's promotion.

"His files on our clubs do not contain a hundredth of what he keeps in his head. He tells us only what he wants to tell us. He knows all the players who belong to us, all the players who belong to the other teams in the NHL, their names, their ages, their strengths, their weaknesses. It is a living encyclopedia . . . but, I repeat, nobody other than him has access to this knowledge."[9]

It was a knowledge that had been hard-earned. When Pollock took over as the Canadiens general manager, the team had more than four hundred players under contract. In the year before his promotion to the top job, he had travelled one hundred thousand miles and attended over one hundred and fifty games in such far-flung locations as Omaha, St. Paul, Portland, Seattle, Vancouver, San Francisco, and Los Angeles.

Sam Pollock was taking over a team that had not won the Stanley Cup in four seasons. In Montreal, a city that had now grown accustomed to a championship parade down Ste-Catherine Street each spring, the four years without the Cup had been an eternity.

In these years, the Canadiens were going through a transition. Many of the players who had been the superstars of the dynasty team of the fifties were departing the scene. This abrupt changing of the guard commenced at the onset of training camp in the fall of 1960, when Maurice "Rocket" Richard, the greatest player the franchise had ever known, suddenly announced his retirement. The following June, Doug Harvey was traded to the New York Rangers. In the summer of 1963, Tom Johnson was claimed by the Boston Bruins in the waiver draft and Jacques Plante was traded to the New York Rangers. And then, a couple of weeks after Pollock assumed his new post, Bernie "Boom Boom" Geoffrion retired to coach the club's farm team in the AHL, the Quebec Aces. As Sam Pollock assessed his team at his first training camp as the Canadiens general manager in the fall of 1964, he would see only five players remaining from the team that had won a fifth consecutive Stanley Cup a little over four years earlier.

Interestingly, it was another of the mainstays of that fifties dynasty who would provide Pollock with one of his first major decisions as the Canadiens' new boss. Following the conclusion of the 1963 season, Dickie Moore, with both of his knees now ruined, decided to retire from the game. Selke, however, out of loyalty had kept Moore on the team's protected list that summer, hoping he would play again. Over the course of the 1963–64 season, the Canadiens would once again ask Moore if he wanted to come back, but a fractured kneecap suffered in his home workshop scuttled his plans.

Now, in one of his first acts as Montreal's general manager, Pollock had to submit his list of protected players for the 1964 Inter-League draft. The hard question confronting Pollock was whether or not to protect Moore, a player with whom he felt a special bond. Fourteen years earlier in 1950, Moore had captained the Montreal Junior Canadiens to the Memorial Cup. The manager and coach of that team was Sam Pollock, who with that win celebrated his first hockey championship.

If the decision had been based on sentiment, then Moore would have always remained a Montreal Canadien. Sam Pollock, however, didn't operate his team on sentiment. Moore was left unprotected, and at the Inter-League draft, the Toronto Maple Leafs picked him up.

With the Moore decision, Pollock had established one of his most central tenets by which he would run the organization. In managing the fortunes of the team, he felt that nothing was more important than the long-term health of the franchise. He would later famously say that no one season, even if it meant winning a Stanley Cup, was more important than the future of the organization.

"People build teams certain ways," Pollock said later. "I've always traded for futures – not pasts."[10]

Sam Pollock had been the Montreal Canadiens general manager for less than a month when he presided over his first amateur draft, held on June 11, 1964, at Montreal's Queen Elizabeth Hotel. With many of the best junior players of the time bound to teams by the C-Form, the draft was open to those born between August 1, 1947, and July 1, 1948, who hadn't signed the binding document. The draft was only made up of four rounds with the majority of the players taken coming from the Ontario Junior B, Junior C, and midget ranks. Of the twenty-four players selected that day, only nine would ever so much as play a game in the National Hockey League.

There would only be one goalie selected in that day's draft. The Boston Bruins, with the second pick in the third round and the fourteenth pick overall, selected Ken Dryden, a Junior B goalie who played for Etobicoke.

Seventeen days later they would trade his professional rights to the Montreal Canadiens. The deal worked out between Sam Pollock and Lynn Patrick, the Bruins general manager, was a simple one. The Canadiens dealt Guy Allen and Paul Reid, the twelfth and eighteenth picks in the recently completed draft, for Dryden, the fourteenth pick in the draft, and for Alex Campbell, the second pick. At the time, the trade received little, if any, attention in the press. It would take a while, years in fact, but this trade would not only haunt the Bruins, it would also be remembered as one of the most one-sided swaps in hockey history. For three players in the trade, Campbell, Allen, and Reid, a career in professional hockey would remain a dream unfulfilled. None of them would ever play a game in the NHL.

Ken Dryden, however, would be a different story.

In Pollock's first year at the helm, a boatload of young players were culled from the Canadiens farm system to make their debut with the team. They were labelled by the media as "Sam's boys," and included Jacques Laperrière, Yvan Cournoyer, Claude Larose, Terry Harper, and Jim Roberts. They would be augmented by the last remnants of Selke's dynasty, Jean Béliveau, Ralph Backstrom, Jean-Guy Talbot, Charlie Hodge, Claude Provost, and Henri Richard, as well as a group of younger veterans like Bobby Rousseau, Gilles Tremblay, and J.C. Tremblay, each of whom had played a year or two with the Canadiens. Throw in Gump Worsley and Dick Duff, two future Hall-of-Famers acquired by Pollock from the New York Rangers in separate trades, and a second dynasty was soon in the offing.

And while Pollock was on his way to building another hockey powerhouse in Montreal, the real test of his aptitude and intellect came less than a year into his stewardship of the Canadiens. On March 12, 1965, NHL president Clarence Campbell announced that the league would soon add a second division of six expansion teams, thereby doubling the league's size to twelve. It was decided that the new twelve-team league would begin operations at the start of the 1967–68 season, with an expansion draft scheduled to take place in the summer of 1967.

Many questioned the Canadiens' future in the wake of the expansion announcement. The system that Frank Selke had built would have to be torn down as the C-form was slowly phased out of existence. Starting in 1969, all twenty-year-old junior players would be available to all the teams in an annual entry draft. Under these new rules, the Canadiens would no longer be able to immediately sign the best young junior prospects in Quebec and the rest of Canada. Instead, all of these prospective players would be available to the other teams, putting an end to the Canadiens' seeming monopoly on the best young players, particularly those coming from the province of Quebec.

As was his way, Pollock set about studying the intricacies of the league itself. He began attending NHL board of governors meetings, as an alternate, gaining an understanding of the league's inner workings, including the upcoming expansion, that none of his contemporaries possessed. It wasn't long before Clarence Campbell, the president of the NHL, often deferred to him on league issues.

It seemed only natural, then, for Campbell to appoint Pollock to the committee that brokered the rules for the coming expansion. In the years that followed many pointed to this decision as a misguided one at best, feeling that Pollock had used the committee to craft a set of rules that benefited the Canadiens. Pollock vehemently denied their accusations, as did Clarence Campbell, but in the aftermath of expansion it certainly looked that way.

The expansion draft was held on June 6, 1967, in the ballroom of the Queen Elizabeth Hotel, and was scheduled for twenty rounds, with the first two dedicated to goaltenders and the next eighteen dedicated to forwards. For each player claimed by a Western (expansion) team, the East would be allowed to protect another player off their roster. Each Western team would select eighteen forwards, while each Eastern team could lose no more than eighteen forwards.

Players subject to the expansion draft were all those professionals belonging to the East Division clubs (the original six) with the following exceptions:

1. The eleven players and one goalie on the protected lists,
2. Those who were eligible for junior hockey in 1966–67 but instead played in any professional league,
3. Players who had been sold outright to minor pro teams before June 1, 1966,
   and finally,
4. Players who had made their professional hockey debut in 1966–67. These players could not be drafted until after the East Division clubs had two goalies and eighteen other players on their protected lists.[11]

For those hoping to see a downward turn in the Canadiens' fortunes it was this fourth rule that caused the greatest consternation. In effect, this rule made the previous season's rookies undraftable until the beginning of the eighth round of the expansion draft. Many saw this rule as nothing more than a way for Pollock to protect the most valuable assets in his organization. Because he didn't need to protect his best young prospects, he could use his protected list to preserve the veteran core of his team. As soon as the draft began and the selections commenced, the fears of Pollock's most vehement critics were realized. When the California Golden Seals selected Montreal goalie Charlie Hodge with their first pick, the Canadiens quickly announced that they would protect Rogatien Vachon, a rookie goaltender, who had just led the team to the Stanley Cup Finals a month before. And so it went, with the Canadiens losing veteran role-players such as Gord Labossiere, Dave Balon, Jim Roberts, and Noel Picard with the first few selections of the draft and at the same time quickly protecting their stars of the future, like Carol Vadnais, Serge Savard, Danny Grant, and Jacques Lemaire.

In addition, Pollock was able to work out various side deals with some of his new expansion brethren to keep many of his most valuable players in the Canadiens uniform, as players like Claude Larose, Claude Provost, and Dick Duff stayed put. Of the twenty-eight players who had played at least a game the season before for the Canadiens, Pollock was able to retain nineteen of them. And so, the Canadiens had emerged from the expansion draft largely intact. Pollock had remained a step ahead of the competition, and thanks to a combination of smarts and shrewdness he was able to preserve the Canadiens' present and future. The true measure of Pollock's achievement in the expansion summer of 1967 was revealed the following season, when Montreal finished in first place and won the Stanley Cup while only losing one playoff game along the way.

Somehow, in another one of Pollock's most famous machinations, he convinced his fellow NHL owners that it would be beneficial to both them and the league if the Canadiens maintained the right to draft the two best French-Canadian junior players. Unbelievably, the owners agreed with Pollock's argument that it was important for the league that the Canadiens maintain their stature as the "Flying Frenchmen."[12]

Pollock astutely deferred the use of this option. He waited through the first few drafts, then employed it to full effect in both the 1968 and 1969 entry drafts, scooping up players such as Michel Plasse, Réjean Houle, and Marc Tardif, each of whom would play an important role with the team in the coming years.

Pollock's understanding of both the league and the expansion process allowed him to maintain the Canadiens' pre-eminent position in the NHL. Not only was he able to fashion ways to keep his championship team together, he was able to take advantage of the new franchises in a way that would keep the Canadiens on top in the decade following the 1967 expansion.

For some of the new expansion teams, success right out of the gate was essential. Faced with trying to sell a new game in a non-traditional hockey market, many of these new owners and their front offices were desperate to ice a winning hockey team immediately, thinking that this would help establish them as a valuable sporting entity in their own home market.

No one understood the desperation of some of the new franchises better than Sam Pollock, who began providing them with players who would instantly help their teams. However, he exacted a high price in return. After much thought and consideration, Pollock came to the realization that all of these new franchises truly had only one valuable asset: their future draft picks. As soon as the new teams were constituted, he was able to put his plan into action. Finding himself with surplus players who weren't a factor in the Canadiens' upcoming plans, he traded them to the new expansion franchises – where they would instantly become considerably more valuable to their new team. Since Pollock had no interest in many of the players on the new expansion teams (many of whom he had originally discarded in the expansion draft), he instead chose the expansion teams' draft picks as compensation in any trade, many of whom would turn out to be among the first picks in a future draft. In the coming years, the Canadiens would use this surplus of high draft picks to help build another dynasty.

"Restocking the team was important to us and we quickly realized that the draft was going to be the major area of importance," Pollock later recalled. "That meant we had to increase our scouting staff, to ensure that we saw all of the best players available and were able to assess them. That also meant that we would draft for specific players with specific talents."[13]

On the surface, the era of expansion changed things very little for the Canadiens, as the team captured the first two post-expansion Stanley Cups in 1968 and 1969, giving Pollock four championships in his first five years on the job.

Looking at the teams in the 1968 Stanley Cup playoffs, the first post expansion, one can see the true extent of Sam Pollock's considerable influence. His Canadiens won the Stanley Cup, defeating the expansion St. Louis Blues in four straight games, a Blues team that had nine players Pollock had discarded over the past year. The team that the Blues beat in the West finals, the expansion Minnesota North Stars, also had nine players on their team who had been deemed superfluous by Sam in the last year.

Pollock began to find it increasingly difficult to stay out of the spotlight. With the Canadiens' continued success, people started whispering about Pollock being a genius. It was a term that a defensive Pollock openly rejected and dismissed.

"I don't believe that there are any geniuses in the world. There are just people who work harder than others. Discipline is the most important thing. Players must have discipline. Anybody who has been successful has had it. We're as good as the accumulation of our experience."[14]

Born on August 8, 1947, in Hamilton, Ontario, to a mother who taught kindergarten and a father who was a manufacturer's agent in building supplies, Ken Dryden grew up in Etobicoke, Ontario, located in the western part of Toronto.[15]

His choice to play goal was a simple one: he wanted to emulate his older brother Dave, who doubled as his childhood hero. Separated by six years in age, Ken would tag along behind his idol, doing as he did, and since Dave played goal, so did Ken. Taking notice of his two sons enthusiasm for the game, Murray Dryden constructed two goalie nets, built from two-by-fours and chicken wire, and placed them at opposite ends of the family driveway. Wearing a catcher's mask and a football helmet, the younger Dryden, all of five years old, faced the neighbourhood competition from one net while his brother manned the other. The next year the Drydens moved into a new home, and their father subsequently paved the whole backyard, giving the boys a year-round ball hockey rink.[16]

"We played from September until May," Dave Dryden recalls. "Eight guys to a side and away we'd go. Neither Ken nor I ever wanted to play anything but goal. I think what helped us both was that we played ball hockey when we were kids. Not too many boys can lift a hockey puck when they are starting out, but they could really zip a tennis ball at us. Ken has fast hands and stopping that tennis ball coming at him from a kid six years older made them even faster."[17]

At the age of seven, Ken Dryden began playing organized hockey for a Humber Valley team in a local Atom League. The next year, at his father's insistence, he played for the Humber Valley peewee squad, even though he was two or three years younger than his teammates. Murray Dryden felt that his son would improve more as a goaltender if he faced the older competition. Dryden was in goal for Humber Valley teams until he was fifteen, when he made the switch to Junior B hockey with the Etobicoke Indians. At the conclusion of that season, at the age of sixteen, he was drafted by the Bruins, before being quickly dealt to the Canadiens.

In the days after the 1964 draft, the Bruins learned that Dryden planned to continue his education beyond high school. Almost overnight they sought to trade him. In truth, Dryden had not been their first choice the day of the draft. They had wanted Guy Allen, the player taken two picks ahead of him by the Canadiens. The subsequent trade with Montreal saw the Bruins acquire the player they originally wanted. The Canadiens in return received Dryden.

"We knew about him from Roger Neilson, our Toronto-area scout, but we were sort of concerned about his ambition," Scotty Bowman, then a Canadiens scout and later the team's head coach, recalled. "He kept talking about going to school instead of playing Junior A."[18]

Sam Pollock and his management team debated the merits of trading Dryden for hours. In an effort to reach a conclusion, Pollock asked another of his scouts, Claude Ruel, to phone Neilson for a final report on Dryden. Neilson told Ruel that Dryden had the potential to be the best goalie in Junior A the following year. As soon as Ruel relayed Neilson's positive assessment to a waiting Pollock, the deal was done.

"They wanted me to go to Peterborough, Ontario," Dryden recalled a decade later. "They had a strong team there but needed a second goaltender. But my schooling was the hang-up. I was planning to attend Grade 13, the most important academic year in Canada, and there would be a lot of pressure on me to do well in the classroom. I could not see how living away, playing hockey and trying to go to school in Peterborough would work, so I stayed in Toronto."[19]

For a player to turn down the overtures of the Montreal Canadiens at the time was unheard of. But for Ken Dryden, school always came first, even if the alternative path held the potential of being a professional hockey player. In addition, the young Dryden had witnessed many of his friends follow the professional route, with very few of them ever reaching the NHL. With the amount of talent in the Montreal organization, he calculated that his road would be that much more difficult.[20] It would be close to another five years before he heard from the Montreal Canadiens again.

"In Pollock's time, players didn't challenge constituted authority," Red Fisher reflected later. "If a general manager instructed the player to jump, the only acceptable response was: 'How High?' That's the way it had worked for years, and that's the way it was supposed to work forever."[21]

In addition to being a desired goalie, the young Dryden was also a basketball standout. Upon graduating Grade 13 he received a few offers from Canadian schools promising a basketball scholarship, and one from an American school offering a combined scholarship in basketball and hockey. He also received an interesting offer from Michigan Tech. "They told me I could play basketball my freshman and sophomore years and then, when Tony Esposito graduated, I could switch over to hockey."[22]

Dryden rejected them all, setting his heart on the prestige of Princeton University. That is until he received a personal visit from Clinton Rossiter, a distinguished professor of government from Cornell University, who had written extensively on the role of government in American history. On the Cornell campus that fall, Dryden began working his way toward a Bachelor of Arts degree in history. Any thoughts of a future in professional hockey were long gone. At the time he firmly believed that his decision to pursue higher education had put an end to any professional aspirations. Furthermore, the number of future NHLers who hadn't played Junior A hockey was miniscule and the number of future NHLers who had played American college hockey was even smaller.

"Had Ken been thinking about a pro-hockey career he would have gone elsewhere," Dave Dryden confirms. "Eastern hockey was not that big then and Cornell wasn't even at the top of the East."[23] However, with Dryden in the nets, Cornell won two national championships in his three varsity seasons, and he was named a collegiate All-American all three years.

And then in February 1969, in Dryden's last spring at Cornell, Sam Pollock instructed his chauffeur, Brian Travers, to prepare for the six-hour road trip to Ithaca, New York, so he could watch Dryden in action for the first time. As was his custom, Pollock feverishly worked in the back of his limousine, as Travers made his way to Cornell University.

Ken Dryden had originally thought that this particular game would be a much tougher affair. He stood alone in front of his net, resting his chin on his blocker and trapper, which in turn rested on the top of his goalie stick. Dryden surveyed the ice in front of him and watched the game play out. He maintained that nonchalant pose throughout the course of the game, only abandoning it when the opposing team made its way toward his end of the ice. Tonight was one of those games in which he didn't have to take his chin off his stick very often. Out of boredom and in an effort to pass the time, he would look into the stands and try to calculate how much popcorn the vendors at the Lynah Rink had sold that night.[24]

He had expected much stiffer competition from the University of Toronto, who many considered to be the best college team in Canada. This may have been true, but on this occasion the Varsity Blues were no match for the Cornell Big Red, who cruised to a comfortable 7–2 victory. In many ways it wasn't that unusual a game for Dryden and the Big Red. Now in the final spring of his collegiate career, he had been almost perfect, amassing a sterling record of 76 wins, against only four losses and a single tie, with a minuscule goals-against average of 1.59.

Despite the gaudy statistics, he had gone virtually unnoticed throughout the greater hockey world. At the time, collegiate hockey in the United States was ignored by elites of the National Hockey League. Unbeknownst to Dryden, though, there was one team keeping an eye on him, the same team that had patiently held his professional rights for nearly five years. A few weeks prior he heard an unsubstantiated rumour that the legendary Toe Blake, the recently retired Montreal Canadiens head coach, had been in the crowd to see him. Now, as he sat there in the victorious Cornell dressing room, slowly peeling off layers of sweat-soaked equipment, he was startled to see before him a short, stocky man carrying a fuzzy felt fedora in one hand and putting forward his free hand for him to shake.[25]

Ken Dryden had never met Sam Pollock before. However, despite playing in relative obscurity for the past five years, Dryden had never been far from the thoughts of Pollock and the Canadiens front office. In truth, most other teams at the time would have long ago given up on a player who spurned their initial offer of a professional hockey career for higher education.

But then again, Sam Pollock did not operate like any other general manager in the National Hockey League.

After assuring a shocked Dryden that he would be in touch at the conclusion of that spring's NHL playoffs, Pollock took his leave and began the six-hour journey back to Montreal. For the next couple of months Dryden and Pollock exchanged phone calls, striking up what was, from Pollock's point of view, hopefully the beginning of a professional relationship.

A few months later, in the midst of the 1969 NHL playoffs, Ken Dryden found himself in Boston attending a sports banquet. As it happened, the Canadiens were in town playing the Bruins. On an impulse Dryden gave Pollock a call to ask if he could get him a ticket for that night's game. Despite the short notice, Pollock did find him a seat – six rows behind the Montreal bench, alongside some of the Canadiens executives. But Dryden had forgotten to mention one little detail: since his earliest days he had been a Boston Bruins supporter. "I was a big Bruin fan," he admitted later, "and I could barely restrain myself. I kept wanting to jump up and cheer for Boston."[26]

With his studies at Cornell completed, Dryden was once again offered a professional contract with the Canadiens. Rare was the prospective player who had said no to Sam Pollock once. Unheard of was the youngster who had done it twice. But unlike many of those prospective players, Ken Dryden had multiple options available to him. An unsure Dryden was sure of one thing: he wanted to go to law school and, if it were possible, to still play hockey. He was accepted at Harvard and considered going there, even going so far as to begin discussions about possibly playing in the Massachusetts Senior League. The Canadiens were another option, offering him a spot with their top farm team, the Montreal Voyageurs of the AHL, and a contract worth $50,000. But, in the end, it was the Canadian National Team that won out, with a contract worth $37,000 over the next three years. In addition, with the team based in Winnipeg, Dryden was free to attend the University of Manitoba law school.

"Had I gone to Harvard, hockey would have been out," Dryden told Frank Orr of the *Toronto Star* at the time of his official signing with the National Team program. "The main factor in my choosing to join Hockey Canada is that it provides the money for me to go to school comfortably and I can continue in hockey. I'd like to play in the Olympic Games in 1972. The Montreal offer was more money, but no school. The Harvard thing was school, but no hockey. This way I can have them both."[27]

With his decision made, all that remained was a call to a soon-to-be jilted Sam Pollock. Ken Dryden nervously dialled the pay phone that hung inside the dingy little roadside bar in Canoga, New York. Located just south of the state thruway it seemed like an unlikely location for a young Canadian hockey player to make such a momentous decision on his future.[28]

But then again, Ken Dryden was not a conventional hockey player. He had never taken a predictable path. He wasn't about to start now.

Sam Pollock was enjoying a rare day out of the office. A few months before, his Canadiens had won their fourth Stanley Cup in his five seasons at the helm. Training camp was still a couple of months away and this summer Montreal day was a gorgeous one. For the briefest of moments, thoughts of hockey didn't cloud his mind. He was just preparing to dive into his backyard pool when the phone rang. Sam looked back and decided to change course and pick up the phone. In truth, when it came to a debate over whether to answer or ignore the phone, the phone always won out.

On the other end of the line was a nervous twenty-one-year-old Ken Dryden. The news that he had wasn't what Pollock wanted to hear and came as a bit of a surprise. As soon as the phone call ended, Sam returned the phone to its cradle, quickly turned toward the waiting pool, and dove in.[29]

It would be another year before Sam Pollock and Ken Dryden spoke again.[30]

A GIFT FROM GOD

Vancouver, British Columbia, December 20, 1969. Standing in front of his net, Ken Dryden felt like an island onto himself, a man lost and struggling to find his way back to where he had been just a few hours before. Back then, he was both confident and self-assured. Now, with the arena clock counting down the game's final moments at what seemed a snail's pace, he could sense what remained of his confidence slipping away goal by goal.

The 13,157 people who had poured in to Vancouver's Pacific Coliseum that Saturday night had expected to see a spirited contest between the Canadian National Team, a motley crew of former professionals, college players, and the like, against their national counterparts from the Soviet Union. This exhibition series, played in arenas across the country, had been intended as something of a preview of the upcoming World Championship, which in three months' time would be the first to be held in Canada. Instead the crowd was witnessing an almost clinical display of Russian hockey efficiency, in which the Soviets not only dominated the overmatched Canadian squad, they embarrassed them.

"The Russians just toyed with Canada at the Coliseum," wrote the *Vancouver Province* the following Monday. "They confounded the Nationals with checkerboard passes and appeared able to score at will. In fact, at times they looked invincible. Every open spot on the ice seemed to be Soviet territory. The puck carrier would fire to an opening and sure enough, there would be a Russian cruising all alone."[1]

The final outcome of the game was never in doubt as the Russians held a commanding 4–1 lead by the end of the first period, extended it to 7–3 after the second, before adding two goals in the third period to make the final score 9–3.

Manning the Canadian goal for all nine goals was an overmatched and, on this particular night, outclassed Ken Dryden. It was the first time that he had ever played against the Russians, and it was unlike any game he had heretofore experienced, leaving him with a mixture of emotions, ranging from frustration to admiration.

"I was never so tired after a game," Dryden wrote years later. "They fired forty-five shots at me, not an incredible amount by NHL standards but an indoor record for the Russians. As I've said, the Russians rarely shoot until they have the perfect shot. That night they had forty-five perfect shots. And I'm not just trying to defend my reputation, either. I felt like the ball in a pinball machine. All night long I got ready for a shot, moved, went down, got up, got ready, moved – and then fished the puck from the net. Once I got so frustrated that I yelled out, 'Damn it, shoot the thing.'"[2]

The Soviet's supremacy had been so complete that in the span of sixty minutes Dryden went from being the most cerebral player on the ice to a man emotionally tattered. As the game neared its end, a slightly emasculated Dryden was reduced to celebrating little victories. "I had to make one of my better saves with ten seconds to go – turning away a deflection – to keep the score from mounting into double figures," he proudly remembered later.[3] Crouched in his crease and drenched in his own sweat, he looked intensely at his tormentors that evening and noticed that they appeared much the same as when the game started, their freshness and energy in stark contrast to his own exhaustion.

For the beaten Dryden there was one moment that stuck in his memory. After the Soviets had put a fifth or sixth goal in the Canadian net, one of their best players, Alexander Maltsev, slowly skated past the dejected goalie, who wearily looked up at him. The two made eye contact. Maltsev, looking every bit the conqueror, winked at the vanquished Dryden.[4]

Spending sixty minutes under constant bombardment by the Soviet offence gave Dryden little time to study his counterpart that night in the Soviet net. Wearing a white helmet with what appeared to be a white lacrosse-style cage covering his boyish face, the seventeen-year-old Soviet calmly stared out from his goal, the picture of composure. Unlike Dryden, over the course of the game he had dealt with considerably less pressure, facing only twenty-three shots in the 9–3 Soviet victory.

The Russian goalie's name was Vladislav Tretiak.

Stockholm, Sweden, March 17, 1963. It had been nine years since the Soviet National Team had won their first World Championship by defeating the East York Lyndhursts in this same city, sending shockwaves throughout a stunned Canada. In the intervening years the sport of hockey, once seen as being the sole preserve of Canada superiority, had gone through its most competitive period, with Russia, Sweden, and the United States, in addition to Canada, all sharing in championship gold.

Much as it had been on that warm Stockholm day nine years before, Canada and Russia would meet in the final game of the 1963 world championships. And just as it had been two years ago, when Canada last captured the gold medal, the country would be represented by the Trail Smoke Eaters, the best senior team in the nation and the defending Allan Cup champions. However, the Canadians who proudly skated out onto the ice that day were not playing for a gold medal; at best, a win by the Smoke Eaters would guarantee the disappointed squad a bronze. The Soviet Union, on the other hand, thanks to Sweden's unexpected 3–2 victory over Czechoslovakia earlier that afternoon, were playing for the championship. A victory over Canada by at least two goals would give them the gold medal, which would be their first since their triumph at the 1956 Olympics seven years before. A win by Canada, however, would give the host country, Sweden, a second consecutive World Championship.

As the two teams skated out before a packed crowd of sixteen thousand spectators, the tension in the air was undeniably thick as the fans, many of them from Sweden, urgently cheered on the Smoke Eaters.

Standing behind the Russian bench was the blustery figure of Anatoli Tarasov. An excitable mixture of nerves and energy, he was eagerly pacing, jotting down notes in his ever-present small black book. Tarasov, a man who had become accustomed to enjoying absolute power over his team, was now for the first time forced to share the coaching duties for the Soviet National Team. Positioned beside the emotional and explosive Tarasov was Arkady Chernyshev, a quiet man who impressed those who knew him with his sense of diplomacy, communication skills, and, above all, his ability to remain calm in the most turbulent of situations.

Tarasov, the Red Army boss, and Chernyshev, the head coach of the Moscow Dynamo, were the two most successful coaches in the Soviet Elite League. Each had been given an opportunity to be the sole head coach of the national team. Chernyshev had been the man behind the bench for Russia's greatest triumphs, the gold medal victories at the 1954 World Championship and again in the 1956 Olympics. Yet, in the eyes of his demanding political bosses, he had been unable to win on a consistent basis. As a result, in 1958 the Kremlin gave an eager Tarasov a second opportunity to pilot the national team. He proceeded to lead them to two silver medals and two bronze medals at the World Championships, but not the much-coveted gold.

Desperate to capture the gold, Leonid Khomenkov, the Soviet Union's vice-minister for sport, came up with the novel idea of pairing Tarasov and Chernyshev as co-coaches for the upcoming 1963 World Championship. The two men were a study in opposites; they looked at the game in different ways, were of contradictory temperaments, and did not get along on a personal level. Needless to say, neither particularly wanted the marriage, but faced with no alternative, they reluctantly agreed.[5]

Led by this new coaching duo, the Soviets had won five of their six games in the tournament by a combined score of 45 to 5. Their only loss of the competition had come at the hands of the host Swedes by a margin of 2–1. The Smoke Eaters had also lost to Sweden, but it was their tie against Czechoslovakia that had scuttled their hopes of bringing a gold medal back to Canada.

Facing the Canadian squad, it took all of seventy-six seconds for the Soviets to score the game's opening goal before quickly adding two more goals. With the wind now taken out of the crowd's collective sails and with each passing minute their hopes for a Swedish gold medal slowly evaporating, the Russians added another goal to their tally and entered the third period with a 4–0 lead. Then, much to the delight of the crowd, the Canadians tried their best to close the gap, assailing Viktor Konovalenko with twenty-one shots, closing the gap to a precious two goals late in the third period. However, with only four seconds remaining, it was too late: and the Soviets hung on for the 4–2 win and the gold medal.

"The Russians outclassed the Canadians by skating better and passing more accurately," wrote the *Globe and Mail* the next day in an article that could have been read as a metaphor for the state of the two national programs at the time. "Their precision teamwork contrasted with the Canadian attacks that appeared disorganized."[6]

The win touched off a nationwide wave of celebration throughout the Soviet Union. The final game had been the first one to be televised to the entire country. Much as it had in Canada a decade before, the advent of televised hockey led to an unprecedented explosion in hockey's popularity. This particular game was seen as a major turning point in the history of the sport and was regarded within the Soviet Union as the beginning of a golden age.[7]

"The hockey boom began," wrote Lawrence Martin in his book *The Red Machine,* the definitive book on the history of Soviet hockey. "Government financing of the sport expanded, more hockey schools were set up, and more teams, such as the one in Kiev in the Ukraine, were established. The boom brought with it an immensely popular national children's tournament, The Golden Puck."[8] At its most popular the Golden Puck tournament saw over three million school-aged boys participate. With the increased exposure, the sport became the hottest trend in the Soviet Union, and tickets became increasingly hard to acquire.

Meanwhile, Canada was undergoing a bitter self-examination of the game it had once so easily dominated. The loss to the Russians resulted in a disappointing fourth-place finish for Canada, the poorest result ever for a team representing the country. Instead of crediting the Russians for the win, Smoke Eaters head coach Bobby Kromm lamented the absence of outside players who would have augmented his Allan Cup championship team. "Time after time I asked for reinforcements but we just didn't get them. We had good goalies, we had some good forwards but we didn't have three complete first-class lines and we didn't have the defensemen we should have had."[9]

The irony, no doubt lost on Kromm, was that only a few years earlier the presence of the Allan Cup champions would have guaranteed a Canadian gold. Now those days seemed to belong to the history books. The 1963 World Championship would turn out to be the last time that Canada sent the Allan Cup champions as its representative.

"Something has to be done to stimulate national pride in Canadian hockey," claimed an exasperated Art Potter, the president of the Canadian Amateur Hockey Association. "It was obvious that the Russians were much fitter, in better condition than our boys. They had the bench power and they were skating better and shooting better." The county's newspapers chimed in with their suggestions on how to solve the problem. The *Ottawa Citizen* wrote that "Canada never again will win the world title unless it sends the pick of its best players and gives them plenty of time to work as a team before the championships."[10]

Even before the final siren wailed, signalling the Smoke Eaters' defeat in Stockholm, plans were afoot to change the way Canada selected its international team. The next year would be an Olympic one with the games being held in Innsbruck, Austria. Rather than sending the country's pre-eminent Senior team, Canada would instead build a truly national team, primarily made up of collegiate players, under the supervision of Father David Bauer. For the first time in years the country would be represented by a truly amateur team, one that would begin practising with each other months in advance of the Olympics, just like the Soviets. This bold move represented, for many in a discouraged country, a return to the purest ideals of Canadian hockey. And in the personage of Father Bauer, those in charge of international hockey at the Canadian level felt that they had found a possible saviour.

Twenty years earlier, David Bauer had been one of the premier junior hockey prospects in the country. A strong believer in the benefits of a proper education, he had resisted overtures of a professional contract with the Boston Bruins in order to attend St. Michael's College while the Second World War raged. In 1943, on loan from the school he helped the Oshawa Generals to a Memorial Cup championship. Though he had hoped to lead the Majors to their own Memorial Cup in 1945, he instead chose to enlist in the Canadian Army in the war's waning days. At the end of the war it was generally assumed that Bauer would join the NHL, but in a decision that sent shockwaves throughout the hockey world, Bauer entered the novitiate of the Basilian Fathers to study for the priesthood.

In 1953, Bauer was ordained as a priest, and a year later he returned to St. Michael's College, this time as a teacher and as a coach in various sports. In 1961, he coached the school's hockey team to a Memorial Cup championship. Months later however, still basking in the glory of that victory, St. Michael's made the surprise choice to withdraw from Ontario Junior A hockey, citing the demands of a lengthy season, considerable travel, and the adverse effect of all this on the player-students' academics. On the heels of the decision, the Basilian Fathers reassigned Father Bauer to St. Mark's College at the University of British Columbia in Vancouver.

In 1962, Father Bauer attended his first World Championship in Colorado Springs, and saw Canada finish as the runner-up to Sweden.

Watching the competition with Canadian Amateur Hockey Association president Jack Roxborough, Bauer shared his concept of a permanent national hockey team. He envisioned a collective with a core of collegiate players, supported by a handful of players from the senior ranks. Bauer presented his plan to the executive on August 26, 1962, and it was unanimously approved. Besides giving Bauer some start-up funding, the CAHA also agreed to pay residence and tuition fees for the players who would be schooled and housed at the University of British Columbia. Jim Coleman, one of Canada's leading sportswriters, later called this plan "the most nobly conceived of all hockey enterprises."[11]

Father Bauer patterned the nascent national team after his experiences at St. Michael's College. He strongly believed that if he gathered together a like-minded group of young players who had some natural ability and then instilled in them a sturdy discipline, in tandem with a thorough grounding in the game's fundamentals, he could then shape them into a collective unit that would transcend its individual parts. Father Bauer felt that his team should project a good image of the nation and stressed the importance of fair and clean play.

It was a noble concept, but in practice the Canadian National Team program wasn't much more successful than its predecessors had been on the international stage. The team's first test came at the 1964 Olympics. They finished in fourth place. They would once again finish in fourth place at the 1965 World Championship, before scoring back-to-back bronze medals at the 1966 and 1967 World Championships, culminating in a bronze medal at the 1968 Olympics in Grenoble, France. Perhaps most galling was that in each of these events Canada failed to defeat the Soviet Union, even once.

The Canadian team was not alone in its ineptitude. The victory of the Soviet Union at the 1963 World Championship over the Trail Smoke Eaters was just the first in what would become an unprecedented run of ten consecutive World Championship gold medals for the Soviets, which also encompassed both the 1964 and 1968 Olympics. The one constant during the Russians dominant reign was the coaching duo of Anatoli Tarasov and Arkady Chernyshev.

As coaches working in tandem, Tarasov and Chernyshev stood in stark contrast to the accepted hockey wisdom of the time, particularly as practised in the NHL, where the concept of a single coach, standing alone behind the bench, still prevailed. In addition, the Russian duo pioneered other new methods that were unheard of in Canadian hockey circles.

In a radical move, the two Soviet coaches began involving their players in running the team. For example, when a dispute came up, it was usually settled in a session held with the players. If a player needed to be disciplined, his teammates would be the ones to vote on an appropriate punishment. In addition, Tarasov and Chernyshev also consulted the players on game strategy and on some occasions they would even ask them which new recruits should be promoted to the national team. After the conclusion of each game, the two coaches would rate the performance of each player on a five-point scale and then would later discuss the rating with the spotlighted player. Tarasov and Chernyshev also instituted a coaches' council on the national team, composed of five players and the team's trainer, which would meet and talk about the business of operating the team.[12]

Despite giving their players much more input than their NHL counterparts, there was never any doubt about who ran the team. As the years went by, the two of them would come to perfect their good cop-bad cop routine. The volatile Tarosov would loudly and publicly push his players, then the calm and composed Chernyshev would sit the players down and quietly engage them, smoothing over any sore feelings created by the often gruff Tarasov.

"You can't find more different personalities than Tarasov and Chernyshev," remembered Boris Mayorov, one of their players. "I can't imagine Chernyshev talking loud as well as I can't imagine Tarasov talking soft. I've never seen Chernyshev out of balance, losing his temper. Even in the moments when we were losing a game. I haven't seen Tarasov relaxed even when there were no reasons for worries."[13]

Tarasov and Chernyshev perfectly complemented each other, working to accentuate the other's strengths while minimizing their own weaknesses. Tarasov was at his best on the ice or behind the bench running the team in practice and in the game. Chernyshev preferred to remain in the background, taking time off the ice, away from the pressures of a practice or a game, to counsel the players one on one. The end result was that Tarasov became the public face of the duo. They would take turns addressing the media at post-game press conferences; the animated Tarasov would always draw a large crowd, while the calm, hushed tones of Chernyshev were frequently delivered to a stack of empty seats.

Together, the two men constructed a hockey dynasty, the likes of which had never been seen before on the international stage. They had made the World Championships, and the Olympics, their own, defeating all comers, hounding the post-tournament All-Star selections, and making a mockery of the scoring race.

Yet, for the ever-competitive Tarasov, there was still one weak spot on his successful team, one position in which he felt that the Soviet Union still trailed behind Canada. Throughout their dominant run of gold medals in the sixties, it was the one position where the Soviets failed to place an all-star, and the one spot that caused the Soviet bench bosses the most apprehension.

It had been a problem he had thought long and hard about, that elusive, final piece of his complex puzzle.

Moscow, Russia, July 1967. The young man quietly stood there in awe of the presence of Anatoli Tarasov. Fifteen years old and still physically immature, he was patiently waiting off to the side, among his teammates on the Central Red Army Juniors. It was not uncommon for Tarasov to watch the juniors practise and play. After all, Tarasov hoped that these young men would grow into the future stars of the Red Army squad and, in turn, the Soviet National Team.

Straining to hear the conversation between their coach and the imposing Tarasov, the juniors heard Tarasov say, "Let this boy come to practise with the seniors," and then turning his attention to the eager but nervous group of young men, pointed to the goaltender in their midst.

Singled out by the great Tarasov, a surprised Vladislav Tretiak began practising with the prestigious Red Army team a few days later. The Red Army already had three goaltenders on their roster in the summer of 1967, but Tarasov wanted to add a fourth goaltender to make the practices and training drills more efficient. But there was more to his selection of Vladislav Tretiak.[14] Tarasov, as was his custom, had closely monitored the Red Army Juniors the season before from afar. Increasingly, he found his focus drawn to one end of the rink. Tarasov was instantly smitten by Tretiak and his potential, who had been nicknamed Gosling by his teammates because of his long neck and high-pitched voice.

"Gradually in my consciousness, I was developing a concept of the ideal goalkeeper," Tarasov later recalled. "I moulded it slowly, avoiding borrowing automatically the traits of other outstanding goalkeepers. I tried to study and improve every aspect of the game, critically looking at the old established teachings of goalkeeping school, and questioning them."[15]

Now into his second decade of coaching, Tarasov had thought long about the role of the goaltender. A natural forward himself, he had no instincts for the position, so he avidly studied various goaltenders, taking from each of them the bits and pieces that he would one day incorporate into his own unique philosophy. Tarasov set out to make Tretiak a hybrid of his favourite goalies: Bohumil Modry, who led Czechoslovakia to two World Championships in 1947 and 1949; Jacques Plante, the great Montreal Canadiens puckstopper; and Seth Martin, who had led the Trail Smoke Eaters to Canada's last World Championship in 1961. Tarasov had long dreamed of finding his ideal goaltender and felt that this young, raw prospect in front of him was the answer to his prayers.

"I decided that it was absolutely necessary to upgrade the overall level of play of our goalkeepers in order for them to gain more respect on our team," Tarasov later recalled. "It became important for them to develop a high sense of intelligence and the ability to analyze our rivals quickly. The goalkeeper had to become a major figure on the team. Just as I was coming to all these conclusions, I saw a tall boy by the name of Vladislav Tretiak. I liked his outward appearance; I immediately recalled Bohumil Modry. They looked alike, with the same mighty stature, the same huge hands. Tretiak was the person I was looking for. I started to work with him immediately. It was like he had been sent to me."[16]

Vladislav Tretiak was born in Orudyevo (a district of Moscow) on April 25, 1952. His father was an armed forces pilot and his mother a gymnastics instructor.[17] Growing up in Dmitrovo (a small town outside Moscow), a young Tretiak was often inseparable from his favourite toy, an old wooden club with a curve on the end. The well-worn stick was a remnant from his mother's days as a field hockey player in the 1930s. Young Vladik would run around the house and the backyard, tightly clutching the stick, using it to hit rocks, all the while pretending to be a hockey player. Like most boys his age, he often played the game at school, where the sight of the older boys in their hockey uniforms endlessly fascinated him.[18]

At the age of twelve he tried out for a place at the Red Army sports school. With only four openings available, and dozens of kids attending the tryouts, Tretiak was initially overwhelmed. However, the testing at that particular time was both crude and unrefined, which worked in his favour. If Tretiak possessed one skill at this age it was his natural athletic ability, which had been honed through the summer camps he had attended since he was five. Besides being active in volleyball, swimming, basketball, and cross-country running, Tretiak was taught how to skate at the age of seven by his mother. One of the tests required the prospective students to skate backwards, which he excelled at. Another skating test had all the young prospects chase an older player, to see which kids could catch him. Tretiak did.

In spite of his initial skepticism, Tretiak was one of just four applicants who won a spot at the school. After being accepted as a forward, he grew increasingly frustrated when, after six weeks at the school, he wasn't provided one of the much desired but scarce uniforms. Tretiak devised a scheme to get one. His coaches hadn't been able to find a person to play goal. The astute twelve-year-old made them an offer, proposing that he would play goal, on one condition – that he get a uniform. It wasn't long before a jubilant Tretiak was pulling on his beloved sweater and skating toward the open net.[19]

Now, three years later, Tretiak was practising with the country's elite players as the members of the Red Army peppered him with shots. Tretiak gave it his all in every practice. In truth, he was thrilled to be in the company of his idols, even going so far as to help them carry their sticks. For the young and eager Tretiak, being there was sheer bliss – even though it only lasted fifteen days. In the middle of the month the Red Army headed south to continue with their training. Tretiak was left behind.[20]

Having had a brief taste of being with the stars of the Red Army, Tretiak made his return to the Red Army Juniors, leading them to the Moscow championship, which named him the tournament's top goaltender. A year later, he was the goalie on the Soviet Union team that won the European Junior Championships held in Garmisch-Partenkirchen, West Germany.

Revelling in his junior success, and with some spare time on his hands in the spring of 1969, Tretiak decided to venture to the Luzhniki Palace of Sports to watch the Red Army team practise. It didn't take long for him to be spotted by Tarasov. A proud Tretiak began to saunter over, thinking he was going to be the recipient of the coach's congratulations for the Juniors' recent win. As he made his way toward Tarasov, and saw the sternness with which he was being viewed, Tretiak's assuredness was quickly replaced by a strong dose of unease.

"And you, young man, why aren't you on the ice? Hurry up!" barked the Soviet coach.[21]

Tretiak hastily ran to the dressing room, threw on his equipment, then rushed out to join the Red Army practice, already in progress. His days of playing for the Red Army junior team were suddenly over.

Tarasov set out to mould the young goaltender. Tretiak had natural gifts, but the demanding Tarasov wanted more. He would personally oversee his development with an almost fanatical zeal. He would experiment with him, instil discipline in him, and train him rigorously all the while – physically and mentally pushing him past the point of exhaustion. An obsessive Tarasov had never taken such an interest in one player, such was the importance he placed on the young man's shoulders.

"I was growing up," Tretiak later recalled, "avidly absorbing not only hockey wisdom, but more importantly, perceiving the essence of such things as team work, responsibility, and courage. From the very beginning my coach trained me to think creatively of my role as a goaltender."[22]

Tretiak was the perfect student; where others may have broken, he stiffened. He put his complete trust and faith in Tarasov, and followed his orders with an almost religious fervour. In addition to suffering through three practices a day, he had to endure a wide variety of new exercises, specifically composed for him, all coming from Tarasov's prolific mind. On the ice, in practice, he was subject to a shooting gallery from his teammates, in addition to playing a full game almost every day. If he allowed as much as one goal, Tarasov would make him stay after the players and the coaches had gone home and do countless numbers of off-ice exercises. Often finding himself alone at night, Tretiak never considered not doing what he was told.

"I could have cheated and not done them at all, since nobody was watching me," Tretiak wrote later in his autobiography. "But I wouldn't even have considered doing one less lunge or somersault. I trusted Tarasov, trusted his every word, even when he criticized me for letting the pucks in my net during practice. There was a method to his madness . . . I understood, then as now, that Tarasov had only one goal: to make Soviet hockey the best in the world."[23]

One day, in the middle of yet another exhausting workout, a tired Tretiak asked Tarasov if the purpose of all this hard work was to make him the best goaltender in the country. A visibly upset Tarasov looked sharply at his young charge and told him, "Not country . . . In the world! Remember this once and for all; in the world!"[24]

"I will never forget Tarasov's lessons," Tretiak wrote later. "Now looking back after many years, I clearly understand that he was not only teaching us hockey, he was teaching us life."[25]

In the fall of 1969, Tretiak was seventeen years old, an age at which his Canadian counterparts would still have been three years away from being allowed to play professionally. Despite the goalie's youth and the disapproval of those who made up the Soviet hockey establishment, Tarasov defiantly made Tretiak his starting goalie at the 1969 Izvestia tournament. Named after the newspaper that inaugurated it, the tournament took place every December in Moscow and brought together the teams who would contest the World Championship the following spring.

It was at this tournament that Tretiak would first face Canadian competition. As Ken Dryden watched from the end of the bench, the Canadian National Team, with Wayne Stephenson patrolling the Canadian goal, managed to gain a tie with Tretiak and the powerful Soviet team. However, a loss to the Czechs scuttled Canada's hopes of winning the tournament, and the Soviet's 8–2 drubbing of the same Czech team clinched their third consecutive Izvestia crown. Tretiak rewarded the faith of his mentor by not only leading the Russians to victory but also by being honoured as the tournament's top novice.[26]

Standing on the ice celebrating the victory, Tarasov looked upon his prize pupil in a way that only a proud teacher can. Here, in Tretiak, was the solution to the problem that had long plagued Soviet hockey. What had once been a weakness would soon become a strength. Tarasov now set his sights on what had always seemed to be an impossible goal: a showdown of his players against a team of NHL professionals.

Toronto, Ontario, January 1, 1970. Ken Dryden's time with the national team had all begun on such a promising note. The previous March, the young goaltender had flown over to Stockholm, where in his international debut he shut out a surprised American team in a 1–0 Canadian victory at the World Championship. Dryden's debut however was only a small bright spot, in another dismal tournament for Canada, which once again finished out of the medals, in fourth place.

A few months later Dryden turned down the Montreal Canadiens and signed a three-year contract with Canada's National Team. The next day's edition of the *Toronto Star* proclaimed that his signing "was considered a major breakthrough for Hockey Canada . . . as Dryden became the first player on such an arrangement with the new group."[27]

Now, a mere twelve days after being bombed by the Russian National Team in Vancouver, Dryden was once again patrolling the Canadian net. Five nights earlier, the Canadian National Team had concluded the Russian part of the tour in the same arena. On that occasion the Maple Leaf Gardens had accommodated a boisterous crowd of 15,614 fans and a television audience who cheered as the Nationals edged the Soviets and their teenage goaltender, Vladislav Tretiak. A disappointed Dryden had watched that entire game from the end of the Canadian bench.

Now, he was the one in the nets as the Canadian National Team faced off against the Czechoslovakian National Team at the same Maple Leaf Gardens. However, for whatever reason, this particular game didn't seem to resonate as much with the public as the Soviet game from a few days before. The contest with the Czechs would only be attended by 7,109 spectators, less than half of what had been in the building against the Russians, and the game would not be televised.

Despite that, the evening was undoubtedly a special one for the young goaltender. For the first time, he was playing for Canada on the Gardens' hallowed ice in his own hometown. Unfortunately, it would not be one of Ken Dryden's greatest nights. Early in the third period, he left the game with a pulled leg muscle, though by then the game wasn't in doubt as the Czechs rolled to an easy 4–0 win. Six months earlier, Dryden's signing had been touted as a major coup for the Nationals. Now, as the team continued to flounder, he was an easy target for criticism.

"All four goals were counted against Dryden, the All-American Canadian from Cornell University," wrote Frank Orr the next day in the *Toronto Star*, "who's been a big disappointment to Nats after he signed a fat contract."[28]

Undergoing treatment inside the dressing room, a discouraged Dryden slowly lifted his Team Canada jersey over his head and put it aside as the team's trainers stimulated his injured leg. He had no way of knowing it at the time, but he wouldn't put on a Team Canada jersey for another thirty-one months. And in that interval, neither would anyone else.

Three days after losing to the Czechs, Hockey Canada made the stunning announcement that it was immediately withdrawing from all international hockey tournaments. This decision meant that the World Championship, scheduled to be held three months later in Montreal and Winnipeg, would now be moved to Stockholm. Canada's withdrawal from international hockey was rooted in the decision by the International Ice Hockey Federation to revoke a previous verdict that would have allowed Canada to add professional players to the national team. Those in charge at Hockey Canada had long held the view that

their Russian counterparts were professional players. The IIHF respectfully disagreed, declaring them to be amateur players. Canada, for so
long the dominant team in international hockey, had now abandoned
the scene. It would be seven years before a team made up of Canadian
amateurs faced off against international hockey competition again. As a
result, almost overnight, the Canadian National Team lost its reason
for being.[29]

Less than a year after signing with the national team Ken Dryden
was left in hockey limbo. Though the team had been disbanded, he still
had two years left on his contract with Hockey Canada. In theory, he
could collect his salary and focus entirely on his studies at the University
of Toronto, where he had been accepted into the law program. Maybe
he could even sign up and play goal for the Varsity Blues, the school's
hockey team.

His professional rights were still held by the Montreal Canadiens, but
after turning them down twice he didn't feel that they were a viable
option. Besides, he was still determined to continue with his legal studies,
and that fact alone, he surely felt would scare off Sam Pollock.

5.

YOU'VE GOT TO DIE
TO BE BORN AGAIN

Montreal, Quebec, April 7, 1970. Sam Pollock sat alone in his office. In a few minutes he would have to leave the comfort of his surroundings and stand before a Montreal media that looked to him for all the answers. Pollock was not a fan of such gatherings, but he realized they were a necessary evil. Two days earlier had seen the completion of the NHL's regular season, and for the stunned Canadiens and their fans, it would be their first spring watching the playoffs, and not participating, since 1948. Even worse, the NHL playoffs would begin without the participation of a single team based in Canada.

Spoiled with the Canadiens' regular success and the team's Stanley Cup win the previous year, the fans and media reacted predictably. The lead headline on the front page of the next day's Montreal *Gazette* put the disappointment in stark terms.

R.I.P. – A STANLEY CUP PLAY-OFF DYNASTY ENDS:
CANADIENS (1949–1970)

The blame was widespread. Many held the whole team responsible, claiming they were bloated on success. Some blamed Jean Béliveau, the team's captain, for spending too much time on his off-ice activities. Others blamed Rogatien Vachon, the team's goaltender, for letting in questionable goals in the final game against the Black Hawks. Many blamed the embattled Claude Ruel, who was now being compared unfavourably with his predecessor, Toe Blake. Only a year earlier, all three men had been the toast of Montreal, celebrating the Canadiens' fourth Stanley Cup in five seasons.

Now Sam Pollock, the man who had constructed those teams as well as this one, was meeting the media in an attempt to put a positive spin on what had been nothing less than a devastating season. Pollock, always a firm believer in the big picture, was ready to put last year in the past and look to what he assured the assembled reporters would be a brighter future. Where others in his position might have panicked, Pollock was a study in tranquility.

"We blame ourselves," Pollock answered. "We lost. It's not just one game, it's a whole season that decides it. That's the crux of the whole bloody thing . . . we should've made it ourselves.[1] No excuses, there are reasons but no alibis."[2]

Not everyone bought his message. Instead of seeing the season as a one-year aberration, many commentators saw it as the end of an era.

"Stung by the defeat," wrote noted hockey scribe Stan Fischler, "the Canadiens' management set about the business of rebuilding the crumbled empire . . . No one questioned that the empire had crumbled."[3]

Sitting at home, the Canadiens watched that spring as the Boston Bruins, a team they had vanquished from the playoffs the previous two springs, won their first Stanley Cup in twenty-nine years. Many in the media and in the Boston front office proclaimed the Bruins, led by the incomparable Bobby Orr and Phil Esposito, as a future dynasty.

"Orr may be the greatest athlete who ever lived," pronounced Harry Sinden, the Bruins coach, to *Time* magazine in the aftermath of Boston's championship:

> "And the rest of the team? Well, let's see," says Sinden, "they've got courage, spirit, harmony, talent, size, youth." Sinden has every right to be effusive. Since taking over the Bruins four years ago, he and General Manager Milt Schmidt have built a budding Boston dynasty. At 22, Orr is just one of a phalanx of young skaters with their best playing years still ahead of them. The flamboyant, mop-topped Derek Sanderson, for example, at 23, is already one of the best centers in the league. He spells Phil Esposito, 28, who set two play-off records this year with 13 goals and a total of 27 points. They are backed by such elder skatesmen as John Bucyk, 35, and Johnny McKenzie, 32, who with Center Fred Stanfield, 26, scored a total of 53 points in the playoffs, an N.H.L.

record for a line. Immediately after the Bruins' victory last week, Sinden said: "The first championship is the sweetest, but there'll be more, many more."[4]

Meanwhile in Montreal a few weeks earlier, as the media conference that doubled as a post-mortem was coming to a merciful conclusion, Sam Pollock had offered a parting shot to the assembled reporters before beginning what would be, for him, his longest summer yet.

"Remember, you've got to die to be born again."[5]

Montreal, Quebec, September 10, 1970. Sam Pollock had admitted, both publicly and privately, that his Montreal Canadiens were a team in transition. Fifteen months removed from winning the Stanley Cup, the team began their training camp in the fall of 1970 with only thirteen of the players who had started the year before on the Canadiens roster. Seventy-four prospective players skated onto the ice before Pollock and the Montreal coaches on that first day, but it was one player who stood out, quite literally, from the rest. Among the twelve goalies on the opening day of training camp, it would have been impossible to miss the imposing figure wearing an off-white threadbare mask that appeared to have its front cage held in place by tape. Not only was he the tallest goaltender on the ice, he was easily the biggest.

Over the course of the summer Sam Pollock and Ken Dryden, after a year of silence, once again began talking with each other. Having turned down a professional contract with the Canadiens on two occasions, Dryden was highly skeptical that Pollock would be still interested in his services. After all, the list of people who had rejected Sam Pollock's overtures was a short one. What Dryden didn't know was that his rebuff of the Canadiens' advances had made a positive impression on Pollock. In a world where every young player was desperate to play in the NHL, Dryden was the exception. Dryden, however, was unaware that his insistence on continuing his education would play a critical part in his professional future. Pollock had come to realize that if he were ever going to sign Dryden to the Canadiens, he would have to include an education component in the terms of a potential contract.

After a few phone conversations, Pollock received confirmation of what he had long suspected. Carefully choosing his words, Dryden nervously confessed that he had turned down the Canadiens offer the summer before because there were no provisions in the contract that would have allowed him to continue his studies. Pollock responded with a novel idea, one that caught Dryden by surprise and was unique in the NHL of the day. He suggested that Dryden transfer to McGill University in Montreal for the fall semester and complete his final two years of law school while practising and playing part-time with the Canadiens' American Hockey League affiliate, the Montreal Voyageurs. Once Dryden completed his studies, he could give professional hockey a real chance, playing full-time, at least for one year.[6]

On the other end of the line sat a stunned Ken Dryden. He couldn't believe what Pollock was offering him. It didn't take long for him to say yes to the unusual agreement.

"I am sure, absolutely sure, that there was not one other General Manager in the NHL who would have been willing to sign me to a full-time law student/part-time hockey player contract," Dryden recalled. "Everyone else would have forced me to make a choice. They would have said that you can't do both so you can't try. You will fail and we will be the ones to pay the price. They would have said that unless you commit completely to us, why should we commit to you. And because coming out of Cornell and the National Team I was absolutely not sure that I was good enough to make the NHL, it is very, very likely that, forced to make a choice, I would have given up hockey and gone to law school."[7]

After years of negotiation and countless efforts to find common ground, Pollock had finally signed his most elusive property to a professional hockey contract. Such was Dryden's loss of stature in the aftermath of the national team debacle that there was nary a mention in the media of the goalie's contract signing. For a player still unsure if he was of professional calibre, joining the Montreal Canadiens organization was daunting.

"You're walking into Montreal, the Montreal Forum, and you're walking into a dressing room with people who only exist on a television screen," he later admitted, "and very soon you're going to go out and share the same ice surface with people who are only on that ice surface on a television screen and that's the real them and that's the fraudulent you."[8]

As the Canadiens training camp began that fall, Dryden became a popular topic for the local media both for his on-ice performance as well as his status as a full-time law student at McGill. With so many prospective players filling the training camp, the recruits were split into separate inter-squad teams, with some playing in the mornings and some in the afternoon. Dryden stood out from the other rookies. Pursuing his education was still his top priority, as evidenced by his switching inter-squad teams in the first days of camp so he wouldn't miss an afternoon class at McGill.[9]

During the Canadiens' exhibition schedule, Dryden saw action in three games, defeating the Black Hawks in his first outing before losing to the Philadelphia Flyers in the second. In the third game, on October 4, he skated out on the ice at the Boston Garden to confront his stiffest test yet, the defending champion Bruins, who were playing their first game at home since winning the Stanley Cup five months before. Making that evening's task more daunting for the inexperienced Dryden was that four Canadiens regulars were beset by injuries and sat out the game. In response, the Canadiens head coach Claude Ruel inserted eight players (including Dryden) who were destined for the AHL in the next few days.

"The game started out as though the big, bad Bruins were going to skate the Habs out of the rink as they stormed around the Montreal zone for the first five minutes," wrote the Montreal *Gazette* the next day. "But Ken Dryden, the big college kid who looks better every time out, came up with save after save to inspire his young teammates . . . Dryden was outstanding. He made a total of 43 saves."[10]

Despite a late Boston onslaught, the Canadiens held on for the 5–4 win. Having entered training camp a few weeks before unsure if he truly belonged, Dryden now felt a surge of confidence as it dawned on him that a professional career might not be so far-fetched. Others, apparently, agreed.

"The six-foot-four, 215 pound college standout may emerge as the rookie goalie of the season," wrote Pat Curran in the *Gazette*, "provided he can mix enough NHL appearances with his law studies at McGill. He has been impressive in every outing and has faced Chicago and Boston sharpshooters without flinching."[11]

Despite his strong pre-season showing, when the Montreal roster was announced Dryden's name was nowhere to be found. As per his agreement with Sam Pollock, he would begin his season with the Montreal Voyageurs of the American Hockey League.

"We had a good talk and I think we're both satisfied," Pollock told the assembled reporters. "He has a three-year contract with us which covers a lot of eventualities. We had to go with our two known quantities and I think Ken understands this."[12]

Pollock was not a man inclined to rush his young prospects; he preferred to give them some seasoning in the AHL. Dryden was no exception to this rule. Pollock also had concerns about how much time Dryden could devote to the Voyageurs, let alone the Canadiens.

"So with a three-year contract and two years of law school remaining, Dryden has – in effect – a year to spare before giving up the ghost on the big team," the *Montreal Star* wrote in the aftermath of Dryden's demotion. "Unless, and he crosses his fingers it won't happen, an emergency recall forces him to re-evaluate once again."[13]

Halifax, Nova Scotia, March 7, 1971. With the NHL's deadline for bringing up AHL players fast approaching on March 7, Ken Dryden had plenty on his mind. In addition to hearing and reading rumours, largely emanating from the French media, that he was about to be elevated to the Canadiens, he had just completed two lengthy paper courses at McGill.

The last few months since the Canadiens training camp had gone well. Dryden had quickly settled into his dual life as a full-time law student at McGill and a part-time goaltender with the Montreal Voyageurs.

"I attended McGill full time, practiced once or twice a week and played one home game a week with the Montreal Voyageurs in the American League," Dryden later recounted. "I figured I could handle that much hockey along with law studies. But at Christmas, after the first term, I felt I could accept a heavier hockey load. I joined the Voyageurs full time and made the road trips. It was all working out well."[14]

In thirty-three appearances that year with the Voyageurs, Dryden had won sixteen games, lost seven, and tied eight, with a goals-against average of 2.68. Without him patrolling the nets, the Voyageurs were a radically inferior team, winning only eleven games, losing twenty-four, and tying six, with a collective goals-against average of 3.83.

Now, on March 5, two nights before the NHL's deadline for bringing up AHL players, Dryden walked into the Montreal Forum for that night's contest between the Voyageurs and the Hershey Bears. Restless from the rumours, he soon confronted his coach, Floyd Curry, in the dressing room.

"You don't have to tell me if I'll be called up or not. But at least tell me 'no' or that it's conceivable." Responding directly to his anxious goaltender, Curry admitted that there was a chance Dryden would be called up.[15]

That night at the Forum, in front of the Canadiens management, a highly motivated Dryden turned in a performance that was nothing less than superb. The game saw the Voyageurs and Bears combine for sixty-four shots but didn't feature a single goal. Hershey's Andre Gill set aside twenty-seven shots, while Dryden turned away thirty-seven Bears shots, including three separate breakaways.[16]

The next morning, the Voyageurs left for Halifax to play a Sunday afternoon contest against the Providence Reds. Fully aware that it was the last possible day that he could be called up to the Canadiens, Dryden backstopped the Voyageurs to a 5–2 win before three thousand spectators at the Halifax Forum.[17] In the dressing room after the game, Curry calmly walked over to a waiting Dryden, said, "You're going back to Montreal," and handed him the precious ticket.

"It was the kind of scene you'd see in a movie script," Dryden later recalled. "It's the symbolic gesture, you just don't say you're going to Montreal, it's handing you the plane ticket. There it is, now take it."[18]

An excited Dryden immediately flew back to Montreal. By sheer coincidence, the Canadiens, having just played an afternoon game in Philadelphia, arrived at the airport at the same time. Running into his new teammates, Dryden noticed the reaction of Phil Myre, the Canadiens' backup goaltender, who couldn't hide the surprise and dismay that was etched on his face.

Dryden remembered later what Myre's unspoken expression really meant: "What are you doing here?"[19]

Quebec City, Quebec, April 4, 1971. On the final night of the NHL season, the Montreal Canadiens travelled to Boston to face the same team that in three days' time would oppose them in the first round of the playoffs. Contrary to the season before, the Canadiens had already secured their playoff position and were destined to finish the season in third place regardless of the outcome of their last game. The Bruins were in a similar predicament having clinched first place in the East division well ahead of their final game. Now on a Sunday afternoon, before a North American television audience, the two teams would once again meet in a preview of their first-round playoff series.

Sam Pollock did not go to Boston with his team. Like many he would watch the game on television that afternoon before making the long trip by car that night to Quebec City. With his chauffer, Brian Travers, doing the driving, Pollock sat comfortably in the back of his limousine, sorting through his paperwork and running through different scenarios and schemes. The purpose of Pollock's multi-hour trip that night was to scout a specific player in an effort to try to come to a final decision for the approaching draft, scheduled for two months later.

This was no simple decision. Last summer on May 22, 1970, while the rest of the hockey world was praising Bobby Orr and the Bruins on their Stanley Cup triumph, the canny Pollock had made a small trade with the California Golden Seals. In exchange for giving up Ernie Hicke and the Canadiens' number-one draft pick in the 1970 entry draft, the Canadiens received François Lacombe, a sum of cash, and the Seals' first-round pick in the 1971 entry draft.

In the end that left the Canadiens holding the Seals first-round pick in the 1971 entry draft. At the time of the deal, not much was made of the Seals' pick. After all, in 1970 the Seals had made the playoffs and looked to be a team on the rise. However, as the 1970–71 season evolved it became apparent that the Seals' fortunes had plummeted and the team found itself in a battle with the Los Angeles Kings for last place in the NHL. On January 26, 1971, the Seals were stuck in last place in the NHL standings, five points behind the Kings, who had two games in hand. On that very day Sam Pollock shipped out a disgruntled Ralph Backstrom to the Kings in exchange for Gord Labossiere, Ray Fortin, and future considerations. For a relieved Backstrom it was a trade that he had long hoped for. A veteran of the Canadiens since winning the Calder Trophy as rookie of the year, in 1959, he had been a valuable contributor to six Stanley Cup championships. However, the 1970–71 season had been a trying one for him. He appeared in only sixteen games, saw limited ice time, scored only one goal, and had four assists. At the start of the season, Backstrom had publicly threatened to retire and openly declared to the media that he wanted to be traded to a team located in a warmer climate. Now, three months later, Pollock granted Backstrom his wish.[20] In 33 games with the Kings, a rejuvenated Backstrom scored 14 goals and added 13 assists, and Los Angeles, only five points ahead of the Seals at the time of the trade, went on to finish 18 points ahead of them in the final standings.[21] Normally, that would have given the Seals the first selection in the upcoming NHL entry draft. However, thanks to their trade a year earlier, the first pick now belonged to Sam Pollock and the Canadiens.

No trade has contributed more to the legend of Sam Pollock. Not only had he been able to swing a deal for the first overall draft pick a year ahead of the 1971 entry draft, but the trade of Backstrom, who improved the Kings' fortunes in the season's final months, was seen by many observers as a very clever move to ensure that the Seals would finish in last place. Pollock vehemently denied this, maintaining that the trade with the Seals had been done a year in advance and no one could have known that the Seals would finish in last place the following season. As for the Backstrom deal, Pollock stressed that he had simply been accommodating the wishes of a long-term member of the organization.

Very few believed him.

"Such was Pollock's reputation by then that everybody began reading ulterior motives into virtually every transaction he made," wrote Chrys Goyens and Allan Turowetz in their book, *Lions in Winter*. The legend only grew in the years ahead with each retelling. There were even rumours that Pollock had acquired the retransmission rights for the Montreal Forum to screen the first Muhammad Ali–Joe Frazier fight from Kings' owner Jack Kent Cooke as part of the Backstrom trade.[22]

Whether it was another example of Pollock's brilliance or just a coincidence, the fact remained that on June 10, 1971, at the Queen Elizabeth Hotel in Montreal, Sam Pollock and the Canadiens would be making the first overall pick of the NHL entry draft.

For many in the media and in the hockey world, the obvious choice with that first selection was Guy Lafleur. He was undoubtedly the most highly prized prospect to come out of Quebec since Jean Béliveau, a generation before. In 56 games with the Quebec Remparts the previous season, Lafleur had accumulated 103 goals and added 67 assists for a total of 170 points. Now, in his final season of junior hockey with the Remparts, he would score an incredible 130 goals, add 79 assists, for an astounding 209 points in only 62 games.

Lafleur was the consensus number-one pick, he had always dreamed of playing for the Canadiens, and they held the first selection in the upcoming draft. On the surface, it seemed like the ideal marriage of team and player. But Sam Pollock had cold feet. The other top player he had to consider was Marcel Dionne. In order to come to a decision he was making yet another trip to Quebec City.

A fellow Quebecer, Dionne had left the province to play junior hockey in Ontario. At the time many felt that Dionne was facing a better calibre of opposition than was Lafleur, with whom he was often compared. In 1971, when Lafleur won the scoring title in the Quebec league,

Dionne claimed the same prize in the Ontario league. Both players had been exhaustively evaluated, appraised, and compared with the best players of the past and the present. Countless reports were filed by numerous scouts, analyzing each man's talent, style, and liabilities. While in the minority, there were those who thought that Dionne was the better player and some of those opinions resided within the Montreal front office. Ron Caron, the Canadiens' assistant general manager, was in favour of selecting Dionne with the first pick. Claude Ruel, up until a few months before the Canadiens' head coach, favoured Lafleur, as did his predecessor, Toe Blake, who professed that Lafleur was "a complete player with a genius for hockey."[23]

However, whenever Pollock had shown up to watch Lafleur play, he had walked away a disappointed man. Claude Ruel had at first felt the same way. But the crafty Ruel had soon figured out what was going on. Whenever the nervous Lafleur was told that Ruel was there to see him play, he seemed slower, slightly awkward, mistake-prone, and tended to be held off the scoreboard. Then, a few days later, Ruel would read in the paper how Lafleur had just dominated a game with his powerful but accurate shot, his uncanny instincts, and his ability to begin the play, give or take a pass at full speed, and to do it all at the highest level. Ruel soon began arriving at Lafleur's games in secret, sitting among the crowd. As a result, he had seen Lafleur at his best and was now his strongest and most persistent advocate.

Finally, after meticulously going through all of the scouts' reports and soliciting a wide range of opinions, a conflicted Pollock took Ruel's advice to watch Lafleur without his knowledge. Arriving at the Quebec Colisée on the evening of April 4, Pollock made his way to the box office and bought two tickets for the game between the Trois-Rivières Ducs and Lafleur's Remparts. Standing in the arena's hallway alongside his chauffeur, he attempted to blend in with the crowd, gently pushing his fedora lower in an effort to hide his famous face.

Paul Dumont, a scout for the Remparts, saw through Pollock's meagre disguise. Waving his hand in the air to get Pollock's attention, Dumont waded through the crowd to offer him a pair of complimentary tickets. Pollock discreetly revealed his bought tickets to Dumont and quietly made his way to his seat. Instead of watching the game, a curious Dumont spent the evening closely examining Pollock, who in turn was watching Lafleur, who was unaware of his presence. On that particular night, Lafleur was outstanding, and exactly how Ruel had described him. After two periods he had scored three goals and added three assists. Dumont couldn't help but notice that despite the display of offensive wizardry by Lafleur, there didn't appear to be even the slightest change in Pollock's demeanour, as he sat there passively watching the action on the ice. As the second period ended, Pollock rose from his seat and made his way toward Dumont.

"Paul, my decision is made."

Close-lipped as always, Pollock said no more and left the arena. Dumont stood there as the crowd rushed past him to the concession stands, wondering what it all meant.[24]

Back in the comfort of his limousine on the way home, Pollock was now a man at ease. With the future settled, he could focus on the present. That afternoon in Boston, the Canadiens dropped the final game of their season, humbled by a score of 7–2. Leading the Bruins' onslaught was Phil Esposito, who recorded his seventh hat trick of the year, shattering the NHL record for goals with 76. This new mark represented only one of the thirty-seven NHL records the Bruins had broken that season.

The Bruins cruised to a first-place finish with a record-breaking 57 wins and 121 points. Scoring 399 goals during the year, they bested the previous mark by almost a hundred. In addition to setting a new goals record, Esposito established a new scoring record with 152 points. Bobby Orr captured the Hart Trophy, as the league's Most Valuable Player, setting a new record with 102 assists. For the first time in NHL history one team had the season's top four scorers and seven of the top ten. Such was the scope of the Bruins' domination that year that they set a new record at each position for points in a season: centre (Esposito, 152 points), left wing (Johnny Bucyk, 116 points), right wing (Ken Hodge, 105 points), and defence (Orr, 139 points).

That week's edition of the *Sporting News* said it all, in a feature entitled, "There's No Way to Stop Bobby Orr."

A Bruins dynasty appeared to be a foregone conclusion. And the playoffs were expected to provide the coronation.

More than any other, the Montreal Canadiens' 1970–71 season required all of Sam Pollock's acumen and expertise just to keep the team afloat. In addition to Ralph Backstrom's retirement, return, and eventual trade to the Los Angeles Kings, there also was the retirement on season's eve and subsequent return of John Ferguson. Bowing to the continued pressure and stress of the position, Claude Ruel resigned as the Canadiens' head coach less than two months into the season. He was quickly replaced by his assistant coach, a reluctant Al MacNeil.

With the Canadiens lodged in third place, Pollock had pulled off a blockbuster trade on January 13, 1971, sending Mickey Redmond, Bill Collins, and Guy Charron to the Detroit Red Wings, in exchange for a player he had long coveted, Frank Mahovlich. Two weeks later, Serge Savard, one of the team's best defencemen, fractured his leg for the second time in two years, ending his season and potentially his career. On February 11, the Montreal Forum erupted in celebration as Jean Béliveau scored a hat trick, the last goal being the much cherished five-hundredth of his glorious career. A month and a half later, a capacity crowd jammed the Forum on Jean Béliveau Night, raising $155,855 for his newly created foundation, which would benefit children in need.

Over the season's last month, Ken Dryden appeared in six games as the Canadiens goalie, winning them all. After being called up from Halifax, he had waited almost a week before debuting on March 14 in Pittsburgh, backstopping Montreal to a 5–1 win. He would go on to beat Buffalo, Toronto, Chicago, and the New York Rangers twice, allowing only nine goals in the process.

Fresh from his visit to Quebec City to scout Guy Lafleur, Pollock gathered the Canadiens brain trust of Caron, Ruel, Blake, and head coach Al MacNeil to discuss the impending playoff encounter with the heavily favoured Bruins. Realizing that they were the overwhelming underdogs, the group struggled to come up with a strategy that might give them a chance. It was MacNeil who proposed the radical idea of starting the series with the unknown Dryden in the net.

"In the game in Chicago we hardly got out of our own end," MacNeil said later. "In fact, I don't think we got out at all in the third period, but we won 2–1. They had a powerful club . . . Chicago isn't an easy rink for a visiting goaltender, especially a rookie just starting. Dryden put on an amazing show. Anyone who was there couldn't have been surprised at him starting the first playoff game . . . Our other goalies, Vachon and Myre, were inconsistent. Dryden had the hot hand."[25]

"We felt that just maybe, just maybe there might be a chance that he could be spectacular in the playoffs," Sam Pollock recalled. "We didn't feel we were going to win any other way and we decided to start him in the series with Boston."[26]

Pollock and MacNeil reasoned that since the Bruins had barely seen Dryden before it would take them a while to figure him out, and that time might give the Canadiens a much needed edge. If Dryden didn't perform well, at least they had taken a chance.

Just days before in the season's last game, the Bruins had thrashed a Canadiens team with the diminutive Rogie Vachon in the net. Now with the playoffs beckoning, most assumed that a similar outcome was in the offing. Boston's Johnny McKenzie confidently announced to the Associated Press on the m ____ing of the first game that "nobody can beat us at home. We're too good."[27]

Before he got dressed in the aged confines of the Boston Garden, Ken Dryden received a telegram from his father, Murray, made up of three simple words: "Ruin those Bruins."[28] Later on that evening he skated out onto the ice of a hostile Boston Garden. Two years ago he had sat in the stands at the same arena watching these same two teams in the playoffs. Now he was on the ice, facing the onslaught of the greatest offensive juggernaut in league history.

"It was such an overwhelming experience, when you're thrown into deep waters and you don't know whether you can swim, you don't notice how fancy your strokes are, you're just trying to keep your head above water," Dryden admitted later.[29]

"Fifteen months ago Ken Dryden was a second string goalie for Canada's national hockey team," wrote Jim Coleman in the *Ottawa Citizen* the next day. "Last night he performed magnificently as he turned back 42 Boston shots." However, it wasn't enough, as the Bruins skated off with a 3–1 win in the opening game of the series. Despite the score, Dryden had been named the game's first star.

The next evening the two teams faced off again in the series' second game. From his home in the Islington part of Etobicoke, Murray Dryden attempted to listen to the game on the radio, since it wasn't being televised in the greater Toronto area. Much to his dismay, the reception on the house radio was sketchy at best. Murray headed outside to listen to the game on the car radio, which was fortunately much better, but halfway through the second period the car battery went dead.

With the Bruins leading the game 5–1, many would have given up on a game that for all intents and purposes was over. However, Murray was nothing if not persistent, and after a quick phone call to a local mechanic for advice, Murray got the car and, more importantly, the radio operating again. The elder Dryden then left his driveway and spent the rest of the game trying his hardest not to stop the car for fear of losing the only link to his youngest son, who at that moment was facing what seemed to be a hopeless cause.

On that cool, spring night along Toronto's lakeshore, as Murray drove back and forth, he heard through the crackling voice of his car radio one of the greatest comebacks in NHL playoff history.

It all began innocently enough with less than five minutes remaining in the second period. Controlling the puck outside his own blue line, Bobby Orr was the epitome of calm as he looked up the ice. However, at that very moment the puck loosened from what had been the tight grip of his stick and got away from him. Just as the puck began to leave the comfort of Orr's blade, an alert Henri Richard popped the wobbly puck between Orr's legs and skated down the left wing. Expertly using his body to shield the puck, Richard slickly moved it from his backhand to his forehand and back again, all within the blink of an eye, before sliding the puck into the net past a thoroughly confused Eddie Johnston, the Bruins' goalie. Still, the score remained 5–2 at the end of the second period, and with only twenty minutes to go, the Bruins seemed firmly in command.

On that evening, Jean Béliveau was in his tenth and final year as the Canadiens' captain. The team's elder statesman was the embodiment of class, grace, and dignity. Tall and handsome, he skated on the ice like a prince, carrying an air of elegance never seen before or since. At the age of thirty-nine, he was playing the final games of his splendid career. He had wanted to retire the year before, but the combination of Montreal missing the playoffs and the gentle persuasion of Sam Pollock had convinced him to stay for just one more year. With the third period about to begin and the Canadiens down by three goals, the proud Béliveau took charge of the game.

"In that second game in Boston, what I remember is the way Béliveau played," Frank Mahovlich later recalled. "He ignited things. He was the one who got us going. That was his last year, but that night he was awesome, and we went on from there."[30]

With Phil Esposito in the penalty box, all five members of the Canadiens power play expertly moved the puck from start to finish, with Béliveau passing to Phil Roberto, who backhanded a cross-ice pass to Guy Lapointe, who fired the puck down to the left side of the net and a waiting Yvan Cournoyer, who redirected the puck to John Ferguson, who shot on net. The puck took a fortuitous bounce off a prone Johnston, and Béliveau, in the right place at the right time, slipped the puck into the yawning net, making the score 5–3 for the Bruins. Less than ninety seconds later, Béliveau gathered the loose puck on the left boards, expertly skated directly into the slot, and after a nifty bit of stickhandling slid the puck between Johnston's legs. The scoreboard now read Bruins 5, Canadiens 4.

With the Bruins on edge, they attempted to regain their lost momentum but were unable to beat a suddenly impregnable Dryden. Attacking in the Montreal zone, Ken Hodge on the boards tried to pass the puck back to the blue line and a waiting Orr. His pass, however, didn't get past the outstretched stick of Jacques Lemaire, who now had a clear breakaway from his own blue line. One on one with the shaken Johnston, he quickly roofed the puck into the top of the net, tying the score at five.

The Boston Garden, so raucous a mere hour ago, was now stone silent.

With only five minutes remaining the game is still deadlocked. Behind the Bruins goal, Béliveau is pinned up against the boards, yet manages to slide the puck to an unmolested John Ferguson, waiting all alone in front of the net, who taps it in to the back of the Bruins net. It is Béliveau's fourth point of the game and the Canadiens have now taken a 6–5 lead.

As the clock winds down, the desperate Bruins press inside the Montreal zone. The Canadiens' Phil Roberto gathers a stray puck along the boards and shoots a pass to the centre of the ice that catches the stick of a streaking Frank Mahovlich, who with his long strides goes in alone on a waiting Johnston. Crossing the blue line he raises his stick high in the air and from twenty feet out blasts the blur of a puck past a helpless Johnston. It is the Canadiens' sixth unanswered goal. The score is now 7–5, which is what it will remain as Montreal evens the series at one game apiece. The loss is the Bruins' first in their last twelve playoff games. A period ago, the Bruins looked invincible. Now they appeared to be mortal.

With the game over, Murray Dryden is finally able to drive his ailing car home.

Chicago, Illinois, May 13, 1971. After the epic game-two victory in Boston, the invigorated Canadiens returned to Montreal and took game three by a 3–1 score. The Bruins evened the series with a 5–2 win before winning the pivotal fifth game by a resounding 7–3 score. After this game there were some calls for MacNeil and the Canadiens to put Dryden on the bench and bring in the experienced Vachon.

"[Dryden] is a great goaltender," a defensive Sam Pollock told the media. "We knew that when he was at Cornell. Then he went away for that year with the National Team and that was a wasted year. But we took a chance on him this year and look what he's done. How can anybody give up on him?"[31]

MacNeil, with Pollock's blessing, stayed the course with Dryden, and Montreal responded with an 8–3 blasting of the Bruins in game six. Before a national television audience in the United States and Canada, the two teams would clash one final time in a conclusive game seven on Sunday afternoon, April 18.

With the Canadiens holding a 4–2 lead in the third period, and Réjean Houle sitting in the penalty box, the Bruins unleashed their potent power play "and they led with their ace," wrote Frank Orr the next day in the Toronto Star. "Phil Esposito, their 76-goal shooter during the National Hockey League season, unloaded from the slot, the most productive move in history. Montreal Canadiens elongated rookie goaltender Ken Dryden flicked up his arm, deflected the puck to the ice and fell on it. Out of sheer frustration, Esposito slammed his stick against the glass. The mighty Bruins were dead."[32]

"The Bruins laughed their way through the 78 game schedule," added Milt Dunnell. "Then Dryden came along and proved the big, bad Bruins were a myth."[33]

In the afterglow of the upset victory, Ken Dryden took time the next morning to send a telegram to his father. The message was only three words in length, "Bruins ruined, Ken."[34]

In the midst of the Canadiens' playoff success, one could find Ken Dryden using his time away from the rink rifling through his law books in an effort to maintain a modicum of concentration on his studies. Back at McGill, he found it increasingly difficult to make all of his classes with the Canadiens playing every other night, so he had friends take notes for him. For many, the sight of Dryden during the day, a serious young student struggling to hold on to his law books while adjusting his glasses, gave the impression of a Clark Kent type. Of course, when he skated out to guard the Montreal net at night, he more closely resembled Superman.[35]

After brushing the Bruins aside, the Canadiens faced off against the Minnesota North Stars, then in only their fourth year of existence, in the semi-finals. Montreal was widely expected to walk over a pesky Minnesota team but required six games to finally advance to the Stanley Cup Finals against the Chicago Black Hawks.

After four games in the finals, the Canadiens and Black Hawks were deadlocked at two games apiece.

An hour and a half before the opening faceoff of game five, Sam Pollock sat by himself in the corner of the Chicago Stadium. Alone with his thoughts he had the satisfied look of a man vindicated. A year ago his team had been left for dead. Now here he was, two wins away from bringing home another Stanley Cup to Montreal, a potential championship that not even the team's most ardent supporters had thought was possible as recently as a month ago. Relaxing in the quietness of the empty arena before this most crucial of games Pollock was surprised to see an old associate coming toward him.

Sam Pollock had first met Scotty Bowman in 1947, the same year that Pollock had signed on for a position with the Montreal Canadiens. Bowman had started as a player under Pollock, but after a career-ending incident, he started working his way up through the Canadiens organization, first as an assistant coach in the junior leagues, then as a successful head coach, and eventually, in the sixties, as one of the team's top scouts. But when the 1967 expansion came along, Bowman took a position with the brand-new St. Louis Blues. Soon he was promoted to the head coaching position and led the Blues to three consecutive Stanley Cup Finals. However, in the past year the Blues had slid down in the standings and, after a power struggle with the St. Louis ownership, Bowman was out of a job. Despite the dismissal, Bowman was considered by many to be the league's best coach.

"I started talking to him," Pollock recalled. "He had just been let go by St. Louis one or two weeks before." Bowman told him he had received a couple of offers from both the Los Angeles Kings and the California Golden Seals, each of whom had offered the dual titles of general manager and head coach, but he was reluctant to go. Pollock immediately offered him a position within the Canadiens organization.[36]

The Canadiens lost that night to the Black Hawks 2–0, but the story of the game was quickly overshadowed by what took place afterwards in the Canadiens locker room. Henri Richard, next to Jean Béliveau, was the team's longest tenured player, and he had spent most of the game anchored to the bench. Furious, Richard blurted out after the game, for all to hear, that Al MacNeil was the worst coach he had ever played for.

Richard wasn't alone in his frustration. John Ferguson had also publicly spoken out against his coach days before. But in the Quebec of 1971, a year removed from the FLQ crisis, which had seen the

Canadian military sent in to quell a separatist uprising, Richard's words were political, social, and cultural dynamite. A media frenzy ensued along linguistic lines, with the French-speaking Henri, the younger brother of the still-worshipped "Rocket" Richard, on one side and his English-speaking coach, Al MacNeil, on the other. Many noticed the silence that emanated from the Canadiens management, as no one rushed to defend MacNeil. A shaken MacNeil received death threats as the controversy escalated out of control. For game six, held two days later on a Sunday afternoon, MacNeil took his spot behind the Montreal bench with a bodyguard on either side. Facing elimination, the Canadiens won the game 4–3, setting up a winner-take-all game seven in Chicago.

The setting for this mounting drama was the same building where a year ago the Canadiens had been eliminated from the playoffs. A successful novelist couldn't have crafted the story any better, with an amazing cast of characters, and all the surprise, controversy, and twists and turns that had marked this most memorable of seasons. And on the morning of the final game, May 18, the Montreal media would break the news that, win or lose, that night would be Jean Béliveau's final game. The stage was set in Chicago for a dramatic finale.

Chicago, Illinois, May 18, 1971. Midway through the second period, the Black Hawks held firm to a 2–0 lead. With all of the circumstances seemingly in their favour the Black Hawks appeared to be well on their way to a Stanley Cup championship. Then Jacques Lemaire of the Canadiens, who had decided to go for a line change, skated over the red line and uncorked a booming slapshot. Turning toward the bench, he soon heard a commotion from the crowd and turned to see that the puck had ended up in the Chicago net behind a dejected Tony Esposito.

With the score now 2–1, the tension in the building reached a fever pitch. Tonight, in the steamy Chicago Stadium, in the seventh game of the finals with the Stanley Cup on the line, Henri Richard, motivated by the events of the last few days, would put an exclamation point on an unforgettable spring.

A few minutes after Lemaire's shocking goal, a motivated Richard tied the score at two, setting up a third period for all the marbles. With only two and a half minutes gone, Richard, much as he had in his crucial game-two goal against Boston a month before, swept in on the left wing and, using his body as a shield for the puck, lifted what would become the Cup winner over a prone Tony Esposito.

To no one's surprise, Ken Dryden was awarded the Conn Smythe Trophy as the MVP of the playoffs. Within two months he had gone from being a curiosity to a media sensation, and the reporters stumbled over themselves as they reached for superlatives to describe the young man who guarded the Montreal net.

"I never saw a goaltender before who, when the play becomes ultra confusing in front of him, stretched out across the goal like a lady on a chaise lounge," wrote Scott Young in the *Toronto Telegram*. "Low shots plunked into his pads and the high ones he caught. Resting all the time. That is a very engaging habit he has, too, no matter how hot the action has been, of greeting every stoppage of play by folding his arms over the top of his stick and leaning there like a street cleaner resting on a broom."[37]

In the jubilant Canadiens locker room, the players revelled in the surprise Stanley Cup championship. "The best, the best of the 10 Stanley Cups I've won," proclaimed a relieved Henri Richard. "This one is the best because we were so much the underdogs, it wasn't even funny."[38]

A few days later, after the Stanley Cup celebration was slowly subsiding, Scotty Bowman placed a phone call to Montreal accepting Sam Pollock's offer of employment. Pollock quickly sent him a plane ticket.

Montreal, Quebec, June 10, 1971. Sam Pollock stood at the podium in the crowded ballroom of the Queen Elizabeth Hotel, a man triumphant. Still beaming from the glory of another Stanley Cup win, Pollock stood and looked out at his contemporaries, many of whom privately grumbled about his success. Today, though, there was another prize in the offing for the victorious Pollock, in the form of the first overall selection. To add to his competition's indignation, Pollock not only held the first pick of the draft but, thanks to his machinations, seven of the draft's first twenty-eight selections. The remaining twenty-one picks would be spread thinly among the other thirteen teams.[39]

Pollock and the Canadiens not only had control of the upcoming draft but also dominated the headlines. The day before the draft, the great Jean Béliveau had made his retirement official.

Then, an hour before the draft commenced, Pollock announced Scotty Bowman's appointment. Going forward, Pollock opined, that Bowman would be the best head coach for the Canadiens.[40]

"It certainly wasn't difficult for me to accept the [head coaching] job when it was offered," Bowman told the assembled media. "I was born here. I played here, and I got my first breaks with the organization here . . . I hope I can stay in Montreal and don't have to make another move."[41]

His predecessor, Al MacNeil, was named the head coach and general manager of Montreal's AHL affiliate, the newly transplanted Halifax Voyageurs. Though MacNeil had won the Stanley Cup, Pollock had been concerned about his deteriorating relationship with the Canadiens players, both English and French.

"I'm looking forward to the job with a great deal of optimism and I feel a lot of gratitude toward the organization," said MacNeil, forcing a smile in spite of what must have been an awkward situation for him. "I wanted the chance to get into management, because I love hockey and want to stay in it. I feel this experience will help my future." And then, in a moment of candour, he added, "It's been a fantastic year in many areas, but I do leave with a little bit of heartbreak . . . I want to wish my successor Scotty all the luck in the world."[42]

After the photographers snapped pictures of Bowman and MacNeil shaking hands, the two men made their way to the Canadiens draft table. Pollock now turned to the business of his team's future. He stepped to the podium to announce the first overall selection of the draft. And so it was that Guy Lafleur, wearing a brown, broadly checkered sports jacket, in the ballroom of the Queen Elizabeth Hotel, officially became a member of the Montreal Canadiens.[43]

The two months that made up the time between Dryden's elevation to the Montreal Canadiens roster and the drafting of Guy Lafleur may have represented the zenith of Sam Pollock's managerial career. In the span of a year he had wisely guided his organization to another Stanley Cup, only one season after it appeared his team was in shambles. Ken Dryden, a virtual unknown just two months ago, was now the hottest young star in hockey. In addition, Pollock had been able to secure a much in demand Scotty Bowman as his head coach and added the most highly prized hockey prospect in a generation, Guy Lafleur. In the coming years, these three men would form the backbone of the next great Canadiens dynasty.

6.

CHANGING OF THE GUARD

Moscow, Russia, May 11, 1969. In the Soviet Union the game was the Super Bowl, the World Series, and the Stanley Cup all rolled up into one giant spectacle. In a life where boredom was the pre-eminent emotion of the populace, a hockey game between the Central Red Army and Moscow Spartak had the ability to relieve a nation from its collective stupor.

At the time there were only two channels on state-sponsored Soviet television. The programming was, in a word, dull, as the strains of classical music vied with heavy doses of political propaganda and films praising the victory of the Soviet Union in the Second World War. Television was not the only form of cultural deficiency since all forms of creativity including music and the literary arts were stifled as censorship reigned supreme. Politics was an exercise in the operation of a dictatorship, and dissent was outlawed. The result was a country that was culturally lacking, with its citizens drudgingly living an existence best characterized by long stretches of tediousness and monotony.

On a Sunday afternoon in the spring of 1969, the Red Army and Spartak teams, their relationship described by one onlooker as the Russian equivalent of the Toronto Maple Leafs–Montreal Canadiens rivalry, would play each other on the final day of that season's Soviet Elite League schedule. At stake was that season's championship. Over the last eleven seasons the Red Army had won the league championship on nine separate occasions. In the two years that the Red Amy failed to finish in first, it was Spartak who was able to take the crown. For an eager television audience, it was a dream encounter.

Broadcast live throughout the Soviet Union on Soviet 1, it was estimated that a television audience of over 100 million looked on that day. Moscow's Luzhniki Sports Palace had a sell-out crowd of fourteen thousand, among them Leonid Brezhnev, the general secretary of the Communist Party. Outside of the Soviet Union, however, this colossal event received very little, if any, attention, as did the entire country's flourishing hockey scene. Instead, the small contingent of Canadian media operating out of Russia at the time was focused almost exclusively on politics. It wasn't until 1987, almost two decades later, that a Western journalist would be issued a press pass to cover the activities of the Soviet Elite league. In his history of Soviet hockey, *The Red Machine,* Lawrence Martin noted that "the march of the Red machine to the 1972 (Summit) series took place behind closed doors. All Westerners saw of the Russians was their infrequent foreign ice appearances, and that wasn't enough."[1] In a time before satellites and the Internet, and at the height of the Cold War, the Soviet Union was truly a closed society, shielded from all external influences, and a mystery to those in the outside world, including Canada.

As the climactic game inched toward the halfway mark of the third period, Spartak held on to a 2–1 lead over the Red Army. Under the rules of Russian hockey at the time the referee would whistle the play dead at the ten-minute mark of the third period, allowing the two goalies to switch ends. It was a uniquely Russian trait and a tradition hearkening back to the days when most of the games were played outdoors in the wind and snow. At the 9:59 mark of the period, the Red Army's Vladimir Petrov appeared to score the tying goal. The timekeeper, however, claimed that the period had reached the halfway mark and it was time for the two teams to switch sides. Asked to look at the scoreboard clock, which read 9:59, the timekeeper claimed it was wrong and once again ordered the two goalies to switch sides. Petrov's tying goal was disallowed.

Standing on the Red Army bench, Anatoli Tarasov, a fiery, temperamental man at the best of times, exploded. Consumed with rage, he stopped the game, vehemently demanding that the goal be counted or else his Red Army team would leave the ice. When the referees refused to make the change on the scoreboard, Tarasov went through with his threat, and the Red Army players marched to their dressing room. The spectators in the arena sat in a stunned silence and millions of viewers sat captivated in front of their television sets. In the strict regimentation of the Soviet Union, none of the populace had ever witnessed such an outward expression of naked emotion.

Sitting in his private box, enclosed in a case of unbreakable glass, visible to all the arena's spectators, Brezhnev sat alone tapping his fingers, his expression stoic. As various Soviet hockey officials pleaded with an enraged Tarasov in the inner bowels of the rink, the time slowly ticked by.[2] After thirty minutes had passed, the assembled crowd began to grow restless, the television producers nervous, and Brezhnev finally decided that he had seen enough. Motioning for one of his top aides, he quickly dispatched him to the Red Army dressing room with a single, stern message for Tarasov: It is the view of the general secretary that you should bring your players back on the ice. It was a message that left Tarasov with no alternatives.[3]

Soon after the delivery of the message, the Red Army slowly trudged back onto the ice. The original decision of the referee stood and the game resumed. Shortly after the puck dropped to restart the game, Brezhnev left the arena early, as he always did, in an effort to avoid the people. In the wake of Tarasov's outburst the rest of the game was anticlimactic. Spartak would add an insurance goal three minutes later, making the final score 3–1 and giving them the championship of the Soviet Elite League.

Tarasov would pay a steep price for his outburst. The Soviet media, an organ of the Communist Party, loudly denounced him. Meanwhile, Tarasov's walkout became a topic of wild discussion and speculation among the Soviet populace. The Canadian media, alerted to what happened after the fact, reported on the story, but with no embedded journalists they were forced to rely on Soviet newspaper accounts. There were no comments from any of the principals, including Tarasov, just proclamations from the government.

"The disputed goal and Tarasov's behavior have been the subject of constant debate here," wrote the *Globe and Mail,* three days after the incident. "In a bus yesterday morning, for instance, the driver, a Spartak fan, became so angry with a passenger who claimed the goal should have counted that he almost lost control of the vehicle."[4] *Sovietskaya Sport,* a newspaper devoted to the Soviet sporting scene, ran an editorial accusing Tarasov of always holding a disdainful attitude toward both judges and spectators. Claiming that Tarasov's action should have been expected, the paper noted that the delay in the game "disorganized the work of the central TV studio for the whole day."[5]

Such was the fallout from the incident that many of the newspapers within the Soviet Union questioned Tarasov's position as the head coach of the national team and his bestowed title of merited coach of the USSR.

"This title is given only to people not only with high accomplishments in their field, but who also are real pedagogues who educate in their pupils the best qualities of a Soviet person . . . A question arises, is Tarasov worthy of this high and responsible title?"[6]

As was often the case in the Soviet Union, the criticism in the newspaper was the prelude to the official action taken by the government a few days later. Five days after the game, and only a few days after the condemnation of Tarasov appeared in the Soviet press, the government removed the title of merited coach of the USSR from him. According to the Soviet media, a meeting of the government's sports committee claimed that the besieged Tarasov was guilty of "crudely violating sports ethics" and that despite his past accomplishments "he had begun to show intolerance of criticism," a veiled reference to Tarasov's continued defiance in the face of his government-sponsored reprimand.

In a closed society where everyone was expected to subjugate their individual wants and desires to those of the collective, Tarasov was guilty of placing himself solely in the spotlight. It was now the time for the government to put the stubborn Tarasov in his proper place. Such was the backlash from the walkout that his position as co-coach of the national team was now open for debate.

For the next six months, the usually outspoken Tarasov was muzzled and his name was rarely, if it all, mentioned in the pages of the Soviet newspapers. With the passage of time, however, the controversy slowly began to recede. In the autumn of 1969, Tarasov quietly, and without any fanfare or enlightenment, had his title as merited coach of the USSR restored. And then on November 13, without any mention of the incident or explanation, Tarasov's name was included in the announcement of the national team coaches for the upcoming Izvestia tournament.[7] That year's national team was made up of twenty players, seventeen of whom played for either the Red Army or Spartak. With Tarasov behind the bench and as always accompanied by his co-coach Arkady Chernyshev, the Soviets once again claimed the gold medal.

While his position as the head man of the national team was growing increasingly tenuous, there was never a doubt or a question on the Central Red Army hockey club as to who was the man in charge. With the Red Army Anatoli Tarasov went far beyond what would be considered the normal duties of a head coach, especially in a Canadian sense. He held full control over every aspect of his players' lives, including whether they would be allowed an off-site apartment or a car. His control over their lives was complete. For example, on two separate occasions, his star pupil, Vladislav Tretiak, asked his mentor for permission to get a day off and was refused. As a result, Tretiak was forced to postpone his wedding. It was Tarasov who dictated how the team spent its free time and in some cases what the player did for a post-hockey career.[8]

Under Tarasov, the Central Red Army hockey team trained in Arkhangelskoye, located twenty kilometres west of Moscow. Best known as an artists' village, nestled deep inside a birch forest, Arkhangelskoye is primarily made up of shabby, well-used wooden cottages and homes dating back to the days of the Tsars. The seclusion allowed an undisturbed Tarasov to put many of his theories into practice.

"I can honestly say that there wasn't one practice to which Tarasov came without new ideas," Tretiak recalled later. "He amazed all of us every day. One day he had a new exercise, the next an innovative idea, and the next a stunning combination to remove the effectiveness of our opponents. Inspiration was always one of Tarasov's main motives, and his training procedures were based on solid principles developed over a long period of time."[9]

Despite their status as Russian hockey royalty, the players on the Red Army team lived in far from luxurious settings.

"The players' residence is a light coloured structure of heavy concrete which, like a routine hotel, is comfortable but hardly a compliment to the venerable surroundings," wrote Lawrence Martin in his book *The Red Machine*. "The athletes are normally required to take their heavy, meaty meals at the compound's eatery. They live two to a room and the base has only one telephone. They have limited opportunity to talk to people other than themselves."[10]

The members of the Red Army team lived an existence that was highly regimented, with a routine that was both strict and firm in its organization. The players woke up every morning a little past seven, quickly showered, and then left the building for a session of open-air calisthenics. After completing their exercises they were served breakfast before hitting the gym and pumping iron for an hour. Arkhangelskoye at the time did not possess an ice surface, so the players were herded onto a bus that made the daily trek to Moscow and the Central Army sports club facilities, which included two ice surfaces. The team began their first on-ice workout at eleven in the morning, with the practice usually lasting for ninety minutes. When practice ended the players were bussed back to Arkhangelskoye, where after lunch they were given a two-hour break, which most of the players made use of by catching up on their sleep. Then it was back on the bus to Moscow for the second on-ice workout of the day, this one lasting a full hour longer than the first. Once the second practice was finished, the Red Army players were bussed back a final time to their compound, where the team was served supper. Following the team dinner, there were classroom sessions with the coaching staff. Then, with only a few precious hours left in the night, the players were permitted to watch television. In addition, the diets of the players were closely monitored, with smoking and the use of alcohol prohibited. At eleven o'clock the players were ushered off to bed.

Other than Sundays, when the players were usually allowed to get away from the compound to visit their friends and family, this was the Soviet players' routine for six days a week, eleven months out of the year. Since they technically were part of the country's army, they essentially worked for the government, where a simple day off was quite often discouraged. Working under a communist regime meant that all of the players were paid the same salary. But there were advantages to playing for the Red Army. Prospective Soviet youth dreamed of playing with the Red Army, as their championships brought with them more prestige as well as a better chance of playing with the national team, and the guarantee of a post-hockey occupation as an enlisted officer in the military.[11]

In the end, the Central Red Army as created, shaped, and moulded by the guiding hand of Tarasov became the most successful hockey club in the world. After the controversial loss to Spartak in 1969, Tarasov promptly led the Red Army to four consecutive Soviet Elite League titles. With Tarasov behind the bench, the Red Army's championship record was unparalleled, as they would win an astounding 18 league championships over 28 seasons. By way of a comparison, the Montreal Canadiens, the NHL's most successful franchise, over the space of their most successful period from 1953 to 1979, a span of 27 seasons, were able to capture 16 Stanley Cups.

On the international front, Tarasov was no less successful as the sixties slowly turned into the seventies. Alongside Arkady Chernyshev, he led the Soviet Union to victory at both the 1970 and 1971 World Championships, stretching the Red Army's consecutive streak to an amazing nine gold medals in a row.

Perhaps nothing better illustrates the successful dynamic of the Tarasov/Chernyshev duo than what took place in the Soviet dressing room in the final game of the 1971 championship. Needing a victory over Sweden to clinch the gold medal, the Soviets, after jumping out to a quick 2–0 lead, allowed three unanswered goals, and after forty minutes were trailing on the scoreboard 3–2.

"During the intermission in the dressing room, Tarasov berated us," Vladislav Tretiak recalled later. "Everyone got a piece of it, even the most famous veterans . . . Then our assistant coach, Chernyshev, took over. Chernyshev never raised his voice. His well-balanced, wise, calm and confident manner of conducting himself had a calming influence on the team . . . Chernyshev had found a few happy words, woke us up, and made us smile again. 'You are strong, you little devils. There is no other team like you.'"[12]

Skating out onto the ice, with Tarasov's stinging criticism and Chernyshev's soothing praise running through their heads, the Soviets scored four unanswered goals of their own on their way to a 6–3 win and their ninth consecutive gold medal.

As his teammates were receiving their gold medals, a proud Tarasov walked over to Tretiak, who was attempting to savour the moment. The year before Tretiak had played goal in some of the early games at the World Championships, but when the games began to matter he was watching from the bench as the more experienced Victor Konovalenko led the team to the 1970 World Championship. This year Tretiak had replaced a slumping Konovalenko, and now led the Soviet Union to the 1971 World Championship. Shaking his hand, Tarasov congratulated his prized pupil, and told him that from now on he was the primary goaltender for the Soviet National Team.[13]

A few months later, as Ken Dryden was leading the Montreal Canadiens to their most improbable Stanley Cup, Vladislav Tretiak was for the first time named the top goaltender in the Soviet Elite League.

The Soviet Union had reached the apex of the international hockey world. Yet for Anatoli Tarasov there was still something missing, the one achievement that had always remained out of his reach. He was concerned that his team and his country's hockey program were in danger of going stagnant, in large part due to the absence of Canada from the international hockey scene. And now, after an unprecedented two decades of success in international hockey, he felt that he had finally built a team that could compete and even defeat the best that only the NHL could provide.

Tarasov's long-range goal had always been to test his theories, his teachings, and ultimately his players against the best that Canada had to offer. At first it was a desire that he kept to himself. However, as the sixties progressed and his teams became even more dominant on the international scene, his desire to play Canada's best suddenly became more overt, and after years of shifting the discussion he now began to openly challenge the NHL.

In advance of an exhibition tour in January 1969, an audacious Tarasov created a minor media stir in Canada by openly challenging the Toronto Maple Leafs and the Montreal Canadiens to a game against his Soviet Nationals. In addition, he boldly predicted that his team would emerge as the victor in such a matchup. His offer was met with indifference by Stafford Smythe, the Leafs owner, who dismissed the challenge as mere propaganda. David Molson, the owner of the Canadiens, openly doubted Tarasov's sincerity.[14]

Tarasov remained undaunted. He was given the unique opportunity by the *Toronto Star* to write a column giving his impressions on the National Hockey League. Printed on December 30, 1969, the piece claimed that the NHL game had grown stale, with no noticeable improvements in the decade. Interestingly, he proposed that one NHL team was the exception, the one team that was willing not only to improve their techniques, but also to change them over time.[15]

That team was the Montreal Canadiens.

A month later, in another article written expressly for a Canadian audience, Tarasov went a step further, claiming that "we (Russia) and not you are the champions . . . Canadian amateurs are no longer a match for our team . . . We assure you that our boys will be able to knock the eagerness for rough-housing out of anybody who tries to play rough against a Soviet hockey team . . . It is time for Canadian game officials to forget their arguments against the match and let the world see a most interesting, most gripping spectacle."[16]

Despite the events of three years before and his clash with the Soviet government, and even after a mild heart attack suffered in the autumn of 1971, his second in a little over two years, the indomitable Tarasov refused to slow down. He now put his energy into preparing his national team for the 1972 Winter Olympics held in Sapporo, Japan. In the days leading up to the tournament, Tarasov and Chernyshev accepted an offer from the host country to play in two exhibition games. According to the terms of the agreement, each Soviet player would be reimbursed for their participation in the two exhibitions, with a payment of $200 for each game. At that time accepting any form of financial payment from any foreign country was considered anti-Communist by those in the government. Warned by the Kremlin, and for reasons still unclear to this day, a defiant Tarasov blatantly ignored their order and the players received their money.[17]

It was an irritated Tarasov who was behind the Soviet bench when the Olympic tournament began in Sapparo. After a pasting of Finland in the opening game, the Soviets' second game against Sweden was a different matter. Led behind the bench by former NHLer Billy Harris, the Swedes were able to overcome a two-goal deficit in the third period by scoring three goals against the powerful Russians. When the final buzzer sounded, the game ended in a 3–3 tie. As was normally his custom, Tarasov flew into a rage behind the bench after the third Swedish goal. Tarasov, however, was not the man he had once been, and his daughter, mindful of his recent health issues, frantically rushed to the bench and succeeded in calming him down.[18] The tie with Sweden would turn out to be a small impediment to the Soviets' march to the gold medal. Outscoring their opposition in their next three games by a combined total of 21 to 7, Tarasov and Chernyshev would lead the Soviet Union to their third consecutive Olympic gold medal. With the Olympics now over, however, there were serious consequences awaiting a disobedient Tarasov and Chernyshev upon their return to Russia. Ultimately, neither one of them would ever again coach a team representing the Soviet Union.

The man who made the decision to release the two legendary coaches upon their return was Andrei Starovoitov, the general secretary of the Soviet Ice Hockey Federation. One of the top bosses in the Soviet hockey hierarchy, Starovoitov had waited long and hard to exact his retribution on Tarasov. Upon taking control of the national team in the mid-1950s, one of Tarasov's first acts was to cut a disappointed Starovoitov from the team. Now years later, a patient Starovoitov had his revenge.[19]

The removal of Tarasov and Chernyshev was swiftly executed. The Soviet newspapers did not carry the news of their dismissal. The players on the national team were brought before the headquarters of the sports committee and informed of the coaching change. Ironically, within the Canadian media, Tarasov's firing was big news. The Russian government maintained he was departing for health reasons. In addition, a

Soviet spokesperson let it be known to the Canadian media that despite winning nine consecutive World Championships, as well as three consecutive Olympic gold medals, "that the quality of the Russian team has been declining."[20]

In 1969, the first time Tarasov had been removed from his post, he had been granted a reprieve by the Soviet government. Now, three years later, there would be no amnesty forthcoming.

Prague, Czechoslovakia, April 19, 1972. The early seventies were witness to a gradual thaw in the Cold War. With the United States mired in the throes of the Vietnam conflict and the Soviet Union economically burdened in an effort to keep up in the arms race, both countries began looking for alternatives to what had been almost three decades of escalation. Talks began about reducing the proliferation of weapons, and the historic visit by President Richard Nixon in May 1972 to the Soviet Union signalled a détente in the relations between the world's two superpowers. After Nixon met with his Soviet counterpart, Leonid Brezhnev, the US and the USSR signed the first treaties that specifically dealt with arms control.

A month before, with the spirit of détente in the air, Canadian and Soviet hockey officials gathered in Prague, Czechoslovakia, the site of the 1972 World Championship, and finally hammered out the details of a Summit Series. This encounter would finally put the best of the Soviet Union against the best of Canada on the same ice surface, and would start that September. After years of back-and-forth talk, proposals, and discussion, the announcement that Anatoli Tarasov had waited his entire life for had finally come. Originally billed in the media as the World Series of hockey, Toronto Maple Leafs owner Harold Ballard upped the ante by proclaiming the upcoming series to be "the greatest sports event in our history."[21]

Anatoli Tarasov would now see his long-held dream come to fruition. The system he had constructed and the players he had trained would now undergo the ultimate test. The Summit Series would also put his theories, his methods, his techniques, all under the microscope, in effect placing the last twenty-five years of his professional life on trial.

But Tarasov would not be an active participant in the upcoming confrontation between the two hockey superpowers. He would travel with the team to Canada, but he would view the series as a spectator.

However, his towering presence would hang over the Russians for the entire duration of the series. The once volatile and outspoken bear, the father of Russian hockey, would be watching from afar, silenced by his own government.

THE SUMMIT SERIES

Vienna, Austria, June 25, 1972. Alongside his wife, Lynda, Ken Dryden was enjoying a well-deserved vacation in Vienna. It had been over ten weeks since he had last worn the goalie equipment that had brought him such sudden fame. Now he was taking a brief respite from the bright spotlight of success and trying to put the events of the last fifteen months into some sort of perspective.

A full-time law student at McGill University, he had become an overnight sensation, leading the Montreal Canadiens to a surprising Stanley Cup triumph in the spring of 1971. After being awarded the Conn Smythe Trophy as the playoff's most valuable player he had spent the summer working for consumer advocate Ralph Nader, campaigning for fishermen in Chesapeake Bay, Virginia, who sought to preserve the quality of their clean water.

Solidly established as the Canadiens' number-one goaltender, Dryden would prove that his playoff success was no fluke. Because he had only appeared in six regular season games the spring before, when the 1971–72 season began he was still considered a rookie by the NHL standards of the day. Starring in 64 games for the Canadiens in his first full season, he led the league in wins with 39. Dryden was rewarded at season's end with a spot on the second All-Star team and the Calder Trophy as the league's rookie of the year, becoming the first and only player to capture that trophy after winning the Conn Smythe Trophy the season before. Despite the trophies Dryden's first full season ended in disappointment, as the Canadiens were bounced from the playoffs by the New York Rangers.

Now among the beauty of a summer day in one of Vienna's numerous cafés, the Drydens were taking pleasure in a relaxing brunch. However, the tranquility of the scene couldn't satisfy an anxious Dryden, who kept consulting his watch as the time slowly approached one in the afternoon. Knowing that he had to return an important phone call, he tried to determine what time it was back in Rochester, New York. According to his calculations, it would now be eight o'clock in the morning. His wife warned him that Harry Sinden would probably be still asleep in bed, but Dryden was unable to resist the urge. He placed the collect call and awoke a sleeping Sinden.[1]

Sinden had been the captain of the Whitby Dunlops' team that had captured the World Championship for Canada in 1958. In 1966, he was named the head coach of the Boston Bruins, whom he led to a Stanley Cup championship four years later. Because of a contract dispute, however, he had left the team soon thereafter. Now, two years later, he suddenly rejoined the sport, this time as the head coach of Team Canada for the upcoming Summit Series.

Dryden eagerly accepted Sinden's offer of a spot on Team Canada. In addition to fulfilling his desire to once again test his skills against the Soviet Union, Dryden figured that playing in the series would be much more enjoyable than the alternative, the Montreal Canadiens training camp, which would be held that fall in Kentville, Nova Scotia.

Sinden informed Dryden that the training camp would start on August 13 at Maple Leaf Gardens in Toronto. Sinden went on to tell him that the squad would include a number of Dryden's Montreal teammates such as Yvan Cournoyer, J.C. Tremblay, and the brother duo of Frank and Peter Mahovlich. With his law exams at McGill scheduled for the end of July, Dryden assured his new coach that he would be ready.[2]

Toronto, Ontario, July 12, 1972. Standing before an eager press Harry Sinden announced to the world what would be described in the media as the greatest team ever assembled. True to his word to Ken Dryden a few weeks before, Sinden included on the prospective roster more than a few members of the Montreal Canadiens. Many of them were widely predicted beforehand. However, there was one selection that raised more than a few eyebrows, that of injury-riddled defenceman Serge Savard.

The twenty-three-year-old had burst onto the NHL scene with the Canadiens in the spring of 1969. In addition to winning his second

Stanley Cup in as many years, he scored ten points in fourteen playoff games, becoming the first defenceman and at that time the youngest player to ever win the Conn Smythe Trophy as the most valuable player in the playoffs. It seemed that he was ready to assume the mantle, now solely held by Bobby Orr, as one of the game's premier defencemen.

"Serge Savard, in fact, belongs in the present tense," wrote Dick Beddoes that spring. "He revealed in the Boston series that he is 1–2 with Robert Orr as the prodigal young defensemen in hockey, and not necessarily 2."[3]

The respected Beddoes wasn't alone in his praise or in the heady comparison. "He is like the Boston Bruins' Bobby Orr when he breaks out of his own zone," Louis Cauz of the *Globe and Mail* observed, "swiveling around the forecheckers and driving in on goal or passing and charging in looking for the rebound."[4]

However, less than a year later, on March 11, 1970, all that changed. With less than a month left in the season the Canadiens were chasing a playoff spot that would ultimately prove to be out of reach. That night's opposition was provided by the New York Rangers, who would eventually capture that elusive last playoff berth. Caught up the ice in the third period, Savard tried to catch an onrushing Vic Hadfield, who was bearing down on Canadiens goaltender Rogie Vachon. At the last possible moment, a desperate Savard lunged forward and managed to strip the puck off the stick of the Rangers star. However, the move had left him in a vulnerable position, as his momentum carried him full speed into his own goal. Suddenly his left leg violently collided with the foot-long steel pegs that made up the net's goalposts. The vicious impact shattered his leg in five places.

The doctors put Savard, who was in immense pain, in a hip-to-ankle cast that night at the hospital. That same night, however, a sleeping Savard refractured the same leg when the shattered limb twitched inside the plaster cast. A second, similar break convinced the doctors to remove the cast and insert two steel pins in an effort to keep the broken bones in place. Despite undergoing three separate operations that week, Savard never felt as if his career was in jeopardy. He was in the minority. "Maybe I was never aware of the danger. I read in the papers that my career was finished, but I never believed it."[5]

After missing the first month of the 1970–71 season, a determined Savard made his return to the Canadiens lineup, but on January 30,

1971, he would once again break the same bones in his seemingly brittle left leg. "Bobby Baun of the Maple Leafs hit me with a clean hip check – hard and low," Savard admitted. "He caught me right where the pins were, but it didn't seem to bother me."[6] Feeling no pain, Savard got up, retrieved a loose puck in the Canadiens' end of the rink, and cleared the zone before making his way to the Montreal bench. As soon as he sat on the bench, the pain began.

Faced with a second broken left leg in ten months, the doctors decided to remove the pins and instead graft bone from Savard's right hip to the broken bones on his left leg. For the next year a rehabilitating Savard would be a fixture in the dressing room, spending endless hours pedalling a stationary bicycle and rehabbing the battered leg in a hot tub.[7] When the Canadiens opened their training camp in the fall of 1971, Savard tentatively took his first steps back onto the ice.

"The first time I came back I don't think I was conscious of my broken leg," Savard later recalled. "The second time I couldn't help thinking about it. For instance when I jumped over the boards onto the ice to practice I always made certain that I landed on my right skate, not my left. Then one day I jumped over and came down on my left foot without even thinking about it. After that I wasn't worried anymore."[8]

The doctors, however, didn't share their patient's confidence and refused to allow Savard to scrimmage with his teammates in training camp. It would be another four months before the doctors would clear him to play for the Canadiens. Starting on February 4 in California, a relieved Savard would see action in the team's next seventeen games before an unlikely return to the hospital ward.

After defeating the hometown St. Louis Blues 5–1 on the evening of March 9, the Canadiens returned to their hotel at the Hilton Inn. In the early morning hours of March 10, a fire broke out on the hotel's fourth floor, leaving a number of the hotel's guests trapped in their rooms, including Canadiens head coach Scotty Bowman.

Alongside his teammates Savard helped with the rescue by climbing ladders and kicking out the windows of rooms that were rapidly filling with smoke. As a result of his selflessness, Savard suffered a badly cut right leg, which required eighteen stitches, and an ankle with chips of glass imbedded in it. In addition to rescuing their coach, the Canadiens were credited with saving the lives of a number of the hotel's patrons.[9] Thankfully Savard's injuries weren't serious and he returned to the

Canadiens lineup in time for the playoffs – only to see the team eliminated in the first round by the New York Rangers.

Relaxing in the summer of 1972, Savard wasn't expecting an invitation to play for Team Canada that fall in the Summit Series. Ironically, it was an injury to Bobby Orr, with whom he once been favourably compared, that paved the way for his own participation. Despite his own well-known history of injuries, and thanks to the intervention of his old teammate and now Team Canada's assistant coach, John Ferguson, Savard was asked to come to the team's training camp. He was surprised but philosophical about the invitation. "Why kid myself? Bobby Orr was hurt. I was named as a fill-in."[10]

Guy Lapointe's placement on the Team Canada roster in 1972 was almost as improbable as Savard's. Unlike many of his teammates in Montreal, Lapointe had never dreamed of one day playing for the Canadiens for one simple reason: he never considered himself to be good enough. The son of a long-time Montreal fire captain and the brother of a Montreal police officer, the young Lapointe had already enlisted and begun training with the Quebec Provincial Police department. And then one day in the mail he found an invitation to the Montreal Canadiens training camp starting in the fall of 1968.

"I had no interest in going to the Montreal Canadiens camp," Lapointe admitted later. "At that time, they were inviting over a hundred kids just for a try-out. My Dad said, 'You gotta go. You can still put in your application to be a policeman and you can always go back to it but you will never have another chance to go to the Montreal Canadiens' camp.' After our discussion, I thought my chances were almost zero to make the team. For once, I listened to my Dad and I went to camp."[11]

After having an admittedly average camp, Lapointe was offered a contract with the Canadiens and soon he was playing in far-off Houston for the Apollos. A seriously homesick Lapointe, who spoke only French and was away from home for the very first time, struggled to adapt. Thanks to his father, who urged him to stick it out, and his Apollos roommate Phil Myre, who taught him the nuances of the English language, Lapointe soon began to assert himself on the ice, to the point where he even saw a few shifts with the big club on October 27, 1968, as the Canadiens dropped a 4–2 loss in Boston.[12]

"The thing I will never forget is going into the room," Lapointe later reflected. "It was like I was walking on a cloud, just looking around and seeing players like Henri Richard and J.C. Tremblay. But I do remember just looking at Jean Béliveau and I was hardly able to tie my skates, I was so nervous."[13]

The next season the Canadiens moved their primary farm team from Houston to Montreal and Lapointe suited up with the AHL's Voyageurs, in addition to seeing action in five games for the 1969–70 Canadiens. The following year he became a regular with the team, in large part due to the continued injury troubles of Serge Savard. Under the tutelage of veteran Canadiens rearguard J.C. Tremblay, the inexperienced Lapointe learned what it took to be a professional and a Montreal Canadien.

"I do remember playing with J.C. Tremblay and I would yell at him to pass the puck. He told me that if my stick wasn't on the ice he wouldn't pass the puck to me. He used to say, 'Kid, show me the stick on the ice, I want to see the blade, and then I'll make you a pass.'"[14]

Lapointe listened well and made an immediate impact, leading the team's defencemen in scoring in 1970–71 with 15 goals and 44 points. That spring, he lived out a childhood dream by winning the Stanley Cup.

"The first time is a dream. For myself, I was a kid who grew up in Montreal about a half hour away from the Forum. You don't even think that one day you're going to play for the Montreal Canadiens. As a kid, you used to wait outside to get the players' autographs and then one day, you end up in the same room with the guy who was my idol – Jean Béliveau – the same as guys who I used to watch on television. It was unbelievable!"[15]

"There are players who come along every once in a while and after about three games in the NHL, you don't think they're a rookie," says broadcaster Dick Irvin. "Guy Lapointe, after about three games his first season, you never thought of him again as a rookie. He just fit in so quickly and played so well right off the bat."[16]

Though he followed his rookie season with an equally superb second season, Lapointe was not the first choice of Team Canada's Harry Sinden in organizing his roster for the upcoming Summit Series. Instead, Sinden hoped to persuade Lapointe's teammate and long-time Montreal rearguard Jacques Laperrière to join Team Canada. However, because Laperrière's wife was expecting a child, he respectfully declined.[17] Lapointe was in the same position as Laperrière, his wife was also expectant, and he knew that if he accepted Sinden's offer he was likely going to miss the birth of his son.

"It was a tough decision for me," Lapointe admitted later, "but I had to go because it was a great chance."[18] He still harboured some doubts as to whether he truly belonged. "I was just beginning to find my way around the NHL and I was trying to learn all the tricks of the trade. When I arrived at the Team Canada training camp, I was in awe of all the great names there. I kept wondering: 'Why Guy Lapointe? Why me? Why not a more experienced guy?'"[19]

Over the course of a month Lapointe would not only prove his worth but once again exceed all expectations.

Savard and Lapointe were only two of the six Montreal Canadiens players moonlighting that fall on the Team Canada roster. No other NHL team would place so many players on the Canadian squad. Five of them would play a crucial role in the final outcome of the series. One of them would reportedly become unglued.

As the story goes, upon his arrival in Moscow, a suspicious Frank Mahovlich conducted a thorough search of his hotel room, scouring it for listening devices. According to Dick Beddoes, the famed *Globe and Mail* columnist, the frantic Mahovlich discovered a metal object, hidden underneath the rug. After peeling the rug back, he then proceeded to unscrew it, convinced that it was exactly what he was looking for. Suddenly he heard a loud crash. It turned out that a light fixture had dropped to the floor below his.

Whether the story is true or not is known only to those who were there. What can't be disputed is that Frank Mahovlich, the senior member of Team Canada, was not in full command of his game or his faculties throughout the series.

"He was psyched about Russia," Serge Savard recalled later. "We don't know what happened to him over there."[20]

However, his younger brother, Peter, to the surprise of many, emerged as one of the key players throughout the series.

More than eight years younger than his famous brother, Peter Mahovlich seemed destined to be an afterthought. Renowned for his hulking size (he stood six-foot-five and weighed 210 pounds), famous last name, and untapped potential, he was viewed by many in the hockey world as a disappointment, and after six lacklustre seasons in the Detroit Red Wings organization, he was dealt to the Montreal Canadiens in a four-player swap on June 6, 1969.

"Peter's problem was that he was brought up when he still had a year or two of junior hockey left," explained his new boss in Montreal, Sam

Pollock. "And he was brought up to a team that didn't use him. But he looked good enough at Fort Worth for us to go after him."[21]

Beginning the season with the AHL's Montreal Voyageurs, Mahovlich was called up for good to the Canadiens on March 14, 1970. Over the course of thirty-six games that season he emerged as an offensive threat while also showcasing a renewed commitment in the defensive end and a previously unseen mean streak. Answering a group of eager reporters looking for an explanation for his sudden turnaround, Mahovlich was quick to credit a chance meeting a few months before with John Ferguson, the noted Montreal pugilist.

"It was in the (early) winter of 1970, which was my first season in the Montreal organization," Mahovlich explained. "I met Fergie in the Forum one day and he said 'come with me, kid. I want to talk to you.' He said he couldn't understand why, when I was the biggest man in the National Hockey League, I was playing the way I was. He told me I should be skating right over top of people, instead of skirting politely around them. He said I had nothing to fear from anybody in the league so I should be playing that way – aggressively, going after people."[22]

The 1970–71 season saw the flourishing Mahovlich play his first full season with the Canadiens, as he transformed himself from a lackadaisical player to a more belligerent foe, tallying 35 goals and 61 points to go along with a team leading 181 penalty minutes.

"Mahovlich was a perfect fit with the Canadiens," Red Fisher later wrote. "They needed his size. They needed his skill with the puck. They needed the joy he brought to the ice, and off it. Hockey was a game, something to enjoy – and Peter enjoyed it to the fullest."[23]

Reunited with his older brother, Frank, who was traded to the Canadiens in January 1971, the younger Mahovlich shone in the playoffs, scoring six goals and adding ten assists while excelling on the penalty kill. Like his teammate Guy Lapointe, also a second-year player, Mahovlich was able to take his first sip from the Stanley Cup that spring.

The following season he repeated his thirty-five-goal season and, despite a disappointing playoff performance where he was held to only two assists in the Canadiens' six-game exit from the post-season, Mahovlich was an easy selection for the Team Canada brain trust in 1972.

"Frankly, I was surprised when I was asked to play for Team Canada against the Russians," a modest Mahovlich informed the press at the squad's training camp. "I didn't have such a good season. Somebody must have put in a good word for me. It probably was Fergie [assistant coach John Ferguson]. Now I've got to vindicate him."[24]

Winnipeg, Manitoba, June 28, 1972. Three days after Harry Sinden's long-distance discussion with a vacationing Ken Dryden, the hockey landscape was forever altered. Standing on the corner of a packed Portage and Main, Bobby Hull, one of hockey's greatest stars, was photographed holding an oversized certified cheque for $1 million. That upcoming fall he would abandon his Chicago Black Hawks jersey in favour of the brand-new threads of the Winnipeg Jets, who would begin play as one of the original teams in the nascent World Hockey Association.[25]

The World Hockey Association had quietly been founded the year before. Before Hull's blockbuster signing, the WHA had received little notice. For the most part the talent that signed up for the upcoming WHA season were college and minor-hockey journeymen players. But Hull's signing with the Jets changed everything and virtually overnight the WHA became a viable alternative to the long-established NHL. In a sport that had the lowest average salary of the four major sports, other NHL superstars followed Hull's lead, with each of them receiving a drastic increase in pay. Sixty-seven NHLers that summer, including Gerry Cheevers and Derek Sanderson of the Stanley Cup champion Boston Bruins and J.C. Tremblay of the Montreal Canadiens, joined the new league.

Hull's defection to the WHA caused a major ripple through a still-forming Team Canada. Like Dryden, Hull had accepted Sinden's invitation to join the team. But Clarence Campbell, the long-time president of the NHL, who had painstakingly overcome the objections of many in his ownership to secure the players' participation in the upcoming series, publicly declared that if a newly defected Hull were permitted to play, no NHLer would participate. Campbell's threat was clear and for Alan Eagleson, the head of the NHL Players' Association and the man most responsible for the series' creation, "My choice was either blow the tournament or blow Bobby Hull."[26]

Despite a national uproar and the intervention of Pierre Trudeau, Canada's prime minister, Hull – alongside Cheevers, Sanderson, and Tremblay, each of whom would have also been on Team Canada – would sit on the sidelines when the series began. They would be joined by Bobby Orr, hockey's greatest player, who would sit out the entire series with an injured knee. In the end, the controversy subsided when Team Canada opened its training camp on August 13.

For many in the media, caught up in the excitement of the event, the absence of Bobby Hull and Bobby Orr quickly became a non-story. After all, with such a collection of Canadian superstars on the ice, and all on one team, it was not as if the visiting Soviets were going to be able to provide much competition.

Leningrad, Russia, August 22, 1972. Training for the upcoming show-down against Canada, the players that would represent the Soviet Union were enjoying a more relaxed atmosphere under their new coach, Vsevold Bobrov, himself a former star with the national team two decades before. Unlike his predecessor, Anatoli Tarasov, Bobrov had relaxed the strict regimentation and given his players more individual freedom, both off and on the ice. No player took advantage of this more than the team's goaltender, Vladislav Tretiak. On two prior occasions, he had asked Tarasov for a day off so he could get married, only to have his request denied. Now, with Bobrov's permission, he finally had time to get married to his long-time girlfriend, Tatiana, on August 23, 1972.[27]

On the eve of his wedding, Tretiak patrolled the net for the Red Army team in an exhibition contest against the Soviet team that would square off in a few weeks against Canada. Since many of the players starred for both teams, it was agreed that, with the exception of Tretiak, all of the best players would side up with the Nationals, leaving a Red Army team made up primarily of lower-tier players who normally didn't see action with the team.

The evening before the game, Tretiak and his compatriots from the Red Army had celebrated his upcoming nuptials long into the night. The next morning, Tretiak, on the eve of his wedding, and still feeling the effects of the night before, skated to his goal for what was, to him, a meaningless exhibition game. Surrounded by a shell of his normal Red Army team, up against the powerful Soviet National Team, and with his condition severely weakened from the night before, Tretiak's performance was not up to his usual standards. He and his Red Army "imposters" were trounced by the national team by a score of 8–1.[28]

Unbeknownst to Tretiak, two representatives from Team Canada, Bob Davidson and John McLellan, were watching the exhibition game from a jammed press box. McLellan, the head coach of the Toronto Maple Leafs, and Davidson, the Leafs' chief scout, would spend only four days in the Soviet Union and see only two games, including this one. Unaware of Tretiak's "condition," they came away thoroughly unimpressed as they watched eight goals get past him. On their arrival back at Canada's training camp, the two scouts informed John Ferguson, the team's assistant coach, that Tretiak was definitely a weak spot, to the point that Canada would have a five- to six-goal advantage in each game of the upcoming series. It didn't take long for the scouting report to spread within the ranks of Team Canada and then throughout the media. Ken Dryden, the only member of the team to have played against Tretiak, was skeptical.

"McLellan and Davidson did not come back with glowing reports," Dryden recorded in his diary of the series. "But I'm not convinced . . . we shouldn't take the reports from Leningrad too seriously."[29]

On August 26, three days after his wedding, Tretiak, alongside his teammates boarded a plane for Canada.

A LITTLE PIECE OF ALL
OF US DIED TODAY

Montreal, Quebec, September 2, 1972. For many in Montreal, the Sunday of the 1972 Labour Day was best enjoyed outdoors; the temperature reached into the high eighties, and the sun shone brightly and hot. The mood across the city was one of celebration as people enjoyed the last weekend of summer.

Meanwhile, Team Canada spent the morning of the first game inside the cooler confines of the Montreal Forum. Before a morning meeting in which Harry Sinden went over some last-minute details, the confident Canadian players engaged in a loose morning skate. Reflecting the relaxed atmosphere, Ken Dryden shed his goalie equipment and took some laps around the ice, all the while pretending he was a forward as he spent the morning shooting the puck.

In the middle of the Canadian practice, the opposing Soviets entered the Forum. The Russian players spent the night before at the movies, enjoying a screening of the popular movie *The Godfather.* Now they sat in the stands and observed the Canadian stars shooting the pucks loudly against the Forum boards, creating a sound that reverberated through the empty arena.

"They were shooting pucks so fast that we thought there were bullets in the air," Tretiak remembered later, as if he were describing a scene from the film the night before. "The speed of the Canadians was also incredible . . . it looked as if they were flying slightly above the ice."[1]

Watching in silence the Soviet team appeared star-struck. After the Canadian team concluded their morning practice, the Soviets took to the ice.

Eddie Johnston, the third goalie on Team Canada, wasn't too impressed by what he saw.

"I remember sitting in the Forum watching the Russians practice and it looked like it was going to be a blowout. They screwed around, nothing went right, and they just looked awful. You couldn't help but wonder about this team."[2]

Before the watchful eyes of Team Canada, the Russians had spent the days before the opening game deliberately practising at a slow speed. At this, their final practice, they continued the charade. In their display of ineptitude they seemed to confirm the opinions that McLellan and Davidson had brought back from Russia in their scouting report. Their shots appeared soft; their defenceman, clumsy; and their goalie, Tretiak, seemed stuck deep in his net, flubbing shot after shot. Their laissez-faire attitude led many to question whether the Soviets were even taking the whole event seriously.

Among the Canadian media, many of whom had never seen the Russians up close and in person until five days ago, the vast majority believed that the Soviet squad was overmatched, a fact confirmed in an informal poll taken by the Montreal *Gazette* on the eve of the series opener:

Red Storey, former NHL referee: "Canada in eight straight – but the toughest will be the opener."

Jim Coleman, Southam News Services: "Canada will win seven, with one game tied on Russian ice."

Jacques Plante, Toronto Maple Leafs goalie: "Eight straight for Canada."

Jerry Eskenazi, *New York Times:* "The NHL team will slaughter them in eight straight."

Milt Dunnell, *Toronto Star:* "Canada will win handily; they might lose one in Moscow. Say 7–1.

Claude Larochelle, *Le Soleil:* "We may lose one in Russia. 7–1 for Canada."

Foster Hewitt, *Hockey Night in Canada:* "Canada's two goals a game better. It looks like 8–0 Canada."

Dick Beddoes, *Globe and Mail:* "Canada to romp in eight – it's a Russian team in decay."

Fran Rosa, *Boston Globe:* "8–0 Canada – and that's also the score of the first game."

Mark Mulvoy, *Sports Illustrated:* "Canada, 7–1."[3]

The hyperbole was not limited to the media, however, as Alan Eagleson, the organizer of the series, boldly proclaimed: "We gotta win in eight games. Anything less than an unblemished sweep of the Russians would bring shame down on the heads of the players and the national pride."[4]

The glowing media predictions of their own dominance, the Russians' poor practices, the scouting reports: all of it trickled down to Team Canada. Even Ken Dryden, the most thoughtful of the Canadian players, briefly wondered aloud if the Russians weren't somehow putting on a show for Canada's benefit. But just as quickly as the thought appeared he banished it from his mind, the sheer confidence of his fellow teammates swaying him. Along with the rest of the team he came to believe that Team Canada would defeat the Russians pretty easily.

The Soviet deception was complete.

Getting dressed in the visitors' dressing room at the Montreal Forum that evening, Vladislav Tretiak is feeling rushed, in large part due to to the Russian team arriving at the arena later than scheduled, thanks to heavier than expected traffic congestion.[5]

Suddenly, a surprise visitor enters the room. Accompanied by an interpreter, the legendary Jacques Plante approaches a startled, yet admiring, Tretiak. The two men are not strangers to each other, having exchanged pleasantries and discussed goaltending during the Soviet Nationals' tour of Canada in the fall of 1969. Now, right before the biggest game of his life, Tretiak and his idol sit right beside each other. A piece of chalk in hand, Plante then makes his way to the chalkboard and before a stunned Tretiak and his teammates carefully proceeds to give a detailed description of Team Canada's best players. Phil Esposito, Yvan Cournoyer, Frank Mahovlich: Plante dissects all of them, outlining their strengths, their weaknesses, their tendencies.

For Tretiak, this is a crash course from the master, one that he admitted later was invaluable.

"I am still puzzled by what motivated him to do that. He probably felt sorry for me, the little guy, in whom Esposito was going to shoot holes. I don't know, but I will always be very grateful to Jacques Plante, whose suggestions helped me so much."[6]

Realizing his team is anxious, Bobrov attempts to put them at ease. He tells them that they are better skaters and passers than their Canadian opponents. He tells them to stick to their game plan, and not to panic if

Canada jumps out to an early lead, stressing that it will be a long game.

The sold-out crowd that evening in the Montreal Forum, all 18,818 people, many clad in shirtsleeves, have come to see their team, Canada's team, administer a painful and punishing hockey lesson to these Soviet upstarts. They are joined by millions of television viewers across the country. For close to two decades they have read about Soviet successes at the Olympics, the World Championships, and so on. But in the Canadian psyche, gently stoked by the media, all of those victories are considered meaningless because the country has never been represented by its very best players, until now.

Taking to the ice, the Soviet team is introduced first. Each player's name is broadcast over the Forum loudspeaker and is met with silence. They are all unknown to the home crowd: their faces are interchangeable, their names unpronounceable, each of them are clad in uniforms that look worn and ill-fitting.

They stand in stark contrast to their opponents. The Canadian team is introduced to rapturous applause, as the Forum crowd lets loose a generation of pent-up expectation. It is this revival of Canadian pride that Pierre Trudeau hopes to capitalize on. The day before, the prime minister announced his bid for re-election. As he confidently makes his way to centre ice to perform the ceremonial puck drop, Trudeau is mindful of his new campaign's slogan, "The Land Is Strong."

It takes Team Canada all of thirty seconds to open the scoring.

"There was so much noise," Tretiak later recalled. "I remember the crowd going crazy, people were roaring, laughing, whistling, and yelling. Phil Esposito, who scored the goal, patronizingly tipped me on my shoulder and said 'OK.' It was a clear message: 'Take it easy, don't forget who you're playing against.'"[7]

For Tretiak, who was accustomed to playing in silent arenas across Europe, it was a disconcerting moment. Never before had he experienced anything like it. The sound of the siren pounded in his head, the flashing lights blinded his eyes, and the roar of the crowd made it impossible to think. After the goal was announced the Forum organist broke into the song "Moscow Night." Six minutes later, Paul Henderson made the score 2–0. Tretiak later described the crowd's reaction as "a triumphant rage." This time the Montreal organist began playing a funeral march.[8]

"For the first five minutes it was as if I was in the darkness, couldn't get out in the light. All our players tried to do was get rid of the puck. When it was 2–0 I thought we would lose by a lot."[9] Tretiak comforted himself in the knowledge that at the very least, the series represented an opportunity for him to test himself against the very best competition.

Not only had the crowd begun celebrating in earnest, but some of the Canadian players rushed over each other to get onto the ice to get in on some of the action. "When we got up by a couple of goals we were all saying, 'Here we go,'" said Peter Mahovlich. "Then, all of a sudden it was, 'There they go.'"[10]

While the early 2–0 lead boosted an already overconfident Team Canada, the deficit has a calming effect on the nervous Russians, who now collectively feel as if they have nothing to lose. Gaining in confidence with each passing minute, the Soviets go on the offensive, attacking a bewildered Team Canada in waves, passing the puck from stick to stick with startling precision and ratcheting up the pace of the play. They look to be the equal of an NHL squad rounding into late-season form. Sitting above the ice is a shocked media corps, whose surprise quickly morphs into a sense of wonder.

Team Canada becomes disorganized, playing as a group of individual stars and not as a team. At the 11:40 mark of the first period, the Soviets score their first goal. Over six minutes later, only nine seconds after Canada begins a power play, the Russians tie the game, when Vladimir Petrov taps a Boris Mikhailov rebound past a prone Dryden. The first period ends with the score tied at 2.

After twenty minutes of play, the summer heat has slowly started to infiltrate the Montreal Forum, and an eerie mist settles over the ice. The Canadian players are gasping for breath in the ever more suffocating air. The difference between the two teams at the end of the period is unmistakable: the Soviets appear to have barely broken a sweat; the Canadians look as if they have already played the full sixty minutes.

Mixed with the exhaustion in the atmosphere of the Canadian dressing room during the first intermission are feelings of anger, disillusionment, and confusion. Sitting there, Phil Esposito realizes Team Canada's predicament. The first period was much faster paced and as a result more tiring than he ever thought it would be.

Later, Esposito compared the intensity of the first period to a Stanley Cup Finals game. "These guys can really motor," he acknowledged before expressing a thought shared by all of his teammates: "Whoever scouted them should be shot."[11]

—

By the time the players return to the ice for the second period, a distinctive chill has spread among the spectators in the Forum. The scoreboard may read 2–2, but the sense of dread is impossible to ignore. The shock is twofold: not only is Canada not as good as everyone thought, but the Soviets are much better than anyone imagined.

Over the last two decades the combined forces of the NHL and the media had not only disparaged Soviet hockey, they had disregarded it. There had been countless opportunities throughout the years to study the progress and evolution of hockey as practised in the Soviet Union. However, those who'd expressed the slightest interest had been routinely ridiculed with a blend of arrogance and ignorance by those who represented the Canadian hockey establishment.

Tonight in Montreal, the players wearing the jersey of Team Canada are paying the price for two decades of denial. And if the first twenty minutes of the game had been a surprise, the next twenty would be nothing less than a staggering revelation.

The second period is only two and a half minutes old when Alexander Maltsev, deep in his own end, passes the puck forward to a speeding teammate with the number 17 on his back. Streaking with the puck down the right side, Valeri Kharlamov passes directly in front of a transfixed Team Canada bench. Standing five-feet-six and weighing all of 154 pounds, he is a blur with the puck, skating past his own blue line, the centre red line, and the Canadian blue line unmolested. Confronted by the Canadian defensive pair of Don Awrey and Rod Seiling, he dips his left shoulder, giving the impression that he is going to try to split the two defencemen. Instead, he smoothly moves to the outside of a surprised Awrey, skates around him, then deftly cuts inside. A beaten Awrey turns around and desperately lunges for the puck, but it is too late as Kharlamov calmly wrists the puck between Dryden's legs.

It feels like the air has been sucked right out of the building. As the replay is shown on television, the audience is mesmerized by the virtuoso skill of this unknown player. It is a stunning end-to-end rush worthy of the sport's greatest players. Phil Esposito and Frank Mahovlich turn to each other on the bench. Rendered speechless by what they've just seen, the two superstars can only shrug at each other in disbelief.

A similar sense of amazement is felt by the man who was standing behind the two stars, although he was at pains not to show it. "All of us were impressed but none of us wanted to let on," Harry Sinden later admitted. "I've seldom seen anyone come down on two NHL defensemen and beat them to the outside, going around them and in on the net. It just isn't done."[12]

Less than eight minutes later, Kharlamov repeats the feat. He collects a loose puck off a faceoff just outside the Russian blue line and at a blinding pace streaks diagonally from right to left, crossing centre of the rink. Just like he was on his first goal, he is confronted at the Canadian blue line by Awrey and Seiling. This time he makes no attempt to fake the two defencemen. Skating to Seiling's left, he puts himself farther away from the net. In the blink of an eye he raises his stick in the air and unleashes a powerful, unbelievably accurate slapshot that – before a stunned Dryden can react – catches the end of the net, between the twine and the far post.

Each goal spotlights a different facet of Kharlamov's extraordinary talent. The first goal highlights his exceptional skill with the puck, while the second reveals the precision and power of his shot. Both goals illustrate his astonishing speed and explosiveness, traits that have previously gone unnoticed by both the opposition and the Canadian media. Sharing the ice with the best players in the NHL, Kharlamov proves that he is their equal. The only question left is whether he is in fact their superior.

"Whenever Kharlamov came out on the ice, his opponents never knew what he was going to do the next moment," added Vladislav Tretiak. "Everything he did looked so easy, so elegant. There'll never be a hockey player who could match his achievements. People like Kharlamov are born once in a century."[13]

The two goals by Kharlamov make the score 4–2 for the visiting Russians and break the game wide open, but Kharlamov is not the only revelation in the second period. Labelled by the Canadian scouts as "weak," Vladislav Tretiak, after the second Canadian goal, shuts the door on an increasingly desperate group of Team Canada forwards.

The third period starts off with a dash of hope for Canada as Bobby Clarke makes the score 4–3. It is the first puck in the past forty-two minutes of play that the powerful Canadian squad has been able to put past a purportedly weak Tretiak. Among the suddenly hopeful fans at the Forum there is an obvious boost in morale as they attempt to impart their passion onto their visibly tired troops below. But within a goal is as close as Canada will get that night, as three consecutive Soviet goals take the last shreds of hope away from the Canadian players and their supporters. The frustration of Team Canada is apparent to all those watching as they begin to rough up the Soviets in the last minute of the game.

The crowd at the Forum, or what remains of it, turns on its own, booing the Canadian squad for their brutish behaviour.[14]

The final score reads 7–3 for the Soviet Union.

The fans are shocked. In their own rink, before their own fans, with their best players, the Canadians are beaten, at their own game.

With five seconds left on the clock a frustrated Sinden, knowing that the game is now long lost, leaves the Canadian bench and retreats to the shelter of the dressing room. Slowly but surely, his players follow him. As the final siren wails throughout the arena, the expectant Soviets gather in a line for the post-game handshake but are disappointed to find only three Canadian players waiting for them: Peter Mahovlich, Red Berenson, and Ken Dryden. When the three men realize that their departed teammates are not coming back, they take their leave too. The last to depart is Ken Dryden, who takes a second to glance back at the Soviet team. He slowly nods his head and unhurriedly lifts his stick, in a silent but touching acknowledgement of their fine play.[15]

Left alone on the ice, the triumphant Soviet team hears the most unexpected sound from the Forum crowd: cheering. For a brief shining moment, all that separates the two countries is forgotten. What is acknowledged is the brilliant display of hockey seen tonight. Caught unaware, the Soviet players return the crowd's appreciation by raising their sticks in the air.

The sport of hockey will never be the same.

Toronto, Ontario, September 3, 1972. Ken Dryden can't get to sleep. Following the game, Team Canada immediately flew out of Montreal, arriving in Toronto in the early hours the next day. The opening game loss to the Soviet Union is a little over five hours old and Dryden's mind is racing.

"I keep asking myself all kinds of questions. How did we lose? Why did we lose? What does it all mean now? Questions. Questions. Questions. But few answers."[16]

Dryden is eventually able to get to sleep, but the questions remain.

Moscow, Russia, September 3, 1972. While Ken Dryden is struggling to get to sleep in a Toronto hotel room, halfway across the world Boris Kharlamov is settling in to watch the first game of the Summit Series, which is being shown on Soviet television on tape delay. Because of the delay he has no idea that his son, Valeri, has become overnight the most talked-about hockey player in Canada.

Like many of the fathers of the Soviet National Team, Boris Kharlamov had desperately wanted to travel with his son to Canada to watch the Summit Series in person. The players strongly pushed the Soviet Sports Committee, but they were refused. According to the government, the presence of the players' family in Canada would be distracting.

Boris Kharlamov had to settle for watching the opening game of the series from the comfort of his small apartment. Surrounded by friends, he was one of the 100 million people in the Soviet Union who would watch the game on television. Like many of his fellow countrymen he took the day off work to settle in for the game, scheduled to be telecast at ten o'clock in the morning.

After the Canadian team jumped out to an early 2–0 lead, the mood in the Russian apartment grew sombre as many in attendance immediately assumed the worst. The exception to the dour atmosphere rested with the owner of the apartment, who urged his friends to remain optimistic.

"I knew our players wouldn't give up that easily," the elder Kharlamov fondly recalled later. "And then Valeri scored. And then he scored again."[17] The earlier gloom was suddenly replaced by a mood of celebration as the vodka began to flow.

Nineteen years earlier, Boris Kharlamov, himself a veteran of Russian hockey, had taught his son how to skate. Not having his own pair, little Valeri took the blades from his father's pair of skates and attached them to his own boots. His sheer talent quickly drew attention. As a result, Kharlamov spent his teen years alongside Vladislav Tretiak in the Central Red Army hockey school.

Like Tretiak, he had been recommended for a spot with the Central Red Army team. However, Anatoli Tarasov, the team's coach, was not overly impressed, denigrating both his small stature and his skating abilities. Banished to Chebarkul, a city 850 miles to the east of Moscow, at the time home to a second division team in the Soviet League, Kharlamov prospered, scoring 34 goals in 32 games. Tarasov could not ignore his high level of performance any longer, and Kharlamov joined the Red Army team in 1968.[18]

Kharlamov was twenty when he joined the premier club team in the Soviet Union. He was immediately placed on a line with Vladimir

Petrov, aged twenty-one, and Boris Mikhailov, aged twenty-four. They would soon become the top line on both the Red Army team and the Soviet National Team, and arguably the best line in the sport over the course of the next decade.

Kharlamov was an immediate success. In his first full season with the Red Army, he played in 42 games, scoring 37 goals. The following year he scored at a goal-a-game pace with 33 goals in 33 games. In 1971, his 40 goals topped the Soviet Elite League goal-scoring race, and in 1972, he captured the league's scoring title and was awarded the circuit's Most Valuable Player award. He was just as successful internationally. In the 1972 Olympics, he led the tournament in scoring as the Soviet Union claimed the gold medal in Tarasov's last game as head coach.

Despite all this success and all the accolades, Kharlamov was an unknown quantity to Team Canada's scouts and the Canadian press in the days leading up to the Summit Series. On the day before the opening game, the *Toronto Star* described Kharlamov as "a truculent winger of the Wayne Cashman school."[19] Kharlamov's subsequent performance in Montreal swiftly rendered any comparisons to Wayne Cashman moot, if not absurd. From that point on he would only be compared with hockey's elite.

"Outstanding hockey player," responded Team Canada's Ron Ellis when he was asked years later about Kharlamov. "In my career with the NHL, I had to shadow a number of superstars, Bobby Hull being one of them. I would certainly put Kharlamov on a par with Hull in terms of talent and ability. There is no doubt in my mind he would have been a star in the NHL."[20]

Ellis's boss in the NHL, Harold Ballard, was in full agreement. In Toronto, on the morning after the game, the bombastic owner of the Maple Leafs announced to the world that he would be willing to pay $1 million for the services of Valeri Kharlamov, proclaiming that Kharlamov "is the best young forward in the world."[21]

Toronto, Ontario, September 3, 1972. Ken Dryden finally awoke from a restless sleep at one in the afternoon. Wrapped in the cocoon of his hotel room, he wonders to himself what awaits him outside the door. His hope on waking was that the game the night before had been just a bad dream. But as he slowly regained his bearings, he came to the realization that his world had suddenly changed.

After getting dressed, Dryden dared to open his hotel door and made his way downstairs to the lobby of the hotel. Red Fisher, the beat writer for the *Montreal Star*, met up with Dryden and told him he was suffering from the same emotions.

"It's like something has been taken away from me," Fisher confessed.

"I too have lost the feeling that the Canadian professional hockey player, by definition, is superior to all other hockey players in the world," Dryden later recorded in his journal. "Disillusionment, call it."[22]

The next day's edition of the *Globe and Mail* in four words summed up the melancholy that had suddenly afflicted an entire country:

CANADA MOURNS HOCKEY MYTH.

The loss to the Russians in the opening game of the Summit Series was a serious body blow to the collective psyche of Canadian hockey. For an older generation, it sparked memories of the 1954 World Championship when the East York Lyndhursts lost to a country making its debut on the international stage: the Soviet Union.

However, this loss was far harder to take. In 1954, the country could console itself with the fact that the Lyndhursts didn't represent the best that Canadian hockey had to offer, that it had been a game contested in a foreign land in a hostile environment. Those same excuses were not available in 1972.

In the days that followed the Montreal game, Canada was a nation living in disbelief, caught between anger and despair. Harry Sinden's words expressed what the entire country was feeling: "A little piece of all of us died today."[23]

9.

THE TEAM WITHIN THE TEAM

Toronto, Ontario, September 4, 1972. In the wake of the stunning loss in the opening game of the Summit Series, the second game in Toronto took on an added importance as Canada sought not only to tie the series but to somehow regain a measure of confidence after the debacle in Montreal.

Yvan Cournoyer arrived early that afternoon at Maple Leaf Gardens. The stunning result of the first game had solidified concerns he'd felt on the eve of the series. "A bit before the Summit Series, I told Frank Mahovlich, 'Gee, Frank, I'm afraid. I don't know what to expect. We've never played these guys. I have no idea what they can do, and I don't like that. At least when you play in the playoffs, you know what to expect. We've never played the Russians before, we're not familiar with their style."[1]

Now, less than two nights removed from that defeat he stands motionless against the boards, staring out at the ice surface. Alone with his own thoughts he doesn't move for a half-hour. He battles his fear of losing by repeating in his mind the same five-word mantra – "We're going to beat them'" – over and over again. Then he quietly makes his way to the Team Canada dressing room.[2] It is a side of Cournoyer rarely seen and stands in stark contrast to his usual joyful manner.

With the retirement of Bernie "Boom Boom" Geoffrion in the summer of 1964, many had assumed that the young Cournoyer would easily slide into his role as the Montreal Canadiens' newest superstar. The season before, the nineteen-year-old played in 53 games with the Junior Canadiens, scoring an astounding 63 goals and adding 48 assists for a total of 111 points. That same season he scored four goals in a five-game tryout with the big club.

The next year saw Cournoyer stick with the Canadiens, but he struggled to get ice time in a frustrating rookie season where he only scored seven goals in 55 games. Toe Blake, the Canadiens' head coach at the time, loved his young prospect's speed and willingness to shoot the puck, as well as his ability to consistently put the puck in the net. He was less enamoured, however, with Cournoyer's lack of defensive acumen.

"If Yvan has a fault it is that he forgets to come back at times," Blake explained. "He forgets his defensive responsibilities because he's so offensive minded."[3]

If there was one main tenet that sustained the Montreal Canadiens in those years it was the firm belief that everyone on the roster had to be a responsible two-way player, excelling on both offence and defence. Because of his defensive deficiencies, Cournoyer in his first years with the Canadiens was exclusively employed by Blake on the power play. His rookie season would climax in the 1965 Stanley Cup Finals. In the decisive game seven, he scored a crucial power-play goal in the first period, as Montreal opened up a comfortable 4–0 first-period lead. As a reward for his goal, Cournoyer found himself anchored to the bench for the rest of the game as he watched his teammates help him receive his first Stanley Cup.

"When you play for the Montreal Canadiens, it's not just hard to make the team, it's hard to stay on it," Cournoyer admitted later. "You have to work harder even after you make the team if you want to be with them for a long time."[4]

It didn't take long for him to become the league's most celebrated specialist. In his first three years with the Canadiens, 40 of his 50 goals came on the power play. With his enthusiasm and blinding speed – a *Sports Illustrated* reporter came up with his nickname of "The Roadrunner"[5] – he became one of the most popular players in hockey. And behind the scenes, thanks to Blake's constant tutoring, Cournoyer began to learn the nuances of playing defensive hockey.

In the spring of 1968, things looked up for Cournoyer. Not only did he claim another Stanley Cup with the Canadiens, but Blake began letting him take a larger role. "He [had] just got into a habit of letting somebody else do the checking for him," explained Blake. "We worked on him. Now he's one of the best checkers on the club. I wouldn't be afraid to use him as a penalty-killer."[6] The end result was that the polished Cournoyer led the team that spring in playoff scoring.

With Claude Ruel behind the bench the following year, Cournoyer became one of the top players in the NHL, scoring a career-high

87 points, winning his fourth Stanley Cup, and being named to the NHL's All-Star team at the end of the season. He would also be named to the All-Star team again at the conclusion of the 1971 and 1972 seasons. In addition to being a key contributor to another Canadiens' Stanley Cup win in the spring of 1971 – his fifth – the explosive Cournoyer was developing a reputation as a clutch performer who played his best in the big games and who could score timely goals in pressure situations.

As the third period begins in the crucial second game of the Summit Series, Team Canada clings to a fragile 1–0 lead. Opening the period on the power play, the Canadian squad is desperate to double their advantage, as Brad Park circles around his own net before bursting up the ice. Hitting centre ice, he quickly glances up to his right and fires the puck directly onto the stick of a streaking Yvan Cournoyer, who crosses the Soviet blue line unmolested. Both Alexander Ragulin and Vladimir Lutchenko, the Russian defence pair, suddenly resemble a set of statues, watching as the determined Cournoyer blows right past them before shooting the puck through an opening between Tretiak's pads. Two nights before, Kharlamov had left the Canadian players in awe. In a flash, an inspired Cournoyer has met Kharlamov's stunning salvo with one of his own.[7]

At the 5.53 mark of the third period, the Russians score on the power play, and Team Canada sees its 2–0 lead cut in half. With the memory of game one vivid in the minds of not only the players but all those watching, the fans in Maple Leaf Gardens let out a collective gasp. The tension rises to an almost unbearable level twenty-one seconds later when Team Canada's Pat Stapleton is whistled by the referee for a hooking infraction, giving the dangerous Soviets another power play. Clinging to a precarious 2–1 lead, Team Canada has arrived at the most crucial part of this must-win game.

The power play calmly sets up in the Canadian zone, the Soviets methodically moving the puck, looking for that perfect opportunity to tie the game. Such is their skill level, their precision with the puck, that a Russian goal takes on the helpless feeling of being almost inevitable. But, as they slowly close in on the Canadian net, patrolled this evening by Tony Esposito, the Soviets unexpectedly lose their control and the puck is suddenly up for grabs. Guy Lapointe makes the first unsuccessful attempt at clearing the puck. When the Soviets barely manage to keep the loose puck inside the blue line, it comes to rest on the stick of Canada's Phil Esposito along the boards. With his back to the play, he blindly throws the puck out past the blue line and three Soviet skaters.

As if somehow guided by providence, the puck lands on the blade of Peter Mahovlich's stick. Only one Soviet defender, Evgeny Paladiev, stands between him and Vladislav Tretiak. What unfolds next is one of the most spectacular plays in the history of hockey.

With his long strides, an awkward-looking Mahovlich purposefully moves the puck toward centre ice. He now bears down on a retreating Paladiev at the Soviet blue line, slowly lifting his long stick in the air for an apparent slapshot. It is the expected move, the smart move, the slapshot that he would always take – but tonight is different. The mere threat of a slapshot paralyzes the overmatched Paladiev, and Mahovlich spots the opening. Without the slightest hesitation he makes his move. Swiftly stepping to his right, Mahovlich goes around the defeated defenceman and bears in alone on Tretiak. Taking the loose puck from his skate to his stick, Mahovlich jerks to his left, giving the Soviet goalie the impression that he will shoot off of his forehand. Tretiak buys Mahovlich's fake, plunging to the ice as his adversary somehow pulls the puck to his backhand, then forces it over the outstretched Tretiak's skates and into the net, his momentum carrying him on top of the goalie. With the puck resting in the back of the net, Mahovlich untangles his large body from that of the prone, stunned Tretiak. Emerging triumphant, Mahovlich bounds out of the net, his arms in the air, as his teammates engulf him in a scrum that is equal parts joy and relief.

Tretiak will never forget the goal, or stop asking himself how Mahovlich managed to put the puck past him.[8]

"Coming off the very lowest moments, the bitterness and humiliation we suffered in Montreal in game one where we lost big-time, that spectacular goal by Pete helped us to a victory at Maple Leaf Gardens," Harry Sinden said later. "It was a goal I'll never forget, an uplifting moment for the team in a game we urgently needed to win."[9]

The beauty of the goal was immediately recognized, and repeated viewings fail to tarnish its magnificence. The goal is one of the greatest in hockey history, but at that moment it signified two things. First, the goal effectively iced the game for Canada, who would go on to win the series' second game 4–1. Second, the goal cemented Peter Mahovlich's claim to hockey superstardom. At the age of twenty-five, "the Little M" had taken his first bold steps out from under the shadow of "the Big M."

—

Toronto, Ontario, September 12, 1972. Flying out of Toronto on September 12, it is a disconsolate group of players that makes its way to Moscow, where they will play the final four games of the series. A week before they had stood on the same tarmac, full of enthusiasm after squaring the series at one with an emotional win at Maple Leaf Gardens. But after a tie in Winnipeg and an embarrassing loss in Vancouver, Team Canada and the country at-large are reeling. The team's departure for Russia is greeted by the public with less than lukewarm support. In fact, there are only a handful of well-wishers at the airport to see them off.[10]

Needing to win three of the final four games to win the series, Team Canada digs itself a deeper hole by losing again in game five. The agonizing defeat puts the Canadian team in an almost impossible situation. Now they have to win the next three games, on foreign soil, in a hostile environment, against a team they have only been able to beat once in the first five games of the series.

Moscow, Russia, September 24, 1972. In time, Peter Mahovlich and Yvan Cournoyer, along with their Montreal teammates Serge Savard, Guy Lapointe, and Ken Dryden, would, when it mattered most, vindicate the faith and hope that Team Canada's management had originally placed in them. All but Dryden had played a significant role in Canada's critical victory in the series' second game. Now facing elimination, starting in game six in Moscow, Canadian head coach Harry Sinden calls on them again. Each of the Montreal Five will play a vital role in Team Canada's comeback. In the media, most of the credit will be given to the scoring exploits of Paul Henderson and the dogged tenacity of Phil Esposito. But without the contributions of the Montreal contingent, it is quite possible that Canada would not have grasped that ultimate victory.

"My only worry was to win," Cournoyer admitted later. "In Moscow, I didn't know what was going on back in Canada or what was happening anywhere else. I thought of nothing else but winning."[11]

"We could not afford to lose that series," recalled Lapointe. "I don't even want to think of how we would have been able to explain to all the people back home how we lost that series. We had everything to lose."[12]

In addition to the now expected Montreal troika of Mahovlich, Cournoyer, and Lapointe, Team Canada would bring Serge Savard and Ken Dryden back into the mix for the sixth game. The surprising reinsertion of Savard and Dryden back into the Canadian net was a desperate gambit by head coach Harry Sinden.

Savard had watched the opening game of the Summit Series from the press box, then was back in action for the pivotal second game in Toronto. In that game, won by Canada, and in the following game, a tie in Winnipeg, it was clear to many observers that Savard was the best defenceman on the ice. Once a superb rushing defenceman, his injuries had forced a change in his game. Savard now chose to play closer to his own end and transformed himself into a steady defensive rearguard, allowing his blue-line partners to lead the rush while he stood guard in the background.

However, at the Team Canada practice following game three in Winnipeg, the injury bug once again unbelievably bit a luckless Savard, this time in the form of an errant shot from teammate Red Berenson. Savard had been standing by himself in the corner of the rink, a few feet from the end boards, when the puck struck him squarely on the right ankle. At first it was thought to be a less than serious injury, but on the flight to Vancouver the ankle ballooned and an immobile Savard had to depart the plane in a wheelchair.

"One doctor in Vancouver told me I had a bone bruise," he remembered later. "Another said I had a hairline fracture of the ankle. I didn't know what to think." Forced to fly back to Montreal, he had to endure the pilot's increasingly dire updates of the fourth game over the intercom, a game in which his Canadian teammates were booed off the ice in the aftermath of their 5–3 defeat. Upon his return to Montreal, it was determined that Savard had indeed fractured his ankle and would have to keep off his skates for at least a month.[13]

"Team Canada considers Savard lost for the remainder of the series with the Soviet Union Nationals," announced the *Globe and Mail*, "but it's not known how long he will be out of the Canadiens uniform."[14]

But in spite of the newspaper's report and against the wishes of the doctors, Savard joined his teammates in Sweden and began practising with them. In the aftermath of the crushing game-five defeat in Moscow and facing the dim prospect of having to win three games in a row in Moscow if they were to win the Series, a desperate Sinden, quickly running out of options, inserted Savard into the lineup for game six.

Guy Lapointe, Savard's teammate with the Canadiens and defence partner with Team Canada, was one of the few not surprised by his return. "Some people said he was through for the series. They didn't know Serge.

He came back for game six in Moscow – not fully recovered from his ankle injury but still one of the best defensemen in hockey history."[15]

Just as surprising as Savard's return was Dryden's reappearance in Team Canada's net. After losing the opening game of the series in Montreal, Dryden had sat out the following two games before getting back in the nets for the fourth game in Vancouver – which ended in a 5–3 defeat and a bombardment of boos from the team's own fans. The final tally wasn't pretty for the underperforming team, and for Dryden in particular. So far in the series he had stood in the Canadian goal for six periods of action. The Soviets had put the puck behind him twelve times.

"I'm playing very stupidly," a candid Dryden recorded in his journal. "It seems that I've hit rock bottom. I'm doing everything wrong. My confidence is zilch. I've forgotten how to play the game."[16]

Such was Dryden's despair that he now considered the series over, at least in terms of his participation in it. As a result he had turned his mind toward getting ready for the upcoming NHL season with the Canadiens. Upon arriving in Moscow, he went for a walk in Red Square with his wife, Lynda. The two of them took in the changing of the guard at Lenin's tomb, where an underdressed Dryden, standing in the harsh thirty degree weather, freezes, resulting in a cold virus a few days later. Normally, this would have concerned him, but Dryden was feeling more like a tourist than a hockey player. More than any other player he was eager to put the Soviets, the Series, and the two games in Montreal and Vancouver into the deepest recesses of his memory.

At practice the morning after watching Canada lose game five of the series, Dryden is going through the motions. He is battling not only the puck but the flu bug he had acquired a couple of days before. Taking a break midway through the workout, he slowly skates over to the boards to grab a quick shot of water. John Ferguson, the assistant coach for Team Canada, ambles over and asks his former teammate how he's doing. A relaxed Dryden, now feeling almost detached from the day-to-day workings of the team, gives the standard answer before admitting that he is "still making stupid mistakes."

"Don't worry about them," Ferguson reassures him, "so long as you don't make them tomorrow night."

Dryden is caught off-guard. All he can muster is a single word that expresses the confusion and apprehension that are suddenly fighting for space in his mind.

"What!"

He has not played a game in more than two weeks, and when he did play before he performed poorly, and now he's feeling less than 100 per cent physically and considerably less than that mentally. He finishes the practice, but he's distracted. At the conclusion of the practice Harry Sinden comes over and confirms what Ferguson has already told him. Facing the first of three consecutive must-win games, Dryden would once again be entrusted with guarding the Canadian net.[17]

He wakes up the next morning, the morning of game six, so beset by nerves that he can barely stand in his Moscow hotel room. He hasn't felt this way since Vancouver, almost four years ago, when he had first faced the Soviet National Team. So much had changed since then, but that same fear of failure has returned with a vengeance.

It is only when the puck is dropped that night, and after making three key saves in the early moments of the game, that Dryden will feel his nervousness subside. In its stead will come a sensation that he hasn't experienced in a long time: it is the welcome feeling of confidence. The first period ends in a scoreless deadlock, largely due to his twelve saves. The Russians will finally break through a little over a minute into the second period, but a reassured Dryden doesn't crumble, instead he soldiers on, and just over four minutes later Canada ties the score at one. Then, after another minute of play, Cournoyer will give the Canadians the lead before Paul Henderson adds an insurance goal fifteen seconds later.

And then Ken Dryden will be tested in a way that he has never been tested before. He had felt NHL pressure for the past year and a half, but this is something entirely different. Two minutes after Henderson's goal, Canada begins a steady procession to the penalty box that will see them play shorthanded for most of the remainder of the second period. Defending against the vaunted Soviet power play, Dryden will bend, but he will not break.

"They came at us in brigades," Dryden excitedly recorded in his journal that night, "but our defensemen, particularly Serge Savard, repeatedly broke up their passing plays near the net."[18]

With a little less than three minutes left in the period, and Canada playing two men down, the Russians put the puck past Dryden and come within one goal. But they will score no more as Canada gains its second victory of the series. Dryden will be rewarded as one of the game's MVPs but of more importance to him is that he has overcome a stigma that he has often wrestled with. He has now, finally, beaten the Soviets. After the game, an unburdened Dryden is told by the coaches that regardless of the outcome, Tony Esposito will be the goaltender in game seven and that he would be given the duties in game eight.

Moscow, Russia, September 26, 1972. Two nights later, sitting nervously among the crowd for game seven, Dryden witnesses a seesaw battle. After the Russians tie the game at three apiece with a little over five minutes expired in the third period, the two teams settle into a fight for survival that will test the limits of both the players and the spectators alike. In the end, it will be two of Dryden's Montreal teammates who will help deliver salvation for Team Canada. With a little over two minutes remaining in the game, Guy Lapointe shoots the puck behind his own net on to the stick of his defence partner Serge Savard, who carries the puck up the boards. Out of the corner of his eye, he spots a streaking Paul Henderson darting through centre ice. Thanks to Savard's amazing precision and awareness, the puck and Henderson meet at the Soviet blue line. Confronted by two Soviet defencemen, Henderson manages to get around them and, while falling, pinches the puck between Tretiak's arm and body for the winning goal.

"It is no coincidence that the revival of Team Canada in this hockey showdown with the Soviet Union dates back to Serge Savard's return to the defence corps," writes Jim Proudfoot in the *Toronto Star*. "Nor is it any accident that the Canadians have won three and tied one of the four games in which Savard has been available to add mobility and offensive thrust to an otherwise awkward rearguard."[19]

As improbable as it seemed just days before, the series is now tied at three games apiece, with one tie. Two nights later a winner will be decided.

Moscow, Russia, September 28, 1972. The third period of the climactic game eight begins with Team Canada facing another obstacle, this time in the form of a 5–3 deficit on the scoreboard.

At the start of the final period of the Summit Series, the necessary spark for Canada is provided by Peter Mahovlich. With a little over two minutes gone on the clock, he passes the puck from behind his own net to Yvan Cournoyer, who quickly returns it to him. Blasting his way up the boards to the right corner of the Soviet end, pursued by three Soviet defenders, Mahovlich is finally brought down to the ice. But as he falls he desperately throws the puck to the front of the net. With the loose puck, floating high in the air, the indomitable Phil Esposito bats at it with his glove. With the puck now rolling at his feet, he instinctively swings his stick like a golf club, missing on his first try, but swatting it on his second. Somehow the puck finds the opening between Tretiak's pads.

The Soviet lead, suddenly more tenuous, is now 5–4.

Ten minutes later, the play begins this time with Esposito charging up the right wing. With four Soviets in close pursuit, he carries the puck over their blue line before cutting toward the centre and letting go a high blast from fifteen feet out. Tretiak blocks the powerful shot but is unable to control it, and the loose puck deflects off a rampaging Esposito behind the goal. Surrounded by three Soviet players, Esposito somehow finds a way to centre the puck to the waiting stick of Cournoyer, who wastes no time in shooting the puck. Tretiak makes the stop but once again is unable to corral the rebound. Recovering his own rebound, Cournoyer is confronted with not only Tretiak, but the three Russian defenders clumsily covering their own goal. Despite the pileup of Soviet mass, he is able to put a backhander over the prone Tretiak and through the phalanx of arms, legs, and torsos. The puck stretches the twine at the back of the Soviet net.

The game is now tied at five goals apiece.

There are ninety seconds remaining. There is no overtime, no shootout. The game and the series will conclude in ninety seconds. Fuelling the sense of urgency are the Soviet officials who have already informed Team Canada that if the game ends in a tie they will claim victory in the series based on the fact that over the course of the entire series the Soviets have scored more goals.

In response, the officials are angrily informed that the game isn't over yet.

In Canada's end stands Phil Esposito. Throughout this critical third period it seems as if he has never left the ice. He is surrounded by Montreal Canadiens. Standing watch over the Team Canada goal is Dryden. Pete Mahovlich is to Esposito's left, Cournoyer is to his right. Behind him stand the defensive pairing of Savard and Lapointe. A month ago, Esposito and the Montreal players were sworn enemies, warring combatants in hockey's fiercest rivalry: the Boston Bruins versus the Montreal Canadiens. All of that is forgotten now. The day before, Lapointe is sent word that his wife has just given birth to a baby son. A proud father, in ninety seconds he will be free to deal with both the emotions and the logistics of what's happening at home. But like every one of his teammates, at this moment he is thinking only of the task at hand.

"There was a lot of tension," Cournoyer confirmed later, "but when you're confident like we were, it takes care of that. And we had all been through similar situations."[20]

Recognizing the magnitude of the moment, Esposito takes the strange step of huddling with the rest of the players. Dryden remains anchored to his net, stoic. The tension in the Luzhniki Palace is almost unbearable. However, there is a familiar sound piercing the air. It is the battle cry of "Go Canada Go," being yelled by the three thousand Canadians dotted among the Soviet crowd. It gives the Canadian players strength. It also gives a nervous nation hope.

After the puck drops, the Canadian team deliberately moves it from their own end into the Soviet's. With the clock running down, and fatigue coursing through their legs and lungs, the players on the ice are forced to make a pivotal decision. As the bench hollers for them to get off, each of the three forwards wrestles with a crucial choice.

Standing impatiently on the bench is Paul Henderson, the hero of games six and seven. He yells out for Mahovlich three times, his desperation growing with each successive holler. The closest of the three forwards to the Canadian bench, Mahovlich makes what will turn out to be a monumental decision and leaves the ice. An eager Henderson leaps over the boards and assumes the left wing.

Esposito hears his teammates calling but pays them no heed. There is nobody alive who could take him off the ice at this moment.

Standing at the far end of the ice along the boards is a tiring Cournoyer. Holding the puck he shoots it into the Soviet end. The teachings of his old coach immediately spring to mind. "Toe Blake used to tell us if the score is tied and the puck is in the offensive zone and you're tired, get back to the bench,"[21] he later remembers. Accustomed to playing in the smaller NHL-sized rinks, he begins to tentatively head toward the bench. But when he realizes how far he has to go he contradicts his mentor's edict, shifts gears, and skates instead into the Soviet zone.[22]

Gathering the puck behind his own net is Soviet defenceman Valeri Vasiliev, who proceeds to clear it around the boards. The puck finds the stick of a surprised Cournoyer, standing along the boards, just inside the Soviet zone. With not a single Russian near him, he spots and directs a pass to an onrushing Paul Henderson. The pass, however, is just behind

Henderson, who is hooked by Vasiliev and spun to the ice behind the Soviet net. The wayward pass ricochets off the end boards and past three Soviet players, onto the stick of Esposito, who immediately shoots the puck from the left faceoff dot at Tretiak. Once again, the Russian goaltender can't control the loose puck. Slowly emerging unnoticed from behind the net is an opportunistic Henderson, who suddenly finds himself all alone in front of the Soviet netminder. He immediately stabs at the loose puck, which is stopped by Tretiak's pad as the Russian goaltender sprawls out. The rebound comes right back to Henderson. He shoots again, at the only opening he can see, a tiny space between Tretiak's body and the right post. Henderson's aim is true.

There are thirty-four seconds remaining on the clock when the puck comes to rest in the back of the Soviet net.

"I have no on-ice recollection," Ken Dryden later admitted, "except of sprinting down the ice when the shot went in. But I don't remember anticipating the play, I just remember jumping out of the starting blocks and hurrying down the ice. I remember the celebration, then thinking, my God, there are still thirty-four seconds to go. I've got to get a hold of myself."[23]

The longest thirty-four seconds that anyone can remember uneventfully tick off the clock.

For those who watched Team Canada's 6–5 victory over the Soviet Union on September 28, 1972, it is one of those rare shared moments in the history of a country, an unforgettable experience, a defining moment.

"Nothing in hockey ever brought me so low or took me so high. And nothing meant so much," an emotionally drained Dryden later concedes.[24]

Amid the hoopla in the crowded Team Canada dressing room sits an exhausted but proud Yvan Cournoyer. As the media descends on the game's twin heroes, Henderson and Esposito, the man who instigated the most famous play in hockey history is alone with his thoughts.

"I often think if I hadn't changed my mind on that final shift, what would have happened? If I hadn't stayed on the ice, there wouldn't have been a Paul Henderson goal. Who would have been over by the boards to intercept the puck? Who would have kept it in the zone?"[25]

For the players in the jubilant Canadian dressing room, there are mixed feelings. They have won the most important series of their lives, but this will be their last moment as a team. They will soon leave

Moscow behind, touch down in Canada to wild celebrations, and then make their way to their NHL training camps. It will be a return to normalcy, a sense that the last month had been some sort of a dream. But the reality is that in the course of one month the world of hockey has been forever changed.

"I think we have all grown up these past six weeks," a reflective Dryden recorded in his journal. "From the unswerving commitment to the belief that Canadians are unquestionably the best in the world and that our style is right because we invented the game and developed it, the feeling now seems to have changed to an awareness that the Russians have something going, too. Now there seems to be an appreciation for discipline and passing and skating, and at the same time, there is a questioning of the old NHL standards of conditioning and preparedness. Both the Russians and the Canadians have an amazing amount to learn."[26]

The schedule decreed that nine days after Team Canada's victory the Montreal Canadiens would open their season at the Montreal Forum with a game against the Minnesota North Stars. But after the excitement of the just concluded Summit Series, the upcoming NHL season felt like an anticlimax.

The Soviet Union's threat to Canada's domination of the sport was real. Now, in the wake of September 1972, the media, the public, and the players, all once so dismissive of Soviet hockey, found themselves eager for more of the ultimate in head-to-head competition.

No one knew it at the time, but the next confrontation would be more than three years away. On the last day of 1975, the two most decorated hockey teams in the world would congregate at the Montreal Forum for a sixty-minute display of the sport at its highest level, played by the finest players in the world in a single match still referred to simply as "the greatest game ever played."

МЕЖДУНАРОДНАЯ
ХОККЕЙНАЯ ВСТРЕЧА
КОМАНДА ЦСКА
ИЗ МОСКВЫ
ПРОТИВ
«КАНАДИЕН»
31-го ДЕКАБРЯ 1975 г.
ФОРУМ В МОНРЕАЛЕ

International
Hockey Game
**Central Army
vs Montreal
Canadiens**
December 31, 1975
Montreal Forum

Rencontre internationale
de hockey
**L'Armée Centrale
vs le Canadien
de Montréal**
le 31 décembre 1975
Forum de Montréal

On December 31, 1975, the Montreal Canadiens and the Central Red Army
– the two most successful teams in hockey – would play each other for the first
time. Pictured here is the game's program.

The dominant hockey figure in the Soviet Union for a quarter-century, head coach Anatoli Tarasov is remembered as "the father of Russian hockey."

In his fourteen years as the team's general manager, Sam Pollock guided the Montreal Canadiens to an amazing ten Stanley Cup championships and established a reputation as one of the most shrewd executives in hockey history.

Initially regarded by Canadian observers as the weak point on the Soviet national team, goaltender Vladislav Tretiak would become the first Russian-born player to be inducted into Canada's Hockey Hall of Fame.

Goaltender Ken Dryden was a complete un-known when he first joined the Canadiens in the spring of 1971, but he would lead Montreal to a Stanley Cup two months later. He would add five more before retiring from the game eight years later.

In only their seventh year of existence, the Philadelphia Flyers became Stanley Cup champions. They were led on the ice by Bobby Clarke (left), their incomparable captain, and off the ice by Fred Shero (below), their eccentric head coach.

The Flyers' rise to prominence coincided with a spike in on-ice hockey violence. Christened the "Broad Street Bullies" by the media, they became the NHL's top attraction, loved by some, loathed by many. Their head enforcer, Dave "The Hammer" Schultz, set many penalty minute records that still stand.

The on-ice brutality quickly generated a backlash. Leading the charge was Bill McMurtry, who chaired a commission for the Ontario government in the summer of 1974 that targeted the rise in violence at all levels of the sport.

Seen as the heir to the legacy of Maurice Richard and Jean Béliveau, Canadiens'
forward Guy Lafleur almost collapsed under the weight of expectation. By the
mid-seventies, however, he had established himself as the game's top player.

With his breathtaking speed and a stunning arsenal of moves, Soviet forward Valeri Kharlamov became the first hockey superstar from outside of Canada.

Arguably the two most exciting forwards in the sport, Lafleur and Kharlamov would first cross paths on December 31, 1975.

With the New Year's Eve game against the Red Army, Montreal Canadiens' Scotty Bowman would start burnishing his reputation as the sport's pre-eminent coach. A quarter-century later he would retire with a record nine Stanley Cups to his credit.

For many throughout Canada, Danny Gallivan was the voice of the Canadiens and the only English-television play-by-play commentator that the team had ever known. The New Year's Eve matchup would be the first time he had called a game involving players from the Soviet Union.

10.

A DYNASTY DELAYED

Chicago, Illinois, May 10, 1973. The Chicago Stadium is without a doubt the loudest arena in the entire NHL. Referred to by its patrons as the "Madhouse on Madison [Street]," the brick-and-limestone building is an imposing structure for any visiting team. Tonight twenty thousand rabid fans have conjugated at 1800 West Madison Street to cheer on their beloved Black Hawks. Deep in the bowels of the packed arena, that evening's opponent, the Montreal Canadiens, can not only hear the fans, but can also feel them. The sound level inside the building has at its highest been measured at 130 decibels – louder than the loudest rock concert, and past the accepted pain threshold. Tonight will be no different.

Sitting in their dressing room, directly underneath the shaking grandstands, the Canadiens are patiently waiting to take to the ice for the sixth game of the 1973 Stanley Cup Finals. A win tonight will bring the franchise an unprecedented eighteenth Stanley Cup championship. The task that lies ahead of them is a daunting one, however. Not only will they have to defeat the Black Hawks on the ice, but they will also have to overcome the hostility of the fans and the distinctive quirks of the uniquely shaped old building.

Less than two years ago, the Canadiens had surmounted all these obstacles and exited the building as the Stanley Cup champions. Surely these thoughts of old triumphs helped to reassure them as they prepared for this pivotal game. But while many of them could take some form of comfort in past glories, there were just as many in that dark and dingy dressing room who had never been this far before, for whom this was a new and frightening, if exhilarating, experience. This was especially true for a quiet youngster named Murray Wilson, who found himself seated in the dressing room between Henri Richard and Frank Mahovlich. The threesome provided a stark contrast in appearance and especially in terms of experience. It was not by accident or coincidence that Wilson, a twenty-one-year-old rookie left winger, was positioned between the two oldest players on the Canadiens who had at this point collectively won a total of fifteen Stanley Cups. For an impressionable Wilson it was learning through experience and the latest step in the gradual process that constituted his education in becoming a Montreal Canadien.

A little less than two years before, Murray Wilson had been an eager spectator at the Queen Elizabeth Hotel waiting for his name to be called at the NHL's annual entry draft. The son of an RCAF navigator, Wilson was a gifted athlete who excelled in track and field in high school but whose true passion was always hockey. Despite having spent the previous three years in England and playing very little hockey, at the age of fourteen he made the Ottawa 67's "B" team. It didn't take long for him to make a positive impression, and before the end of the season Wilson graduated to the "A" team, a considerable achievement in light of his recent past and the fact that the 67's were established as one of the top teams in Canadian junior hockey. Wilson's resulting junior career, however, was marred by injuries: "Mention any broken bone and I've probably had it broken," he readily admitted.[1] Despite his history of injuries, the brittle Wilson was an attractive target for prospective NHL teams. Possessing a beautiful skating style characterized by long strides, he was also a gifted scorer, averaging over a point a game throughout his junior career.

Entering through the lobby of the Queen Elizabeth Hotel, Wilson knew that he would be selected in the first round of that day's draft. From what he had been told in the time leading up to the event, he was reasonably sure that his name would be called by the Philadelphia Flyers, the holders of both the eighth and ninth picks. Yet when the time came, the Flyers took a pass on Wilson, leaving the Montreal Canadiens, the recent winners of the Stanley Cup and the holders of the eleventh overall pick, to select a suddenly downcast Wilson.

"I was disappointed when the Canadiens drafted me because they had just won the Cup and they had a wonderful team," Wilson candidly admits today. "With an expansion team like the Flyers I would get a better opportunity. Landing with the Canadiens I knew that I wasn't going to take Frank Mahovlich or Marc Tardif's spot with the team."[2]

After some thought and then attending the team's training camp, Wilson warmed to the idea of joining the Canadiens organization, admitting later that "I kind of liked the environment, I liked my teammates, and it was close to my home in Ottawa."[3] As was customary for nearly all Canadiens prospects during Sam Pollock's tenure, Wilson was sent to Halifax in the fall of 1971, where he would play for the AHL's Voyageurs and begin the process of learning how to become a professional hockey player. Arriving at the Halifax airport he was greeted by his new coach, Al MacNeil, who had just coached the Canadiens to a Stanley Cup championship the previous spring. For the young, unpolished Wilson, as well as for many other Canadiens prospects who would later emerge as stars in Montreal, playing under the tutelage of MacNeil proved to be a fortuitous break in his path to the NHL.

"The Canadiens really believed in developing their players into their system through people like Al MacNeil and Claude Ruel," says Steve Shutt, who followed a similar path. "They would spend the time in building the player. If you grew up in the environment, the pressure and all that that entailed would become second nature to you."[4]

MacNeil's primary responsibility in Halifax was to act as a teacher/mentor to his recruits, enlightening them as to the tenets of defensive hockey, exposing them to situational hockey, and all the while preparing them for the responsibilities of being a professional hockey player. Coming out of junior, the great majority of players were accustomed to measuring their success solely by goals and points. However, within the Montreal Canadiens organization, it had long been a principle that each and every player could not and would not be one-dimensional but a complete player able to excel in any given situation, well versed in the basic skills of shooting, passing, and checking. In addition, each player would be taught to think of the team's achievements and goals as paramount, even if it meant subjugating one's individual statistics. The team's success over the past quarter of a century spoke to the wisdom of this approach.

"They [the young players] follow the rules," pronounced Sam Pollock, "because if they don't, we let them know they're not welcome. If they want to act like future Canadiens, they can stay. If not, they're out."[5]

"They would test you in different ways and see if you could accept it," Wilson remembers today. "Certain guys couldn't adapt or didn't want to because they wanted to continue playing their own style. Once the Canadiens management identified these players they were shipped out."[6] Such was Montreal's wealth of amateur talent that they could afford to discard those who didn't fit into their system.

Away from the rink many of the Voyageurs players clustered within three Halifax apartment buildings. As a result there quickly developed a shared closeness among the members of the team. On the ice the team thrived as the Voyageurs went on to win the Calder Cup that spring, symbolizing the championship of the AHL. An extremely gifted collection of players, they showed the depth of talent within the Montreal organization. In all, seventeen members of the team would go on to star in the NHL, nine of them with the Canadiens.

Murray Wilson was one of them. In the fall of 1972, he attended the Canadiens' training camp. With six of the team's top players away participating in the Summit Series, he was given an even greater chance to showcase his developing skills, particularly his checking, and along with many of his Voyageurs teammates from the season before, he made an immediate impression.

"It's quite amazing what a difference a year can make in the career of a young athlete," remembers Larry Robinson, a teammate of Wilson's in Halifax who also joined him with the Canadiens. "If attitude is everything, then I was an entirely different person when September 1972 rolled around." As was true for many of the Voyageurs' young players, his maturation reflected the teaching and coaching skills of Al MacNeil. "Just traveling to Montreal knowing that many of my Calder Cup teammates would be there gave me a big psychological lift."[7]

In light of the tremendous talent gathered throughout the organization, the Canadiens were confronted with a problem that every other team in the league envied – there simply weren't enough positions on the team to satisfy all the talent, a fact duly noted in *Sports Illustrated* and by the opposition.

"Stated simply, the Canadiens have the best goaltender (Ken Dryden) and the best group of defensemen (Jacques Laperriere, Guy Lapointe and Serge Savard) in the game; and in Frank Mahovlich, his gangling brother Peter, Jacques Lemaire, Yvan Cournoyer, Guy Lafleur, Marc Tardif and Chuck Lefley, among others, they have more than enough firepower to storm the Bastille. The Montreal bench, meanwhile, is stocked with talented rookies, particularly Goalies Michel Plasse and Wayne Thomas, Defenseman Larry Robinson and Wings

Murray Wilson and Steve Shutt, who play like the Drydens and the Laperrieres and the Mahovliches whenever Coach Scotty Bowman finds time to use them. Impressed? Hold on a minute. Down east on the farm at Halifax, Nova Scotia shrewd Sam Pollock, the general manager of the Canadiens, has assembled a team comprised of the best young talent outside the NHL."[8]

One of the youngest members of the team, twenty-one-year-old Murray Wilson ended up seeing action in 52 games during the 1972–73 season, his first in the NHL. Despite scoring an impressive 21 goals, he served mainly as a situational player when called upon. "You filled a role with the team and my role was to make sure that my opposing player didn't see the puck that night whether it was Eric Vail, Mickey Redmond, or whomever," he explains. "We had plenty of guys who could score goals. My specific assignment was to make sure that the other team didn't score. It became a matter of personal pride. I remember telling guys at the start of the game 'you better get your goal on the power play because you're not going to get it off me tonight.'"[9]

As a young player in the bubble, Wilson, along with the other rookies on the team, was expected not only to work out with the team on a daily basis but to stay on after practice concluded for some one-on-one instruction with Claude Ruel.

In the story of the Montreal Canadiens dynasty of the seventies, Claude Ruel is truly the forgotten man. A list of his most prominent pupils shows his importance to the success of the team throughout the decade. Larry Robinson, Steve Shutt, and Bob Gainey, among many other Habs stalwarts, took that next step under his tutelage. The team's head coach a few years before, Ruel was now in the position of director of player development with the Canadiens. This job allowed him to engage in his twin passions of scouting amateur talent, in addition to tutoring the franchise's youngest players on the fundamentals of the game.

"Claude was the first assistant coach in the NHL," remembers Steve Shutt, himself a rookie in 1972–73. "He had us work on our basis skills. All of the guys on the Canadiens had one thing in common, their basic game was good. Using that as a foundation we were able to then showcase our individual talents."[10]

Ruel's main role with the youngsters was to prepare them for duty with the Canadiens. "You learned as a young player to be prepared and to be in shape when you got your opportunity," says Murray Wilson. "Scotty Bowman expected you to play up to a certain standard and if you didn't they would find somebody else who would. It was Ruel who helped us get to that standard. I can still remember him not only working our tails off, but just repeating the same basic principles, over and over, day in, day out, until they stuck in your head; 'shoot the puck through the net,' 'skate hard,' 'finish your check,' 'pass the puck tape to tape, not in the skates' . . . 'get ahead, move the puck."[11]

Thanks to Ruel and his specialized instruction, the youngest Canadiens possessed a maturity and a pride that was lacking in their contemporaries.

For many players, gaining a roster spot on an NHL team was the final step on their journey to becoming a professional hockey player. This was not true in Montreal, however, where upon entering the Canadiens' locker room at the Montreal Forum one truly became aware of the awesome responsibility that awaited them. Spread across the top of one wall, just below the ceiling, were the faces of those who had come before, the members of the team who had been enshrined in the Hockey Hall of Fame. In the dressing room one couldn't escape their gaze, nor ignore the words written above their heads, "To You from Failing Hands We Throw the Torch, Be Yours to Hold It High." Skating out onto the ice, one only had to look upward at all the Stanley Cup banners to understand not only what had been accomplished but what was expected.

The width and expertise of their scouting, their shrewd moves at the draft table, their bountiful array of minor league teams, the expertise and personal one-on-one instruction, and the lessons imparted from the team's veteran players all were signposts on a player's indoctrination to becoming a Montreal Canadien. Orchestrated by Frank Selke Sr. and finetuned by his successor, Sam Pollock, the Montreal system was unlike any other developmental process in the league. The Canadiens' numerous Stanley Cups spoke to its success.

Trudging up the stairs that led to the ice surface at the Chicago Stadium that warm night in the spring of 1973, the Canadiens were a collection of superstars (eleven of them would eventually be enshrined in the Hockey Hall of Fame), but they were also a team, the best in the NHL. During the 1972–73 season, the team had romped to a first-place finish with an astounding record of 52 wins, against a measly 10 losses, with 16 ties for a total of 120 points, 13 ahead of second-place Boston. The 10 losses represented at the time the least for any NHL team in the modern era. In the first round of the playoffs, they had dispatched the Buffalo Sabres in six games, before eliminating the Philadelphia Flyers in five games in the second. Now they stood one win away from the Stanley Cup.

For Yvan Cournoyer, this game would be the culmination of not only his longest year but his greatest as a professional. In spite of having drained himself both emotionally and physically in the Summit Series, he was able to follow his heroics for Team Canada with another 40-goal season and another place on the league's post-season All-Star team. He had followed that up with a playoff to remember, leading all post-season scorers with 22 points in the 16 playoff games the Canadiens had played up to that point. "There's nobody on the Chicago Black Hawks staff who is equal to the task of covering Yvan Cournoyer, the fireplug right-winger Montreal Canadiens call the Roadrunner," wrote the *Toronto Star*. "That glaring deficiency is prominent among the reasons the Montreal club is one victory away from capturing the Stanley Cup for the 18th time . . . He has been Montreal's most consistently good player and, just as important, the individual who's wrecked Hawks' overall battle plan."[12]

"There is no doubt that Cournoyer is now the cement which holds the Habs together," added journalist Al Rosenberg. "He is the man they look for for the big one."[13] Henri Richard, the Canadiens' captain, wholeheartedly agreed, proclaiming Cournoyer "our big gun."[14]

What wasn't as widely known was that Cournoyer was attempting to ignore constant, searing pain incurred four months earlier on January 8 in a game against the Minnesota North Stars. "I got hit by Ted Harris," Cournoyer later recalled. "I kept playing that night but after the game I had a problem with my stomach for a long time, right to the end. But when you start with a good feeling like in 1972, you want to do it all the way . . . I had to be frozen in the stomach before every game because the muscles were really hurting."[15]

In the first period, the hometown Black Hawks, facing elimination, quickly opened up a 2–0 lead. Yet, like Henri Richard had done so many times before, the thirty-seven-year-old captain of the team led by example, putting the Canadiens on the scoreboard with only twelve seconds left in the first period. After a wild second period in which the two teams scored five goals, the third period began in a 4–4 deadlock. With so much on the line both teams pressed hard for the tiebreaker.

As is so often the case, the path to a monumental goal seemed to start innocently enough. A few seconds after passing the eight-minute mark of the final period, Montreal's Jacques Lemaire fired a shot that missed the Chicago goal. Before anybody else could react, the puck careened right off the backboard and flipped in the air, only to be batted by the waiting blade of Yvan Cournoyer's stick. And before Tony Esposito, the Black Hawks goalie, could react, the puck was in the back of his net. For the indomitable Cournoyer it was his fifteenth goal of the playoffs, a new record. With the Canadiens on the power play a little over four minutes later, Lemaire and Cournoyer teamed up again, setting up Marc Tardif's insurance goal, which put the Canadiens ahead to stay in a 6–4 Cup-winning victory.

As could be expected, the scene in the visitors' dressing room, so quiet and focused only hours before, was now one of unrestrained celebration. Yvan Cournoyer, the freezing slowly wearing off, was able to combat the approaching pain with sheer exhilaration, as he tightly grasped the Conn Smythe Trophy awarded to him as the playoff's Most Valuable Player. His teammates on Team Canada the previous fall and now with Montreal – the Mahovlich brothers, Ken Dryden, Serge Savard, and Guy Lapointe – all revelled in the end of their longest season, one that had seen them emerge victorious in both Moscow and Chicago. In his part of the crowded room, Henri Richard, never letting the Stanley Cup stray far from his sight, savoured his eleventh Stanley Cup, a new record. "I guess it's my biggest moment," he said. "My 11th Cup and first as captain . . . Yes, I may have contributed something to a few of them, but I was lucky to play with so many great teams and great players since 1955. They did more for me than I did for them."[16] Scattered through the dressing room were his youngest teammates, Murray Wilson, Guy Lafleur, Larry Robinson, and Steve Shutt, all savouring the moment and champagne of their very first Stanley Cup, as was their head coach, Scotty Bowman. "Could anything be better than this?" Bowman asked the gathered media. "This will always be my greatest thrill, this moment now."[17]

In the days following Montreal's latest championship, the media began asking whether anybody could stop what seemed inevitable, another extended reign at the top of the hockey world for the Canadiens. On its front cover *Sports Illustrated* proclaimed them "The Now and Future Champs." In the *Globe and Mail*, Dick Beddoes wrote, "Beat Canadiens? Cadge a phrase from a television program. Mission Impossible."[18]

Even Ken Dryden, a normally careful, thoughtful speaker, couldn't resist the opportunity to openly discuss the Canadiens' seemingly impending dynasty. A few months before the playoffs a reporter had casually asked him about the chances of the New York Rangers winning the Stanley Cup.

"If they don't win the Cup this year," a pensive Dryden confidently responded, "it probably will be a long time before they do."[19]

Montreal, Quebec, September 14, 1973. To say the very least, it had been a difficult summer for Sam Pollock. While the rest of the hockey world was contemplating how to knock the Canadiens off their championship pedestal, a rival league was doing what no NHL team could. Pollock's team would not be defeated on the ice; instead the cause of their downfall would be death by pocketbook. After completing its first season of existence, the rival World Hockey Association once again began the process of raiding NHL rosters for talent. For a nascent league eager to gain a measure of respect and widespread acceptance, the easiest target was NHL players who had fulfilled their contractual obligations.

Marc Tardif was one of these players. Drafted with the second overall selection in the 1969 entry draft, the twenty-three-year-old Tardif had moved through the Montreal developmental process, spending a year with the Voyageurs before becoming a full-time member of the Canadiens in 1970–71. In his three full campaigns with the team he had been a key contributor to two Stanley Cup winners, and seemed poised to take the next step toward potential NHL stardom. In the 1972–73 playoffs, he had scored twelve points in the team's fourteen games, including two game-winning goals, good for sixth-best on the team.

Tardif, who had made $40,000 in his last year with the Canadiens, suddenly found himself in an enviable position. Since the advent of the WHA, the real winners had been the players who, thanks to the competition, saw their salaries wildly escalate. Offered a three-year contract with the Los Angeles Sharks of the WHA at $125,000 per season, including a no-trade clause, Tardif signed on the dotted line. "I want that stability in my life and that's the main reason for coming to Los Angeles," Tardif admitted. "My first consideration was for a no-trade contract and my second consideration was money. The money here is better than I was offered in Montreal so I felt I had better come here."[20]

In truth, paying Marc Tardif a salary of $125,000 per season and offering him a no-trade clause went against all of Sam Pollock's beliefs in paying his players based on performance. Henri Richard, the longest tenured player on the Montreal roster, was also the highest paid, receiving a new two-year contract that same summer at $200,000 per season. He was followed by Frank Mahovlich and Yvan Cournoyer, who each made $125,000 a season. Tardif, who was an emerging star according to Pollock, simply hadn't earned on the ice a salary equal to those of his top players.

"I felt that a player would have to prove his worth as an individual and team member before he could be considered a superstar," Pollock said later. "Some were quite upset to hear my definition of superstar. I felt that a superstar was a player who had produced well-above-average performance for a period of time. This definition was given a severe test during the WHA war. Teams in that league were giving journeymen $100,000-plus a year, teams in our league were following suit, and I was trying to convince our players that their paydays would come if they produced for the best hockey team in the world."[21]

A few weeks later, another player that the Canadiens had drafted, cultivated, and developed walked away from the team for greener pastures. Réjean Houle had been drafted with the first overall pick of the 1969 entry draft, one selection ahead of Tardif. A prolific scorer who averaged two points a game in his last year of junior, Houle had transformed himself in his three years with the Canadiens into a valued checker who became noted for his ability to shut down opposing forwards. At the same time Houle had gradually seen his point totals steadily rise from 19 to 28, culminating in a 48-point campaign in 1972–73. Like Tardif before him, Houle was approached by a WHA team, this time the Canadiens' provincial rival, the upstart Quebec Nordiques. Sticking to his principles Pollock refused to match the Nordiques' offer to Houle of a three-year contract at $100,000 per season.[22]

In the space of one month, Sam Pollock had lost both of his top selections from the 1969 entry draft. Though it may have been very little consolation at the time, in truth the Canadiens had a lot of young players ready to step into the breach created by the departure of Tardif and Houle. However, the loss that the team suffered on the eve of the team's training camp in the fall of 1973 would not be as easy to fill.

Soon after the completion of his first full season with the Canadiens, Ken Dryden signed a new two-year contract with the team, which paid him $70,000 in the first year and $90,000 in the second. Vacationing in Vienna with his wife in the summer of 1972, he quickly wished that he had been more patient. When Bobby Hull signed his famous million-dollar contract with the WHA's Winnipeg Jets mere weeks after Dryden had signed with the Canadiens, the amount paid to premium players changed overnight. Soon, other players would make the jump to the new league, all lured by extremely lucrative contracts. In response, the management of the New York Rangers in a collective panic renegotiated the existing contracts of their biggest stars, resigning them to multi-year, higher salaried deals. Before long, other teams throughout the NHL followed suit.

In light of these rapidly escalating, staggering salaries Ken Dryden made a quiet, secret visit upstairs to Sam Pollock's office in the confines of the Montreal Forum, where he raised concerns about his new contract, which in his view was already hopelessly outdated. Receiving a promise that Pollock would consider his concerns, Dryden then left for the Summit Series. Mingling with his new, temporary teammates, in particular the members of the Rangers, he came to the conclusion that he was being underpaid. Upon returning from Moscow, Dryden once again asked to renegotiate his new two-year contract. "After we came back from overseas on the Tuesday before our opener, which was a Saturday night game," Dryden recalled later, "I asked them what they planned to do about my contract. When the answer was nothing, I decided to quit right there and then."[23]

Thinking it over in the days before the opening game, a hesitant Dryden calmed down and decided to play the 1972–73 season, feeling that another spectacular season would enhance his stature and lead to a fair renegotiation of his contract. In his mind he fulfilled his part of the deal, helping lead the Canadiens to a dominant first-place finish that season plus another Stanley Cup, his second in three years. On a personal front, he would lead the league in wins, post the lowest goals-against average, and put up the most shutouts. At the end of the season he would be awarded the Vezina Trophy for the first time and would be named to the first All-Star team. Amazingly, he had done all of this while attending McGill University as a full-time law student, completing his studies in the first months of 1973. He was now widely considered the best goalie in all of hockey, possessing a list of accomplishments that would make a goalie ten years his senior jealous with envy.

Now, with the season behind him, he fully expected that his contract would be renegotiated. He would be bitterly disappointed. In the summer months of 1973, there was no movement in talks between the two parties. The stalemate echoed the earlier problems between Pollock and Dryden from a few years before, as both stood their ground, waiting for the other to flinch. Dryden was at a loss as to why the Canadiens couldn't pay the going rate in the NHL for a top goalie, which he undoubtedly was. On the other side, Sam Pollock feared that if he gave in to Dryden, then his other stars would come knocking on his door to revise their contracts. In order to prevent that from happening, he had to make a stand, to send a message to all of his players – and unfortunately it would be at his star goaltender's expense. Each man stood to lose a tremendous amount. When neither party moved an inch, Dryden took a fateful step on the eve of the Canadiens' training camp, hastily calling a press conference at the Windsor Hotel on September 14, 1973.

Standing there alone, uncomfortably, at the podium before a group of reporters in the hotel's Prince of Wales room on a warm Friday afternoon, Ken Dryden stunned the hockey world by announcing that he would sit out the 1973–74 NHL season instead of fulfilling the second and final year of his contract with the Canadiens. With his hands nervously fumbling in his suit pockets he struggled to explain, with an uncharacteristic show of emotion, that this decision was the most difficult of his life.

"You look around the league and you see somebody else who you feel is making no more, no less of a contribution to his team than you are and then you see where he's at," said Dryden. It was clear to those assembled that the situation had taken an incredible emotional toll on a man noted for his composure. Getting a hold of himself, he informed the gathered media that he knew of at least six NHL goalies whose salaries the previous year had been more than his. "And it will be even more this year," he added. "It's very difficult to accept, and something that gets harder all the time."[24]

When asked by a reporter if he felt he was "reneging" on his signed contract, Dryden firmly answered that because of the changing circumstances and the altered hockey landscape, he didn't share the opinion of Sam Pollock, who felt he had gone back on his obligation to the Canadiens. Realizing how important the loss of Dryden was, *Montreal Star* reporter Red Fisher in the days afterward suggested to Pollock that he should talk to Dryden in an effort to come to some sort of agreement. "He's got a contract," a testy Pollock replied. "He hasn't honoured the contract, so we may go to court. If he wants to talk to me, he knows where I am."[25]

Sam Pollock and Ken Dryden would not speak to or see each other for eight long, excruciating months.

Dryden's announcement sent shockwaves throughout the hockey world. The Canadiens, proclaimed as a dynasty-in-waiting mere months before, were now seen as a beatable team without the services of their all-star goaltender.

"The single shot required to bring Montreal Canadiens down to the mediocre level of the rest of the National Hockey League has been fired," predicted the *Globe and Mail*. "Suddenly, in Dryden's desertion, the Canadiens became less than overwhelming favourites to retain the Stanley Cup through to the year 2000. His departure is the vital factor in the other 15 teams in the NHL achieving parity with Montreal."[26]

Instead of tending the Canadiens' net, Dryden announced that he would spend the year articling with the Toronto legal firm of Osler, Hoskin, and Harcourt in order to complete his law degree. Starting in three days' time, he revealed that he would be receiving a modest $134 per week, a steep decrease in pay from what he was walking away from in Montreal.

The newspapers openly speculated that Dryden was seeking a four-year contract that paid $150,000 per season, and that Sam Pollock was only willing to provide a two-year contract that paid $110,000 in the first year and $125,000 in the second.

Montreal would attempt to defend their championship minus Dryden, but the team was clearly not the dominant one that had carried off the Stanley Cup in the spring of 1973. The Canadiens would employ three different goalies that season in an effort to compensate, but none of Wayne Thomas, Michel Larocque, or Michel Plasse could adequately make up for the loss. The Canadiens goals-against would rise in Dryden's absence by a staggering 56 goals over the course of the 1973–74 season. The year before had seen Dryden lead the NHL in shutouts with six. The troika that replaced him the following year could only muster one. The three goalies would post a cumulative goals-against average of 3.04, which paled next to the 2.26 that Dryden had posted the year before.

"We can't gloss over Dryden's loss," Scotty Bowman admitted as the season neared its conclusion. "The truth is we sorely missed him. He's the kind of pro who comes to play every game. He was especially good in games where we got behind and had to open up. You put real pressure on a goalie in situations like that. Dryden generally came up big to handle it."[27]

Bowman wasn't alone in his opinion. Sam Pollock shared it, but as the season went on he stubbornly resisted pressure to make any sort of accommodation or overtures to Dryden. It was painfully apparent to both of them and to all who watched that the team's weakness lay in the nets.

But a determined Pollock never wavered. As a result, his team was ushered out of the playoffs in the very first round by the New York Rangers.

Dryden's departure from the Canadiens had quickly and suddenly created a void at the top of the hockey world. Many observers openly predicted that the Boston Bruins would reclaim past glories, while others felt that the New York Rangers' time had finally arrived. Instead, the team that would fill the power vacuum created by Dryden's absence from the NHL would be a collection of misfits, an unruly assortment of stars, grinders, and goons. In the wake of the Canadiens' implosion they would controversially emerge as the league's new standard bearer. They would be equally celebrated and vilified, striking fear in the hearts of their opponents, revelling in their notoriety and making no excuses for their conduct, which sometimes bordered on criminal.

They were the Philadelphia Flyers, a.k.a. the "Broad Street Bullies," and with their ascendance the sport of hockey had entered its darkest age.

PART TWO

THE DARK AGES

"If they cut down on violence, people won't come out to watch. Let's face it; more people come out to see Dave Schultz than Bobby Orr. It's a reflection of our society. People want to see violence."

BOBBY CLARKE, *Sports Illustrated,* 1975

11.

THE WILD BUNCH

Philadelphia, Pennsylvania, April 6, 1969. Ed Snider was not a happy man. The thirty-six-year-old owner of the Philadelphia Flyers had just watched his hockey team go down in defeat, eliminated from the playoffs at the hands of their expansion brothers, the St. Louis Blues, for the second consecutive season. Coached at the time by Scotty Bowman, the Blues were the most successful of the six expansion franchises, appearing in the Stanley Cup Finals in each of their first three years of existence. Like the other expansion teams, the Blues were forced to deal with a lack of skilled players and had to look for ways to compensate. Bowman's Blues were renowned for their tight checking, their superior goaltender, and for playing a tough brand of hockey.

Compared to the season before when the Flyers had taken the Blues to the seven-game limit before bowing out, this loss was a painful setback for the organization. Outscored 17–3 in a four-game sweep, the smaller, softer Flyers had been pushed around and bullied by the physically dominant Blues squad. Horrified by what he had seen from his owner's box, an enraged Snider immediately approached the gathered media after the conclusion of the game and promised that "this will never happen to the Philadelphia Flyers again."[1]

At the time, many dismissed his comments as the rantings of a frustrated owner, but they underestimated the level of determination and desire in the Flyers' young boss. Snider followed up on his pronouncement and soon made it abundantly clear to his hockey people that he wanted a team made up of tougher players. The first test of Snider's new mandate would come two months later at the Queen Elizabeth

Hotel in Montreal, the site of the 1969 NHL entry draft. In the fifth and the sixth rounds, the Flyers would begin the process of fulfilling Snider's wishes for bigger and tougher players, drafting two prospects from Saskatchewan, Dave Schultz and Don Saleski, who would in a few years' time combine to run roughshod throughout a frightened league. But it was with their second-round selection that the Flyers would hit the jackpot and find the player who would quickly become the cornerstone of their franchise.

The 1969 NHL entry draft was the first modern draft. For the first time, all junior-age players were eligible to be drafted, sounding the final death knell of the sponsorship system. In addition, this draft represented the first time that the draft order was determined by the team's finish in the NHL standings the season before. This was also the last draft in which the Montreal Canadiens could lay claim to the top two French-Canadian prospects. Sam Pollock chose to exercise this option, and with the first two selections in the draft chose Réjean Houle and Marc Tardif. As a result of this decision, Pollock forfeited both of the Canadiens first- and second-round draft choices. With Houle and Tardif in the fold, the Canadiens were now left with no other selections until the third-round of the draft.

However, Sam Pollock had no intention of waiting that long. In the days leading up to the draft the Canadiens had compiled their own list of the top prospects available. Houle and Tardif occupied the top-two positions. The third spot belonged to a nineteen-year-old from Flin Flon, Manitoba, named Bobby Clarke. In spite of all of his talent and potential, it appeared that the Canadiens were the only team that had him ranked so high. Most of the other teams were frightened to take a chance on the young Clarke, who was a diabetic. Pollock had hoped and subsequently correctly predicted that because of his malady Clarke would not be selected in the first round of the draft, but he could not be sure if the same teams would pass him up the second time around.

The Philadelphia Flyers were one of the teams that had passed on Clarke the first time around. Sitting at their table, they were debating their next selection, the seventeenth pick of the draft. As opposed to Clarke, the Flyers had chosen a centre by the name of Bob Currier in the first round. Now, as the time for Philadelphia's pick slowly approached, Pollock made his way to their table, prepared his best sales pitch, and offered the Flyers "a deal they couldn't refuse."[2] In exchange, all he wanted was their upcoming pick.

In the first round, when the Flyers announced that they'd chosen Currier, Gerry Melnyk, the team's top Western scout, couldn't hide his exasperation. Over the past year he had extensively scouted Western Canada, travelling up and down snowswept roads. Shocked that Clarke hadn't been taken, he began pleading his case to a skeptical set of ears at the Flyers' draft table. "Our second pick comes up and still nobody's taken Clarke and holy bleep, I can't believe it," Melnyk later remembered. "I'm saying, 'We have to take him,' and they're all saying, 'No, he has diabetes.' I'm saying, 'I don't care what he has. I played pro for fourteen years and this kid is already a better player than I ever was.'"[3] With the time to decide fast approaching, Melnyk took the unusual and desperate step of phoning a medical specialist in Philadelphia. Patched through to the team's draft table, the doctor assured the wary group that Clarke's diabetes, if properly monitored, would not hamper his playing career. Melnyk's impassioned argument, combined with the medical opinion, helped sway the Flyers' vote toward taking a chance on the youngster from Flin Flon.

Among the expansion teams, the Philadelphia Flyers were the one team able to consistently brush off the persuasive Sam Pollock because of their conviction that as a developing franchise their amateur draft picks were by far the most, and in some ways the only, valuable currency they possessed. Rejecting Pollock's proposal, the Flyers proceeded to go ahead and select Bobby Clarke with the seventeenth pick in the 1969 draft.

"If I had Clarke on the Canadiens, we would have won six or seven Cups in a row, instead of just four," Scotty Bowman, by then the Canadiens coach, later ruefully reflected.[4]

Located directly on the border between Saskatchewan and Manitoba, in 1915, the area that would soon be named Flin Flon was the site of a rich volcanogenic massive sulphide (VMS) deposit. Capitalizing on the strike the Hudson Bay Mining and Smelting Company soon established a functioning mine with one of the largest smelters in Canada. With the onset of the Great Depression, many unemployed men made their way to Flin Flon to find work down in the mines. Among them was a sixteen-year-old boy named Cliff Clarke. "I came to see my uncle and never left," he recalled later. "I worked in a hardware store for about two years, and the mining company hired me on the third day after my 18th birthday."[5] For the next thirty years Cliff Clarke spent his days working five thousand feet underground in the mines. In all that time he only missed half a shift of work. These twin attributes of dedication and devotion to hard work were passed on by Cliff to his son, Bobby.

As a boy, Bobby Clarke was determined to play hockey, even if it meant fudging his true age. "According to the setup in Flin Flon," his father remembered later, "you couldn't play in the Tom Thumb program until you were nine years old. Then you were guaranteed nine minutes a week of live hockey on indoor ice. Well, you know Bobby. He found out they never checked the birth certificates and just took the kid's word for his age. So when he was eight he told them he was nine. Right then I figured someday he'd make the big time."[6]

In Flin Flon, it was expected that boys would go to work in the mines once they'd finished their schooling. Bobby Clarke was no different. At the age of sixteen he left school and started working alongside his father, a drilling inspector. For the next three years Clarke toiled away in the mines, working full eight-hour shifts in the summer months and four-hour shifts in the winter. "We got paid for eight hours in the winter," he later recalled. "I loved it." Leaving the mine at noon, he was free to indulge in his favourite pastime: hockey.

The following year suggested that his future didn't lie in the mines of Flin Flon. "He was wearing glasses, had buckteeth and looked kind of thin on ice," described Pat Ginnell, his junior coach. "But once he started moving, there was no doubt in my mind that this was going to be one of the best kids I ever coached."[7] With a rabid hometown crowd that always filled the two-thousand-seat arena beyond capacity, the seventeen-year-old Clarke, fresh from his shift in the mines and clad in the maroon and white uniform of the Flin Flon Bombers, led the Manitoba Junior Hockey League in goals (71), assists (112), and points (183) while only playing in 45 games. In addition, he led the Bombers to a seven-game loss in the Memorial Cup quarter-finals that spring. Absorbed into the newly formed Western Canadian Hockey League in the fall of 1967, Clarke proved that what had happened the year before was no fluke by finishing first in both assists and points; he then repeated the feat in what would be his last year with the Bombers, a year that also saw him capture the Western League's Most Valuable Player trophy.

But the true value of Bobby Clarke, even as a teenager, was not limited to his scoring totals. "Bobby's leadership qualities really came forward his last season at Flin Flon, even in practice," remembers Ginnell. "One day a bunch of the guys were goofing off during a scrimmage and that got Bobby good and mad. 'I want to play hockey for a living and you guys are hurting me and the team,' he screamed . . . By setting an example Bobby made sure everyone fell into line."[8]

Bobby Clarke was now the top prospect in Western Canada but faced several obstacles on his way to a professional career. Despite his impressive statistics, many of those in the NHL had rarely seen him play, especially in remote Flin Flon, which was a ten-hour bus ride north from Winnipeg. But that problem paled beside the questions many in the NHL asked about Clarke's health.

At the age of thirteen, Bobby Clarke, for reasons unknown, began to rapidly shed weight from his already smallish frame. In addition, he began experiencing problems with his vision. After a battery of tests, it was discovered that he had diabetes.

"I got diabetes when I was 12 or 13. I never had anything to compare it too. [Taking my injection shots] was what I had to do to live," he later recalled. "As far as playing hockey, I don't know if it hurt me, but I never worried about it. I wanted to be a hockey player. I didn't give a darn that I had to take needles. That never bothered me. I just asked the doctor if I'd be able to play hockey and he said, 'Sure.'"[9]

Aware of the rumours that his young star would be passed over in the 1969 entry draft because of his diabetes, Ginnell, the head coach of the Flin Flon Bombers, took the initiative and drove down with a nervous Clarke to the Mayo Clinic in Minnesota and was able to produce a signed doctor's note. The note simply stated that in the doctor's opinion Bobby Clarke could play professional hockey if he kept his diabetes under control.

NHL executives were not the only ones who doubted Clarke's ability to succeed in the professional ranks. Despite all of his achievements in junior hockey and even after being drafted by the Philadelphia Flyers, Clarke himself wondered if he could play in the NHL. After much consideration he decided to take a leave of absence from his job at the mine rather than give his final notice.[10] In September 1969, he nervously attended his first professional training camp with the Flyers, held in Quebec City. Understandably hesitant to discuss his diabetes, a quiet and reserved Clarke provoked a panic in the first few days of camp, when after oversleeping and pressed for time he decided to skip breakfast. As a result his blood sugar level was dangerously low, and as he was returning from that morning's practice he had a diabetic seizure in the taxi, feeding the fears of the Flyers management.

After the scare, Flyers trainer Frank Lewis, took an active interest in the diet of the young rookie, drawing up a complete plan, convincing the naive Clarke of the benefits of having a full meal to start the day. In addition, Lewis would carefully monitor Clarke's blood sugar level, having him drink a Coke that contained three spoonfuls of dissolved sugar before each game. In between periods and after the game, he would give Clarke fruit drinks that were high in sugar, and during the game Lewis would always carry chocolate bars and a tube of 100 per cent glucose in his trainer's kit, in case of emergency.

Clarke followed his trainer's instructions to a tee and began confounding those who had doubted whether he could survive at the professional level. His rookie season resulted in Clarke representing the Flyers in the NHL All-Star Game and dressing for all seventy-six of the team's games. In fact, over the course of his first six seasons in the NHL he would suit up in the All-Star Game and play in each and every Flyers game but two. But it was an incident in Flin Flon, in the summer after his rookie season, that forever changed Clarke.

Telling the story later, Clarke confessed that after spending a season in the NHL he had returned to little Flin Flon with something of a swelled head. "I was driving along with three girls in my big new car with the big engine one night. We'd had a few drinks, and all of a sudden I hit the gravel on the side of the road, the car flipped and I found myself on the roof."[11] Fortunately, no one was hurt, but the accident and a similar one the following day in Quebec had a sobering effect on him.

Michel Brière was also a rookie during the 1969–70 season. Much like Clarke in Philadelphia, he had been a pleasant surprise for the Pittsburgh Penguins, finishing third in team scoring with 44 points. Only twenty years old, and on the verge of marrying his childhood sweetheart, it seemed that a bright future was beckoning for him. However, on the night of May 15, 1970, near Val-d'Or, Quebec, all that changed when he lost control of his car along Highway 117 and was ejected through the front windshield. Suffering from major head trauma, he would never wake from a coma, and finally passed away a little less than a year later.

"It made me think about a lot of things in a different way," a sombre Clarke later admitted.[12]

In his second season, a more mature Clarke led the Flyers in scoring and to an appearance in the playoffs. His third season in 1971–72 saw him crack the NHL's top-ten scorers, and those who once questioned him now lined up to praise him. At the end of the season he was rewarded with the Bill Masterton Memorial Trophy for perseverance and dedication. Even more important than the statistics, however, was that the young Clarke, amid a host of older, more experienced players, had slowly established himself as the team's unquestioned leader. "It didn't matter whether it was a game or a practice, he went 100 miles an hour," recalled teammate Tom Bladon. "I know there were times when everybody was dragging like when we practiced a day after a game. There was Clarkie going all out. We would think, 'Jeez, if he can go like that, what's stopping me?'"[13]

Meanwhile, as Clarke was establishing himself as the foundation of the franchise, the Flyers organization, led by General Manager Keith Allen, was beginning to surround him with talent. The 1970 draft brought Bill Clement and Bob Kelly into the fold while the 1972 draft added Bill Barber, Tom Bladon, and Jim Watson, all of whom would pay immediate dividends. In addition, valuable players like Rick MacLeish, Ross Lonsberry, and André Dupont would come through trades. The new recruits joined with original Flyers Gary Dornhoefer, Joe Watson, and Ed Van Impe to form the core of a team ascendant.

At the same time, the team as a whole began to improve, not only at the gate as the Philadelphia Spectrum started to routinely fill to capacity, but also in the standings. Rounding them into shape was the new Flyers head coach, the enigmatic Fred Shero.

The son of Russian immigrants, Shero attended the University of Manitoba for a couple of years before serving in the Second World War as a member of the Canadian Navy. During his war service, many noticed his proclivity toward two sports: hockey and boxing. In fact, he was both a lightweight and a welterweight champion in the Navy, and was offered but rejected $10,000 to turn professional, choosing instead to follow his hockey dreams. Shero became a journeyman defenceman and in his career, spent mainly in the minors, managed to play a little over two seasons with the New York Rangers in the late 1940s. By the age of thirty-two, his playing career came to a lacklustre end. The next year he began his second career in hockey, as a head coach in the New York Rangers minor league system. In only his second year as a coach, he led the St. Paul Saints to the championship of the International Hockey League. Jumping from league to league, Shero was a consistent winner. In 1969–70 he coached the Buffalo Bisons to the championship of the American Hockey League, and the following year he won another championship, this time with the Omaha Knights of the Central Hockey League.

Looking for a new coach in the summer of 1971, the Flyers set their sights solely on Shero. "I didn't know Freddie well, but I had followed his career and he had won everywhere," explained Keith Allen.[14] Fred Shero was named as the third head coach in the history of the Flyers on June 1, 1971. At the press conference announcing his hiring, Shero went into detail about the nature of his relationship with his players. "You've got to be ready to defend the players from criticism. In fact, once the season starts, I think I'll do more for my players than I'll even do for my family."[15]

In his first year at the helm, Shero watched his team make tremendous strides, but a loss on the season's last day dropped them out of a playoff position, a heartbreaking end to the 1971–72 season. Despite these dashed hopes, the Flyers seemed to be a team on the upswing. "Fred Shero was the ideal man to mold the new Philadelphia players into a cohesive team," wrote Frank Orr a few years later. "He was a firm believer in solid positional play and an excellent tactician."[16]

Before the Flyers could begin their next season, their most valuable player answered the call of his country, and more specifically the call of Team Canada's head coach, Harry Sinden, for that fall's Summit Series. In his first three years in the league, Bobby Clarke had emerged as one of the brightest young stars in the sport. Nonetheless, Clarke couldn't help but find himself in awe of some of his superstar teammates when the team's training camp opened at Maple Leaf Gardens in the late summer of 1972. In the beginning, the feeling ran only one way. Among names like Esposito, Cournoyer, Mahovlich, and the like, Bobby Clarke was an afterthought. In fact, he had been one of the last players chosen for the thirty-five-man roster. On the first day of training camp, Sinden placed Clarke in the middle of a line between Paul Henderson and Ron Ellis, two veteran players on the Toronto Maple Leafs. Henderson later admitted to at first being disappointed at the thought of playing with Clarke. He would have preferred to play with a more veteran centre like Stan Mikita of the Chicago Black Hawks.[17]

However, a skeptical Henderson was quickly won over by the young Clarke's desire to make the team. "Bobby Clarke turned out to be one of the most dedicated hockey players that ever played the game. The best thing that could have happened to Ron Ellis and me was to get this young kid making plays for us. He was terrific!"[18] In training camp not much was expected from Clarke, Henderson, or Ellis. But their tenacity, enthusiasm, and willingness to give their all in both the offensive and defensive ends of the rink endeared them to the Canadian coaching staff. Ironically, this line, among all the others on a superstar-laden Team Canada, would be the only one to remain intact throughout the entire Summit Series.

"I was in the normal process that a young player goes through," Clarke said later. "I was getting more confident, I was gaining some experience. When you go to a series like that and get involved in that level of play with that level of player and you find out you can play at that level, it escalates your career by two or three years."[19]

For Bobby Clarke, the Summit Series was a decisive turning point in his hockey career. At the conclusion of the series he was standing third among all scorers on Team Canada. But more importantly he had learned that he belonged in the company of hockey's greatest players. In the wake of Canada's victory and his rags-to-riches story, Bobby Clarke should have been a bona fide Canadian hockey hero, on par with such superstars as Bobby Orr and Ken Dryden. Instead, he went on to become the most controversial hockey player of his time, beloved in some circles, utterly vilified in others. No one doubted his determination or his talent, but there were questions about his methods, which many found distasteful.

And the controversy all started in game six of the Summit Series . . .

Facing the daunting task of having to win three consecutive games on Russian ice to win the series, the embattled Team Canada is resting in the dressing room after playing to a scoreless opening period. The series has long ago transformed from its announced exhibition status and is now fraught with life-and-death consequences for the Canadian squad. At this moment, any feelings of sportsmanship and ideals of fair play are long forgotten. And if there is one player above all who inspires dread in the desperate Team Canada players, it is Valeri Kharlamov. Every time his skates touch the ice he strikes fear in the collective heart of the Canadian squad. Perched at the end of the bench is John Ferguson, the team's assistant coach. Retired from the game for over a year, he had carved out a reputation as the NHL's pre-eminent enforcer during his NHL career.

"Kharlamov had been eating them up," remembered legendary columnist Dick Beddoes. "Clarke told me the story back at the reunion [in 1987]. It's the end of the first period and Sinden tells Fergie to give the pep talk. He says, 'Someone in this room has got to get that sonovabitch Kharlamov.' Clarke tells me, 'I'm looking around the room and I came to the conclusion he was talking to me.'"[20]

At the halfway mark of the second period Clarke senses that now is his chance. Skating with the puck, the fleet Khalamov moves toward the centre of the Canadian blue line. Skating on a parallel course is a predatory Clarke, who glides down toward the Canadian blue line, slowly moving his left hand to the top of his stick and linking it with his right. Kharlamov bears down on the two Canadian defencemen in front of him and doesn't see Clarke closing in on his left. Clutching his stick like he's wielding an axe, Clarke puts all his effort into swinging it at Kharlamov's left ankle. When the stick makes direct contact, Kharlamov recoils in pain. The two will have words, as an unrepentant Clarke is escorted off the ice to serve a two-minute minor penalty for slashing, as well as a ten-minute misconduct. The consequences are far more dire for the injured Kharlamov, who has a fractured ankle. He will sit out the next game, then attempt to play in game eight, but he will be ineffective, scarcely resembling the player that the Canadian team learned to fear at the start of the Summit Series.

After the series concluded, many pointed to Clarke's actions as a cruel turning point. His brutal slash divided the hockey world. Some saw Clarke's actions as barbarism cloaked under the banner of sport. Those who viewed the Summit Series in its most patriotic terms, as a meeting that Canada had to win, applauded and justified Clarke's actions. As for Clarke, he never regretted it.

"Having Kharlamov out of the lineup made it a little easier for us," an unapologetic Clarke later admitted. "It's not something I would've done in an NHL game; at least I hope I wouldn't. But that situation, against Soviet players, at that stage in the series, with everything that was happening, it was necessary. If I hadn't learned to lay on a wicked two-hander, I would never have left Flin Flon, Manitoba."[21]

If nothing else, Bobby Clarke had loudly proclaimed for all to see how far he would go to win a hockey game. He would carry this win-at-all-costs attitude with him back to Philadelphia, where his coach would build a philosophy around the same principle that his teammates eagerly adopted. With his long curly hair and his missing row of front teeth, Bobby Clarke would not only become the face of the Philadelphia Flyers, he would become the face of hockey in the mid-seventies.

Upon returning from Moscow, an emboldened Clarke arrived in Philadephia and continued to play in the early months of the 1972–73 NHL season at a level with the NHL's best. Even more surprising, the Flyers too were performing apace with the league's best teams. But much like their young superstar, who at the age of twenty-three was made captain, the youngest in the NHL history to that point, the Flyers were beginning to gain attention for more than just wins and losses. Their ensuing success was largely attributable to the team buying into a notorious, yet effective, system propagated by their mysterious coach.

In a time in which systems were a rarity in professional hockey, Fred Shero went against the grain. "There are four corners in a rink," he philosophized, "although a lot of players don't believe it, and there are two pits, one in front of each net. To win a game, you've got to win the corners and the pits. You give punishment there, and you take it, which is why we have more fights than most teams."[22]

The main tenet of Shero's system was its reliance on constant pressure from his team toward the opposition. In an era when players routinely spent two to three minutes on the ice per shift, Shero stressed that his players were to always skate at full speed, always pressuring the opponent, and then get off the ice in less than a minute. In Shero's eyes, if the puck carrier was constantly facing stress and anxiety, he would eventually relent and give up the puck, and more importantly would think twice about wanting it back. Famously quoted as saying, "Take the shortest route to the puck carrier, and arrive in ill humour,"[23] Shero had his Flyers perfect the skill of dumping the puck into the opposition corner and going in at full speed, and then upon arrival doing everything and anything, within and outside the rules, to reclaim it. For Shero, the game of hockey was nothing less than a constant test of one's manhood, one in which skill could be subjugated to brawn and all-out rampaging aggressiveness.

"We know if we do our thing, we'll beat the other club," a confident Bobby Clarke boasted. "Let them worry about us. In the old days we worried about them. Not anymore."[24]

The Flyers' main weapon against other teams was not talent or speed but sheer intimidation. It permeated everything they did. By playing such a physical style, the Flyers dictated the game's overall style, regardless of their opposition. Suddenly many of their opponents were forced into playing a Flyers type of game, often unwillingly, which only worked in Philadelphia's favour. The Flyers weren't the first team to play an aggressive style; many NHL teams in the past had to rely on their physical attributes to make up for a skill gap against its opponent. The Flyers, however, were the first to take it to the extreme, making their form of controlled violence and constant hostility a fundamental part of their game plan. By following that particular style of play, the Flyers also embraced its natural conclusion: fighting. Fighting had always been a part of the game, but Shero and the Flyers were the first to encourage and integrate it within their game plan.

"Hockey," Shero openly declared, "is just a love affair when it doesn't have fighting."[25]

Teams that had more skill were overmatched by the ferocious Flyers. "All of a sudden we went from getting pushed around to getting even," Clarke proudly admitted. "St. Louis and the Bruins bullied everyone before us. We were accused of starting it all, but we were the ones who got tired of being beat up. When we got to the top we took full advantage of it. It felt pretty good actually."[26]

In 1972–73 the Flyers were charged with 1,756 penalty minutes, almost 600 more than their closest competition, establishing a new, if dubious, NHL standard.

By the spring of 1973, the Flyers had become the sport's most popular draw, loved at home and reviled on the road. But not everyone was overjoyed with their increasing notoriety. NHL president Clarence Campbell sent a message to the team's ownership threatening disciplinary action if they didn't step in to control their rampaging players.[27] The Flyers' ownership, now riding the wave of the team's popularity and revelling in their newfound outlaw image, ignored the missive.

The Flyers finished second in the NHL's Western Division at the conclusion of the 1972–73 season. Bobby Clarke ended the season in second place in the scoring race and was rewarded with the Hart Trophy as the league's Most Valuable Player. Rick MacLeish scored the third-most goals in the league with an even 50. "Although the fighting Flyers were often criticized for their belligerent ways," wrote Frank Orr, "it was clear that the team had more than toughness going for it."[28] In the first round of the playoffs, they defeated the Minnesota North Stars in six games. That victory garnered them the honour of facing the Montreal Canadiens in the semi-finals. It would be a close series, but the Flyers lost to the eventual champion Canadiens in five hard-fought, closely played games.

"Although we lost to the Canadiens, the fact that we gave a tough battle to the best team in hockey was good for our confidence," Clarke later said. "We knew that we were just a little bit away from being a Stanley Cup team."[29]

From the point of view of Flyers' management there was a simple solution to closing that gap. Less than a month later, on May 15, 1973, they remedied their deficiencies at the goalie position with the acquisition of Bernie Parent, an original Flyer, who after a stint with the Toronto Maple Leafs and a year with the Philadelphia Blazers of the WHA, returned to his first professional home. The addition of Parent in goal, combined with the subtraction of Ken Dryden from the Montreal Canadiens roster a few months later, tilted the unstable axis of the NHL's elite teams. What had once been a source of strength in Montreal, in Dryden's absence was now an obvious detriment. And while the Canadiens clearly struggled, the Flyers became even bolder with Parent in net, slashing 92 goals from their previous year's total and finishing the 1973–74 season a single point away from being the NHL's best. In the playoffs they would dispose of the Atlanta Flames, before vanquishing the New York Rangers in the semi-finals, and then conquering Bobby Orr, Phil Esposito, and the Boston Bruins in the Stanley Cup Finals. In only their seventh season of existence, and only five years after their owner's bold proclamation, the Philadelphia Flyers had become the first expansion franchise to capture the Stanley Cup. As Bobby Clarke and Bernie Parent paraded around a raucous Philadelphia Spectrum there could be no doubt that the NHL had now entered a new age.

12.

THE LOST BOYS

Toronto, Ontario, November 11, 1973. Brought together for their usual Sunday-night game in the Lakeshore Commercial Hockey League, the members of the Vulcan Industrial Packaging Team slowly pull on their purple and gold uniforms as the clock winds its way toward their 8:15 start time. Like the other three teams that make up the league, the Vulcans are a group of young professionals who are looking to have fun on the last night of the weekend before they return to their jobs Monday morning. Among their ranks are a fireman, a policeman, a lithographer, and a young man who has just began articling for the law offices of Osler, Hoskin, and Harcourt.

As he approaches the ice at the Lakeshore Arena, Ken Dryden is starting to draw a crowd. In large part due to his participation, the league's attendance is on the upswing. Tonight, around 417 spectators, arranged on seven rows of seats on the two sides of the rink will pay sixty cents each to watch the league's weekly double-header. Divided by thin iron arms, the well-worn wooden seats were acquired at a cost of fifty cents each from the old Maple Leaf Baseball stadium torn down four years earlier.

The moment his skates touch the ice, a little murmur rises among the crowd, as many of them strain to make sure it is in fact who they've come to see. A month earlier, Ken Dryden had quietly begun attending the Vulcans' Friday-night practices in an effort to get some exercise. Like every member of the team he would deposit his two dollars at each practice to help pay for the ice time that night. Without any equipment, he would aimlessly skate around while the rest of the team practised.

Then, after a month of practice, he had taken the next step and decided to play alongside the Vulcans in their regular Sunday-night game. His presence had stirred hope within his new ice-mates, who imagined the future of their team with him in goal. But Dryden had other ideas. He was there to play defence.

"I already know what I can do in the goal," he explained at the time, "but I've never been a defenseman or a forward and I've always wanted to try it."[1]

It was a rough beginning for Dryden. In his first game with the Vulcans two weeks ago, an errant stick clipped him over the eye, necessitating a quick visit to the hospital and seven stitches. A week later, in his second game, he was awkwardly dumped into the boards and hurt some ligaments on both sides of his collarbone. As a result, he skipped out on the Friday-night practice two nights ago.

But now with his injured shoulder tightly strapped, he gingerly makes his way across the ice. Tonight is a crucial game against the Christie's Bakeries team, with first place in the Lakeshore Commercial Hockey League at stake. It is an unusual sight for those perched on the old wooden seats, who have only seen the famous Ken Dryden on their televisions, calm and composed and sporting the Montreal Canadiens colours. For the most part he carefully plays his position, but he shies away from carrying the puck, preferring to quickly pass it off to a teammate.

However, midway through the second period, he decides to leave his comfort zone. Playing short-handed he finds himself with the puck and a swath of clear white ice in front of him. Taking off, he visualizes breaking in on the goalie and swiftly putting the puck in the back of the net, with all the speed and elegance of Yvan Cournoyer, his former teammate in Montreal. But the reality is far less graceful and successful as two Christies players catch him from behind and, in the resulting tangle, come away with the precious puck. Stripped of the puck, Dryden somersaulted into the cold air and landed with a thud right on his stomach.

Ken Dryden had proved himself mortal, after all.

Four nights earlier he had been reminded of his not-too-distant past when the Canadiens made their first visit of the season to Maple Leaf Gardens. At the end of the game, won 4–1 by Montreal, a nervous Dryden carefully made his way through the mob that enveloped the visitors' dressing room. Dryden was invited into the inner sanctum by his former coach Scotty Bowman, under the pretense of collecting his Stanley Cup ring from the spring before. Though at first a little timid,

Dryden soon felt at home. As he laughed and talked with his old team-mates, he suddenly began to feel what he had missed most, the camara-derie that only comes with being a part of a team. "Things suddenly seemed natural again," he later recalled. "I was hit by towels and by flying bars of soap, and I was hopping over skates."[2]

Much to his chagrin, it came to an end all too quickly as his former teammates started boarding the waiting bus reserved for the team. Dryden walked alone to his parked MGB-GT.[3]

The next morning, like many of his fellow working Torontonians, he stepped on the subway for the commute to his new office. Located in the heart of the city's financial district at King and Yonge, the offices of Osler, Harkin, and Harcourt occupied three full floors of the Prudential Building and accommodated 60 lawyers and 150 employees. Each of the three floors was divided into seemingly endless rows of small offices. Outside each office, a small sign on the door identified the occupant. The sign on the door of Dryden's own office simply read "Student."

His day's work usually started with his sorting through a limitless supply of legal briefs and law books, and responding to requests for his attendance at countless events. Then he settled down to what he got paid to do: defend clients for the firm.[4] "I was a rookie again in another game," Dryden later admitted. "I wasn't given the most important as-signments and I had to make the most of my opportunities."[5]

For the firm's most famous student, this small office fulfills a second function, as a sort of sanctuary, away from the question he is repeatedly asked by strangers in the building: "When are you going to stop messing around here and go back to Montreal?" He knew that his decision to walk away from the Canadiens was a difficult one for those on the out-side to understand. After all, from their point of view he had been living the Canadian dream and being paid for it.

At 5:00 p.m. every day Dryden would head home to his wife, Lynda, and his newly built highrise, about twenty minutes' north of downtown Toronto. His pastimes revolved around sports: hockey on Friday and Sunday nights, squash at the beginning of the week, basketball with a team named the Islington Press on Thursday nights. In addition, he moonlighted as the colour commentator for the Toronto Toros, the city's entry in the World Hockey Association. In fact, it was his role as an analyst that would prematurely end his playing career with the Vulcans, since his announcing duties often clashed with the schedule of the Lakeshore Commercial Hockey League.

As for his professional future, Dryden remained evasive throughout the winter months as the calendar turned from 1973 to 1974, as many speculated that there was more to his broadcasting job and his articling than met the eye. Further fuelling the conjecture in the media was the seeming relationship between his legal firm and the Toros, which led many to assume that Dryden, despite repeated denials on both sides, had already secretly reached an agreement for the following year and beyond.

"It must be plain to Sam [Pollock] that Dryden never will be back with the Habs," concurred Milt Dunnell in the *Toronto Star*. "Sam's only hope of salvaging something out of what remains in Dryden's contract is to make a deal with some other NHL club."[6]

As the year wore on and the Canadiens struggled in Dryden's absence, the other teams in the NHL fell over themselves trying to swing a trade with a beleaguered Sam Pollock. Holding his ground, however, Pollock turned down each and every request. On the other end, as the holdout lengthened, Dryden held out very little hope of ever playing for the Canadiens again. In the days following Montreal's defeat in that spring's playoffs, Dryden found himself a free man. After spending a season on the sidelines, he was now contractually free to explore other professional hockey options, though he couldn't deny that he still felt a keen connection to his old team. In part, his longing for the team was satisfied by a tenuous connection he had maintained to the Canadiens throughout his holdout – a regular and constant dialogue with Red Fisher of the *Montreal Star*.

"Sam Pollock knew that Dryden had kept in touch with developments within the organization through regular telephone calls to me. Similarly, Pollock delivered several 'unofficial' messages to Dryden through me . . . The temptation to write off Dryden was great, even though he had led the Canadiens to a Stanley Cup in 1972–73 against Chicago. However, Pollock was a businessman. As the 1973–74 season wore on, it was clear that there was a weakness in the nets, which is why the Canadiens were eliminated in the first round of the playoffs . . . Each knew exactly where the other stood."[7]

"It wasn't a happy year for me," Dryden later admitted. "I don't think it was a happy year for Sam Pollock. We never saw each other. We never spoke. I wondered what he was thinking. I didn't know if he wondered about me. After the Canadiens' season was over, I thought of doing it [calling Pollock], then stopped again several times over a few days. Finally, I called him. He wasn't in. I spoke with his great and long-time assistant, Miss Lee Dillion. She said he would be back in a few hours and that I should call back then. Then she stopped herself. 'No,' she said, 'it's his turn to call."[8]

On May 24, 1974, less than a week after the Philadelphia Flyers had won the Stanley Cup, the Canadiens and Ken Dryden once again stunned the hockey world, this time by announcing the return of Dryden to the Montreal fold. The new contract was for three years with an annual salary of $200,000, which finally put Dryden in the elite category of the best at his position. On the surface, the contract seemed to vindicate Dryden and his decision to take a year off. Knowing that his team was in desperate need of its star goaltender, Pollock swallowed his pride, put any personal issues aside, and once again did what he felt was best for the Montreal Canadiens organization.

Ironically, it was Dryden's time spent in the broadcast booth watching the Toronto Toros that convinced him that he belonged in Montreal. Watching the action in the WHA, he became convinced that the best hockey, in addition to the biggest challenge, still resided in the NHL. In preparation for his return to the NHL in the fall of 1974, Dryden worked out throughout the summer months, in the words of his wife, "like a madman." Subsisting on a diet heavy on yogurt, fruit shakes, honey, apples, and fruit salad, he ran two miles each night, played a daily game of squash, and undertook frequent tennis matches. And on one particular night he even resumed playing hockey, and once again took up a position on defence, but with a twist. In addition to playing on the blue line, he now wore his full ensemble of goalie equipment out on the ice.[9]

Bracebridge, Ontario, Summer 1974. In the same summer that Ken Dryden was running himself ragged through the streets, courts, and arenas of Toronto to get fit for that fall's training camp, his young teammate Steve Shutt was taking a slightly different, more relaxed approach. Renting a farm in Bracebridge, an area a few hours' north of Toronto and known for its picturesque settings and waterfalls, the twenty-two-year old Shutt arrived *sans* automobile, in the company of only his dog and his thoughts.

Two summers before he had been enjoying all the attention that came with being the fourth overall pick in the 1972 NHL entry draft. "I had scored 63 goals in my last year as a junior," he later recalled. "I'd scored 70 the year before. I was a big star with the Toronto Marlboros and I figured there was no reason I couldn't do the same in the NHL."[10] However, for the overconfident Shutt, that first training camp was a rude awakening. Unlike many rookies on the Canadiens he made the team out of training camp, only to find himself alternating between two positions, a lonely seat in the press box and the even more frustrating position of being anchored to the side of the bench. Suddenly, the young player who had arrived filled to the brim with confidence found himself at the opposite end of the spectrum, struggling with every player's worst enemy – doubt.

"They had a stacked team and it was extremely difficult for a rookie to break in there," he says today. "For the first two years, I really didn't play that much, but it was a real learning curve I never forgot . . . It made me appreciate my job a lot more and really respect how hard it is and how long it takes to be a regular on any NHL team."[11]

At the end of his rookie season with the Canadiens, Shutt lived the dream of every young boy by winning his first Stanley Cup. But even this wonderful moment had a downside, and while his name was engraved on the trophy, the truth was that Shutt felt somewhat detached from the celebration. "It was a great feeling winning the first year, but it was a little empty in the sense that I dressed for the game against Philadelphia (in the semi-finals) and played one shift and that was my whole playoff experience . . . It was a little empty for me because I didn't feel like I was part of it."[12]

Shutt's sophomore season with Montreal was no less frustrating. At times he would see a regular shift, but then would spend considerable time nailed to the bench, and still have to stay after practice to hone his basic skills. It was admittedly a difficult time for him, but in retrospect he considered it a very valuable one. "Later on, I realized I didn't know a lot of the little things it took to play in the NHL, especially about the defensive side of the game."[13] "Only after you have made the team and gone past the first couple of years do you realize the benefits of the way the Canadiens work you into their system."[14]

Despite a disappointing conclusion to the 1973–74 regular season for Shutt, caught in a late-season slump, he was benched, the playoffs offered him a shot at redemption. Finally, after two seasons marked by frustration and disappointment, he was able to harness his talent and desire together into one productive package. And while the Canadiens bowed out in the first round of that spring's playoffs, it was not because of Shutt's valiant effort. Over the course of the six-game defeat to the

Rangers, he scored five goals and added three assists, to lead all Montreal scorers. For Steve Shutt, the spring of 1974 represented a brief but significant turning point in his professional career and helped him regain a measure of the confidence he had lost over the past two seasons.

Now with the playoffs in the recent past, he sat in the gorgeous, tranquil summer setting of Bracebridge, repeating a silent vow to himself. "I decided I was either going to make it as a hockey player the next season or I wasn't going to make it at all," he later explained. "I disciplined myself to concentrate on thoughts like that."[15]

Montreal, Quebec, September 16, 1974. As summer came to an end the letters started arriving in the mail. Tucked in white envelopes, the invitations to the Montreal Canadiens training camp to be held in Montreal that fall began with the announcement that the players were scheduled to undergo the standard medical assessment on September 14. The remainder of the invitation was simple and direct. "The message simply stated that our goal was to win the Stanley Cup," remembers Bob Gainey, "that we had failed the year before and that there was nothing else in between."[16]

Without a doubt, the biggest story of that fall's training camp was the return of Ken Dryden after sixteen months away from the game. In his first appearance before the media and his teammates, he didn't disappoint. Thanks to his rigorous summer regimen, he showed up at camp a new, and lighter, man, carrying a trim 193 pounds on his tall, imposing frame. In his first fitness test he showcased the results of his hard work, only needing a minute to perform 53 situps, when 36 was considered an optimal result.[17] He also unveiled a brand-new bull's-eye mask that only added to his daunting on-ice persona.

In a training camp dominated by the news of Dryden's return, Steve Shutt quietly went about his business, motivated by the silent vow he'd made that summer. As it happened, circumstances outside his control dictated a sudden shift in Shutt's importance to the Canadiens.

"When I went to camp the next season (1974) I was really helped by the fact that Frank Mahovlich, Réjean Houle, and Marc Tardif had all gone to the WHA," he later recalled. "The Canadiens were at a point where they had to play me. But at the same time I was at a point in my life where I was mentally prepared to do the job."[18] For a player looking to prove himself in a crowded training camp, Shutt was also extremely fortunate to be placed on a line with Pete Mahovlich and Guy Lafleur.

"At the time Pete Mahovlich was a star," Shutt later said. "Guy Lafleur hadn't lived up to expectations, and I hadn't lived up to expectations. They put Flower and me with Pete right from the start that season. Pete took us under his wing and said, 'Come on, guys, this is how we're going to play.' And he showed us. He really looked after us after a while. You could see Lafleur starting to get confidence, and I started getting my confidence."[19]

Guy Lafleur had spent the first three years of his professional career burdened by the immense weight of failed expectations. Unlike many of his teammates he did not spend his first few years working his way through the Montreal system, learning how to become a professional hockey player. From the first time that he donned his sweater he was expected to step in for Jean Béliveau, who had announced his retirement on the day before the Canadiens drafted Lafleur. The media, both inside and outside of Montreal, wrote that the nineteen-year-old Lafleur was the one who would assure the elongation of the dynasty and be responsible for upholding the tradition of the Montreal Canadiens. "When I first came up with the Canadiens I had tremendous publicity," Lafleur later admitted. "So everybody was expecting me to replace Jean Béliveau and at the beginning I really didn't think about it but as soon as we started training camp and playing a few games I realized what it meant to the public. It was a lot of pressure."[20]

Guy Lafleur made his much-anticipated debut with the Montreal Canadiens on the evening of September 18, 1971, in a pre-season game against the Boston Bruins. He didn't disappoint. On that one magical night, before the then largest crowd the Montreal Forum had ever seen at a game, he flourished under the harsh spotlight. Taking the opening faceoff, a nervous Lafleur found himself centring Frank Mahovlich and Yvan Cournoyer, just as Béliveau had the spring before. Winning his first puck drop from Phil Esposito, he skated into the Bruins' end, quickly stole the puck from an unsuspecting Ken Hodge, and passed to an open Mahovlich, who put the puck in the back of the net. It had taken all of forty-one seconds for him to record his first point. That Saturday night, the 18,906 in attendance saw their hopes realized as Lafleur set up three goals in the 7–4 Montreal win.[21]

For the next three years, nights like this slowly became fewer and farther between as Lafleur struggled to find his place and role on the superstar-studded Canadiens roster.

"Tremendous things were expected of Guy Lafleur when he came in the league and of course, he was coming into a great hockey club," explained Sam Pollock years later. "It just took a couple of years for him to feel right at home."[22]

Facing off against Phil Esposito, Bobby Clarke, Alex Delvecchio, Dave Keon, Jean Ratelle, and Norm Ullman, Hall-of-Fame centres all, proved to be an intense learning experience for the young Lafleur. Despite playing head to head against the league's best, he was able to score 29 goals and 64 points that first season, which also placed him a respectable fifth in team scoring. But expectations were too high and the media and the fans who expected him to step directly into Béliveau's skates viewed his rookie season as a disappointment, especially in light of the success of Marcel Dionne and Rick Martin, each of whom had been picked in the draft after Lafleur, and each of whom collected more points in their first NHL seasons. Viewed as a legend-in-waiting only seven months before, Lafleur was judged on what he wasn't rather than on what he was.

For Lafleur, a very private and shy man, his problems on the ice were only a part of the larger issue. Off the ice he was lonely, living by himself and without any friends or family in Montreal. On the days when he didn't have to go to the rink, he would hop in his car and make the 180-mile journey to Quebec City to reconnect with those he still felt closest to. Such was his deep sense of isolation that he would often travel to the provincial capital just to get a simple haircut. The trips to Quebec also granted him a brief, if fleeting reprieve from the intense suffocation he felt in Montreal.

Lafleur's sophomore season in the NHL actually saw him take a step back. Instead of building on his rookie point totals, an overwhelmed Lafleur failed to match them. Even worse, Dionne and Martin continued to outscore Lafleur. On a team that lost only ten games and went on to win the Stanley Cup, he quickly became a forgotten man. At the same time his original two-year contract with the Canadiens was set to expire, and Lafleur began to obsess over his future.

Sam Pollock was faced with a huge decision. After two years of misery in Montreal, a depressed Lafleur was being tempted by the Quebec Nordiques of the WHA, who offered him a return to where he felt most comfortable. The pressure for Lafleur to return to Quebec City was immense. Still bitter over the loss of Jean Béliveau to the Canadiens a generation before, the Nordiques now offered the city hope that it could reclaim his heir apparent. With the 1973 playoffs set to start, the Nordiques, publicly urged on by the media and privately supported by some of the city's largest financiers, boldly made their move, offering Lafleur a three-year contract at $90,000 per season with a $50,000 signing bonus. Expecting something more substantial, Lafleur was not impressed with the Nordiques' offer, especially in light of some of the other salaries being doled out to NHL stars. After a counter-proposal from his agent, the Nordiques made their final offer: a three-year package, with a salary that escalated annually by $10,000, from $125,000 in year one to $145,000 in year three, and a signing bonus of $60,000.

Faced with the prospect of losing Lafleur, a calm and calculating Sam Pollock now made his move. Despite Lafleur's disappointing first two seasons, Pollock still believed he was a potential superstar. Of equal importance was the rivalry between the Canadiens and their provincial counterparts, the Nordiques. "This is the one young man we cannot afford to lose," Pollock told the Canadiens' ownership. "He will lead us to the Stanley Cup in a couple of years, and probably more than once. If he goes to the other league, he will help them establish credibility in Quebec, something they have in only a few places, with people like Bobby Hull. We'll lose in several ways."[23]

Another consideration was timing. For Pollock, it couldn't be any worse, as the tug-of-war over Guy Lafleur took place just as the Canadiens were preparing for that spring's playoffs. In order to ensure Lafleur's future in a Montreal uniform, Sam Pollock was prepared to hand out the biggest contract in the team's history. Pollock's subsequent contract offer somehow managed the impossible, by tying Lafleur's yearly salary into the team's current money structure. On a yearly basis, Lafleur would receive a lower salary than his more accomplished teammates, but in the long run, his contract would be far more lucrative. The offer on the table was a ten-year, million-dollar deal, plus a signing bonus and additional bonuses tied into his on-ice performance. At the end of the third year of the contract, and again at the end of the sixth, Lafleur would be free to renegotiate, if NHL salaries had escalated beyond the terms of his deal.

With the approval of the Canadiens' ownership, Pollock offered Lafleur the contract. It had several advantages over the Nordiques' proposal. Most importantly, in the Canadiens' offer the million dollars was guaranteed, even if Lafleur didn't play another game (Pollock and the Canadiens were wise enough to take out a million-dollar insurance policy on Lafleur to meet this risk), whereas the Nordiques were unwilling to guarantee any more than a quarter of that amount. With the instability of the WHA (just the week before Bernie Parent had walked out on the Philadelphia Blazers over non-payment of his contract), this was no small issue. Another major factor that helped sway Lafleur to the Canadiens' offer was that he would retain all of the money he gained from endorsements, whereas the Nordiques wanted a third of such royalties.[24] The stability of the NHL's pension plan, health benefits, and various league bonuses also combined to persuade Lafleur to sign the Canadiens' offer.

Other players did not go the same route. Over the next few months, the team would lose both Marc Tardif and Réjean Houle to the WHA. In time they were replaceable. Sam Pollock had known that Guy Lafleur was not.

His new contract safely signed, Lafleur promptly went out and in his third professional season had his worst year yet. In a season of widespread disappointment for the Canadiens, Lafleur seemed to be lost in the shuffle. In their third seasons, both Marcel Dionne and Rick Martin cracked the NHL's top-ten scorers, as opposed to Lafleur, who dropped to a new low of 21 goals. Even worse, in Montreal's first-round playoff loss to the Rangers, Lafleur had produced one measly point.

"The first three years weren't easy," Lafleur later said. "I was always nervous, before the games, during the games, after the games. I was worried that people would think I wasn't working and that they would compare me to Béliveau and Richard. I worried all the time."[25]

Behind the scenes, however, Lafleur had been taking the first, tentative steps toward reversing his fortunes. Before the beginning of the 1973–74 season, Sam Pollock instructed Claude Ruel, his organization's greatest teacher, to pay special attention to the team's newest millionaire. When Ruel first started working with Lafleur, he was shocked to see how little confidence resided in his young charge.

"I realized right away I would have to sweat like a pig to get him out of the rut he was in. His motor was stalling and he was spinning his wheels in the mud," recalled a blunt Ruel a few years later. "It was unbelievable. Somebody should have handled his situation long before that. I am sure they would have been able to root out his great talent as early as his sophomore year, if they had put their minds to it right from the start."[26]

Ruel had been assigned a daunting task by Pollock. He was asked not only to halt Lafleur's regression but to help reinstate his confidence. In short, he was to work at bringing back the player who had starred for the Quebec Remparts only a few years before. Whereas he had once been so bold, the new Lafleur was tentative, hesitant, and afraid to take charge. As the 1973–74 season progressed, Lafleur slowly began the long climb out of a very deep hole.

"Lafleur is going to become a great hockey player," predicted Toe Blake in the summer of 1974. "Don't jump to conclusions about his behaviour. Up to now the various events and tensions shook him in brutal fashion, but you will see him break out of it. He passes the puck unlike anyone else. He has a wealth of puck sense. I would take him anytime on my club from the '60's back in the days of the six-team pre-expansion league."[27]

But Blake's comments were widely disregarded. In truth, the public and the media had given up on Lafleur, a fact of life that Lafleur himself would discover in the summer months of 1974. He no longer was hounded everywhere he went and was for the first time in years able to go through life unmolested. Gradually, however, the old, confident Guy Lafleur began to reappear. Newly married and armed with a contract that guaranteed financial security, he purchased a country property on the banks of the St. Lawrence, thirty miles outside Montreal, and welcomed the impending birth of his first child, a son.

Much like his teammate Steve Shutt, over the summer he was able to relax. "I found myself right at home in Verchères," Lafleur later admitted, "on a property I really liked. I swore to myself that the moment had come to roll up my sleeves if I wanted to keep my post with this team for the duration of my contract."[28]

The criticism of the press, the disparaging remarks of the fans, now served as motivation. "I'm going to show those bastards that I can play hockey," he quietly vowed.[29]

Guy Lafleur arrived at the Canadiens training camp in September 1974 in excellent physical condition. With the re-arrival of Ken Dryden, however, Lafleur was relegated to the background as the media chose to focus on the returning goalie and some of the team's other superstars. The new and rejuvenated Guy Lafleur, however, wouldn't stay under the radar for long. On the second day of training camp, he skated out onto the ice at the Forum in a barely contained rush. In his haste he had forgotten to put on his helmet. That day as his teammates on the ice and the media in the empty stands watched, Lafleur put on a spectacle that left all those who witnessed it awestruck and amazed. Where he had once been hesitant, he now took charge on the ice, giving his all in the workout, all the while showcasing an intensity that many had doubted he possessed. As the practice came to a conclusion, there was scattered applause from his impressed teammates as well as from a formerly skeptical press corps. Resting up against the boards, in front of the Canadiens bench, Guy Lafleur couldn't hide his smile.

Normally not the superstitious type, he decided right there and then to discard the helmet he had worn for the first three years of his career in Montreal. In his mind, this simple piece of headgear represented the past and all that was associated with it. Minus the helmet, he was a completely different and better player as the energy and inventiveness that had long laid dormant now flourished every time his feet touched the ice. The change in Lafleur was like night and day.

Equally important that fall was a personnel move made by the astute Scotty Bowman, who started playing Lafleur on the power play and the penalty kill, giving him a bounty of ice time he hadn't had before. "The extra responsibility seemed to work wonders," said an impressed Bowman.[30]

"What really helped me then is Scotty decided to play me more," Lafleur explained later. "When you feel that they have confidence in you, you find you get back the smile that you left, three or four years ago."[31]

"He was skating aggressively, shooting accurately, was much tougher in the corners, and he was throwing moves I'd never seen anyone throw before," claimed Bowman.[32] "I think it's a case of confidence and getting results."[33]

Sam Pollock later echoed those thoughts. "He just gained confidence in training camp and he never looked back," he recalled. "It took time for him to realize all his talents and blossom. Certain players take time to do it and he finally did it this year."[34]

In addition, Scotty decided to move him to the right wing on a line with Steve Shutt and Peter Mahovlich. Almost overnight, the trio formed one of the top lines in hockey and soon they were all household names.

"A lot of people look at Guy Lafleur's first three years and forget that he was playing out of position and not complaining," says Claude Ruel. "The centre position demands a lot more than the wing and it is quite a change for a player coming off the wing. Going from centre to wing is much easier."[35]

But in the Canadiens' first seven games of the season, Lafleur had been held without a goal. He seemed to be on the verge – hitting posts, missing the net by inches, the goalies making unbelievable saves, sometimes through sheer luck – but the puck remained on the outside of the net. On the edge of a complete breakdown, his hard-won confidence on the brink, Lafleur decided to go upstairs at the Forum and talk to the one man he had always idolized above all others: Jean Béliveau.

"I told him that the way he was playing lately, the law of averages just had to start working in his favour," Béliveau later recalled. "There was no way, I told him, that a player could continue to play as well as he and not score a lot of goals. I told him to be patient, don't worry about any criticism, and just play the ...y he had been playing."[36]

In his very next game, the Canadiens' eighth of the season, he finally bulged the twine – and the floodgates were released. He quickly added six more goals over the next two weeks and never looked back. After three years of struggle, Lafleur had finally blossomed. "The most complete player in the game today," claimed Béliveau as the season reached its halfway point.[37]

Claude Ruel, who had taken on Lafleur at his lowest point, expressed pride and satisfaction in his pupil's progress. "The thing he's doing much better this year that he never did before is now he wants the puck. He's skating all the time . . . Now he's hungry. It's that little black thing he wants. He's fighting. Now he's skating, he's moving, he's playing hockey exactly the way it's supposed to be done."[38]

As if by magic, Guy Lafleur quickly emerged as one of the greatest players in the game. Suddenly, the comparisons to Marcel Dionne and Richard Martin were rendered moot, as Lafleur vindicated the patience and understanding of Sam Pollock, Scotty Bowman, and the Canadiens ownership. But aside from his statistics, which were at the top of the league, it was the way he played, his explosive style, that made Guy Lafleur the most exciting player in hockey.

In response to Lafleur's sudden emergence the sportswriters who had long written of his shortcomings tripped over themselves to come up with new superlatives. "Lafleur typifies what is best about this sport," wrote Bill Libby in the *New York Post*. "He is an artist on skates, creating scoring plays the way a painter puts a vivid scene on a canvas with a brush. His start is explosively quick and his stride is swifter than the others. He sees where his opponents and teammates are and anticipates where they will be. He is a spectacular athlete in a spectacular sport and it is wonderful watching him work."[39]

Guy Lafleur finished the 1974–75 season with 119 points, the most ever scored in a season by a Montreal Canadien, and good for the fourth-best total in the NHL. He became the third player in Canadiens history to reach the 50-goal mark, then set a new team record as well as a record for NHL right wingers with 53 goals, which was the second-highest total in the league. Playing in his first All-Star Game, he was named to the post-season All-Star team as the NHL's top right winger.

Peter Mahovlich would finish only 2 points back of Lafleur with a total of 117 points, the fifth-best in the NHL and a 44-point improvement from his previous career best. Steve Shutt would crack the 30-goal mark for the first time as the Canadiens' 374 goals scored as a team led the league. Ken Dryden, after some early-season struggles, in part attributable to his one-year sabbatical from the team, slowly regained his prior form and then played in the mid-season All-Star Game, as the Canadiens gave up the fourth-least amount of goals in the NHL.

The resurgent and recharged Canadiens would finish the season in a three-way tie with the Philadelphia Flyers and the Buffalo Sabres for the league's top spot. Lafleur would continue his superior play in the play-offs, scoring 19 points in the Montreal's eleven post-season games. In the six playoff games won that spring by the team, Lafleur would be the player responsible for the game-winning goal in four of them. After dispatching the Vancouver Canucks in five games, Montreal faced off against the Sabres in the semi-finals. In what Red Fisher later referred to as a stumble, the Canadiens bowed out to the Sabres in six games.

In the first Stanley Cup final between two expansion teams, the Philadelphia Flyers again captured the main prize, defeating the Buffalo Sabres in six games. By winning the Cup twice in succession, the Flyers proved that their win the year before hadn't been a fluke. In the wake of their success, there were many eager to follow their lead. Skill now became subordinate to brawn, speed to size, and, finally, beauty to brutality, as the sport entered a new, dark age.

13.

WAR ON AND OFF THE ICE

The Bramalea Legion was like most of its counterparts in the mid-seventies: a private establishment for war veterans and their fellow members to congregate. Gathered together around a table with a group of like-minded souls, Gerry Henderson was enjoying a leisurely pint of draft and some good conversation. One of the topics that particular night in 1972 was the looming exodus of six teams from the Metro Junior B League to the new Ontario Provincial Junior A League. With the jilted Metro League desperately searching for new teams, someone floated the idea that now would be the ideal time to form their own squad, based in Bramalea and stocked with local players. It was a noble endeavour, especially in light of the rapid changes that were quickly overtaking the sport.

In less than a decade the National Hockey League had undergone a sweeping and unprecedented transformation. It had tripled in franchises, from six to eighteen, and as a result the number of openings for professional hockey players had also tripled, from 120 to 360. For many players who would never have made it to the professional ranks otherwise, expansion proved to be a boon to their careers.

"The money-hungry businessmen of the NHL initially hurt their sport by expanding from six to eighteen teams in just seven years," wrote *Time* magazine in 1975. "There simply have not been enough quality players to staff all the teams."[1]

This lack of quality players was exacerbated by the arrival of the World Hockey Association, which among other consequences, further thinned the ranks of available talent. In a time in which the two professional leagues overwhelmingly relied on Canadian-born players to make up their rosters, skilled players were now more than ever at a premium. However, the swift ascent of the Philadelphia Flyers to the top of the NHL altered the equation. Many desperate general managers, pressured by the owners, often began to fill their teams' rosters with players whose main attribute was a pugilistic attitude. Scouring the ranks for prospective players became far easier when it devolved to locating the local thug, who would not only play for less money but bring to the rink the elusive paying customer. Suddenly the people who had been watching pro wrestling, roller derby, and auto racing crashes on television went out and spent their precious entertainment dollar on hockey and flocked to their hometown arenas to see the fights.

Thanks to the successful example propagated by the Flyers, teams now lined up to sign a wide variety of players whose primary asset was their brawn. Besides fighting a couple of times each night, these players were employed to help a team of lesser skill compete against a more talented team. Suddenly, the line that had always separated aggressive play from mindless violence blurred. Dave Schultz, the noted Flyers enforcer and poster child for this new violent era in hockey, put the new style in its simplest terms: "It makes sense to try and take out a guy who's more important to his team than I am to mine. If I take out Brad Park, that's not a bad trade, is it?"[2]

"The rationale seems to be something like this," wrote *Sports Illustrated* at the time, "if violence is what it takes to win these days, and winning violently is what makes the turnstiles sing, then bring on the raw meat."[3]

Now that this way of thinking had infiltrated the professional leagues of the sport it was only inevitable that the same attitude would trickle down the ranks, and soon the methods and tactics of the Flyers and others were being emulated in various amateur and junior leagues. It was this new wave of play, characterized by intimidation and brutality, that would violently collide with Gerry Henderson's idealistic dreams one night at an arena in North York, Ontario.

With Henderson in place as the new team's president, the Bramalea Blues began play in the Metro Junior B League in the fall of 1972. "We began the club to develop the hockey players, but also to help them become good citizens," Henderson stated a few years later. "Our goal was to keep the boys in Bramalea as citizens of the community who could perpetuate the organization."[4] Made up of boys aged fifteen to nineteen, the Blues quickly became one of the circuit's best teams. In only their second year of existence they defeated Owen Sound to win the league championship, and on April 16, 1974, hosted the first game of the Sutherland Cup All-Ontario Junior B finals at their North York Arena. Their opponents that evening, for the first game of a best-of-seven affair, were the Hamilton Red Wings. While the game ended as a 3–2 victory for the Blues, the final score reflected only a small part of the larger story.

Because of a brawl in the second period, it took almost four hours to complete the contest, with a total of 165 minutes in penalties handed out, as well as four game misconducts – not to mention the uncountable number of fights that broke out, both on the ice and in the stands. The Blues watched as four members of their team were taken to the hospital, one with a scratched cornea, one with a broken nose, one with a shoulder injury, and one to receive a tetanus shot for bites he had suffered during a fight.[5] After the game was finally over, the Blues players would steadfastly claim that the Hamilton players had used "foreign objects" during the brawling between the two teams. Members of the Blues team, as well as some of the police officers on the scene, alleged that Bert Templeton, Hamilton's coach, had not only urged on his players – who used bottle-cap rings and taped hands – during the brawl, he pointed out opposing players as potential targets and vocally gave his approval as his rampaging players excitedly described the results of their actions.[6]

The Blues head coach and general manager took immediate action. The very next morning, in advance of the series' second game that night in Hamilton, and responding to the anger and fears of many of their players' parents, they both resigned their posts rather than continue the series. The final straw for Henderson came that afternoon when the local newspaper received an anonymous phone call threatening that "if the Blues came to Hamilton, before they left, there would be a bomb on the bus."[7] Rather than travelling for the second game, Henderson sent a letter of withdrawal, on behalf of the Bramalea Blues, to the offices of the Ontario Hockey Association claiming that "we fear for the lives of our players."[8] The ensuing forfeit (the only one in the history of the trophy) awarded the Sutherland Cup to the Hamilton Red Wings. As a further consequence of the withdrawal, the traumatized Bramalea players, under the league's rules that expressly forbade forfeiture, faced the threat of a one-year suspension, with Gerry Henderson himself potentially facing a lifetime banishment from the league.

"Of course we realize the consequences," a disheartened Henderson told the media. "But the safety of our players is more important. Several of the boys' parents were afraid to let their sons go back into the series."[9]

The resulting media coverage brought attention to the incident from Ontario's highest political circles. A week after Bramalea's withdrawal from the Sutherland Cup, Patrick Reid, a Liberal MPP from Rainy River, stood up in the provincial legislature and denounced the brawling in North York, declaring that, "We're training kids from the time they learn to skate that the aim in hockey is to go out and injure somebody. Professional hockey is giving a bad example. It looks more like Saturday Afternoon Wrestling or Saturday Night at the Fights than Hockey Night in Canada." Robert Secord, the director of the Ontario Government's Sports and Recreation branch, echoed Reid's concern. "The professionals are making hockey into Roller Derby on ice. It's a horrible comment when a kid can't go and play this great game without fearing injury on the ice."[10]

The two men's condemnation of the violence received widespread media coverage and precipitated a flood of letters and phone calls to the provincial legislature. In response to the barrage, on April 25, 1974, the provincial government of William Davis ordered a public inquiry into violence in amateur hockey, with the goal of a final report on the subject in a month's time. Put in charge of presiding over the inquiry and producing the final report was Bill McMurtry, a prominent Toronto lawyer.

The son of a lawyer, and a native Torontonian, McMurtry had long been one of the city's most vocal advocates for the disadvantaged. One of four brothers in a politically privileged family, he had played hockey, as well as rugby and football, while attending first the Royal Military College and then Osgoode Law School. Since becoming a lawyer he had stayed close to hockey by playing in a recreational league, coaching his son, and being one of the three thousand hardy souls who attended the last four games of the Summit Series in Moscow two years earlier. And while McMurtry had been instructed to focus his report on the Bramalea/Hamilton situation, when it was announced that Clarence Campbell, the NHL's long-time president, would be appearing at the inquiry, it quickly became apparent that his true target would be the National Hockey League. McMurtry would justify Campbell's appearance and tie the NHL into his inquiry on the grounds that "it appears that the conduct and standards applied by NHL coaches, players and officials are having a very real and possibly detrimental effect on all of amateur hockey."[11]

By the date of the inquiry, June 3, 1974, Campbell was approaching the end of his third decade as the president of the NHL. During his tenure he had been a tireless worker and a steadfast defender of the owners who paid his salary. If the probing McMurtry had thought that Campbell would agree with some of his theories, he would learn when the president appeared before the inquiry how mistaken he had been. In an often contentious exchange between the two men, a defiant Campbell boldly claimed that "fighting is not undesirable, because it's the best safety valve I know of in hockey . . . in the framework of our operation, the elimination of fighting could encourage other offences. Fighting is the least dangerous of fouls, perhaps fourth or fifth on the list of violent occurrences where the number one concern is the risk of injury . . . I've said it many times before and I'll say it again: Fisticuffs inhibit more serious offences." Campbell went on to assert that the NHL was less violent now as compared to any time in its long history. "It's just not true that hockey has become a more violent game," maintained a condescending Campbell. "We've been through a whole series of crises. We've had it all before. Please credit us with the intelligence to want to improve the game in all areas. We certainly will not sanction any anti-social behaviour or reprehensible tactics. Of course, some teams have used the approach of intimidation. Perhaps the Philadelphia Flyers [who had won the Stanley Cup a week before]use that approach more than any other team now, but I think it's correct to say that their skill carried them to the Stanley Cup."[12]

In addition to Campbell, several sociologists and psychologists spoke at the inquiry, as did Bobby Hull, via an interview filmed the week before the hearings. Critical of how both the NHL and the WHA failed to enforce the rules against those who instigated the fights, Hull also lashed out against the necessity of having to fight to establish one's "manhood" and the continuing employment of those players he labelled as goons. "What concerns me is that 99 per cent of the WHA and NHL scouts are looking for the 20-year-old animal."[13]

Two months later, on August 21, 1974, McMurtry delivered his final forty-seven-page report and to nobody's surprise placed the blame for the proliferation of violence in the game squarely at the feet of the National Hockey League. Naming the NHL as the strongest influence on the increase in violence in amateur hockey, McMurtry wrote that "big-league hockey is perhaps the only sport that encourages the use of physical intimidation outside the rules as a legitimate tactic. The NHL obviously still sets most of the standards in hockey. The irony is that if they continue to encourage the present trends in hockey, where skill is secondary to physical intimidation then it is likely that every hockey nation will surpass North America in actual hockey skills."[14]

A defensive and annoyed Campbell publicly asserted that McMurtry had gone beyond the boundaries of the inquiry. "He was assigned to investigate one small incident and turned it into something unnecessarily grand."[15] Two days later at the Royal York Hotel in Toronto, the leading executives from the NHL gathered for a meeting of the board of governors. With the reporters pressuring him for a response to McMurtry's scathing report, an insolent Campbell once again stressed that there was no violence in the NHL and informed the assembled media that in the day-long meeting there had been no discussion of the report. When asked about Premier Bill Davis's support of the report, Campbell retorted, "What does Davis know about the NHL."[16]

Campbell and his NHL owners had always firmly believed that the government had no place in their shared business, but their dismissive manner and blatant disregard of McMurtry's report and, by extension, of the increase in violence in hockey, polarized those both inside and outside the sport. An indignant McMurtry, now thrust into the spotlight by virtue of his report, became the public face of the anti-violence forces, appearing on a variety of radio talk shows and speaking at various public symposiums.

"Hockey is sick," he asserted to a nationwide audience on CBC Radio. "If I could think of a stronger word, I would. I believe the situation is bad and getting worse and a lot of the fault lies with the National Hockey League. There's something wrong with a sport that glorifies a player like Dave Schultz of Philadelphia. His play is hockey by intimidation, not skill. Bobby Clarke of the Flyers is tireless and unceasing, but they taught him in Flin Flon that he needed to spear and slash to survive among the pros."[17]

In what was progressively becoming an overheated war of words, Fred Shero, the Flyers' head coach, waded in to the raging debate, echoing a soon-to-be familiar theme that McMurtry was not qualified enough to criticize the sport before attempting to deflate his argument. "Why's everybody up in arms over violence in hockey? Look at football. Players die like flies in football. There's over 20 deaths a year in that sport. I don't think there's ever been one death resulting from a hockey game." Shero then went on to defend his own players against McMurtry's charges. "I was really upset to hear that some of my players in Philadelphia have been mentioned with regards to this report. I don't think we're all that rough."[18]

Within a few months the NHL began its new season, but the topic of hockey violence refused to go away. Newspapers that had carried the verbal feud between McMurtry and the NHL on their front pages throughout the summer now increasingly showcased scenes of players fighting alongside editorials about the state of the sport. The amplified media attention had an unintended consequence, however, as it only seemed to stimulate interest in the sport. Mainstream media outlets that had never before paid much attention now put hockey on their front covers. Even the much respected *Time* magazine got into the act, putting Philadelphia's Bernie Parent on the cover of its February 24, 1975, issue under the headline "Hockey: War on Ice" and inside devoted a large amount of space to an article entitled "Courage and Fear in a Vortex of Violence," which explored the Flyers' ascendancy, hockey's subsequent rise in violence, and the resulting box-office profits.

"The arrival of Parent and his bruising teammates as the most potent force in hockey has added immeasurably to a growing interest in the sport," concluded the magazine. "For better or worse the Flyers have brought new muscle into the game. Fans cannot resist their intimidating play and all-too-eager fights. In Philadelphia, 17,007 pack the Spectrum for every game to cheer on the 'Broad Street Bullies'; on the road, standing room only crowds come to boo the tempestuous enemy. The cry for blood explodes whenever Flyer enforcer Dave Schultz starts swinging for the nearest hostile jaw. Inevitably, other teams have been infected by the mugging malaise . . . partially in response to the Flyers' fireworks, kids from Florida to California are taking to the ice by the thousands."[19]

This new popularity of the sport only seemed to harden the position of the NHL. With the league's arenas playing to about 95 per cent capacity, a satisfied Clarence Campbell saw no reason to make any changes to what he and the owners saw as a successful formula. Speaking at a Queen's University symposium on hockey violence on February 28, 1975, Campbell once again stressed that violence was simply a part of the game. "Without violence, hockey wouldn't be hockey. Basically there is a social acceptability of violence in the NHL. There won't be any big changes next season. My number one concern is to keep the NHL a viable enterprise."[20]

Campbell's words were a stunning rebuke to Bill McMurtry, who shared the podium that day with the NHL president. "The casual observer isn't competent to make comparative judgment on the degree of violence," Campbell stressed, speaking derogatively of McMurtry, the inquiry, and its subsequent report. "The referees are well conditioned and superbly equipped and their outlook is totally different from one not so well placed."[21]

If it hadn't been obvious to McMurtry and his supporters before, it was more than evident now: six months after McMurtry had submitted his report to the government of Ontario, the likelihood of any change of heart in the high offices of the NHL seemed now very dim indeed. The summer of 1975 would be comparatively quiet on the subject, as the debate over violence in hockey noticeably cooled. However, if Campbell and those who controlled the NHL thought the issue would simply fade away, then they had underestimated the determination of those leading the charge to curb the violence they felt was ruining the game.

Winnipeg, Manitoba, October 24, 1975. It was an unprecedented and bold move made by one of the biggest stars in the sport. A little over a year before, Bobby Hull had been the only professionally active hockey player to answer questions at the province of Ontario's inquiry into hockey violence. At the time he had lamented how the game that he loved, the game at which he excelled like few others, had degenerated into what he termed "goon" hockey. But in the year since the inquiry, he had seen frustratingly very little action in response to what he considered a problem of epic proportions.

He had thought long and hard about what he would do next. Truthfully, he didn't know if what he had planned would make any difference, but to sit still and do nothing was anathema to his way of thinking. So, after informing his superiors with the Winnipeg Jets, Hull took the drastic step of temporarily quitting the game he loved, as a form of protest against what he viewed as the growing violence and brutality in professional hockey. Hull's stand drew front-page headlines throughout Canada. "If something isn't done soon," Hull asserted, "it will ruin the game for all of us. I've never seen so much vicious stuff going on. Instead of making hockey a better game, we're tolerating people and things that are forcing a deterioration of the game."[22]

On the front page the report of Hull's protest shared space with the news from the opening day of the provincial government's Royal Commission on Violence in the Communications Industry. James McGrath, a Progressive Conservative Member of Parliament, caused a stir and was widely applauded when he declared that "the most violent Canadian made program on television is Hockey Night in Canada."[23]

Bobby Hull would rejoin the Jets two nights later and *Hockey Night in Canada* would still be broadcast every Saturday night, but now the pendulum appeared to be swinging to the side that advocated against the violence. The NBC television network, which had openly advertised fighting in an attempt to bring in more American viewers, pulled the plug on its contract with the NHL because of poor ratings. Opinion polls increasingly showed the public growing disenchanted with the direction of the sport. *Sports Illustrated* ran a picture of two players fighting on the front cover of its November 17, 1975, issue under the banner headline, "A Violent Sport Turns Vicious." Inside in an article titled "Wanted: An End to Mayhem," the magazine argued that the NHL should "do away with the fighting once and for all . . . Fear not, hockey fans, good solid hard-hitting play and the healthy sort of intimidation that are integral to all contact sports will not cease and may even intensify. As in football, there is plenty of leeway within the rules for any player to make his muscular presence felt . . . Failing any such miracles, the NHL will continue to be plagued by a split personality that threatens a ruinous alienation of affections."[24]

On October 29, the building frustration of the Ontario government reached its limit, and fourteen months after it had received Bill McMurtry's final report on violence in hockey, and having waited in vain for the status-quo NHL to take action, the government took an unprecedented step directly aimed at curbing hockey violence. Roy McMurtry, Bill's brother and the new attorney-general for the province of Ontario, issued a directive to both the police and the Crown attorneys of the land to "aggressively enforce the law" in an effort to halt the rising tide of hockey violence. Attorney-General McMurtry informed everyone that he wanted to see charges laid against professional hockey players for any Criminal Code offences they committed on the ice. McMurtry also sent letters to Clarence Campbell and Ben Haskin, the chairman of the WHA, notifying them of the impending crackdown:

As Attorney-General of Ontario, I have become increasingly concerned with the continuing violence in the sport of hockey and the fact that millions of television viewers are exposed to acts, on the ice, which may be in contravention of the Criminal Code. I wanted you to be aware that I have instructed my agents, the Crown Attorneys in Ontario and through them the law enforcement officers of the province, to aggressively enforce the law in this area.[25]

Much like the inquiry that begat his decree, McMurtry's attempt to put a criminal face on the violent action on the ice caused a range of reactions. Gordie Howe, a legend equal to Bobby Hull, took a different tack from his compatriot, laughing when informed of McMurtry's edict: "I don't think we need any of his legislation." Harold Ballard, the bombastic owner of the Toronto Maple Leafs, went further and called McMurtry's order "utterly stupid. Violence is what keeps the game alive."[26]

However, McMurtry's bold decision received widespread support both in and out of his own Parliament from the opposition New Democratic Party. "I'm for it completely," said leader Stephen Lewis. "It is about time something was done."[27] Ron Basford, the Federal Justice Minister in Ottawa, also supported McMurtry's decision, urging the attorney-generals of the other provinces to follow suit.

In the midst of all the publicity and heated discussion, many wondered how long it would take for a player to be charged. The answer came a week later.

Toronto, Ontario, November 5, 1975. Brian Glennie, a defenceman with the Toronto Maple Leafs, had just completed what appeared to many observers at Maple Leaf Gardens that night to be a clean, hard body check on Bryan Hextall of the Detroit Red Wings. Hextall's linemate, Dan Maloney, however, took exception. Watching Glennie lay out his teammate, Maloney felt that the hit was "extra hard." In a split-second he made the crucial decision to retaliate and charged toward an unaware Glennie.

Glennie never knew what hit him. Stalking him from behind, an angry Maloney viciously swung his clenched right fist at the side of Glennie's face. Glennie fell to the ice, limp and unconscious, but Maloney kept punching him, then jerked him up and down off the ice, so that Glennie's head struck the unforgiving solidity of the cold ice a couple of times before the referees intervened. Despite the brutal nature of the assault, Maloney was only assigned a five-minute major penalty with no further disciplinary action from the NHL. Glennie spent the night in a Toronto hospital, with a mild concussion. He was released the next day.[28]

Maloney escaped punishment from the NHL head office, but he didn't get off so easily with the provincial authorities. The next day he was charged with assault causing bodily harm. If he were convicted of the charge, Maloney could face up to ten years in prison, with the minimum punishment being a stiff fine.[29]

"Why is McMurtry picking on hockey," protested Maloney's coach, Doug Barkley. "The NHL is the best-run league of any major sport. The league has done an excellent job running itself."[30]

The province of Ontario obviously disagreed.

The fight to stem the increase in hockey violence would now be fought in a provincial court. Attorney-General Roy McMurtry had followed through on his decree. If the NHL wouldn't do anything to curtail the violence now inherent in the game, then the law would.

Montreal, Quebec, November 20, 1975. Two weeks after Dan Maloney was charged for assaulting Brian Glennie, a beleaguered Clarence Campbell released the final details of the upcoming "Super Series." For the first time two club teams from the Soviet Union, the Central Red Army and the Soviet Wings, would each play four exhibition games, opposite eight different NHL teams.

Against the tumultuous backdrop of a sport in turmoil, Campbell announced that as part of the Super Series, the Montreal Canadiens would play an exhibition game against the Central Red Army at the Montreal Forum on the evening of December 31, 1975.

THE RUSSIANS ARE COMING

Moscow, Russia, September 28, 1972. Ken Dryden started hearing rumblings at the reception a few hours after Team Canada's triumph in the Summit Series. Straining closer he was alarmed at what he was over-hearing among the loud din of the celebration at the Metropole Hotel.

"If we [Canada] played them in mid-season with some games under our belts, we'd probably beat them eight straight."

"They couldn't maintain the pace in the NHL for seventy-eight games and then the Stanley Cup playoffs."[1]

Dryden was dumbfounded. He considered the just defeated Soviets to be a team equal to that of Team Canada. After all, they had forced his Canadian teammates to work harder than they ever had before. He thought to himself how easily the end result could have swung the other way. Over the course of the series he had grown to respect and even admire his Russian opponents. He was now distressed to find out that his opinions were not widely shared.

"Even though we won the last three games and the series, they were all one-goal victories," he later wrote. "And now we were talking about our great superiority. To me, it was a sad moment in a great series. These feelings of superiority did not fit the occasion. And I, for one, don't believe that we are superior."[2]

Dryden would later learn that the opinions he was hearing weren't limited to that Moscow reception hall. Though Team Canada had emerged victorious, many in Canada would lament over the next few months and years that the series had been played in the month of September, a time when the NHL professionals had traditionally been in training camp. Many argued that the Russians had an unfair advantage because their national team trained and played with each other year-round, whereas the Canadian squad had only a few weeks before the series started to bring together a collection of professional players from different teams. As time passed the excuses would only multiply as a still-smug Canada clung to the idea that the sport was entirely their own.

In the last days of spring in 1974, the Soviets took the important first step to a future exchange of ideas and tactics with Canada by extending an invitation to the country's hockey elite to come to Moscow and study the Russians' methods first-hand. One hundred Canadian hockey coaches took them up on their offer and flew to Moscow to take part in a joint symposium dedicated to hockey. Among this group of one hundred, however, was just one head coach from the NHL. That there weren't more suggested that the league continued to arrogantly suppose it had little to learn from the Soviets. Instead of embracing the new techniques in hockey as practised and displayed by the Russians, Canadian hockey, only a year and a half removed from 1972, seemed more than ever to be content and comfortable in its belief in the superiority of its own game. Those who could have learned the most from the Soviets – players, coaches, and executives – were satisfied to explain away 1972's challenges with any number of excuses and use them as a reason to resist any type of change.

For many of those in Canadian hockey circles, these lingering doubts from 1972 could only be answered in a game, or a series of games, pitting the Russians against one of the top teams in the NHL. To their way of thinking, an NHL team would be "a real team," one that had trained, practised, and played together over an extended period, much as the Soviets' team had. By holding the potential game or games around the Christmas holidays, halfway through the league season, an NHL team would, it was felt, be in a far better position to face off against the Russians. And this time around, unlike 1972, the professionals would be prepared for the Soviet style of hockey.

However, despite the continued claims of Canadian superiority, in the immediate aftermath of the monumental Summit Series there was an overwhelming clamour from Canadian hockey fans for more clashes featuring NHL professionals on the international stage. To capitalize on this interest, six weeks after the Summit Series finished Clarence Campbell announced to the public that the NHL was in the planning stages of a potential series to take place in the middle of the 1973–74 season. Interestingly, the proposed ten-game series would see Soviet club teams against NHL teams, with six games to be held in North America, two in Moscow, and two in Leningrad.[3]

In the spring of 1973, with the Montreal Canadiens on their way to winning another Stanley Cup, the demand for a contest between them and the Russians only intensified. "No prospect is brighter for next winter than the possibility that the Canadiens will play a series against the best squad in the Soviet Union, presumably Moscow Red Army," wrote Dick Beddoes in the *Globe and Mail*.[4]

It only took a month for that dream to evaporate, however, as rumours surfaced that the NHL brass were only interested in having American-based teams participate. Having lost out on any revenue from the lucrative Summit Series, when the first four games were all played in Canada, the American owners who had lent the services of their players were now expecting their own lucrative payback. However, all the speculation would become moot in the fall of 1973, when negotiations for the potential series broke down for a variety of reasons, many of them political. With the NHL owners unwilling to set up another Summit Series so quickly on the heels of the first one, the rival WHA stepped into the breach and the 1974 Summit Series was born. The format would be the same as the 1972 series, with the first four games contested in Canada and the final four at the Luzhniki Ice Palace in Moscow. However, there were many differences between the two series, not the least of which was that the Soviet Union was widely expected to cruise to victory.

The WHA team was able to ice Bobby Hull, who would finally make his international debut. He was joined by a forty-six-year-old Gordie Howe and other former NHL stalwarts such as Gerry Cheevers and some veterans of the 1972 series who had since jumped to the WHA, such as Frank Mahovlich, Pat Stapleton, and the hero of that series, Paul Henderson. Much like the league they played in, however, Team Canada '74 did not possess the depth of talent that the '72 team enjoyed. In many media quarters, Team Canada '74 was seen as a glorified old-timers team, but for a league desperately searching for acceptance, it was hoped that the series would give the WHA a boost in credibility. This approach stood in stark contrast to their opposition; the Russian National Team was earning its standing on the ice. Since they had last been seen by North American eyes, the Russian National Team had triumphed in both the 1972 and 1973 Izvestia Cups. Their 1973 win was particularly impressive as they won all four of their games with devastating ease, defeating Czechoslovakia 7–1, Sweden 8–3, Finland 7–0, and Poland 10–1. They were just as overwhelming at the 1973 World Championship, where on their home ice at the Luzhniki Ice Palace they romped to the gold medal, winning all ten of their games by a collective score of 100–18. The 1974 World Championship proved to be a somewhat more difficult task for the Soviets; they suffered a shocking loss to Czechoslovakia, 7–2, in the opening game of the tournament but then bounced back and emerged victorious in their next nine games to capture the gold.

Of course, none of these tournaments featured the participation of Canada. In an age when satellite was still in its infancy, the Canadian public could only keep up with the Soviets' triumphs by reading about them in the newspaper. The 1974 Summit Series would give the country their first glimpse of the returning Soviet players (17 of the original 27) since 1972. With the Soviet players on average four years younger than their Canadian opponents, the Russians' strategy going into the series was to try to wear out Team Canada by outskating them and being more physically assertive. Two years ago, on the eve of the first Summit Series, the Soviets had purposefully and successfully lulled the arrogant Canadians into a false sense of security by staging poorly played exhibition games in Moscow and dismal practices in Canada. Unable to repeat that strategy, the Soviets took the opposite approach in 1974, by stunning the Canadian team with a full showcase of their awesome skills in their practice sessions. Skating out for their first practice, Boris Mikhailov, fresh off of leading all scorers in the 1974 World Championship and starting to assert himself as the team's leader, made note of the many Canadian players in the arena and gathered his team together. The practice that followed left all who watched it speechless.

At the conclusion of the fast-paced practice Gordie Howe made his way toward his old adversary and now teammate, Bobby Hull. "Hey, Bobby, put your eyeballs back in your head," said Howe half-jokingly. Both men had stood in wonder as the Soviet team attempted to have the perfect practice, one that they hoped would leave a lasting impression on their Canadian opponents. In that sense, they succeeded. In all of their combined years, neither Howe nor Hull had ever witnessed a practice that was so fast, so concentrated, and so perfect. Howe said to Hull, "Did you see those guys handle the puck? My god, I saw one guy blow a pass in the entire practice. And one of the coaches called him aside and gave him hell."[5] Canada had tried to intimidate their Russian counterparts in 1972. Two years later the roles had been reversed.

Similar to the '72 Series, it was once again Valeri Kharlamov who attracted the most attention. In game one in Quebec City, with fourteen minutes gone in the second period and Team Canada holding on to a slim 2–1 advantage, Kharlamov once again seized the moment and scored a goal that his teammate Vladislav Tretiak later insisted should have been videotaped and screened in classrooms.

Taking the puck just inside his own blue line Kharmalov swiftly turned and dashed straight down the middle of the ice, his blinding speed leaving a clinging but increasingly desperate Réjean Houle in his wake. Waiting for him at the Canadian blue line were Pat Stapleton and J.C. Tremblay. These two defencemen, who had been stalwart, even All-Star defencemen prior to joining the WHA, stood at the ready, fully aware of what the elusive Kharlamov had done to a helpless Don Awrey in 1972. In Montreal, he had burst around Awrey on his first goal before darting to the right and unleashing a crisp slapshot for his second goal. Now in Quebec City, he would confound them by unleashing a third option from his seemingly endless arsenal of offensive trickery. He jumped between the two startled defenders – somehow inching between them and their sticks – then landed back on the ice off-balance, where he had the presence of mind to bring his swinging stick down on the loose puck and promptly flip it over the shoulder of a stunned Gerry Cheevers, the Canadian goalie. Countless replays only further enhanced the beauty of the goal.

Thanks to two subsequent goals from an energized Bobby Hull the first game ended in a tie, but after a win in the series' second game in Toronto, the WHA version of Team Canada begin to slowly fall apart. In the months before the 1974 Summit Series commenced, Team Canada's coach Billy Harris had appeared before the McMurtry inquiry looking into violence in hockey. Eager to build publicity and legitimacy for the upcoming series, and with memories of Bobby Clarke's vicious slash on Kharlamov still fresh, Harris attempted to put the future WHA version of Team Canada on a higher moral plain than its NHL predecessor. "We're not taking any goons to the Soviet Union because we're not going over there and trying to overpower them physically," Harris asserted. "We're taking some class guys and we're going to win or lose with dignity."[6]

However, in Moscow a few months later, Harris's earlier commitments to decorum were quickly abandoned in the harsh light of Team Canada's dire situation. Defeated in the series' fifth game by a score of

3–2, with the superb goaltending of Gerry Cheevers being the sole reason the final score approached respectability, Team Canada was staring at an increasingly impossible situation. Like their 1972 predecessors, they now had to win the last three games of the series, all in Moscow, to claim victory. Unfortunately, the 1974 version of Team Canada was not up to the task. The morning after the fifth game, Harris arrived at the Luzhniki Ice Palace for Team Canada's morning practice only to discover that some of his players were so hung over from the post-game party the night before that they couldn't even skate. Disgusted and disheartened, knowing that it was now all over, he immediately left the arena and began the long, solitary, three-mile walk back to the team's hotel.[7]

In a sixth game characterized by some bizarre officiating, the Soviets gained a 5–2 victory and clinched the series. As the final siren sounded, all hell broke loose. Kharlamov and Canadian defenceman Rick Ley, who had engaged in a spirited battle all game long, were involved in an incident that would mar the series and further stain the international reputation of Canadian hockey. At the game's conclusion, as the two benches emptied, Kharlamov tapped a beaten Ley on the back and then looked at him derisively. Ley snapped. With a forty-pound weight advantage, an enraged Ley pounded on Kharlamov until the ice was stained red. Mercifully separated by a combination of officials and players the resulting scene was one of confusion as Kharlamov, his face a crimson mask, calmly went about the task of picking up his equipment from the ice, then skated off with half the Soviet team following him. For the first time in anyone's memory the Soviets refused to participate in the post-game handshake. The morning after saw tempers subside and a remorseful Ley seek out Kharlamov at the rink and personally apologize to him. Kharlamov, showing far more sportsmanship and class than he had himself received from the Canadian professionals over the course of two Summit Series matchups, immediately accepted Ley's apology. "It's okay," he told Ley. "These things happen between hockey players."[8]

The apology, however, had little impact on the controversy now raging in two countries. Billy Harris's earlier declarations of sportsmanship and friendship rang hollow in the wake of the events of game six. "Team Canada's goodwill mission to Moscow can be listed as a dismal failure following the ugly incidents which dotted last night's 5–2 defeat at the hands of the Soviet Union nationals," wrote the *Toronto Star*'s Jim Proudfoot directly from Moscow. "The World Hockey Association allstars, who had come here determined to show Muscovites and the world what splendid fellows Canadian hockey players really are, today are marked as worse villains than anybody the original Team Canada had in 1972."[9]

No player was more dismayed at the violent turn of events than Bobby Hull, who along with his coach, Billy Harris, had denounced such displays at the McMurtry inquiry a few months before. "There was no need for that kind of crap at the end," said a frustrated Hull in the moments following the melee. "I don't care who was to blame, Ley or Kharlamov, that's not what this series was supposed to be about."[10]

The Russians threatened to pull out of the tournament and the Soviet coach, Boris Kulagin, publicly declared that Ley should be jailed. All of this only served to inflame the already toxic debate over violence in hockey, as Ley was alternately vilified and applauded in the Canadian media and even in the Senate chambers. On October 8, 1974, Liberal Senator John Godfrey stood up and proclaimed that the Canadian government should apologize to the Soviet Union for "the stupid conduct of a hooligan like Rick Ley. When hockey players represent Canada it is of vital importance that every one of them behave in a sportsmanlike manner. By fighting and his inexcusable conduct, Ley injured in the eyes of the world the reputation of Canada . . . he was a disgrace to his country." Godfrey went on to opine that Ley should have been immediately sent back to Canada and that the failure to do so by Team Canada officials had also disgraced the country. As soon as Godfrey concluded his speech, his fellow Liberal Senator, Sid Buckwold, promptly stood up and denounced his contemporary's comments, calling them inexcusable. "I'm proud of Team Canada and what they've done," he said, taking the opposite point of view from Godfrey, claiming that the Canadian team had endured a rough series and had been pushed too far.[11]

What had started as an attempt by the WHA to gain some respectability had now merely served to prove in the eyes of many that they were no better than many of their NHL brethren. Billy Harris's summer vow to engage the Soviets in a series characterized by clean play and sportsmanship had now crumbled in the Moscow fall. The last two games of the series would see another tie, and then a Soviet victory, putting a merciful end to a series that most tried to immediately forget.

Ten weeks after the conclusion of the ill-fated 1974 Summit Series, Kharlamov, Tretiak, and their teammates on the Central Red Army club team embarked on a ten-day tour of the province of Ontario, where they would play in seven exhibition games against some of the best junior teams in the province. At the time, the Central Red Army was a team in the midst of a transition, having lost their four-year hold on the championship of the Soviet Elite League the spring before to the upstart Soviet Wings. In response, Anatoli Tarasov, the only coach the team had ever known, had willingly stepped aside and was replaced by his loyal and long-serving protégé, Konstantin Loktev, behind the Red Army bench. A legendary right winger with the Red Army in the fifties and sixties, Loktev had helped lead the Red Army to ten Elite League championships. In addition, as a key cog in the Russian National Team, he won a gold medal in the 1964 Olympics and three consecutive World Championships from 1964 to 1966. At the conclusion of the 1966 season, he retired from playing the game and took up a position as the assistant coach on the Red Army team under Tarasov. Now in his first season coaching the Red Army, a team that consisted of eleven players who had starred in the 1972 and 1974 Summit Series, Loktev was also making his head coaching debut on the international scene.

In all seven exhibition games the Red Army emerged victorious, despite facing a better than expected opposition from the junior squads that quite often augmented their rosters with outside players. For example, in the final game of the series, the Kitchener Rangers augmented their team with six players from the Peterborough Petes. Of particular interest to the Rangers was a nineteen-year-old centreman who would go on to lead the Petes in points that season while finishing the season fifth in the entire Ontario Minor Junior Hockey League. In less than a calendar year Doug Jarvis would once again face off against the Central Red Army, but instead of the cozy Kitchener Memorial Auditorium the venue would be the Montreal Forum, under the bright lights of a national television audience.

For those in the seven cities, the Soviet exhibition tour against various Ontario junior teams was an unexpected boon. The games represented a rare opportunity for members of the public to watch players they had only seen on their televisions or read about in their local newspaper. At the assorted stops along the way the Soviet players were treated like rock stars, as kids lined up for their autographs and crowds cheered them every step of the way.

A strange phenomenon was taking shape. A little over three years before, the Soviet Union and its hockey players had been unknown to the Canadian populace. However, after two Summit Series that were broadcast nationwide, the country's hockey fans had learned to appreciate the Soviets' speed, skill, and elegant play. And now as North American hockey was mired in a debate over violence, it was to the Russians that many hockey fans looked for inspiration. In the minds of some of those who abhorred the current status of play in the NHL, the style of play exhibited by the Russians provided an alternative, a way to play the game free of the fighting and the brutality that were currently plaguing the sport. For some, they represented the way forward.

Returning home to Elite League play after their successful tour, the Red Army recaptured the Soviet championship that spring. In April, the Soviet Union once again took home the gold medal in the World Championship, winning all ten of their tournament games by a cumulative score of 90–23. Their continued winning only served to heighten the anticipation of a potential showdown in the future against the best of the NHL.

The announcement that the hockey world had long been waiting for came suddenly and without warning. On the evening of May 28, NHL president Clarence Campbell announced that the league would play a series of games against two touring Soviet club teams in a few months' time, in late December 1975 and early January 1976. "For the time being, I believe it is the only way to develop the game of hockey," claimed Campbell.[12]

Over the next couple of months the NHL and their Soviet counterparts engaged in a series of complex negotiations. At the end of July, the details of what would become known as the Super Series slowly started to leak out. The top two club teams from the previous season in the Soviet Elite League, the Central Red Army and the Soviet Wings, would each play four games against NHL opposition. The eight NHL teams that would be participating were the Montreal Canadiens, the Philadelphia Flyers, the Boston Bruins, the Buffalo Sabres, the Chicago Black Hawks, the Pittsburgh Penguins, the New York Rangers, and the New York Islanders.[13]

That October the NHL and its players agreed to a new five-year labour contract. The agreement paved the way for the upcoming Super Series, in addition to future international best-on-best tournaments. "That contract had an international component starting with the Super Series and running all the way through to the 1991 Canada Cup, involving the International Ice Hockey Federation, the NHL, and the NHL players associations," confirms Alan Eagleson, at that time the head of the NHL Players' Association.[14]

On November 21, 1975, a month before the Super Series was set to take place, the NHL released the final details on the upcoming showdown. Through a sometimes intense set of negotiations, the NHL had won the right to play all the games under its own rules while the touring Russian club teams won the right to add some players from other teams in the Soviet Elite League. The games would be officiated by groups of three, two NHL referees and one Soviet official. It was also announced that CBC would broadcast nationwide each of the four games featuring the Red Army as well as the game between the Soviet Wings and the Buffalo Sabres.[15]

The announced schedule was:
Red Army vs. New York Rangers, December 28
Red Army vs. Montreal Canadiens, December 31
Red Army vs. Boston Bruins, January 8
Red Army vs. Philadelphia Flyers, January 11
Soviet Wings vs. Pittsburgh Penguins, December 29
Soviet Wings vs. Buffalo Sabres, January 4
Soviet Wings vs. Chicago Black Hawks, January 7
Soviet Wings vs. New York Islanders, January 10

This series was designed to answer all the lingering questions that had been generated in the past few years. These eight games would pit the visiting Soviets against NHL teams in their own arenas, teams that had half a season of play under their belts. The series would be contested under NHL rules and be officiated by NHL referees.

"In approximately seven weeks, the National Hockey League will begin the most crucial two-week period of its 50-year history," wrote Al Strachan in the November 11 edition of the Montreal *Gazette*. "If they [the NHL] win, they will be saying to their detractors, 'Look, you say that we don't play hockey the way we used to but we just beat the much-heralded Russians. The NHL brand of hockey must therefore be a good-quality game again.' If, on the other hand, the NHL teams get thumped by the Russians' sound, programmed play, the NHL has no excuses. It is only sending its best teams against the Russians anyway. It is their best against our best."[16]

15.

THE NEW BREED

The previous NHL season had been a struggle for Henri Richard. The captain of the Montreal Canadiens, he had only played in the first sixteen games of the 1974–75 schedule thanks to a broken ankle suffered on November 13, which sidelined him until the second round of the playoffs. Though he was regarded as one of Montreal's best players in the semi-final series loss against the Buffalo Sabres, and despite having a season left on his contract, the thirty-nine-year-old decided it was time to leave. The past few years had been a challenge for the proud but aging Richard, as he increasingly found himself at odds with a succession of coaches and frustrated by what he viewed as the limitations of his new teammates, many of whom had been preschoolers when he first joined the Canadiens in the fall of 1955.

"The desire to play hockey was missing a little,"[1] admitted Richard, explaining that the strain of constant travel and his advancing age were two of the main factors that went into his decision, which was admittedly a difficult one for him. "After 20 years I believe a good thing has come to an end and this is the day."[2] Henri Richard's retirement signalled the end of an era, both for the sport and for the Canadiens franchise. For the first time in thirty-five years the Canadiens would begin their season without a Richard in their lineup. The last active player from the great Canadiens team to win an unprecedented five consecutive Stanley Cups, his departure severed the final link to the glory days of the fifties.

The retirement of Richard capped off a tumultuous two-year period for the Canadiens that had begun with the sudden and unexpected departure of Ken Dryden in the summer of 1973 and moved through successive playoff disappointments, consecutive springs that climaxed with the rough-and-tumble Philadelphia Flyers skating off with the Stanley Cup.

For Jim Roberts, who (with Richard's retirement) shared with Yvan Cournoyer the status of longest-tenured player on the team, those two seasons represented a lost opportunity for the Canadiens. "In the two years that Philadephia won the Stanley Cup, we [Montreal] weren't quite ready early in the playoffs to win a series like we usually were. It was the Rangers one year and Buffalo the next that got the jump on us and beat us early, and I always felt that if we hadn't . . . had the letdown early and if we would have gone on to win those series than it would have been very tough for Philadelphia to have won. The two years they won were a big disappointment for us; it was just a case of us not being as sharp as we should have been."[3]

Living in a hockey world that had accepted the Flyers as the standard bearer, and in which skill and ability were being steadily degraded in favour of brawn and bullying, didn't sit well with many of the Canadiens' followers either. As is customary, some placed the blame for team troubles squarely at the feet of the head coach, in this case, Scotty Bowman; others urged the Canadiens to adopt more aggressive tactics such as the Flyers were propagating. The Canadiens were, in fact, changing their approach, but in a different way. In the way characteristic of him, Sam Pollock had spent those two lost years quietly assembling the final pieces of a new championship team. Taking his cue from the Flyers, Pollock began gathering a group of hard-nosed players who brought aggressiveness and enthusiasm to their play, but who also brought with them a complete game rooted in tenacity and defensive responsibility.

If one were to look for the prototype of the player that Pollock began acquiring in the mid-seventies they needn't have looked any further than the Montreal bench and the man wearing the number six: Jim Roberts, whose approach to the game significantly influenced those who followed him into the Canadiens ranks in the mid-seventies.

Robert's long and hard road to employment in the National Hockey League began almost two decades earlier, in the fall of 1956, when he made the hour-long trek from his home in Port Hope to Toronto and tried out for a spot with the Toronto Marlboros junior team. "When I was a kid I always had in mind that I wanted to play hockey but I was afraid to admit it too openly for fear that I would be embarrassed by never getting a chance," he later admitted. "But I always kept my eyes open for a chance to move ahead and when an opening came along to better my position I would grab it."[4] Turned down by Toronto, the persistent sixteen-year-old Roberts began playing Junior B hockey in Peterborough. Two years later, in the fall of 1958, he made the jump to Peterborough's Junior A team, which at the time was sponsored by the Montreal Canadiens. For the next two years, Roberts, a defenceman, would hone his skills under the tutelage of Scotty Bowman, a young head coach only seven years his senior.

Turning professional two years later, Roberts began a slow and daunting climb through the Montreal Canadiens' extensive amateur system of teams, spending the next three seasons in the Eastern Professional Hockey League, first with the Montreal Royals and then with the Hull-Ottawa Canadiens, where he would once again come under the guardianship of Scotty Bowman, in addition to that of the team's manager, Sam Pollock.

"I played for Sam in Hull-Ottawa," remembers Roberts today. "He left Scotty to coach the team, but Sam was on top of everything. Sam knew what the makeup of the team had to be to be very successful. Sam was always thinking ahead."

During this period, Bowman and Pollock made a decision that would change the course of Roberts's career. Standing five-foot-ten and weighing in at 165 pounds Roberts was not an imposing defenceman. Roberts's size, along with the abundance of defensive prospects in the Montreal system and the lack of defensive-minded forwards, led Bowman and Pollock to switch Roberts to the right wing. In short order he became a top checker and a fantastic penalty killer, thanks to his combination of speed and smarts. Roberts may not have been the most robust or gifted player in the Canadiens system and even he harboured doubts about ever making the big team, but there was no one who could match his work ethic or his fierce competitive nature.

The next season saw Roberts at his most transient. He spent most of the 1963–64 hockey season with the Omaha Knights of the Central Professional Hockey League, where he was once again coached by Bowman and managed by Pollock. But he also starred in the American Hockey League, where he had a brief two-game stop with the Quebec Aces and saw action in nine games with the Cleveland Barons. Roberts's stellar play at each stop finally earned him the call he had long dreamed about, and at the age of twenty-four he joined the Canadiens for the last fifteen games of the season and all seven of their playoff games that spring.

Roberts began the 1964–65 NHL season on the team's fourth line and was almost exclusively used in a penalty-killing role, which garnered very little notice from either the media or the fans. His experience stood in stark contrast to that of another rookie on the Canadiens squad that year, Yvan Cournoyer, who received equal amounts of hope and hype from both the fans and media. Cournoyer, the offensive wizard, and Roberts, the defensive stalwart, couldn't have been more opposite, yet their predicaments were eerily similar.

"I think everybody with the Canadiens had an apprenticeship back then," reflects Roberts today. "I used to sit on the bench and just kill penalties, Yvan used to just sit there and play power plays, and if we got down in a game he'd play more, and if we got ahead in a game I'd play more. Every young player that came on that team had to prove himself and had to prove that he could do his job. It was just what the Montreal Canadiens were about then. I used to go to training camp and there would be 120 players showing up for one job, and once you got the job you worked that much harder to keep it."[5]

A decade later Cournoyer and Roberts were the Canadiens' two elder statesman. In the interval Cournoyer had become one of the game's most dangerous offensive threats and most popular players. Roberts would achieve a similar though less popular renown for his defensive prowess and would become one of the most respected, if not best known, players in the league. For a player like Roberts, his value wasn't measured in goals and assists, but in team achievements. It was a state of mind that he passed along to his younger teammates. "I've got specific jobs to do with this team and, if we're going well, it means I'm doing them."[6] He admitted that "I don't know how to judge my individual performance,"[7] but his gutsy and plucky play would be rewarded with Stanley Cups in 1965 and 1966. The team was unable to protect him in the 1967 expansion draft, and Roberts was the very first pick of the St. Louis Blues, where he was reunited with his old mentor, Scotty Bowman.

Respected throughout the league as one of the game's tightest checkers, Roberts would be a valuable cog in the Bowman-led Blues team that made it to three consecutive finals in his first three years with the team. Given more responsibility with the Blues than he ever had in Montreal, he was recognized and rewarded for his performance, which culminated in appearances in both the 1969 and the 1970 All-Star Games. However, things started going downhill for the Blues in the spring of 1971 and Scotty Bowman was soon let go. On December 13, 1971, just a few months into Bowman's tenure with the Canadiens, Pollock arranged a trade to bring Roberts back to the team he had started with. "I always felt pretty good that Scotty seemed to want me wherever he went," says Roberts today. "I learned, and I think we all learned from Scotty and Sam, that it takes more than one kind of player to win. And as long as you go all out, you can help the team win."[8]

In his first couple of years back he would often be shifted back and forth between defence and right wing. "My favourite position was being on the team," he later reflected. "I played wherever they needed somebody, and that changed as the years went by."[9] By the time the team approached training camp in the fall of 1975, however, he had been permanently placed on right wing. From that spot Roberts would line up on the third line or what was known as the checking line with two fellow Peterborough Petes alumni, each of them more than a decade younger than him, and each of them nurtured in the same defensive proficiency and checking approach that he, himself, brought to the game.

Montreal, Quebec, May 15, 1973. Sam Pollock entered the Mount Royal Hotel in a position that made his fellow general managers seethe with envy and cry foul. Five days earlier his Canadiens had hoisted the Stanley Cup in the Chicago Stadium. Now as they prepared to pick over the best amateur players in the annual cattle call otherwise known as the NHL entry draft, Pollock, through a series of shrewd trades and acquisitions, had managed to secure seven of the first twenty-two selections in the draft. He had accumulated all of the picks with one prospect in mind – Denis Potvin.

Potvin, a star junior defenceman with the Ottawa 67's, was the prospective first choice of everyone in the draft. Yet it was the New York Islanders, a team that had just completed their first season in the NHL with an abysmal twelve-win season, that held the precious and highly coveted first pick. And nobody coveted that pick more than Sam Pollock, who envisioned adding Potvin to his burgeoning defence core. He had spent the months before the draft constantly badgering his Islanders' counterpart Bill Torrey with a variety of proposals, most of them including a raft of older players that would help the Islanders in the short term.

Like Guy Lafleur two years before him, Denis Potvin was considered a can't-miss prospect. In his junior career he had broken all of Bobby Orr's scoring records, and had been named the Ontario circuit's top defenceman in each of the past two years. "Denis Potvin was one of the best junior players to come along in quite a while," remembers Jimmy Devellano, then the Islanders' top scout and a future NHL general manager. "He was a legitimate future superstar and a silver lining for the team that could convince him to sign with them, for sure. He was big. He was a presence. He could score . . . anybody could see he was going to be a star."[10] The Islanders' brain trust, in spite of the relentless pressure applied by Pollock, made the decision to keep the pick and promptly took Denis Potvin with the first selection of the draft.

Having been rebuffed by the Islanders, Pollock and the Canadiens were now on the clock, holding the second overall pick of the draft. The consensus number-two selection was a high-scoring centre from Medicine Hat named Tom Lysiak. In the days leading up to the draft, however, Lysiak had made it publicly known that he did not want to play for the Canadiens out of a fear that it would take him longer to make the team. Many in the media speculated that the Canadiens would instead pick André Savard, a talented French-Canadian centre from the Quebec Remparts. The shrewd Pollock chose to go in another direction, trading the pick that became Lysiak to the Atlanta Flames. In exchange, he received the Flames' fifth overall selection in this draft, plus Atlanta's first-round selection in 1977 and second-round selection in 1978.

With the draft's third overall selection, the Vancouver Canucks claimed Dennis Ververgaert, a right winger from London. The Toronto Maple Leafs used their fourth pick to take Lanny McDonald, a teammate of Lysiak's in Medicine Hat. Now owning the fifth overall selection, which he had acquired from Atlanta, Pollock consulted his own self-crafted, handwritten draft sheet and noticed that the first four selections had gone exactly to plan. Glancing at his sheet, Pollock now took a calculated risk.

Holding the pick after the Canadiens, the Boston Bruins were impatiently waiting for Pollock to make his choice so they could select John Davidson, easily the draft's top goaltending prospect. Feeling that the player he wanted would still be available and not wishing to pass up the chance to thwart the Bruins, at the time the Canadiens' greatest rival, a scheming Pollock executed a trade with the Blues, who were also hungering for Davidson. Montreal would give the fifth overall selection of the draft to the Blues in exchange for the Blues' pick, which was the draft's eighth overall. In addition, Montreal would also get the Blues first-round pick in the 1975 entry draft.

Outraged, the vindictive Bruins immediately selected André Savard. The rationale for their pick was the belief that Savard was the player Pollock wanted. It turned out that the Bruins were wrong, and when the Pittsburgh Penguins selected high-scoring winger Blaine Stoughton with the seventh pick, Pollock knew that his gamble had paid off. He had managed to gain more draft picks for the future, while taking the junior player he valued more than any other. With the eighth overall selection of the 1973 NHL entry draft, Pollock walked to the podium and chose Bob Gainey, a left winger with the Peterborough Petes.

"So we got Gainey," said Pollock, "a player who had a reputation of being a great defensive player and who had learned defense under the best, Roger Neilson in Peterborough."[11]

The selection of Gainey was Pollock's first step toward rounding out the Canadiens and making the team a complete one. At the time of the pick, however, no one seemed to grasp his thinking. The choice of Gainey took everyone by surprise and left many dumbfounded. Sitting in his office at the *Montreal Star* that same afternoon, Red Fisher asked a colleague whom the Canadiens had picked. When Fisher heard Gainey's name, he could only ask, Who? Upon being told that Gainey was a pretty good defensive player with the Peterborough juniors, Fisher confessed that he'd never heard of him.[12]

"Who among us has ever heard the name Bob Gainey?" echoed an equally stunned Yvon Pedneault in *La Presse*. "I consulted the statistics to see if they had got the name correct. I expected to find a fifty-goal scorer, at least a centreman – in short, a logical choice for the big team."[13]

The selection of Gainey also caught the player unawares. Still at his parents' home in Peterborough, he was contacted that evening by the Montreal *Gazette*. "Yes, I was surprised. They told me I might go in the first or second round but I was surprised at being the first Peterborough player picked, and at being picked by Montreal," the twenty-year-old admitted. His reaction was notably different from some of his contemporaries', who had stated publicly that they didn't want to be drafted by the Canadiens: "I'm certainly not going to go around worrying about whether or not I can make the Montreal team. If they picked me they must like me a bit."[14]

What wasn't widely reported at the time was that Sam Pollock had never even watched his first-round draft pick play a game.[15] That responsibility had fallen to Ron Caron, who had extensively scouted both Gainey and the Ontario Junior League he had played in. Furthermore,

Gainey's coach with the Petes, Roger Neilson, had long doubled as a scout for the Canadiens. The combined word of Caron and Neilson had been enough to convince Pollock of Gainey's worth.

Gainey's public coming-out party would take place a few months later on September 21, 1973, in Moncton, New Brunswick. Before a sold-out crowd of nine thousand fans he made his Canadiens debut in an exhibition game against the Boston Bruins. For Sam Pollock and the assembled media, the game was their first opportunity to see their first-round pick in action. Skating around in the warmup, Gainey couldn't stop himself from gazing at his reflection in the glass that extended above the boards. For the first time he saw himself in the Canadiens uniform. Surrounded by players he'd only ever seen on television, he felt as if he somehow didn't belong.[16] But it wouldn't take long for him to prove to himself and others that he was in the right place. In one of his first shifts, Gainey was knocked off his feet by a hard check, compliments of the sport's biggest superstar, Bobby Orr. The physical force of the check seemed to knock Gainey out of his initial unease and timidity. Now he did what he had always done from the time he first took to a frozen pond in Peterborough. Skating into the Boston end of the rink with speed and purpose, he returned the favour, chasing Orr on an icing call and crunching him into the boards.[17]

As Bobby Orr slowly picked himself off the ice, Red Fisher glanced at Sam Pollock, who stood with a slight smile creaking out from behind his usually stoic demeanour. That fall, Gainey would spend all of six games in Nova Scotia with the Voyageurs before being recalled to the Canadiens. He never looked back.

"Nobody has ever been more right about a player," wrote Red Fisher years later. "Gainey's first thunderous NHL bodycheck was an omen of things to come . . . He made defense and punishing bodychecks fashionable among NHL forwards. He controlled games."[18]

Gainey took a different tack than most forwards: instead of trying to score goals he went on the ice with the intention of preventing them. It soon became apparent that he possessed the rarest of gifts in his ability to go out and shift the momentum of a game without scoring a goal. He would often be dispatched onto the ice by Scotty Bowman when the Canadiens were in disarray, and by the time he finished his shift not only would the situation have been calmed, but quite often it was now tilted in the team's favour. He could assume control over any situation, using his physical attributes, his fleetness of foot, or through his superior positioning. Standing six-foot-two and weighing 200 pounds, Gainey could physically hold his own and more, and his swiftness on his skates allowed him to keep pace with the league's fastest players.

Gainey took a unique analytical approach to the game. He studied the strengths, weaknesses, and habits of all those he played against. Standing behind the bench for the Canadiens, Scotty Bowman could not believe his good fortune. In Gainey, he had the consummate team player, one who was extremely coachable and ultra-competitive. A player unconcerned with his personal statistics, Gainey always seemed to have his finger on the pulse of the game and could dictate the nature of the action on the ice.

Soon the player that nobody knew took his place among the Canadiens' most valuable. "I can't think of anybody on our team who means more to us than Gainey," asserted Serge Savard a few years later. "A few guys like Robinson, Lafleur, and Lapointe mean as much. But they're not more important than Gainey."[19]

Montreal, Quebec, September 21, 1974. As the Boston Bruins sat in the visitors' dressing room at the Montreal Forum, they could barely contain their anger. They had just suffered a 4–0 defeat at the hands of the Montreal Canadiens in a pre-season game. The loss, however, was not the reason for their rage, although it surely didn't help. No – their fury and resentment were directed at one player on the Canadiens. That player had so infuriated the Bruins that he had provoked a bench-clearing brawl in the game's closing moments.

As he watched the melee that ensued, Scotty Bowman, standing behind the Canadiens' bench, had a hard time suppressing his enjoyment, which he shared with the reporters after the game. "I was just saying to Sam Pollock the other day: it's so refreshing to get a guy who's willing to go out and take the first shot at somebody . . . The big thing is that he's earned respect already."[20]

Across the hall, the still-raging Bruins were inclined to disagree with Bowman, but there was no doubt that the new guy had gotten their attention. "He backstabbed somebody the first time he was on the ice," a visibly agitated Wayne Cashman told the assembled reporters after the game. "He got me the same way. He backstabbed four or five of our guys like that. We're not going to take that crap. Who was he? Number eight? A few of us have that number firmly fixed on our minds."[21]

Number eight was Doug Risebrough, and in just his third pre-season game he was already establishing himself as a new force in the NHL. Much like Bob Gainey had done the year before, the rookie Risebrough brought with him a new attitude to the club, one that was infectious. He was not physically imposing, standing five-eleven and weighing 180 pounds, but Risebrough was an outstanding skater, fast, well balanced, and extremely agile. Like Gainey, he was also blessed with an uncanny ability to read the play, which enhanced his already considerable defensive skills. However, he was different from Gainey in other respects. A relentless agitator on the ice, he reminded many of Bobby Clarke, and like him walked the thin line between being aggressive and being dirty. He could also knock opponents off their game, and backed up this ability by playing a physical style that was above his stature.

The Canadiens' choice of Risebrough with their seventh overall selection in the 1974 NHL entry draft raised some eyebrows. Thanks to a severe knee injury suffered in mid-season, he had only played forty-six games of Junior A hockey with the Kitchener Rangers that year. Normally such circumstances would have lowered a prospect's draft value, and many expected that Risebrough would be taken some time in the second round. However, it was Roger Neilson, whose opinion had been so instrumental in the Canadiens' drafting of Gainey the year before, who helped seal Risebrough's professional fate.

"The head coach of the Peterborough Petes, Roger Neilson, told us about him," Scotty Bowman recalled. "He said that Risebrough will get beat up in a fight, then come back the very next game and pick a fight with the guy who beat him."[22]

For a team like the Canadiens, who were on the lookout for a tenacious, dogged player who took his defensive responsibilities seriously and put the team before his own personal achievement, Doug Risebrough was the perfect fit. Despite an impressive training camp in the fall of 1974, he was sent to Halifax, but Henri Richard's sidelining by a broken leg a few games into the season provided an opportunity for the eager Risebrough. He would make his NHL debut on November 14, 1974, at the Boston Garden against the Bruins, the team he had so infuriated in the pre-season a few months before.

Risebrough was not the only Canadien making his debut that night. Lining up on his right side was a player two years his junior, who shared his relentless attitude and rambunctious style. Mario Tremblay was the youngest player to ever don the uniform of the Montreal Canadiens. In an effort to combat the rival WHA, which had begun signing underage players before they even became eligible for the annual draft, the NHL allowed each team to select one underage player in the first two rounds of the 1974 draft. With the twelfth pick, five spots after selecting Doug Risebrough, the Canadiens selected the seventeen-year-old Tremblay.

Besides sharing the same draft year, there were several startling similarities between Risebrough and Tremblay. In a word, Mario Tremblay was fearless. Standing six feet tall and weighing a solid 190 pounds, he never backed down from anyone, and his fiery temper, found at the end of a very short fuse, often ignited his team. Extremely quick on his skates, he fit in nicely with the Canadiens' new dictum of adding forceful, defensive-minded players to the team's third and fourth lines. Playing on the right wing with Risebrough, Tremblay complemented his pesky centre by always thinking shoot first, pass later. He augmented his offensive game with a crisp, hard shot and an uncanny ability to gather in loose pucks and rebounds in the wildest and tightest of scrums. Like Risebrough, Tremblay, who turned eighteen on the eve of the training camp, began the 1974–75 season in Nova Scotia. However, after fifteen games (10 goals, 8 assists) with the Halifax Voyageurs, where he led the team in scoring, he was called up alongside Risebrough, with whom he would make his professional debut on November 14 in Boston.

Arriving at the Boston Garden, Risebrough and Tremblay were in for a surprise. Scotty Bowman, looking to send a message to the hometown Bruins, and to take advantage of the pent-up aggression in his new call-ups, took the unusual step of pencilling Risebrough and Tremblay into the starting lineup, with Yvon Lambert, a sophomore player on the Canadiens, inserted on their left wing. It would turn out to be one of Bowman's most inspired moves.

After the opening faceoff, the puck made its way into the Bruins corner, where an aggressive Risebrough announced his presence, roughing up Bobby Orr in the corner.[23] Such was the impact of the line that Bowman, notorious for switching up the personnel on his lines, kept his new troika of Lambert/Risebrough/Tremblay intact and gave them a regular shift throughout the entire game, which the Canadiens won 4–1. He couldn't have known it at the time but Bowman had stumbled onto a line he'd always dreamed of. In future games, whenever he found the team lagging, Bowman would deploy his new "energy" line to infuse the Canadiens with a much-needed dose of adrenaline and inspire momentum-changing consequences. Brought up as temporary replacements, the performance of Risebrough and Tremblay made it impossible for the Canadiens to send them back down, and they quickly became entrenched on the Montreal roster.

Such was the success of the Canadiens' new energy line that the trio of Lambert, Risebrough, and Tremblay would be kept intact through-out the remainder of the 1974–75 season and beyond. As further proof of their aggressive nature, Risebrough and Tremblay would finish the season first and second on the team in penalty minutes. The impact of the fourth line on the Canadiens was immense. Their combined aggression and tenacity helped to change the tempo of the game, setting the pace while forcing the opposition to abandon their own game plan to combat their never-ending pressure. The line also contributed to the scoresheet, in particular Yvon Lambert, who finished fourth on the team that season with 32 goals, ahead of such notable sharpshooters as Yvan Cournoyer and Steve Shutt.

In many ways, Yvon Lambert was the unlikeliest player on the Montreal Canadiens roster. The oldest of eight children, Lambert had been raised on a farm in the parish municipality of Saint-Germain, Quebec. With his father working in town, the young Lambert was inundated with responsibilities on the farm, leaving him precious little time for hockey, with the rare exception of sometimes watching *Hockey Night in Canada* on television. At the age of thirteen, he received his first pair of skates as a gift under the Christmas tree, and two years later he played in his first game of organized hockey, which led to a spot in the local Drummondville Industrial League. When he was nineteen, Lambert played one season with his hometown Drummondville Rangers in the Quebec Junior League, scoring 50 goals and adding 51 assists for 101 points in only 52 games.

The Detroit Red Wings were impressed enough to draft the raw, un-polished Lambert with the fortieth selection of the 1970 NHL entry draft. Spending the 1970–71 season in the International Hockey League with the Port Huron Flags (23 goals, 41 points), the tall and lanky Lambert appeared to have a bright future awaiting him with the Red Wings. His eight goals in fourteen playoff games that spring only seemed to solidify his future as he helped Port Huron capture the Turner Cup as the champions of the IHL.

But for some reason, a few months later the Red Wings inexplicably left Lambert unprotected and the astute Sam Pollock pounced, claiming him for the Canadiens in the NHL Reverse Draft, held on June 9, 1971. Like many of his fellow rookies, Lambert spent the entire 1971–72 season in the AHL with the Nova Scotia Voyageurs, where alongside future teammates Murray Wilson and Larry Robinson he helped the team win the Calder Cup. In the fall of 1972, Lambert established himself as the organization's top prospect. The last player cut from the Canadiens' training camp that fall, he returned to the AHL and led the entire league with 52 goals and 104 points. Thanks to his performance and aided by the sudden departures of Marc Tardif and Réjean Houle to the AHL, there was little doubt that Lambert would stay with the Canadiens in 1973–74. But he struggled in his rookie season, admittedly losing his confidence, and appeared in a limited role, finishing with only 16 points that season.

That fall, at the training camp in which Risebrough and Tremblay made their first impressions, Lambert was a man revitalized. For the first time in his hockey career he had spent the summer skating and training, and as a result he arrived at the camp much better prepared than he had been the year before. Soon his confidence returned, as he spent less energy worrying about making a mistake. Thanks to his combination of size and scoring touch, he began seeing time on the power play where he would park himself in front of the opposing goal.[24] At the onset of the 1974–75 season, Lambert blossomed, and when he was united on November 14 with Risebrough and Tremblay he was tied with Guy Lafleur for the team lead in goals.[25] Teaming with his two new linemates didn't halt Lambert's production and he continued to match Lafleur in the goal-scoring department. In fact, the line of Lambert, Risebrough, and Tremblay began receiving, alongside an emerging Lafleur, a boatload of credit for the Canadiens' turnaround, which led to the team's first-overall finish at the season's conclusion.

"Scrappy as bearcats, the Risebrough line is compensating in large part for their lack of experience and refinement with an aggressiveness the team hasn't had since John Ferguson hung up his skates," wrote Tim Burke in the pages of the Montreal *Gazette*.

"Their style has been contagious," added Scotty Bowman. "They've built a fire under the whole team. These young guys have desire and desire is the number one priority today. Everyone wants players who work, because it has been demonstrated that work can beat superior talent.[26] I honestly can't say that I expected that much from either Risebrough or Tremblay, but that line has been the sparkplug of the club. They all play a good aggressive game and give the rest of the team a lift . . . These kids never accept defeat."[27]

Referred to as the "Kid Line" by Bowman and the media, the surprising trio suddenly gave the Canadiens a line similar to the ones employed so successfully by the Philadelphia Flyers. The presence of Roberts, the addition of Gainey, and the unexpected ascendancy of the "Kid Line" helped transform the Canadiens from a team that had relied almost solely on offence to a more balanced squad with a renewed focus on the defensive side of the game.

Winnipeg, Manitoba, Summer 1975. In the immediate aftermath of the Canadiens' surprising elimination at the hands of the Buffalo Sabres in the spring of 1975, Scotty Bowman spent a restless summer lamenting and analyzing what his team could be missing. On a team that had finished the year before with 118 points (47 wins, 14 losses, and 9 ties) there didn't appear to be much room for improvement. But the ever-astute Bowman could detect one flaw. He was convinced that the main factor in the Canadiens' loss was the effectiveness of Buffalo's checking line of Don Luce, Danny Gare, and Craig Ramsay in shutting down the potent Montreal offence. Bowman desperately wanted a line like that of his own.[28] With Bob Gainey entrenched on the left wing and Jim Roberts on the right wing, Bowman wanted to find a centre of similar style and temperament. In addition, he was looking for a centre who was not only defensively responsible but one who excelled in the faceoff circle.

It was on his mind when he went to Winnipeg that summer to attend a coaching clinic put on by his old friend Roger Neilson. Bowman had first met Neilson over a decade before in 1962. At that time Bowman was the Montreal Canadiens head scout for Eastern Canada and he was looking to hire a scout to be the Canadiens' eyes for the midget-age (boys sixteen and seventeen years of age) Toronto Hockey League. In the days before the 1967 expansion and the entry draft, NHL teams would scour the midget leagues looking for players to sign to an affiliated junior-team contract (most notoriously through the document known as the C-Form). Once the player joined your junior-sponsored team, you not only held his amateur rights, you also controlled his professional rights.

A few years after his hiring, Neilson proved his worth to the Canadiens by convincing them to acquire from the Bruins a goaltender from the Etobicoke Indians named Ken Dryden. In the fall of 1966, the

Peterborough Petes, a Canadiens-sponsored Junior A team, had a vacancy at the head coaching position, and Pollock gave the job to Neilson. A year later, the expansion of 1967 put an end to the direct relationship between the Canadiens and the Petes, and by association between Neilson and the team. However, the relationship continued on an informal basis. Neilson would be instrumental in the selection of Bob Gainey by the Canadiens in the first round of the 1973 entry draft, as well as in the selection of Doug Risebrough a year later.[29]

"Roger Nielson was coaching in Peterborough at the time and in the summer I would go to his coaching clinics," says Bowman today. "I was at a clinic in Winnipeg that summer [1975] and we were talking about face-offs and he mentioned to me that he had one of the best face-off men in hockey. And I thought he had meant in junior hockey, and Roger said, 'No, no, I'll stack Doug Jarvis up against anyone in hockey. Keep in mind that over the past two years in the playoffs Bobby Clarke had just dominated everybody on face-offs.'"[30]

A skeptical Bowman asked Neilson to compare Jarvis with Craig Ramsay. Before starring for the Sabres, Ramsay had spent four seasons playing under Neilson in Peterborough before becoming a thorn in the Canadiens' side. Neilson confided to Bowman that Jarvis was more valuable to the Petes than Ramsay had been.[31] In Bowman's eyes there was no higher endorsement. With such an unabashed recommendation, Bowman's doubts swiftly vanished and that night he placed a call to Sam Pollock. Here was the answer to Bowman's dilemma. The only problem was that Doug Jarvis had just been drafted by the Toronto Maple Leafs a few months before.

In that same draft the Canadiens had passed on Jarvis three times. The general feeling among the Montreal scouts had been that Jarvis at five-nine and 170 pounds was too small for the daily rigours of the NHL. But Scotty Bowman was nothing if not persistent, and his constant pestering eventually broke down Sam Pollock's resistance. "We were fortunate in that we had an extra goalie in Wayne Thomas and Toronto was looking for a goalie and we were reluctant to trade him just for a draft pick,"[32] Bowman recalls today. As a result of Neilson's commendation, Pollock structured a deal with the Leafs in two parts. The first part of the deal involved shipping out Thomas to Toronto in exchange for a first-round pick in the 1976 entry draft.

In the meantime, the Canadiens had learned through Neilson that Jarvis was refusing to play for the Maple Leafs. Jarvis had also been drafted by the Houston Aeros of the WHA, and he was poised to go to Houston rather than start in the AHL within the Leafs system. The Maple Leafs were also very interested in Greg Hubick, a defenceman with the Nova Scotia Voyageurs who didn't figure in the Canadiens' future plans. Thanks to the Peterborough influence of Neilson, who had been Jarvis's former coach, and of Gainey, a former teammate, the Canadiens knew they would be able to sign Jarvis.[33] In exchange for Hubick, the Maple Leafs presented Montreal with a list of five players who were available in return. The list included the name of Doug Jarvis.

"Toronto didn't think they could sign him so we jumped in and made the deal," remembers Bowman. "We got Jarvis signed to play in our system and we went to training camp and he was ticketed to go to Halifax, but we had some injuries during the training camp so he saw some action in some pre-season games and he looked really good."

In a pre-season game against the Black Hawks, it was Jarvis's work against veteran Stan Mikita that convinced Bowman the former Peterborough Pete was ready to be a Montreal Canadien. Mikita, a former two-time league MVP, future Hall-of-Famer, and faceoff specialist, ended the evening on the short end of the draws against the young Jarvis, losing almost every faceoff.

"We got to the start of the season and I remembered sitting in Sam Pollock's office and he had Jarvis ticketed to go down to the minors and I said, 'We're going to have to start the season with him, because Jacques Lemaire was injured.' Sam wasn't really sure, but I really persisted, and faced with the Lemaire injury he had no choice, so he relented. Jarvis got involved in starting the season with us and he never went back to the minors. He was just so good on the face-offs. He upgraded our face-offs immensely and of course, our penalty killing. A large degree in the success of your penalty killing is in who wins the face-off and Jarvis was one of the best I've ever had on face-offs."[34]

Doug Jarvis was the final piece to the puzzle for the Canadiens. Bowman had wanted Montreal to become a team that controlled the game through puck possession. As promised by Neilson, Jarvis's faceoff skills were among the best in the league. As a result, with the Canadiens winning an inordinate amount of faceoffs in their own end, they could frequently control the puck. With Jarvis positioned at centre between two fellow Petes alumni, Bob Gainey and Jim Roberts, the team now possessed one of the best, if not the best, checking lines in the sport. Not only did they shut down the top lines on the opposing teams but they also stifled their opponent's power plays by keeping them off their game, besides providing the odd goal. Any notions that the Canadiens were defensively deficient were now put to rest: Pollock and Bowman had achieved the seemingly impossible in constructing one of the finest defensive teams in the league without sacrificing any of the offence that had made the team the most renowned in the hockey world.

Sam Pollock's overhaul of the Montreal Canadiens was now complete. He had constructed a team unlike any other in the NHL, a team so versatile that it had no visible weakness. The Canadiens that opened the 1975–76 season were primed for another run at the Stanley Cup. Pollock had shrewdly assembled a team that excelled in each and every aspect of the game and could adapt to any style of play. The upcoming season would be the proving ground. The Stanley Cup remained the ultimate goal and that trophy still resided in Philadelphia. But before they could get to that contest a different challenge awaited the hungry Canadiens.

PART THREE

THE GAME

"As far as I am concerned, this is what the game of hockey is all about; fast, full of combinations, rough (but not rude), with an exciting plot. I would love to play it over again."

VLADISLAV TRETIAK, *Tretiak: The Legend,* 1987

16.

THE PREAMBLE

Moscow, Russia, Fall 1975. The zone.

In the career of any great athlete there are moments where the athlete is able to elevate his performance to an even higher level. Negative thoughts are banished as the player's self-esteem and confidence swell. Suddenly he is able to sharpen his focus exclusively on the task at hand, allowing him to exercise an almost effortless power and control over his surroundings. Athletes refers to this advanced state as "being in the zone."

In 1975 Vladislav Tretiak was in the zone. That spring he would be named the best player in the Soviet Union for a second consecutive year. The following spring he made it three straight. In recognition of his achievements the Soviet government awarded him the prestigious Order of the Badge of Honour. A virtual unknown only three years before, the twenty-three-year-old Tretiak was now one of the most recognizable Russian citizens not only in his native country, but throughout the Western world.

In the days leading up to the departure of his Red Army team for the Super Series, Tretiak recognized that, in addition to his stature, his performance was taking on a higher level. He had never felt more confident or more comfortable in the net.

"Just before our departure for Canada, I finally reached my peak form," Tretiak later wrote. "Until then I'd had a few problems with my game, but now everything fell into place. The puck 'listened to me,' as if it was trained. I felt great . . . At the end of 1975, I constantly experienced something which could probably be described as 'hockey inspiration.' How perfect that it happened precisely in December."[1]

In addition to playing in the upcoming Super Series, the Russian National Team competed in the annual Izvestia Cup. Led by Valeri Kharlamov's tournament best-seven goals as well as Tretiak's enhanced play, the Soviets captured their fifth consecutive gold medal with victories over Finland, Sweden, and Czechoslovakia. Primed and ready, Tretiak, Kharlamov, and their teammates on the Red Army headed off on the long plane ride to Montreal three days after the successful conclusion of the Izvestia Cup.

Montreal, Quebec, December 24, 1975. The plane carrying the Soviet contingent arrived in Montreal at 6:10 p.m. on Christmas Eve. Stepping out onto the tarmac, the visiting Russians discovered a city still trying to dig out from a large snowfall that had blanketed Montreal a few days before. After being cooped up inside the plane for over ten hours, the members of the Red Army and the Soviet Wings felt the combined effects of jet lag and the bitter cold of the Montreal night as they jumped onto the bus waiting for them and made their way to their accommodations at the Queen Elizabeth Hotel.

Their hosts, the National Hockey League, had scheduled for the touring Russian teams a sightseeing tour of the Laurentian Mountains for Christmas Day. They had assumed that after the flight, and with all of the adjustments that travel entailed, that the two teams would probably enjoy a more relaxed schedule. Instead, and to the complete and utter astonishment of their hosts, the Russians declined the generous offer. Immediately, the management of the hotel was notified that their Russian guests might make some noise in the early hours of the morning. The reason for the commotion was that the Soviet players, upon awakening, were required to perform a series of pushups and then run in place in their rooms.[1] The team's management also decided to engage their players in a strenuous three-hour practice at a Concordia University rink on Christmas morning. They would follow that up with a four-hour practice at the Montreal Forum on Boxing Day, and a three-hour practice on the morning of the 27, before leaving that afternoon for their first game of the series, to take place the following night in New York.[3] Needless to say, the demanding practice schedule signalled to their NHL opposition that the touring Soviets were taking this series very seriously.

Much had changed since their last visit to Montreal. The touring Soviets in 1972 were regarded by both the Canadian media and the public as a mere curiosity. Now, three years later, they were still the object of media scrutiny, but thanks to the results of both the 1972 and 1974 Summit Series they were now considered a serious threat to the treasured ideal of Canadian hockey dominance.

"There's two things that didn't have to do with the New Year's Eve game that made the expectation for the game so high," Bob Gainey acknowledges today, "and that was trying to recreate the feeling between east and west that was very vivid and alive in the mid seventies, the capitalist and communist viewpoints that these two sides represented, difference between philosophies, beliefs, and lifestyles. Secondly, we were in the middle of an attack on our beliefs that as Canadians in ice hockey we were world dominant."[4]

In stark contrast to the nonchalance three years earlier toward the Soviets' methods, each Red Army practice was studied intently by both the media and the members of the Montreal Canadiens. Tretiak couldn't help but notice the distinct change himself. The newspapers that had dismissed them before were now extolling their virtues, some even going as far to predict a Soviet victory in the upcoming series, and complete strangers were approaching the visitors on the street to shake their hands. "Nothing similar had happened in the previous series," Tretiak recalled later. "Again, I could not help remembering September of 1972. So much arrogance, haughtiness, and disregard had been shown to us by the players and the officials of the NHL. Where did it go?"[5]

In 1972, the Russians had been the undisputed underdogs. Now, three years later, in the opening game of the Super Series, they were the overwhelming favourites. The Red Army's first opponent in the Super Series, the New York Rangers, failed to generate much enthusiasm or inspire much confidence among those who championed the NHL cause. "I think it should be said unequivocally that the New York Rangers are not the worst team in hockey; they're just pretending," wrote an indifferent Michael Posner in *Maclean's* magazine, summing up the general expectation for the game. "By dint of some demonic fortune, however, these same Rangers are about to make sporting history. On December 28, they will become the first regular NHL team to play a regular Russian team . . . They will, therefore, also become the first NHL team to lose to the Russians."[6]

Only a few months into the 1975–76 NHL season the New York Rangers had gone from being one of the elite teams in the National Hockey League to a bottom feeder. However, the Red Army players would once again confront the familiar face of Phil Esposito, this time in an unfamiliar uniform. Having joined the team only six weeks before, Esposito was still adjusting to his new life as a New York Ranger. He had been involved in one of the biggest trades in hockey history, a swap in which Brad Park and Jean Ratelle, two of his fellow teammates on Team Canada '72, went the other way and joined the Boston Bruins. Relishing the chance to once again play against the Soviets, Esposito attempted to inspire his new teammates in the leadup to the game. "We're under the gun. The rest of the league will be watching what we do against the Russians. We'll set the tone for the whole series. They'll want to beat us very badly, and we'll want to beat them. It's going to be a helluva game."[7]

Esposito's words were initially prophetic. Twenty-one seconds into the game, he gathered in the loose puck from in front of the Soviet net and dished it to a waiting Steve Vickers, who gently tapped it into the open net behind Tretiak. The New York crowd roared, and a sudden surge of optimism filled the building.

The feeling would be short-lived.

Thanks to a combination of ill-advised Ranger penalties and a lethally efficient Red Army power play, the visiting Red Army slowly sucked all of the enthusiasm out of a raucous Madison Square Garden by seemingly switching to another, faster gear. With frightening efficiency they proceeded to tally seven straight goals against an increasingly helpless, overmatched, and exhausted Rangers team.

With the game now out of reach, New York fans vented their frustrations and threw debris onto the ice, which halted play as the arena's attendants scurried to clean up the mess.

"A rotten egg hit the ice right beside me and the game was stopped," Tretiak later recalled. "I looked up at the stands and saw a policeman holding one of the fans. The police officer began to hit him on the pockets, which were stuffed to capacity. At the end of the game, someone threw a paper cup on the ice. I turned around and pointed toward the scoreboard. I thought: Look at the score, you hoodlum!"[8]

As was now becoming his custom in televised, high-profile games against Canadian professionals, Valeri Kharlamov once again scored a highlight-reel goal, this time in the closing seconds of the first period. With the score 3–1 and the Red Army on the power play, Kharlamov slowly made his way to the Rangers' end of the rink, where he was confronted by all four New York penalty killers stretched across the blue line, forming a protective wall. Approaching Carol Vadnais, Kharlamov suddenly sped up and, thanks to some nifty stickhandling, left the Rangers' best defenceman gasping for air as he made his way around him. Vadnais's defensive partner, Doug Jarrett, was caught flat-footed and, realizing that Kharlamov had split their wall, desperately stuck the blade of his stick around the onrushing Kharlamov's waist in a vain attempt to slow him down. Forward Walt Tkachuk also managed to swing his stick against Kharlamov, but like his two teammates he couldn't stop him. Face to face with John Davidson, the Rangers' goalie, Kharlamov quickly moved the puck to his backhand, then immediately reversed it back to his forehand, and shot it behind the sprawling goaltender.

"We were standing at the blue line," Vadnais explained to the reporters after the game. "We were told to stay up on their power play . . . so we're standing and waiting and then this little guy [Kharlamov] is coming at us and we're still looking at each other after he's through and the puck is in the net."[9]

"I couldn't even hook Kharlamov," echoed an exasperated Jarrett. "I thought he was going to the other side. Even if you get him it takes as much out of you as it does out of him."[10]

Kharlamov's goal was merely one example of the Soviets' supremacy against the overmatched Rangers. Kharlamov and his centre, Vladimir Petrov, would each end the game with four points, while their linemate Boris Mikhailov would chip in three. Two late goals by the outclassed Rangers, after the Red Army had noticeably lifted their collective foot off the pedal resulted only in making the final score of 7–3 appear much closer than the play on the ice had really been.

"What the Russians played was a brand of hockey rarely seen in the NHL these days – lightning thrusts to the enemy zone and players passing all the time when on the fly, not whacking the puck off the board or wasting passes around the net," echoed the *Toronto Star*. "Obviously the Soviets came prepared to play a superior brand of hockey. They didn't find it in New York."[11]

Those who had seen the game were left mesmerized by the Russian display. "They may be better than that team we played in '72," claimed a resigned Harry Sinden, then Team Canada's coach and the third man in the broadcast booth that night. "It's hard to believe, but I think they are."[12]

The Rangers had been ill-prepared for and confused by the Red Army's offensive attack and its dizzying arsenal of moves. Pete Stemkowski said it was as if the Soviet players were on a merry-go-round.[13] "It seemed that our opponents didn't have enough time to understand what was happening on the ice," Tretiak said later, a conclusion shared by the Rangers and those who had watched the game. "Even their goaltender appeared to be in a state of confusion, and could not help his team."[14]

After the game, despite the result, and notwithstanding the one-sidedness of the game, Esposito took all the media's questions, the sweat still dripping from his dejected brow, even as many of his teammates went off to shower and then leave the Rangers dressing room. His pride wounded, an openly embarrassed Esposito admitted that he would love another opportunity to play the Russians, trying to convince himself that he and his teammates could do better. He vowed that if the touring Soviets won every one of the remaining games of the Series, he would personally eat the Russian uniforms in front of the Montreal Forum.[15] To back up his boast, Esposito pointed out the one flaw he noticed in the Soviets' apparently indomitable game.

"There's one lesson the other teams should have learned," he said. "If you really start pushing them and forechecking them, they'll throw the puck away in their own zone."[16]

He needn't have worried. Watching the game on television from the comfort of his home in Montreal, Scotty Bowman had noticed the very same thing. And in the coming days he would find a way to exploit it.

Washington, D.C., December 29, 1975. The morning after conquering the Rangers, a victorious Red Army squad embarked on their return trip to Montreal. When they landed, they were whisked away not to their hotel but instead to the Forum for another rigorous practice. Not content to rest on their laurels, the Red Army prepared for the next opponent with a renewed vigour. There were now only three days before the Red Army would face the Montreal Canadiens, and the anticipation for the New Year's Eve game was reaching epic proportions. In fact, the hype for the clash on New Year's Eve had begun building long before the Russians even arrived in Montreal.

"If you're planning a New Year's party and you don't want to be left sitting alone until 11 p.m. waiting for your first guests to arrive, I'd advise you to take the following precautions," opined John Robertson in the December 5 edition of the Montreal *Gazette,* a full twenty-six days before the game.

1. Rent or borrow an extra colour TV set, and put one in every room if necessary.
2. Make sure you say on the invitation that the guests should arrive between 7 and 8 p.m.
3. Spell out clearly to them that they will have easy access to a TV set so they can watch, from start to finish, perhaps the most meaningful hockey game Les Canadiens have ever played.

Canadiens vs. Soviet Army . . . an exhibition game which in reality is the Super Bowl, the Grey Cup, the World Series and the Stanley Cup, all wrapped into one.[17]

For the first time ever, the two most successful club teams in the sport would clash. On one side stood the Red Army: winners of nineteen championships in the twenty-nine-year history of the Soviet Elite League. On the other side stood the Montreal Canadiens: winners of an unequalled eighteen Stanley Cups in the fifty-eight-year history of the National Hockey League.

Thoughts of the game against the Red Army had long percolated in the minds of the Montreal players. "I think we were anticipating that game right when it was announced that we would play them," says Jim Roberts today. "There hadn't been an individual team that ever played a Russian team before. We were really looking forward to that game. The excitement around the team was right from the moment it was announced."[18]

The prospect of playing the Red Army thrilled the Canadiens and they eagerly awaited the unique challenge that the Russians provided. And though the team focused itself on the main task at hand, the NHL schedule and the Stanley Cup, thoughts of the Red Army were never far away.

The 1975–76 Canadiens had gone out and sprinted to the top spot in the NHL standings, accumulating a record of 25 wins, 5 losses, and 6 ties. Following their coach's advice, the Canadiens showcased a renewed commitment to defensive hockey, without sacrificing any of their offensive skill, and it was paying dividends. As a result, after a few months the Canadiens were among the league leaders in goals scored. However, it was in the goals-against category that Montreal was holding a commanding lead over the rest of the league. With the hype cresting, and the Russians lying in wait in Montreal, the Canadiens took to the ice in Washington, D.C., on the evening of December 29. In only their second season of existence, the Washington Capitals were undoubtedly the worst team in the entire league, and maybe of all time. Having won only three of their first thirty-five games, the Capitals appeared to be at a serious disadvantage to the powerful Canadiens.

The end result, a 6–0 whitewash of the Capitals, was hardly surprising and served as nothing more than a glorified warmup for the Canadiens. With their glittering record and first-place position in the standings, the Canadiens refocused on a new challenge. The Soviets were just as keen to meet their challenge.

"We knew that the most important and most difficult games were yet to come," Tretiak later wrote. "Our next opponents were the Montreal Canadiens, the most famous club in the NHL. They were the trend-setters, the star-makers. The Canadiens have won 18 Stanley Cups and their roster of players includes many of the greatest names in hockey.[19] "Without exaggeration, I think that the whole of Canada was looking forward to this game. The excitement had reached unbelievable proportions. Everyone thought that the Montreal Canadiens would put up a good fight against the Russian hockey players."[20]

Having fulfilled the games on their NHL schedule, the players were now free to focus their energies on their next opponent, the Red Army. On the one-hour flight back to Montreal, the players were quiet and reserved, as the enormity of what lay ahead filled their thoughts.

The young players on the team, like Risebrough and Tremblay, sought out their older teammates, like Dryden, Savard, and Mahovlich, those who had previously played against the Soviets.

"I remember talking a lot to the five guys," Risebrough later recalled, "because they dealt with that emotion in '72 and certainly gave us some insights as to what to expect and the thing that they kind of left us with was, you gotta go out there and play hard, it's going to be a fun time. As much as there was a buildup of nerves, you knew you were going to get a chance to release it when the game was on."[21]

Don Awrey was another veteran from Team Canada '72. However, unlike many of his teammates who had relished the experience, Awrey for the last three years had been haunted by his performance in the Summit Series, in particular surrounding the two goals scored by Valeri Kharlamov in the opening game. Prior to the series, Awrey had enjoyed a solid professional career as a steady, defensive rearguard who sacrificed his personal achievements in favour of team goals. A member of both the 1970 and the 1972 Stanley Cup–winning Boston Bruins, Awrey found himself toiling in the large shadows cast by Bobby Orr and Phil Esposito, his flashier and more famous teammates. Rewarded by Harry Sinden with a spot on Team Canada in the 1972 Summit Series, Awrey only saw action in two of the eight games. Previously overlooked by the public, he quickly became known as one of the defenceman who had been completely overwhelmed by Valeri Kharlamov in the series' first game.

"Everybody talks about that one particular goal," Awrey recalled with some regret in the days before the game. "I can't remember the guy's [Kharlamov's] move but I guess he did a job on me. I don't really know what it looked like. I've still never seen a replay of it. Now, I'm starting to look forward to the game as it's getting closer," he confessed. "I've been thinking more and more lately about what I would do."[22]

Arriving back in Montreal around midnight, the Canadiens were soon confronted with the latest daunting reality. The Soviet Wings had beaten the Pittsburgh Penguins the night before, and the expectations for the Canadiens' performance had intensified. With the NHL having lost the first two games of the eight-game Super Series, the pressure on the team to salvage the pride of the NHL was enormous.

"The reputation of Canada hockey would ride on this contest," Tretiak later wrote. "Not only the stadium, but the entire city, the entire country, was filled with electricity that night. The desire to win and witness that victory had overtaken Montreal."[23]

"In the days before the game we got a sense that we were representing Canada, in addition to the Montreal Canadiens, and how big it was," Murray Wilson confesses today. "I never had the chance in my career to play for Team Canada, but that night was my night to represent Canada, it was so much bigger than the city of Montreal or the province of Quebec."[24]

"The idea that you were playing for the pride of your country, and how we measure ourselves according to how we feel about our ice hockey, I think both of those things created an atmosphere leading into the game that gave it the chance to be a memorable signpost in a lot of peoples' lives," Bob Gainey says today.[25]

"On New Year's Eve in Canada, the nation will come to a virtual standstill between 7 p.m. and 10 p.m.," observed *Time* magazine. "The reason: a hockey game between the Montreal Canadiens and the Central Army Sports Club from the Soviet Union."[26]

—

Montreal, Quebec, December 30, 1975. On Tuesday, the day before New Year's Eve, both the Red Army and the Canadiens took to the ice at the Montreal Forum for their final practices before the next evening's game.

The Canadiens were first out in the morning. The reporters who normally covered the team on a daily basis couldn't help but notice that the team's practices since the Red Army's arrival a week ago had been more rigorous than usual. Skating hard, the players executed a variety of complex passing patterns and concluded with a hotly contested scrimmage. Peter Mahovlich summed up the team's predicament. "We have not much to gain, but a helluva lot to lose. This game means everything to the NHL and the Canadiens."[27]

The intense practices, the careful preparation, the notes and the attention the Canadiens paid to the Red Army's workouts – all were a far cry from Team Canada's approach three years before. In 1972, it had been the Russians who had studied Team Canada, taking notes, observing patterns, and planning strategy. Now the Canadiens, led by Scotty Bowman, were doing the same. Surprisingly, they weren't the only ones who had changed their approach. The Red Army team that entered the Forum that day barely took any notice of the Canadiens' practice and instead confidently made their way to their dressing room.[28]

Another reversal this time around was that the Canadiens, in some quarters, were the underdogs now. And while this opinion wasn't widespread, it didn't stop some members of the team from using the perceived slight as another source of motivation. "It's going to help us to feel that we're the underdogs," Guy Lapointe volunteered to the press. "According to what we hear on TV and radio and read in the papers, everybody thinks we're going to lose. Well, I've got a feeling that we're going to be very well prepared for this game and I can't think of anything that would motivate us more than being underdogs."[29]

Milt Dunnell in the *Toronto Star* took it a step further, openly stating that a Canadiens loss to the Red Army might be in the best interests of hockey's future. "That might be about what's required to convince North American shinny people their gravy trails have hit a blind switch. It might bring home the horrible truth to the elders of the NHL lodge that they no longer are retailing the best brand of their product in the world."[30]

In an era when NHL hockey was widely criticized for its descent into violence, many were starting to look to the Russians to show the way forward.

One thing that hadn't changed in the three years since the Summit Series was the media's difficulty in gaining comments from, much less an interview with, any of the Red Army players. "They wouldn't allow you into their dressing room," remembers Red Fisher. "There still was somewhat of a bit of an iron curtain between the Russians and us."[31] For media clamouring to speak to players like Tretiak and Kharlamov, it was a frustrating state of affairs.

That Tuesday, at the end of their practice, the Canadiens held an afternoon team meeting before they were treated to a private screening of the Rangers/Red Army game from two nights before. Scotty Bowman, meanwhile, took a seat in the spacious Montreal Forum and watched the Soviets practise for two hours.

For as long as he could remember, Scotty Bowman had lived in the shadow of the Montreal Forum and its primary tenant, the Montreal Canadiens. He had grown up during the Great Depression, living just west of the arena in a working-class neighbourhood known as the Avenues. As a young man Bowman had been able to make use of his athletic abilities to get all the way up to a spot on the left wing with the Montreal Junior Canadiens, playing in parts of two seasons (1951–52 and 1952–53) under head coach Sam Pollock. When his playing days ended in the spring of 1954, the twenty-one-year-old Bowman enrolled in a business program at Sir George Williams College. He then found work in the stockroom at a Sherwin-Williams paint plant located on Atwater Avenue. By chance, the plant was located only a few blocks south of the Forum.[32] Quite often, during his lunch break, he would make the trek to the Forum to watch the Canadiens practise. Watching his idol, Toe Blake, run through drills with players named Richard, Béliveau, Geoffrion, and Plante helped plant the coaching seed. Often, as he sat there alone in the arena, he would make mental notes of what he was watching, incorporating much of it into his future coaching repertoire. It was a practice he would keep up for the next decade. He had stayed in touch with Sam Pollock, who couldn't help but notice Bowman's enthusiasm, and in the mid-fifties Pollock gave him a job within the Canadiens organization. Bowman would spend the next ten years working his way through the Montreal system as both a coach and a scout with great success.

With expansion on the horizon, Bowman left the Canadiens in the spring of 1967 and joined the newly formed St. Louis Blues. "Montreal was a very strong team at the time," Bowman commented later. "Toe

Blake was coaching. I got a chance to go to the NHL when they expanded. It's hard to turn down a chance to get into the NHL. I was coaching the Junior Canadiens who had moved back to Montreal. I got the opportunity to go to St. Louis from Lynn Patrick. He was going to be the general manager, and I coached his son Craig in junior hockey in Montreal. When he got the job with the Blues, he hired me as his assistant. I decided I really should take a chance. I was fortunate the league expanded and I got an opportunity to get to one of the expansion franchises."[33]

Bowman would be entrusted with the Blues head coaching job on November 22, 1967, in the wake of Patrick's abdication. The following year he would add the role of general manager to his portfolio. Armed with a collection of veterans, castoffs, grinders, and former underachievers, Bowman was able to lead the Blues to the Stanley Cup Finals in each of his first three years with the team. However, at the conclusion of his fourth season, the Blues' owners unceremoniously dumped him. It was his old friend in Montreal, Sam Pollock, who ensured that Bowman would not be out of work for long, naming him as the Canadiens' head coach on June 10, 1971.

Bowman inherited a team that had just won the Stanley Cup, but it was also a team in transition. In his second year as coach, the Canadiens won the Stanley Cup (his first) and he was widely praised for it. But his failure to repeat the feat in 1974 and 1975 led some to question his fitness as the team's head coach. However, as the game with the Red Army approached, the whispers about Bowman's coaching had been silenced with the Canadiens securely perched in first place.

As head coach in Montreal, Bowman had one objective – winning – which stood him in good stead with his players, many of whom regarded him as a mystery. On a team full of superstars Bowman positioned himself as the common enemy, never allowing the team to become complacent or satisfied with itself.

"Scotty was a guy who knew that what the players wanted more than anything was to win," Ken Dryden reflected later. "They wanted easy practices, a smiling coach, an arm around the shoulder but they could live without those things, but they couldn't live without winning and the players sensed that the decisions he made, the actions he took, would give us a better chance of winning."[34]

By maintaining an emotional distance from his players, Bowman was able to base his decisions on their merit rather than on personal bias.

With Guy Lafleur and Bob Gainey hovering, Vladislav Tretiak turns aside another Canadiens scoring attempt. Scotty Bowman later admitted that Tretiak, on December 31, 1975, "had played as good a game in goal as I can remember."

Canadian Press

The Canadiens' "energy" line of forwards Yvon Lambert, Mario Tremblay, and Doug Risebrough was a constant headache for the Red Army defence. Their perpetual pressure resulted in Montreal's second goal.

Canadian Press

A veteran of the 1972 Summit Series, captain Yvan Cournoyer was one of the Canadiens' best players. In addition to scoring Montreal's third goal, he constantly found himself in and around the Red Army net on December 31, 1975.

Canadian Press

At the conclusion of the game, Alan Eagleson, the head of the NHL Players' Association, attempts to console Peter Mahovlich and Yvan Cournoyer at the Canadiens' bench. Future Canadian prime minister Brian Mulroney is sitting over Eagleson's right shoulder.

The announcement of Vladislav Tretiak as the game's first star is applauded by Peter Mahovlich, soon to be recognized as the second star.

Canadian Press

Vladislav Tretiak, the evening's first star, stands alone at centre ice at the Montreal Forum, basking in the glow of a standing ovation.

The three stars of the
December 31, 1975 game
between the Montreal
Canadiens and the Central
Red Army (left to right): Peter
Mahovlich, Vladislav Tretiak,
and Yvan Cournoyer.

The two teams gather at centre ice for the traditional post-game handshake.

Canadian Press

The 1976 Stanley Cup Final between the Montreal Canadiens and the Philadelphia Flyers was one of the most anticipated in hockey history. Here, Larry Robinson and Bobby Clarke battle for position in front of Ken Dryden.

The Canadiens celebrate their Stanley Cup victory over the Flyers on the ice in Philadelphia (left to right): Yvon Lambert, Yvan Cournoyer, Serge Savard, Doug Risebrough, and Doug Jarvis.

Canadian Press

Old rivals Vladislav Tretiak and Ken Dryden celebrate the retirement of Dryden's jersey by the Canadiens at the Bell Centre on January 29, 2007.

Among his many talents was his uncanny ability to get his best players to produce at their highest peak on a nightly basis, regardless of the level of their opposition. He also treated his players as individuals, masterfully placing them in the specific situations in which they could respond and succeed using their particular skills and talents. His focus was entirely on the team and its victories. Individual success, media pressure, and fan expectations were of no concern to him.

Notoriously secretive about his methods, Bowman took a different approach from his fellow NHL head coaches. Instead of working according to a plan, he often chose to improvise as the game developed. "You have to have a feel for the game," he later said. "When you feel things aren't working, you have to make changes – use a fourth line. Change the make-up of our lines. Play some guys more than you have been. Sit a guy out for a shift or two."[35]

Bowman, in many people's opinion the best bench coach in the history of the sport, thoroughly enjoyed the sixty-minute game-within-the-game against his fellow opposition coach. The characteristics that really set him apart from the competition were his almost photographic memory and his thorough preparation.

"Nobody can match lines or anticipate what's going to happen next like Scotty Bowman," says NHL commentator and former player John Garrett. "Scotty can anticipate what line's coming up next, what pair of defensemen are coming up next, who's going on the power play, whose penalty killing, which penalty killing pair will go against the opposition's best power play unit . . . a lot of that is little subtleties about whose best on face-offs, right hand shot, left hand shot, which point men are they trying to feed, and Scotty has all that, just bang."[36]

Like a great chess master, Bowman was always in command of the board and positioning the right players into the right situations at the right time. He also had the innate ability to know when to take a player off the ice, particularly a tired one, removing him from a potentially harmful situation, for himself and for the team.

Bowman also strayed from the norm when it came to practising with the Canadiens. At the time, the whole idea of systems was in vogue, with some teams employing a style of play based on aggressiveness in the attacking zone, while others took a more cautious, defensive approach. Montreal, however, played a style of game entirely predicated on speed. Whereas the Philadelphia Flyers used intimidation to throw their opponents off-guard, making them hesitant and forcing them to play the

Flyers' style of game, the Canadiens did much the same, but by using speed instead. Bowman was able to play without a system because the Canadiens were not only the most talented team in the league but the most varied. "It's a team good enough to play, and win, any style of game," Ken Dryden later wrote. "For it, a system would be too confusing, robbing the team of its unique feature – its flexibility."[37]

No player escaped his gaze. In order to get the best out of his players Bowman would set up his practices and drills as glorified "game situations." Each practice would always include a scrimmage, in which he placed each of his players in specialized situations. For example, he would often line Guy Lafleur up against Bob Gainey. Lafleur would be forced to work against the best defensive forward in the game on a daily basis. On the flipside, Gainey would have to test his defensive acumen against the game's premier offensive star. The end result was that the practices informed each man's performance in an upcoming game, making each of them better players. "Bowman really pushed players to be better than they ever thought they would be," says Steve Shutt. "Not only did Scotty push us, but our own teammates pushed us. Our practices were probably a lot harder than some of the games we played."[38]

Naturally, Bowman was a student of watching other teams practise. And on December 30, 1975, he watched the Red Army engage in their last practice before the game. Just as when he worked at the paint factory down the street two decades before, he had made himself a fixture at the Russian practices over the past week.

It was at one of these practices that Bowman was introduced to Anatoli Tarasov. The year before Tarasov had relinquished his coaching duties with the Red Army, and also became the first Russian citizen ever inducted into the Hockey Hall of Fame. Though he was no longer actively involved in the day-to-day activities of the Red Army, Tarasov still travelled with the team, remaining for the most part in the background.

"Tarasov had watched our team practise," says Bowman today. "I remember him telling me through an interpreter that there were two or three things he really liked about our practice; he also felt that there were some things we could do that would help us, and we kind of exchanged information. He was impressed with our defence, especially Robinson, Lapointe, and Savard, and he gave me some ideas for designing some plays on how to spring offence in our own end with Lafleur,

Shutt, Mahovlich, and Lemaire. It was pretty enlightening for me to be able to sit down, even though there was an interpreter.

"Tarasov also mentioned to me that Lafleur and Shutt were very dangerous, and if they played up high and near the point men of the opposing team, they could take away a lot of the offence from the other team's defenceman. [Their centre] Jacques Lemaire liked to play a defensive style, down low, working with the defenceman. Of course we had defencemen who could make great passes. I adopted that pattern for the rest of my Montreal tenure. In today's NHL all five [players on the ice] collapse [toward the net], [with the Canadiens] I only collapsed three. That line was so effective, and because Jacques Lemaire was so effective defensively I could play them against any line in the league. Lemaire was a terrific two-way centre, who could play against anybody, solidifying his position."[39]

One of Bowman's strengths as a coach was his willingness to always listen to advice from other coaches and to take their best ideas and incorporate them with his own. Now, with the game only a day away, he took his seat in the empty Forum and watched the Red Army engage in a fast, spirited ninety-minute practice. The team was split into three separate groups, with each group using a specific zone on the ice, to practise rushes, power plays, penalty-killing, and passing. Such was the precision of the drills that the players in each group rarely infringed on the others.[40] For Bowman, the Red Army practice was unlike anything he'd ever seen.

"In watching them practise I was impressed with how they made use of the entire ice surface with all kinds of drills going on," he recalls today. "While it might have looked confusing, it wasn't when it was all broken down. There was no idle time, [they were always in] continuous motion, always taking shots on the goal, passing and skating. It was a pretty unique practice, very different from an NHL practice. I picked up a lot of good ideas watching them practise."[41]

Setting aside several hours, Bowman synthesized all that he had seen in the practices and from his conversation with Tarasov, and combined with what he had gleaned from the Rangers/Red Army clash of a few days before.

"I used up a normal workday to prepare our strategy," he later admitted. "The weaknesses of the Russian game were quite evident and the solutions to them weren't very complicated. Once a plan had been established, all I needed to do was relay the instructions to the players."[42]

The twin tenets of Bowman's game plan against the Soviets were no different than what he preached in any other game against any other opponent: take control of the puck, and take the opponent out of his comfort zone. Simply put, the team that controlled the puck could dictate how the game would be played. Bowman had seen the Rangers, despite all their mistakes, dominate the faceoff zone against the Red Army. Bowman knew that if the Canadiens could do the same, they could not only dictate the terms and pace of the game but also keep the puck away from the most dangerous Soviet players.

Bowman had also made note of one strange little quirk from that particular game. To his eyes it appeared that the Russians did not play along the boards, ever. In response, Bowman told his team that when they had possession along the boards in the Soviet end of the rink they should take their time, since there would be no pressure. He also told his defencemen to clog up the middle in both the neutral zone and their own zone, since it was in these zones that the Russians would try to generate their offence. He further instructed his charges to be aggressive in the middle, to take away the Red Army's space.

Watching the Rangers' game, Bowman had also noticed that the Red Army was not only susceptible to a strong, consistent forecheck but a little soft in their defence, at least by NHL standards, and would often opt to stick check rather than body check. He also tracked the Red Army's tendencies with the puck. He made note of the Soviets' preference to shoot from the middle of the ice or in the slot area. In addition, he become aware of the tendency of the Russian puck carrier, when he hit his own blue line, to make a short pass and then cross across the wing and wait for the return pass. Bowman instructed his players to permit that first pass and then take the passer out of the play, in order to disrupt the flow of the Soviet offence.[43]

In some ways Bowman's approach was audacious and bold. No team before had ever managed to dictate the tempo of the game to the Soviets. But Bowman recognized, perhaps more than anybody else did, that in a single game showdown, such as was coming on New Year's Eve, you only had one chance to make an impression. He and his team were determined not to waste theirs.

"What we have to realize is that we've only got one shot against them," stressed Bowman in the edition of the *Montreal Star* that hit the newsstands on the morning of the game. "We have to be ready for tonight, because that's all we've got. I see where the Rangers and the

Penguins are saying that they'd like another crack at the Soviets. They may get it but not this year and not next year. . . . This game is important for us and it's important for the entire league, because we're supposed to be the best. The only way we can show we're the best is on the ice."[44]

THE CURTAIN RISES

Montreal, Quebec, December 31, 1975. With only one day remaining in 1975 the eyes of the hockey world were on Montreal. That night's game dominated the talk throughout the city and the writing in the city's newspapers, both French and English.

The front cover of the tabloid *Le Journal de Montreal* proclaimed Happy New Year in both Russian and French in its top banner, then filled the rest of the page with a cartoon of Vladislav Tretiak and Ken Dryden nose to nose, captioned "The Better One Wins."

"I know one thing," stated Canadiens forward Jacques Lemaire in that morning's edition of the *Montreal Star,* "I don't want to come out of this game with people laughing at the Canadiens. If we don't play well, we can expect people to laugh at us, and I don't look forward to something like that. No way. All of us saw what they did do against the Rangers. We're a better team than the Rangers. They're rebuilding. They have a lot of new people. We're set."[1]

"I can guarantee we'll be ready," echoed Lemaire's teammate Peter Mahovlich that same morning. "I can't say we're going to beat them or by how much, but we'll be ready. If we don't beat them, we don't have any excuses. We've got to beat them. That's the only way to think going into the game, and we've got to play that way from start to finish."[2]

Mahovlich's desperate words helped betray what everybody, in Montreal and across the country, was thinking but refusing to say aloud. After over twenty years of the Soviet threat to Canada's hockey supremacy, the Montreal Canadiens represented a country's last hope. A loss by the Canadiens on New Year's Eve would leave no more excuses, and the NHL and Canadian hockey would finally have to admit that they had in fact fallen behind, that the Russians had overtaken Canada at its own game.

That evening the Montreal Canadiens and the Central Red Army would play a game of hockey against the backdrop of the Cold War. The storied Montreal Forum would see two teams engage all of these political, cultural, and sociological currents, channelled through a simple sixty-minute game of hockey. In addition, the game would also be played while a civil war over the direction of the sport in North America raged. It was an immense burden for each player on the team to carry, freighted with a pressure many of them had never experienced before.

In an effort to get away from the building tension, many of the Canadiens chose to spend the eve of the game with their families. Ken Dryden took a different approach. He checked into a downtown hotel and spent the night before and the following day cooped up in his room, completely isolated, in the company only of his thoughts, as he slowly built himself up for the game. Trying to focus on what lay ahead, Dryden instead found himself dealing with doubts and anxiety that threatened to overwhelm him.

Jacques Lemaire was dealing with a whole different set of emotions in the hours leading up to the game, as his wife gave birth to their third son.[3] There were many who wouldn't have blamed Lemaire had he chosen to remain with his wife and newborn son, yet when the Canadiens began gathering at the Montreal Forum at around four o'clock that afternoon, there was Lemaire, ready to go.

Jacques Lemaire had first joined the Canadiens in the fall of 1967 to little fanfare. An injury to Henri Richard suddenly brought the young Lemaire to prominence and he made the most of his opportunity, finishing second in the voting for the Calder Trophy as the NHL's rookie of the year. That spring Lemaire's star continued to rise, as he scored 7 goals and contributed 13 points in thirteen playoff games on the way to winning the Stanley Cup. Lemaire also began laying the foundation of his well-deserved reputation as a clutch performer by scoring the overtime goal that clinched the Canadiens' semi-final series win against Chicago. A week later, Lemaire completed the rare feat of scoring another overtime goal in his next game, the first game of the Stanley Cup Finals against the Blues. However, it wasn't enough to guarantee him a spot with the Canadiens at his natural position. Due to a glut of centremen on the team, Lemaire was constantly shifted between his natural position and the left wing. Despite this, he was a remarkably consistent scorer throughout his career. In his fifth season he was finally given the centre position for good and posted a career-best 81 points, cracking the NHL's top-ten scorers. The next year he topped that by scoring 95 points, the fifth-best total in the league, and 44 goals, the fourth-highest total in the NHL. That spring he captured his fourth Stanley Cup with the Canadiens.

Lemaire's scoring exploits soon put him in the spotlight. He was the focus of profiles in both *Sports Illustrated* and the *Sporting News* and the cover subject of many a hockey magazine, and rated among the public as the most likely member of the team to join Maurice Richard and "Boom Boom" Geoffrion as the Montreal members of the exclusive 50-goal club. The media coverage generated still more attention, which Lemaire actively attempted to avoid. In the summer of 1972, he was, surprisingly, passed over for the Summit Series by the Team Canada brain trust. Whereas most players would have been upset, Lemaire was openly relieved, admitting that he wasn't very enthusiastic about participating "because the pressure is too strong."[4] This attitude may have helped to explain why personal honours proved to be elusive for Lemaire. Despite being among the league's top scorers and premier two-way players, he surprisingly never participated in a single NHL All-Star Game. His predicament did not go entirely unnoticed. "Jacques Lemaire has never received the credit due him since he's been a member of the Canadiens," opined Bertrand Raymond in *Le Journal de Montreal*. "When he plays a game equal to his reputation, no one bats an eye. When he plays up to superstar standard it barely causes a ripple."[5]

The 1973–74 season saw his goal and point totals plummet and the reticent Lemaire faced both a media and public backlash. If he had one flaw, it was his inability to take any form of criticism. Often targeted by disappointed fans for booing and the press for criticism, a thin-skinned Lemaire even took to not appearing when named one of a game's stars, feeling that the selectors should have honoured him more.[6]

After getting booed and criticized so much in 1973–74, Lemaire had an epiphany. "Everybody in Montreal expected him to be the next 50-goal scorer," recalls Steve Shutt. "The next year when he scored 29 and got booed, he basically said to his critics, 'The heck with you guys. I'm going to be a defensive player,' and that's what he did. When he played with Guy Lafleur and me he'd score 35 goals, but once he got that 35 he'd say that's it and he would make sure that he didn't score any more, at least until the playoffs. By only scoring 35 goals a season, year after year, his critics would learn to never expect more."[7]

"Jacques was a painfully shy man when it came to all the media attention and adulation that surrounds a team like the Montreal Canadiens," remembers Larry Robinson. "He just preferred to blend into the background, avoiding the media circus altogether."[8]

Two separate events allowed Lemaire to do just that. The first was the rise of Guy Lafleur, who became the third member of the Montreal Canadiens to crack the 50-goal barrier. Not only did Lafleur's success lift that particular burden off Lemaire, but the resulting attention made him, and not Lemaire, the new focal point of the team. The second was the proclamation by Scotty Bowman only a few months before that he wanted the Canadiens to concentrate more on their defensive play.

Bowman, unusually adept at reading the inner psyches of his players, singled out Lemaire in particular. The two men went back more than a decade to when Bowman had coached the young Lemaire with the Junior Canadiens. Reassuring the wounded Lemaire, he personally told him how much his defensive skills were appreciated and how crucial his two-way play was to the Canadiens' future success. Bowman's words eased the pressure that had been building inside Lemaire since he had joined the team, unburdening him of the responsibilities that had always weighed heavily on his sensitive personality. Asking him to focus on his defensive responsibilities, Bowman allowed that any goals scored by Lemaire would be a bonus for a team that now contained so many pure offensive talents. Freed of all that had encumbered him for so long, Lemaire publicly expressed his new level of confidence. "I know my job and I know when I do it well – just like I know when I do it badly. The important thing is that the other players and management know what I do."[9]

"Jacques Lemaire was the total professional, capable in all areas of the game," Larry Robinson later reflected, speaking for many of his teammates. "He was a super checking centre, a tremendous passer to both sides; an important offensive threat with both his speed and incredible shot, and a quiet leader on the ice."[10]

The evening of December 31, 1975, would finally provide the perennially underappreciated Jacques Lemaire a public stage befitting his many talents.

Ralph Mellanby was not a person who would have been recognizable, in name or person, to many Canadians. However, within the hockey world there were very few who carried more clout. Such was the power of the man most responsible for the production and broadcast of *Hockey Night in Canada*.

As soon as Mellanby learned the preliminary details of the Super Series, he and his counterparts in the CBC began plotting a broadcasting strategy. "I didn't think that the New Year's Eve game between the Red Army and the Montreal Canadiens was going to be that big of a deal," Mellanby admits today. "CBC instead decided to focus the majority of their promotional strategy behind the Red Army game with Philadelphia. As a result, for the Philadelphia game, CBC would use four additional cameras compared to the one in Montreal."[11]

It was only when he started looking for a place to hold a post-game gathering on New Year's Eve that Mellanby grasped the anticipation for the upcoming Red Army/Canadiens contest. Mellanby tried to make a reservation at the Beaconsfield Golf Club west of Montreal for its traditional New Year's Eve dinner. Much to his surprise, he discovered that because of the game this year's event had been cancelled. Placing calls to a few other establishments, he heard similar stories. Curious, he began dialling some of his favourite haunts in Toronto, only to quickly learn that many of them were also keeping their doors closed while the game was on, New Year's Eve or not. The same scenario was playing out all across the country.

As the New Year's Eve afternoon sun slowly began its descent, Ralph Mellanby, inside a ghostly, silent Montreal Forum, gathered his own team around for their usual pre-game production meeting. In addition to the usual assortment of technical staff, assistants, and so on, he was surrounded by some of the most recognizable on-air talent in Canadian broadcasting history, many of it first discovered by Mellanby himself.

Howie Meeker, along with Dave Reynolds, would be the evening's host. A former Toronto Maple Leaf, Meeker's squeaky voice and home-spun personality endeared him to a whole new generation of fans, as did his insistence on not replaying the goals. "I don't want to show the goals," a stubborn Meeker maintained. "I don't want to show people what happened, I want to tell them why it happened."[12] Besides running hockey schools and writing best-selling instructional books, he had applied his experience and talents to bring a new level of analysis to hockey broadcasts, popularizing the use of a telestrator to diagram the replays and pioneering the use of videotape. He was also a polarizing figure, the first broadcaster to be openly critical of the game and its players. For Mellanby, Meeker's presence on the broadcast was essential. "Howie Meeker was the true star of *Hockey Night in Canada*," he recalls today, "and the most knowledgeable about the Russians. He also brought his natural passion to the game and I thought that would help to enliven the broadcast."[13]

In laying out the parameters of the broadcast, Mellanby knew he had to retain the Montreal broadcast team of Danny Gallivan and Dick Irvin, but in doing so he faced a unique problem. Neither Gallivan nor Irvin, who had been the English broadcast face of the team for close to a decade, had ever broadcast a game involving the Russians. In an effort to bring some knowledge of the opposition to the telecast, Mellanby enlisted the help of John Ferguson, who would be the third man in the booth. A former Montreal Canadien and the assistant coach of Team Canada in the 1972 Summit Series, Ferguson brought with him first-hand knowledge of both the Russian player and the Russian game, offsetting the inexperience of his two partners in the booth. And on the flipside, Mellanby felt that the tried-and-true duo of Gallivan and Irvin could help Ferguson, who had next to no experience in the broadcast booth, overcome any shortcomings.

As Mellanby mapped out the details of the broadcast to his staff that afternoon at the Montreal Forum, there was one conspicuous absence, although by this point it was to be expected. At that time, no person in Montreal had been involved with the production of *Hockey Night in Canada* longer than Danny Gallivan or been nearly as entrenched. In 1952 when *Hockey Night in Canada* began broadcasting on television, Gallivan was the man calling the play-by-play on the Montreal Canadiens English-language broadcasts. For almost a quarter of a century it had been the perfect match of broadcaster and team.

"There is nothing a broadcaster can do for a hockey team as far as winning or losing is concerned," Dick Irvin, his broadcast partner, later wrote. "But a team can do a lot for a broadcaster and his career . . . the Canadiens reached the Stanley Cup finals in each of Danny's first eight years on the job. Early impressions run deep. The Canadiens were the dominant team on the tube in the beginning of televised hockey and Danny Gallivan was their voice. He gave Canadian viewers and listeners a different style. The sound of his voice was electric . . . his knowledge of the game ran deep . . . and of course, there was his vocabulary. But as long as it was Danny coming up with flowing words and phrases the fans loved it."[14]

Gallivan was widely praised and beloved, but behind the camera he could be difficult, something Ralph Mellanby later alluded to. "Right from the start I couldn't figure Gallivan out. He wasn't a prima donna, but he could be awfully stubborn. He was an independent thinker and a trifle eccentric. I liked him, but I hardly ever saw him because he wouldn't attend production meetings or the morning skates where reporters gathered information about the upcoming game. He had his regimen and he wasn't really interested in what others thought."[15]

Mellanby had a lot riding on Gallivan that New Year's Eve. Worried about Gallivan's lack of experience with the international game, he was even more concerned that his play-by-play man might struggle with the pronunciations of the various names on the Red Army squad. To ensure a smooth delivery, Mellanby had Gallivan pore over tapes of the 1972 Summit Series in an effort to acquaint himself with the Russian players. Now, in the hours before the game, he could only hope that he had gotten it right.

While Ralph Mellanby sweated over the details of that night's game in one section of the Montreal Forum, Guy Lafleur was alone with his thoughts in another.

The game is hours away. He sits by himself in the quiet of the Canadiens dressing room. His teammates, coaches, and trainers won't begin to start showing up for another hour, but Lafleur is already dressed in full regalia for the game with his skates tightly tied and his stick resting at attention beside him. He stares straight ahead, only breaking the trance for the odd drink of water. This is his alone time, away from the spotlight and the harsh glare and expectations of those that surround him.

A curious onlooker would have assumed that this period of solitude might be Lafleur's way of getting prepared for an important game. In that respect he would be half-right. The game against the Red Army is important, but so is the next game against the Washington Capitals and the one after that. In the eyes of Guy Lafleur there are no nights off, each game is an important one, and he will prepare accordingly for each of them, in full uniform with his skates tied tightly – hours before the puck drops.

No player on the entire Montreal Canadiens team feels the pressure of the names, the faces, and the expectations more intently than does Guy Lafleur. He is the proud inheritor of a mantle previously worn by Maurice Richard and then Jean Béliveau, as the game's pre-eminent French-Canadian superstar, the one player who defines the Montreal Canadiens in the eyes of both the media and the public. The demands on his time are immense. In addition to being a Montreal Canadien, he's a pitchman for several companies, a guest at countless banquets, and a frequent visitor to local hospitals. He is also always in demand by those who report daily on his exploits, from those who make up the countless local radio, television, and newspaper outlets in the city to those outside of Montreal who make the trek to win just a moment of his time. It's a role and a routine he once shied away from but now not only readily embraces but dedicates his life to, even to the detriment of those closest to him.

"I really love my family and my kid," he tells the *New York Times*, "but first of all it's my hockey, my career. My family is second and my fans go third. Sometimes my fans go second, and my family is third. It's turning all the time."[16]

Now he is universally recognized as not only one of the sport's premier players but also undoubtedly its most exciting, as evidenced by the sold-out crowds paying premium prices who leap out of their seats as soon as he touches the puck. In a country that elevates its hockey stars to a status approaching divinity, Guy Lafleur is nothing short of a national treasure. Inside the province of Quebec, he is something more akin to a tribal god. Not only does he belong to them, he is one of them.

As the clock ticks closer to four o'clock his teammates start streaming through the door and each of them begins his own routine in preparation for tonight's game. An hour from now the team will have their final meeting; two hours from now they will touch the ice for the pre-game skate; and in three hours the game will begin.

The atmosphere outside the Montreal Forum is electric. This game is important, maybe even more important than a game in the Stanley Cup Finals. The crowd gathering outside tonight is a unique one. Many of the fans are dressed for a formal occasion, and once the game has ended they will head to the various public and private society parties that are traditional in Montreal on New Year's Eve. Many of the men are nattily dressed in suits, while many of their female companions are in full-length gowns, their jewellery sparkling against the dark backdrop of the evening night. The crowd is also sprinkled with celebrities, none more conspicuous than Harold Ballard, the owner of the Toronto Maple Leafs, alongside his running buddy, King Clancy.

"It's the first time in 54 years that I'll pull for the Canadiens to win," announced Ballard, never lacking for words in the presence of a microphone .[17]

The atmosphere of the event lends the game a class and dignity not always assorted with a hockey crowd. As the multitudes slowly find their seats, Danny Gallivan gets settled in the broadcast booth alongside Dick Irvin and John Ferguson. As per his routine, Gallivan will not talk to Irvin about the upcoming game. Instead, the long-time broadcast partners will exchange small talk and prepare for the word from the control truck to go. Inside that truck, Ralph Mellanby slides into the producer's chair.

"For the big events I would assume the production chair," Mellanby explains today. "My feeling at that time was the bigger the event, the more control I wanted. Ultimately, I'm the one who has to answer to the powers that be at the CBC. This didn't always sit well with the regular producers but they had no choice but to accept it."[18]

There was one aspect of the broadcast that the confident Mellanby couldn't control and as the time to air approached he found himself worrying about it. "Before the game I had the feeling that the Russians would dominate the game," he remembers today. "I thought that the game had the potential to be a blowout in their favour."[19] It is only when the people begin filling into the Forum that he begins to realize the enormity of the moment.

All of the major cities in Canada have sent their reporters to the game, as have American publications including *Time, Newsweek, Sports Illustrated,* and the *New York Times.* The result is that the press row that was built to accommodate 140 journalists is grossly insufficient for the 200 accredited media members, and some of the journalists are forced to sit among the crowd.

As game time approaches, Alan Eagleson, the head of the NHL Players' Association and the much-publicized "czar of international hockey," makes his way to the Montreal Forum with his son. "We rushed over in the taxi, it was a very slushy, snowy night with a mild temperature, and as we got out, my fourteen-year-old son took a step and down he went into a pile of snow, slush, and water. He came up absolutely soaking wet in a well dressed set of clothes."[20]

With his son soaked, Eagleson makes his way toward the Canadiens dressing room. One of the first people he encounters is Sam Pollock, who immediately ushers him and his son into the hushed dressing room. The members of the Canadiens are all dressed and ready for the word to go out on the ice. There is a heavy stillness in the room. Meanwhile, Pollock ushers Eagleson and his son off to a side room and they proceed to put the wet clothes into the industrial dryer usually reserved for the team.

Spotting Eagleson hovering around the room, Scotty Bowman, always looking to take advantage of a situation, hit upon a quick idea. Eagleson recalls, "While I was waiting for my son's clothes to dry, Scotty came over to me and said, 'Why don't you come in here and talk to some of these new guys and tell them what we're up against.' It was nothing clandestine, nothing planned, it just happened by coincidence. All of them in that room, we're aware of what was in front of them," remembers Eagleson today. "They knew they were headed for a hockey game, because they had six guys who had played in 1972. Those players had made it clear to their teammates that this wasn't going to be a picnic."[21]

Eagleson, in his imitable way, pleads with players, attempting to appeal to their sense of patriotism. "You're the only Canadian team playing in this series," he began. "Whether you like it or not, you're carrying this country's pride on your broad shoulders."[22] Picking up on the energy in the room, Peter Mahovlich uses the time remaining to stir up the team. Soon they are like a young group of boys, standing and cheering.[23]

"The biggest message I had to give to them was that we have to play another forty-four games together," Mahovlich later revealed. "Let's go out there as a team, win or lose, we'll respect each other after the game. We weren't going to blame anybody and that's the way it had to be before the game and that's the way it's going to be after the game."[24]

"Pete was so intense in the dressing room," recalls Murray Wilson. "You didn't see that too often from Pete. It let the rest of us know how important this was, the veterans bring you up to that level."[25]

"The dressing room was pretty intense," remembers Jim Roberts. "There wasn't a player in that dressing room that wasn't at his best, ready for that game."[26]

———

Down the hall from the Canadiens, the most famous anthem singer in Canada is exercising his voice. Ever the professional, he requires a warm-up lasting ten minutes. Labelled Mr. O'Canada, he is instantly recognizable as soon as he takes his two steps on the ice. Off the ice, he rarely travels far without being asked for his autograph. His vocal talents are so lauded that he receives bundles of fan mail, sometimes as much as some of the players. Despite his widespread renown, however, the majority of the mail is simply addressed to "The National Anthem Singer, Montreal."

His name is Roger Doucet and like every other night at the Forum, he is going through his usual preparations before taking to the ice for his appearance, which always lasts less than a minute. Pulling his suspenders over his stout body he constantly tests his vocal range, the mirror his only audience. He warms up in his usual space – the washroom.

Since tonight is a special occasion he had considered singing the Soviet national anthem in addition to his standard rendition of the Canadian anthem. Doucet does not speak or read the Russian language but had been taking the time to teach himself the nuances of the anthem phonetically. Against Doucet's wishes, it was ultimately decided that the Soviet anthem would be performed instrumentally by the Forum organist. "The reason Roger Doucet didn't sing the words to the Russian national anthem was because the Canadiens didn't want him to sing the words," remembers Ralph Mellanby. "There was kind of a connotation toward communism in the words and Sam Pollock didn't want it sung, and Clarence Campbell agreed."

Slipping his shoes into a set of rubber protectors, Doucet begins the long solitary walk down the hallway, pausing in front of an emergency fire hose for a glance at his reflection in the case's glass. Taking one last deep breath, he opens that last set of doors separating him from the Forum crowd and walks through.

As the clock strikes seven for all those tuned in to the CBC, the voice of Dick Irvin comes across the airwaves and a montage of highlights from the 1972 and 1974 Summit Series fill up the television screen. Canada, however, is not the only country glued to their televisions. It is three a.m. in Moscow and unlike the games in the tape-delayed 1972 Summit Series, tonight's encounter with the Montreal Canadiens will be broadcast live throughout the Soviet Union.[27]

The camera pans to the evening's hosts, Dave Reynolds and Howie Meeker, clad in the their traditional powder-blue sports jackets, both of them located in the wide entrance at the bottom right-hand corner of the rink, traditionally used for the Zamboni's entrance and exit from the ice. It is the voice of Reynolds that starts the proceedings and sets the scene: "There are more than 18, 19,000 people in this building and they're waiting for what may be the key game of Super Series '76. The atmosphere in the Forum is electric because here it's more than just the Montreal Canadiens versus the Soviets, it's Canada." Realizing the trepidation about the potential outcome of the game, a confident and clearly excited Meeker sets out to reassure a skeptical viewing audience. "I don't think the Russians can match Dryden in goal, Lapointe or Savard on defence and all the fellas that play that position with them, and down centre, I think Lemaire, Mahovlich, and Risebrough give us an edge, so Canada sit back, relax, enjoy yourselves and have a ball, the Canadiens are going to win tonight." Somewhat taken aback by Meeker's confidence, a less assured Reynolds can only hesitantly answer, "I sure hope you're right," before switching off and going upstairs to the broadcast booth.[28]

Up in the broadcast booth, both Dick Irvin and John Ferguson had watched intently as the Red Army warmed up and they now share their impressions with the television audience. Ferguson is impressed. "Ten different exercises they did in the pre-game warmup . . . they get something out of that pre-game warmup believe me." For Dick Irvin, getting his first taste of the Red Army's methods, he can't help but notice how much more they work the goalie than the Canadiens do. In addition to taking a lot of shots, the Red Army dutifully practises tip-ins, one-on-ones, and three-on-ones on Tretiak before the final buzzer sounds and both teams leave the ice. The opinions of both Irvin and Ferguson only serve to reinforce the stereotype of the Russians as different from us. The underlying fear in the voices of the two men and all those watching is that the Russians might in fact also be better than us.

"I didn't originally feel much enthusiasm for the game," Irvin admits today. "I wasn't close to the international scene, I had no experience with international hockey and I hadn't been involved in the 1972 series in any way. The whole thing took me by surprise; I didn't think the game would have had much impact. It took me aback at the Forum that night, right from the start you could cut the tension with a knife."[29]

After a short commercial break, the action shifts back to the ice surface where the Canadiens' public address announcer Claude Mouton commandeers the proceedings. His first duty is to introduce the two teams, beginning with the visitors, the 1975 Champions of the USSR, the Soviet Red Army. One by one the players are all introduced, slowly taking their spot on the blue line. Each of them is met with polite applause. Their chests display a hammer and sickle against the dark maroon of their jerseys, which is partially offset by a dash of blue on their shoulders and around their waists. The fronts of their sweaters sport the letters UCKA. Among the group introductions are two players who have been added to the roster for the Super Series as reinforcements for the Red Army, Valeri Vasiliev and Alexander Maltsev, each of whom saw action in the 1972 Summit Series and plays on the Russian National Team. Not surprisingly, the introductions of Kharlamov and Tretiak are saved for last and both are greeted with tremendous cheers. In the three years since they first appeared at the Montreal Forum, each man has been transformed from complete unknowns to recognized superstars, as evidenced by the large amount of fan mail each receives from Canada.[30] A quick scan of the Red Army team on the blue line reveals a squad almost identical to that of the Russian National Team. Of the seventeen players gathered on the blue line, twelve had starred for Team Russia in the 1972 Summit Series. In addition, among the five players who hadn't played in 1972 are three who have spent time with the national team.

"When we take the ice at the Forum, we are greeted by noise like I've never heard before," Tretiak writes later. "During the game, I always try to talk with my teammates, give them advice and encouragement. Here, it is inconceivable. I can't even hear my own voice – and the uproar is bound to continue through the entire game."[31]

Claude Mouton attempts to announce the Canadiens, only to be nearly drowned out by the applause of the energized crowd. Introduced by position (goalie, defence, forward) and in numerical order, the invigorated Canadiens, in stark contrast to their restrained opponents, jump out energetically onto the ice. The biggest ovations are reserved for Lafleur and those who played in 1972. This includes Pete Mahovlich, who skates out with his head lowered, until he reaches the blue line. Lifting his head up, his face a picture of naked emotion for all to see, he vigorously clutches his stick and pumps it into the air to acknowledge the cheers. Yvan Cournoyer, the team's newly minted captain, in the wake of Henri Richard's retirement, is introduced last.

"I've witnessed many pre-game presentations at center ice over the years and I've never seen the Canadiens players as nervous as they were Wednesday night," wrote Bertrand Raymond in *Le Journal de Montreal*. "They were unable to remain still. Their skates shuffled back and forth as they stood, in the manner of a race car engine that is warmed minutes before a big race. Pete Mahovlich looked like a caged lion, hammering his shin pads with his stick. Serge Savard, as experienced as he is in these types of games, fixed his gaze above the ice toward the press box. I caught myself, surprisingly wishing him luck with a hand gesture. Savard responded with an affirmative nod. These things don't happen ordinarily."[32]

After the introductions are complete, it is time for the official faceoff. Of the eight cities that the Russians will visit over the course of the Super Series, Montreal is the only one that will feature a pre-game ceremony and exchange of gifts.

As the red carpet is rolled out, five men gather at centre ice: Jacques Courteois, the Canadiens' president; Viacheslav Koloskov, the head of the USSR Sports Committee; Clarence Campbell; Sam Pollock; and Alan Eagleson. With everyone set, the Forum organist plays the Russian national anthem. At its conclusion, without fanfare, Roger Doucet takes his traditional two steps out onto the ice and begins to belt out "O Canada." As his voice cascades through the arena the tension in the building reaches a fever pitch. The crowd, their palms growing sore from the ferocity of their clapping, vacillates between the extreme emotions of elation and tears as Doucet comes to his grand conclusion.

"Before the opening face-off when they were singing the anthem, the feeling that I got just standing there at the blue line was really something," Larry Robinson later recalled.

"I knew that millions of people were going to be watching the game. It was frightening, to say the least. It gave you a tingle all over . . . It was just a terrific feeling."[33]

Cournoyer and his Red Army counterpart, Boris Mikhailov, skate to centre ice for the ceremonial puck drop, which is performed by the unlikely duo of Koloskov and Campbell. As the ceremony comes to an end, Alan Eagleson visibly urges on the Canadiens.

There is now the traditional exchange of gifts. Although it isn't well known at the time, the process of getting the gifts was arduous. A few days before, when the Red Army was in New York, Ralph Mellanby had notified the Russian official from the Canadian Embassy, who was travelling with the Soviets, that the Canadiens would be presenting the Red Army with gifts at their upcoming game on New Year's Eve. This presented a slight problem. "Well, the Russians didn't have any gifts," remembers Mellanby who was forced into finding a quick, drastic solution. "For our sponsors and directors *Hockey Night in Canada* had made up these glass pieces to put on your shelf that had the two team's emblems and the Super Series logo on it. We now decided that the Red Army would give those to the Canadiens as gifts in the pre-game ceremony. Obviously this left our sponsors in the lurch. So I went to Frank Selke Jr. and we discovered this little place that Aggie Kukulowicz (a Canadian/ Russian interpreter who worked as a conduit between the two sides) found on the Danforth in Toronto that sold Russian dolls, which were imported from the Soviet Union, and that's where we got the souvenirs for the sponsors. We lied to the sponsors and told them that the dolls were a gift from the Soviet team."[34] With no one any wiser, and their sponsors satisfied, the exchange of gifts went off without a hitch.

Finally – after all the pre-game hype, speculation, and anticipation – the time to play has come. A game that has been over twenty years in the making is now a reality. Perched high above centre ice Danny Gallivan attempts to put into simple words all of the conflicting emotions currently swirling throughout the arena and through countless households, restaurants, bars, and anywhere else two or more Canadians could come together to cheer on "their" team, across the country.

"I have never heard this crowd in such a frame of mind as they are tonight."[35]

18.

THE GAME

The First Period. Clutching the puck tightly in the palm of his hand, Wally Harris, the referee, slowly makes his way to the centre dot. Assisting Harris are two linesmen, Claude Béchard and the Russian official, Yuri Karandin. Karandin's presence caused a hint of controversy in the days leading up to the game when it was revealed that he routinely practises and travels with the Red Army team. But now, with the start of the game only seconds away, all that is temporarily forgotten.

Looking to his right, Harris takes in the Russian juggernaut. Konstantin Loktev, the Red Army coach, has chosen to start the game with his best unit of Valeri Kharlamov, Vladimir Petrov, and Boris Mikhailov up front, backed by the defensive duo of Valeri Vasiliev and Alexander Gusev. After counting the Russian five, Harris turns to his left toward the Canadiens. It immediately becomes apparent that Scotty Bowman is operating from a different playbook. He starts an opening line of Guy Lafleur at centre, flanked by Bob Gainey and Murray Wilson on his wings. Not only are Lafleur and Wilson both opening the game out of their normal positions, but they are taken from three different Canadiens lines and have rarely if ever played together before as a unit.

"The opening line had a lot of speed and some size," Murray Wilson recalls today. "I think that's the message Scotty wanted to send them at the start of the game – you're not going to outskate us, you're not going to outwork us – and with Guy we matched them in talent."[1]

Backing them up is the twosome of Serge Savard and Guy Lapointe, who were one of the most valuable defensive pairings for Team Canada in the 1972 Summit Series.

With the preliminaries over, the game can begin. The arena is temporarily blinded by camera flash as Harris drops the puck. Lafleur wins the faceoff from Petrov and quickly shovels the puck to Gainey, who plays it back to Savard, who returns the favour to a now rushing Gainey, who makes his way toward the Red Army blue line. Valeri Vasiliev is standing there waiting for him and forcefully checks an unsuspecting Gainey, who falls to the ice. The loose puck rolls into the Soviet zone in the corner below a watching Tretiak. Vasiliev takes the initiative and attempts to retrieve it but is crunched into the boards by a determined Gainey. The game is only in its first few seconds and already the Canadiens are beginning to reveal some of the facets of their game plan.

"We knew that their D were slow," says Murray Wilson. "The Soviets moved the puck slow, and they wouldn't go after you in the corners; Scotty wanted to set the tone early with some physicality and some speed."[2] Unlike some of the other teams that had played the Russians, the Canadiens were determined to take the game to the Red Army rather than wait for it to come to them.

"The pace of the New Year's Eve game was so much [faster] than [a] regular season game," Scotty Bowman reflects. "There were very few whistles and almost no stoppages, so the pace was kept up. It was an action-filled game. You had to be sharp on the bench because there was no free time to allow you to think. The electricity of the game is what I remember."[3]

Seconds later, Gainey springs the speedy Wilson on a breakaway that is stopped cold by Tretiak. Eighteen seconds later, a frustrated Wilson gets a little overzealous and is whistled for the game's first penalty, a high-sticking minor only thirty seconds into the game. This is a scene that the Canadiens had desperately wanted to avoid. There is no more feared power play in hockey than the mighty Soviet's. With the man advantage the Russians are usually free to improvise, often with spectacular results. Loktev chooses not to change those who are on the ice. Bowman chooses to continue with Savard and Lapointe, but switches up his front end, leaving Gainey on but pairing him with Doug Jarvis, who has all of 36 NHL career games under his belt. With the enthusiasm of youth he hops over the boards and heads right to the faceoff circle. The only rookie on the team, and a player easily discarded by the Toronto Maple Leafs a few months before, tonight Jarvis is one of the game's most critical players. Despite the increased pressure and limelight, Jarvis proceeds to do what he does best, cleanly winning the crucial faceoff.

Thanks to his expertise the Canadiens are able to maintain command of the coveted puck, disrupting the flow of the frightening Red Army power play and negating their man advantage. Over the course of the next two minutes the short-handed Canadiens are the team in control, even when Jarvis and Gainey leave the ice in favour of Jacques Lemaire and Jim Roberts, effectively clogging up the middle of the ice and causing confusion within the Red Army team, rendering their power play surprisingly impotent. When Murray Wilson's skates touch the ice, signalling the end of the Russian power play, the frustrated Red Army are still searching for their first shot on Ken Dryden.

Both teams change their personnel on the fly and the trio of Yvan Cournoyer, Steve Shutt, and Peter Mahovlich take to the ice for the first time with a little over three minutes gone in the opening period. Seconds later, Red Army defenceman Viktor Kuzkin attempts to clear the puck from his own end. Instead he inadvertently shoots the puck into a cluster of Canadiens gathered near the far boards.

Feeling the puck strike him, Shutt instinctively corrals the loose puck onto his stick. Now in his fourth season and blossoming into a pure goal scorer, he seizes the moment. Gaining the blue line, Shutt has every intention of shooting the puck. Recognizing this Cournoyer trails in behind him, and Mahovlich skates toward the slot waiting for a potential rebound. Shutt on his off-wing cuts from the boards to his left, creating more space. With the Soviet defenceman backing off, Shutt takes his time. He gently places the puck in front of him, then violently whips his stick back before recoiling it with all of his strength. Making perfect contact with the puck, it is a wicked shot that becomes a blur right over Tretiak's left shoulder and only slows when it hits the twine in the back of the net.

Canadiens 1, Red Army 0.

In the throes of celebration, Shutt thrusts his arm in the air with such force that one wonders if he might just take off. His exuberant teammates leap off the bench and over the boards to congratulate him, and the raucous crowd rattles the fifty-year-old Forum to its core.

"It was a really quick release and I don't think he ever saw the shot," says Shutt today. "It was a good hard shot in a perfect place, right in the top shelf. On that particular play, because I came in on my off-wing, it made it tough for the Russian defenceman to challenge. If I take a step to my left, the defenceman is out of position so he really was in no man's land. To this day, when Tretiak meets me he puts his glove hand up and waves it in the air and then smiles at me."[4]

With the Canadiens posting the game's first goal, the tension in the Forum temporarily subsides and is replaced by an overwhelming sense of joy, expressed in the crowd's first "Go Habs Go" chant. Amid the carnival atmosphere in the building it is up to Dick Irvin to send out a cautionary note. Cognizant of the fact that the Rangers had opened the scoring against the Red Army a few nights before, and with the lingering memory of the initial game of the 1972 Summit Series, Irvin reminds the television audience, "1–0 leads sometimes don't mean very much."[5]

Trying to switch the momentum, Konstantin Loktev puts his top line of Mikhailov, Petrov, and Kharlamov on the ice. Possessing the last change as the home team, Bowman counters with a line of Jacques Lemaire centring Lafleur and Gainey. It is this matchup of strength on strength that he will strive to maintain for the rest of the game. As Wally Harris motions to drop the puck, a sly Kharlamov slides down past Gainey and attempts to set up all alone by the boards. He is met, however, by Guy Lapointe, who moves up from his blue line position and lines up beside the most dangerous of all Russian players. In the matchup between the two coaches, it appears in the early minutes that the wily Bowman has an answer for each Red Army move.

The Canadiens pick up right where they left off, with their aggressive forecheck pinning the Red Army in its own end. Unable to gain control over the puck and the play, the Russians are on their heels. As the play continues in the Soviet end, Bowman picks the perfect time to deploy the trio of Lambert, Risebrough, and Tremblay, who ratchet up the intensity. Amid the confusion, and finding themselves on the short end of most of the skirmishes, a tired Vasiliev lazily hooks an energetic Risebrough as the young Canadien lunges for the loose puck, resulting in the first Montreal power play.

Despite controlling the tempo of the play and exerting steady and unremitting pressure in the Russian zone for the next two minutes, the Canadiens' power play is unable to convert. With the time ticking down on the man advantage, Bowman taps on the shoulders of Doug Risebrough, Yvon Lambert, and Mario Tremblay in a shrewd move to maintain the stress and strain on the beleaguered Red Army. Under siege in the face of the Canadiens' tenacity, the Russians make more glaring mistakes. Tremblay inexplicably finds himself all alone in front of Tretiak, who calmly kicks out the tenacious sophomore's backhand attempt.

Gathering the puck, the Russians make a vain attempt to relieve the pressure, but their offensive rush is repelled by Serge Savard at centre ice. Much as he will throughout the evening, the commanding Savard takes control and leads the Canadiens' counterattack, calmly distributing the puck to a waiting Lambert. Quickly gaining the blue line, Lambert quickly passes to Risebrough, who immediately fires a quick snapshot that Tretiak stops with his blocker. Tretiak is unable to control the rebound, which bounces in front of the Soviet goal. The loose puck nestles on the nervous stick of a besieged Vasiliev, who tentatively skates in front of his own net, his back to the play. Behind him is a fast-approaching Lambert, who sneaks behind an unaware Vasiliev and coolly picks his pocket. Before anyone can react to his act of larceny, Lambert instantly shovels the puck through the yawning gap between Tretiak's legs.

Canadiens 2, Red Army 0.

The Canadiens bench once again empties out onto the ice to congratulate an ecstatic Lambert. Along with the exuberance a genuine feeling of surprise fills the Forum. "The Soviets have not had a shot on Dryden," intones an incredulous Dick Irvin. "The Canadiens have outshot them 7–0 to this point in the hockey game."

Irvin was expressing the same wonder that was permeating through the broadcast booth, the press box, the Forum crowd, and the millions watching at home. "They're playing a fired-up hockey club in the Montreal Canadiens," echoes his broadcast partner John Ferguson, "there's no doubt about it."[6] In the days, weeks, and years before the game, many had speculated on what would happen when the Canadiens and Red Army finally met on the ice. Nary a one openly predicted that Montreal would enjoy such a one-sided advantage.

Holding a 2–0 advantage, Bowman once again employs the services of Doug Jarvis for the next faceoff at centre ice. Keeping his foot on the throttle, Bowman watches Jarvis win yet another faceoff. With the Canadiens once again in control, Bowman immediately resumes his strategy of quickly changing his lines in an effort to keep the Russians off balance. As a result the pressure continues, and the Canadiens continue to push their advantage: a Robinson blast from the point; a chance close-in by Cournoyer deflected into the crowd; Lemaire and Lafleur on a two-on-one, ending in a blast from Lemaire sailing over a besieged Tretiak and the Red Army net.

"We were happy we were up 2–0, but we just wanted to keep going," admits Steve Shutt. "We knew these guys were a good team and we weren't going to slow down because we knew they could come back.

One of the strengths of that team was when we decided to do something, we just did it."[7]

Taking the rebounding puck the other way, the Red Army finally mounts its first offensive thrust as the period approaches the halfway point. Petrov passes the puck to the dangerous Kharlamov, who finds himself immediately draped by three Canadiens. Despite all of this he records the Red Army's first shot of the game. Gathering the rebound is his linemate Boris Mikhailov, whose errant pass is intercepted by Guy Lafleur. Collecting the puck, Lafleur takes it out of the Montreal end of the rink, ending the Soviet threat.

For Ken Dryden, admittedly beset by nerves, one shot in the game's first ten minutes does very little to calm him. "I would never get mentally free enough just to play," he says later of what will be a sixty-minute struggle.[8]

As the first period enters its second half, the game begins to simmer down, with the checking becoming a little tighter and the initial burst of enthusiasm slightly waning. For the next few minutes the play is generally confined to the middle of the ice as the Russians continue in their efforts to penetrate the Canadiens' defence. As opposed to the Rangers, who let the Russians come to them a few nights before, the Canadiens defence actively challenges the onrushing Red Army, often turning them back at the centre red line, and then counterattacking. In the first period, the Canadiens' defence have thrown a blanket between the oncoming Red Army and Ken Dryden. There are, however, rare occasions when the Russians are able to cross the Canadiens' blue line, but they are continuously pushed out of their comfort zone. One-on-one with Lapointe, Kharlamov is forced to take a wrist shot on Dryden from fifteen feet out. Alexander Gusev finds an opening to take a slapshot on the Canadiens' goal, only to have the puck deflected into the crowd by an alert Serge Savard.

"The crowd was in a frenzy for the first eight or ten minutes and exploded tremendously when the Canadiens got the goals but it's been rather quiet of late," observes Gallivan from the broadcast booth. With the play settling down, Bowman returns to his energy line for an injection of enthusiasm. Risebrough, Tremblay, and Lambert don't disappoint.

Sending in two forecheckers, the Canadiens leave their other three skaters between the Soviet blue line and the red line. Once again the tenacious forecheck pays instant dividends. Holding the puck in the corner of his own end, Soviet defenceman Gennady Tsygankov has his pocket picked by an industrious Risebrough, who immediately throws the puck toward the slot where it is picked up by an onrushing Lambert, whose wrist shot is in turn kicked aside by Tretiak's left pad. The rebound finds its way to the stick of Mario Tremblay, who blasts the puck wide and out of play. Harnessing his youthful enthusiasm, Tremblay plays with a controlled fury that impresses those in the broadcast booth. "Mario Tremblay is playing the best fifteen minutes of hockey I think I've seen him play in a long time," comments an impressed Dick Irvin. "He's the youngest player on the ice. He's just nineteen."[9]

With less than three and a half minutes remaining in the period, the Red Army's youngest player, twenty-year-old Boris Aleksandrov, enters the Canadiens' zone with his two linemates flanking him and two Montreal defencemen in front of him. Trailing on the play, the Canadiens' captain, Yvan Cournoyer, hauls down the speedy Aleksandrov, ending the Russian threat. Whistled for a penalty a demonstrative Cournoyer throws up in his arm in disbelief at Wally Harris, loudly protesting his innocence. "Yvan Cournoyer got very upset," Harris later recalled. "He skated up to me ranting and raving all over the place. I said, 'Take it easy. Settle down. There's pressure on everybody here tonight.' Cournoyer said, 'I know, but we have to beat these bastards.'"[10]

As with their first power play, the Red Army employs their top unit of Petrov, Mikhailov, Kharlamov, Gusev, and Vasiliev. In response, Bowman also sends out the same penalty-killing unit of Jarvis, Gainey, Savard, and Lapointe. In a virtual replay of their first power play, the Russians have trouble gaining traction in the Montreal end of the rink, much less setting up in the offensive zone.

For Danny Gallivan and Dick Irvin, both of whom have seen the most of the Canadiens this season, their enthusiasm is an eye-opener. The Canadiens are doing a lot of things they wouldn't normally do, all of them playing as if this is the most important game of their lives.[11] The second Red Army power play concludes much like the first with the frustrated Russians failing to even garner a single shot.

Reinvigorated by killing another penalty, the Canadiens resume their persistent forecheck, once again pinning the Red Army in their own end. Unable to clear the puck, the Soviets, in a combination of frustration and fatigue, take another penalty with fifteen seconds on the clock, as Viktor Shluktov interferes with an oncoming Bob Gainey.

As the siren sounds, bringing an end to the first period, the departing Canadiens are serenaded by the Forum faithful with a standing ovation. The period ends with the score 2–0 in favour of the Canadiens, who are enjoying an 11 to 4 advantage in shots.

The First Intermission. The first period and the Canadiens' ferocious start has caught many by surprise, not the least of which is Ralph Mellanby. "I was stunned by their start, and their passion," he recalls today. Before the game he had doubted whether the Canadiens could even compete. Now he has just experienced one of the defining moments of his career at *Hockey Night in Canada*. "Part of the appeal of that game was the story being told on the ice, it was a game where you couldn't miss a moment as the story unfolded." As he sits in the producer's chair in the broadcast truck outside the Forum, Mellanby receives a call from his bosses at CBC headquarters in Toronto telling him what he already knows, that he is on to something special.[12]

Returning from the commercial break the television viewer is treated to a discussion between the evening's host, Dave Reynolds, and John Ferguson, who has made his way down from the broadcast booth. "I don't know how many games a year we do, maybe sixty, but this one has got me just like this," admits a still-tense Reynolds, clenching his fists and shaking them in full view of the camera. "The Canadiens are playing just fantastic hockey."

"They've done their homework," echoes Ferguson in agreement. Reynolds then admits to being skeptical before the game about how the younger members of the Canadiens would react to the atmosphere and tension of the game. "When you play against a good hockey club like the Soviets it brings out the best in a lot of hockey players," responds Ferguson, "and the kids are workin' and if they work that way things can happen."[13]

In the second segment, the viewers are once again in the studio, but this time Dave Reynolds is joined by Valeri Kharlamov in an interview taped earlier. "We pre-taped the Kharlamov interview before the game," remembers Ralph Mellanby. "Aggie Kukulowicz was in his earpiece off-camera, translating Reynold's questions. Hence the slight hesitation in Kharlamov's answers."[14] Clad in his Red Army sweater and a pair of jeans the Soviet superstar answers the most basic of questions put to him by Reynolds: "When I'm skating I express my own individuality, otherwise the game would be very, very dull, but I do listen to my instructors." Kharlamov expounds on how the smaller NHL rinks don't have an adverse effect on his game, how he's recovered from an early-season knee injury, and about his life as an honoured master of sport in the USSR.[15]

After another commercial, the intermission returns to the broadcast booth for the analysis by Dick Irvin and Howie Meeker. Explaining to the television audience how the Russians have been caught off guard by the Canadiens' aggressiveness, Irvin give details of how their style of game has been disrupted. "I think they've all got that hockey fever," counters Meeker, "we used to see it here night after night. If you've been in Montreal, you had to catch it."[16]

In the Russian locker room, one might have expected a tinge of panic. After all, they have been completely outplayed, and are behind by two on the scoreboard. Konstantin Loktev does not berate his players. Instead, he attempts a different approach, urging his team to skate harder and pass more accurately. The details of the first period are never mentioned as Loktev assures them all that "it's going to work out."[17] Their coach's confidence in the face of the Canadiens' onslaught helps to keep the team afloat.

In the Canadiens' room, very little is said. There is no need to make adjustments, to fire up the team; after all, they've just played the most perfect period anyone can ever remember seeing. "When the game was close Scotty wouldn't say much," eloborates Steve Shutt. "He trusted that we were going to play the system that he wanted, which we did, and he just ran the bench."[18]

The Second Period. Holding the momentum and a two-goal advantage, the Canadiens open the second period on the power play. In the Russian goal a calm and collected Vladislav Tretiak prepares for what he now knows is to come. It doesn't take long for him to be tested. Storming down the wing Steve Shutt unleashes another slapshot. But this time Tretiak stops the blast with his right pad. The rebound is collected by the Red Army, who then make an attempt to clear the puck. Instead of clearing the zone, the puck comes to a stop on the blade of Montreal defenceman John Van Boxmeer's stick. Positioned at the point with one thought in mind, he launches his own slapshot. Tretiak with his view unobstructed sees the shot all the way and kicks it out with his right pad. The force of the shot carries the rebound to the other point, where Guy

Lapointe immediately fires it right back at a waiting Tretiak. "Three big saves there from the firepower of the Canadiens," exclaims a passionate Gallivan as the Red Army finally eases the pressure by clearing the puck. Gallivan's refrain of "big save" will be referred to so often that it will soon have all the novelty of a broken record before the game is over.

In between action on the ice, the camera often pans to the Red Army bench, and every time finds Loktev and his assistants furiously writing in their notepads. On the other side of the ice is Scotty Bowman, the only person standing behind the Montreal bench, his face an expression of glacial calm with not a notepad in sight.

Staying with the same on-ice personnel, the Canadiens once again hem themselves inside the Russians' end of the rink. Standing in the corner with the puck and with his back to the play is Pete Mahovlich. Remembering what he had been told in the meetings before the game, he takes his time. When he spins around he sees Cournoyer, in front of Tretiak, blanketed by two Red Army defenders. He makes the split-second decision to come out of the corner and carries the puck toward the front of the net unmolested. Quickly gaining ground on Tretiak, Mahovlich is startled to see the two Red Army defencemen are still holding their check on Cournoyer. Switching the puck from his backhand to his forehand, he avoids Tretiak's lunging goalstick. He now has the Soviet goalie at his mercy as Tretiak spreads out in an attempt to cover the shot. Shooting for the corner, Mahovlich is amazed at the sight of Tretiak's right leg springing from underneath his body and stopping the shot from crossing the goal line. In a post-game interview Mahovlich is asked about the play. "Well, I thought it just hit the corner of the post and it came back out at me, I just didn't have enough room. He played it exceptionally well. He didn't move off the post, he just sort of laid off, layered down. There was enough room there but I just didn't get it in."[19]

A besieged Tretiak will later write in admiration that "it seems as if the Canadiens are trying to exceed the limits of their talent. One shot follows another; they are all powerful and accurate."[20]

In the ensuing chaos in front of the Russian net, Shutt gathers in the loose puck and instinctively whips a pass back to the point. At the same time Shluktov's penalty expires, and he races back to the Russian end to help his teammates. Luckily for him and the Red Army, his path meets with that of Shutt's errant pass and he casually relieves the pressure.

In what is rapidly becoming one of the game's recurring themes, the Montreal defence continues to repel each and every Red Army offensive advance, causing turnovers at centre ice, which the Canadiens immediately convert into offensive sorties of their own. With only a few minutes gone in the second period, Murray Wilson is a beneficiary of one of these turnovers. Gaining the Soviet blue line, he passes to his onrushing teammate Jim Roberts, who uncorks a quick snapshot at Tretiak. Flashing out his left pad, Tretiak fends off the shot, but he kicks the puck out into the open slot where Wilson attempts to backhand the loose, bouncing puck. Making contact with the loose puck, Wilson watches it go past the outstretched glove of Tretiak, hears the crowd begin to rise and roar, feels the instantaneous shutter of a thousand cameras, and sees the goal light begin to illuminate – then hears the unmistakable clang of the crossbar as the puck ricochets off the top post and bounces into the corner.

Up in the broadcast booth an excited Danny Gallivan expresses the temporary heartbreak of a nation before yelling "the light went on" as the Forum crowd lets out a mass moan. Replays will prove what no one wants to admit; the puck off Wilson's stick hit the crossbar and the game remains 2–0 Canadiens.[21]

With the faceoff in the Russian end and the game inching toward the four-minute mark of the second period, the Canadiens seem poised to increase their advantage. In a rare instance, however, the Red Army wins the faceoff and Vasiliev retreats with the puck. Refusing to give up their strategy, he attempts to make yet another long, so-called "Hail Mary" pass to one of his forwards. Up until this point this play has been repeatedly thwarted by the active Canadiens defence. But on this one occasion Vasiliev's pass is true, hitting the blade of a speeding Boris Mikhailov at centre ice. The successful pass catches Serge Savard at centre and he is forced to skate back into his own end parallel with Kharlamov. Mikhailov goes one-on-one with Savard's defence partner Guy Lapointe, who stays in front of the charging Russian by backing in toward his goalie. Allowed this smidgen of room by the two Canadiens defencemen, Mikhailov pivots toward the slot and unloads a sudden wrist shot that splits Savard and Lapointe before deflecting right off the heel of Ken Dryden's moving glove and dropping behind him, the puck agonizingly edging over the goal line before a desperate Lapointe can reach it with his stick.

Canadiens 2, Red Army 1.

Mikhailov's goal stuns both the crowd and the Canadiens in its swiftness. It is the Red Army's first shot of the period, and only their fifth of the game. Suddenly a game that had been increasingly one-sided reads

2–1 on the scoreboard. Sensing that their team might need a lift, and with memories of 1972 still fresh in their minds, the crowd rallies, and for the next four minutes both teams go back and forth with Gallivan citing "a dire dearth of whistles here in the second period."[22] Fearful and recognizing the abrupt nature that seemingly characterizes each of their goals, each Russian chance, no matter how minor, is greeted with a yelp from the nervous crowd. This call and answer is only halted when Doug Jarvis is hauled down from behind as he reaches the Soviet blue line. Vyacheslav Solodukhin is assessed a two-minute tripping penalty at 7:38 of the second period.

In the broadcast booth, Dick Irvin turns to John Ferguson and puts voice to what most are feeling at this moment. "Ferg, this is hockey the way it should be played." Ferguson offers no objection: "It certainly is, close checking all around."

Bowman employs the unit of Lafleur, Mahovlich, and Shutt, backed up by Lapointe and Van Boxmeer, to start the power play. Right off the faceoff Mahovlich chases down the puck in the corner before passing to a waiting Lafleur whose one-timer goes to die in Tretiak's pad. "In the pre-game warmup Tretiak was stopping all of his shots on the low corner of the net with his goal pad," explains Ferguson during the resulting stoppage. "Most goaltenders stop them with their sticks."[23]

Once again, the Canadiens win another crucial faceoff, with Mahovlich immediately passing the puck to Lafleur who is in the crease area. This time, instead of one-timing the pass, he decides to take a couple of strides. The cool Tretiak doesn't commit, however, and shadows Lafleur before easily stopping his backhand attempt.

"What I remember most of all is Tretiak," referee Wally Harris later reflected. "When you're two or three feet away from a goalie you get a good look at him. That night, I never saw him make the first move. I can't remember a goaltender who could stare down the guys the way he did that night."[24]

The Russians soon clear the zone, forcing the Canadiens to regroup in their own end. Taking possession of the puck at his own blue line, Mahovlich lumbers his way through to the Russian end, all the way behind the Red Army net where he absorbs a two-hander from Red Army defenceman Alexander Gusev. The referees turn a blind eye to Gusev's two-hander; however, they aren't quite as charitable when he upends Mahovlich in the corner. Whistled at 8:23 for tripping, the Canadiens will now enjoy a two-man advantage for the next 1:15.

The eagerness of the crowd only intensifies in the wake of the second penalty. Bowman adjusts his five-man power-play unit, deploying Lapointe, Lafleur, Lemaire, Mahovlich, and Cournoyer. Their presence and the amount of time of the two-man advantage has the crowd nervously anticipating another Canadiens goal as the puck is dropped. "When you're up against a goalie that's standing on his head, you just gotta keep firing away," says Bowman today. "A goalie can make a difference in any game, especially in a one-game shot. [That night] Tretiak played as good a game in goal as I can remember."[25]

After two missed opportunities the Canadiens set up the power play in the Russian end, and the puck makes its way to Guy Lafleur, who is standing on the blue line at the right point. With plenty of time and space he steps up and unloads a powerful slapshot. Vladimir Lutchenko blocks the shot and the loose puck goes into the right corner of the Soviet end. Cournoyer retrieves it and follows the play to the left corner. He then sends the puck back to a waiting Lafleur, whose cannon of a shot flies over the top of the Soviet net, hitting the back glass before bouncing into the slot in front of Tretiak, causing a commotion, where it touches two Soviet sticks before coming to a rest on Cournoyer's blade. With ten feet between him and a screened Tretiak, Cournoyer fires a well-placed wrist shot that bulges the back of the net. Tretiak never does see the puck.[26]

Canadiens 3, Red Army 1.

While the players and the crowd emphatically celebrate, Dick Irvin attempts to say a few audible words over the crushing noise. The television crowd hears him say only two words – "tremendous atmosphere."

Luckily for the Red Army, Cournoyer's goal comes just after the first penalty expired, so the teams resume play at even strength with a little over ten minutes remaining in the second period. In an increasingly rare occurrence, the Red Army win the faceoff right after the Cournoyer goal and Vladimir Popov and Maltsev break in on a two-on-one with Pierre Bouchard, the only defenceman back. It is a rare shift for the popular Bouchard, the son of legendary former Canadiens captain Emile "Butch" Bouchard. Despite seeing relatively little ice time, Bouchard makes a stellar play on the odd-man rush, smothering the pass and the puck under his large frame. With the whistle, however, the Canadiens go short-handed, as a hooking penalty is assessed to Serge Savard.

In their first two power-play opportunities, the vaunted Soviet power play has failed to register as much as a single shot, yet there is a feeling within the arena that by taking penalties the Canadiens are indeed play-ing with fire.

However, much to the delight of those watching, and in large part due to the continued dominance of Doug Jarvis in the faceoff circle, the Red Army power play is stymied once again, and over the course of their two-minute advantage they are unable to set up in the Montreal end of the rink. For the Russians, the record is dismal, three power-play opportunities that have so far failed to produce even a single shot, much less a scoring chance. "The Soviets have been unable to get on track on the power play tonight," intones Danny Gallivan, "the tenacity of the checking of the Canadiens has been a thing of beauty."[27]

Yet after the power play's conclusion, the Red Army, for the first time in the game, is able to maintain some sustained pressure in the Montreal end of the rink. "Despite the fact that they've only had six shots on Dryden, they're a threat every time they have the puck," John Ferguson reminds the television audience.

With only four minutes left in the second period the enthusiastic Montreal crowd rises in appreciation of the home team's effort, as the Canadiens stymie yet another Red Army attempt to get past centre ice. "Canadiens doing forechecking of a tremendous magnitude right here," says Danny Gallivan.[28]

No sooner have these words left Gallivan's mouth than the Red Army's Vladimir Petrov starts out with the puck behind his own blue line. He is able to skate through centre ice, right past Montreal checker Jim Roberts. Gaining the Canadiens' blue line unobstructed he goes to his right near the far boards and drags three Canadiens (Savard, Lapointe, and Wilson) with him. With all three players focused on him, Petrov saucers the puck in a beautiful pass toward the centre that is picked up by an onrushing Kharlamov, who splits between Savard and Lemaire and softly slides the puck behind a sprawling Dryden.

Canadiens 3, Red Army 2.

In an instant the dangerous Kharlamov had struck. "I think he popped out of a hole in the ice," Dryden later recalled.[29] The goal was undeniably stunning as the three men in the booth readily admit as the replays roll across the screen.

"Beautiful setup," proclaims Gallivan.

"Here's Petrov, he's a great stickhandler, number sixteen. Now watch him slide this puck through to Kharlamov . . . a super goal," says Ferguson.

"One of the few times the Canadiens defense has sort of moved over and been a little too close together," observes Irvin.[30]

For the first time in the game, Bowman had broken up the Gainey/Lemaire/Lafleur line, and instead gone with a line of Wilson/Lemaire/Roberts, which is on the ice for the Kharlamov goal. It was a rare and costly manoeuvre by the Canadiens coach. Bowman returns to using the Gainey/Lemaire/Lafleur line and will keep it together for the rest of the game.[31]

Even though it was only the Red Army's seventh shot (three by Kharlamov and four by Mikhailov), they had closed within one goal of the Canadiens. One might have expected the stunned Canadiens to perhaps tighten up, play it a little close to the vest, in the period's last three and a half minutes, to ensure their lead heading into the dressing room for the second intermission. Instead, the Canadiens press their advantage in the Soviet end, but they are unable to put the puck past Tretiak. Larry Robinson finds Steve Shutt roaming the slot in front of Tretiak, but his shot is deflected over the net. Winning a faceoff in the Russian end, Mahovlich passes to a streaking Cournoyer who moves in unhindered right on Tretiak – who stops him cold.

When the siren sounds ending the second period, the mood in the Forum has slightly altered. There is no doubt that the Canadiens have taken the play to the Red Army. They are leading and have enjoyed a significant territorial advantage, controlled the faceoff circle and the pace, and have the overwhelming advantage in shots, 22–7. But there is an unmistakable feeling throughout the arena that – with just twenty minutes to go – the roof could cave in at any moment.

The Second Intermission. Howie Meeker is shocked. He has seen a lot of hockey in his colourful life and is considered one of the foremost experts on Soviet hockey. He has studied the Russians like few others, admires the way they play and practise. But tonight he has seen them thoroughly outplayed by the Canadiens. That the score is only 3–2 is a reflection of one man's performance.

"I think their [the Soviets'] whole game is built on offence, their defence – "

Meeker, in front of a national television audience, stops, laughs to himself, and then throws his hands up in the air. Then he continues with his original thought, picking up in mid-sentence right where he had left off.

" – Has got to be Tretiak, [he] played a fantastic period there. The Canadiens had four of five excellent scoring chances and I don't think you can't beat anybody." [32]

Following a commercial break, Dave Reynolds conducts a live interview with an enthusiastic Alan Eagleson. After some back and forth about the details of the series, Reynolds asks Eagleson what this series means to the sport and to the country as a whole.

"At the end of the second period, after watching two of the most exciting periods of hockey, I just can't remember anything as emotional with our players in that Canadiens dressing room before the game started tonight. Peter Mahovlich is six three, six four, but he was twelve feet off the ground, Cournoyer, Serge Savard, all these players are wrapped up and caught up in the emotion of playing great hockey players and to me that's what this series is all about. If we want to throw out our chests and say we're proud of our style of hockey and we think that we're the best, the only way to find out is to play the other fellows who think they are the best and the Russians think they are the best. They really do."[33]

The Third Period. "I'm really impressed by Tretiak," reiterates Ferguson, "even now before this period has started he's down doing his exercises, just a great goaltender."[34] The period begins with the matchup that has played out throughout the first forty minutes: Mikhailov, Petrov, and Kharlamov on one side, opposed by Lafleur, Lemaire, and Gainey on the other.

Once again the Canadiens win the faceoff and take control, effortlessly penetrating the Soviet end of the rink. Lafleur sets up a waiting Gainey at the side of the net, but he fires the puck wide of the net. The puck makes its way out of the Soviet zone temporarily, but is brought back in by an onrushing Lemaire. Valeri Vasiliev, the hard-hitting Russian defenceman, is waiting for him, but when he misses Lemaire with a hip check, he compensates by hitting him leg-on-leg, resulting in a tripping penalty with only twenty-seven seconds having expired in the third period.

Bowman switches around his power-play unit, sending out Mahovlich, Lafleur, Lambert, Lapointe, and Van Boxmeer. A power-play goal here will restore the Canadiens' two-goal lead and put the Red Army in a daunting position. "This has got to be a pretty big moment for the Canadiens," says Dick Irvin as the referee sets up to drop the puck.

Winning another faceoff the Canadiens' waste little time. Van Boxmeer unleashes a point shot, tipped by Lambert, Lapointe fires a point shot, and Lafleur unloads a slapshot. All of this takes a grand total of twenty-four seconds and the seemingly impenetrable Tretiak stops them all. In the broadcast booth an awestruck Ferguson can only muster two words, "Super goaltending."[35] Bowman makes some adjustments to his power-play unit. Mahovlich and Van Boxmeer take their leave as Lemaire and Savard enter the fray.

"Pete Mahovlich, Guy Lafleur, and Cournoyer are all playing excellent hockey," Tretiak later remarks, "hockey that is passionate, daring and honest."[36]

Montreal again wins the faceoff and Lapointe holds the puck in the Soviet end before sending it to Lafleur, who calmly moves to the slot and winds up for a slapshot that misses the net, then bounces to Lemaire in the slot. Lemaire immediately fires the puck at the net. Tretiak makes the save but can't control the rebound. Lambert is tightly engaged with Tsygankov, but wheels around and strikes the puck on his backhand. Tretiak deflects the oncoming puck in the air, where it hangs for what seems like an eternity before the Soviet goalie swats it away, then covers it up with help from his other defenceman, Alexander Gusev.

The crowd at the Forum lets out a gasp and stares in disbelief as Wally Harris whistles the play dead. In the broadcast booth, high above the action, Gallivan's voice reaches its highest octave, "Oh, what a save there on Lambert!"

"Boy, what else can you say about Tretiak the goaltender," adds Dick Irvin, giving a voice to what countless Canadians glued to their TV sets are thinking. "The Canadiens have just been all over them on the power play. They've had great chances but they have not scored."

The camera slowly pans to Tretiak who now takes up the entire screen. "There's the man of the hour right here in the hockey game," says Irvin.

Amid the praise for Tretiak, Gallivan points out that Serge Savard "has played an unflappable game for the Canadiens tonight; he's been on the move all the time."

"Murray Wilson started this game with a breakaway on the Soviet goal and the pace really has not slackened since then," claims Irvin. "Territorially, John, it's been all Montreal."[37]

The Canadiens' power play fails to score on the man advantage and after a stoppage in play Bowman sends out a five-man unit of Jarvis,

Wilson, Roberts, Awrey, and Robinson. Quickly gaining the Russian zone, Jim Roberts takes a point shot that Tretiak guides to his right corner, where it comes off the boards onto the stick of a waiting Murray Wilson. Gennady Tsygankov blocks Wilson's attempt at a shot and quickly gives chase at the near board for the loose puck. A pinching Don Awrey leaves his blue-line post and makes a dash for the loose puck at centre ice. Tsygankov arrives a split second before Awrey and chips the puck past him to Viktor Shluktov, who takes the puck in full stride, creating a two-on-one break with Boris Aleksandrov against Larry Robinson. In a valiant attempt to break up the pass between the two youngest players on the Red Army, Robinson attempts to make the most of his six-foot-four frame, spreading in front of Shluktov with his stick outstretched. The patient Shluktov waits for the sliding Robsinson to pass him by and flutters the puck over his stick to a speeding Aleksandrov, who has left a desperate Jim Roberts ten feet in his wake, something the Canadiens forward still retains to this day.

"I remember the winger I was covering, he went way back into his own end, and when he came back he had just too much speed and he went right on by me. It was just something that we hadn't seen too much of."[38]

Alexsandrov briefly carries the puck before wristing it on net, where it trickles through the webbing of Ken Dryden's glove and struggles to eventually cross the goal line.

Canadiens 3, Red Army 3.

"Fergie, these fellows are just annoying," announces an exasperated Dick Irvin, "that was a two-on-one break with Don Awrey trapped on the play. You just don't give them a chance."[39] Ferguson can't help but agree with Irvin.

This was the first and only time in the game that the Canadiens had permitted the Red Army a two-on-one break. Furthermore, it was only the Russians' second odd-man rush in the entire game. They had earlier scored on the three-on-two and now they had just converted the two-on-one.[40] Don Awrey, still haunted by the demons of 1972, has once again found himself on the wrong end of a crucial Soviet goal.

There is a dread that now grips the crowd as for the first time in a few hours they face the real possibility that the Canadiens might actually lose the game. Looking for a scapegoat, some of them focus on Dryden, who receives a smattering of Bronx cheers a few minutes later when he stops an errant puck following a Red Army offside. At this moment his noticeable shakiness doesn't inspire much confidence. With the game hanging in the balance and less than sixteen minutes remaining, the tension in the building rises as every little motion on the ice assumes a larger importance.

With the score now tied, both teams tighten up defensively. As the third period approaches the halfway mark, Lemaire shoots hard into the Soviet end from his own blue line. In what is clearly a set play, Guy Lafleur accelerates and gives chase, beating the icing only to stop at the sound of a whistle. Yuri Karandin, the Russian linesman, has whistled the play dead, under the mistaken belief that the NHL operates with a no-touch icing like they do in international play. The crowd, by now strained to the limit, loudly voices its disapproval and some will later look for something sinister in this mistake as Wally Harris gathers the two teams together for a centre-ice faceoff.

As the game enters its final ten minutes the Soviets seem content to ice the puck. Unlike the Canadiens the Red Army have only used three forward lines throughout the game; Bowman, on the other hand, has made use of all four of his lines. In a game played at such a quick pace, it is only natural that the Red Army team is steadily growing more tired. As a result, and because of the Canadiens' superiority in the faceoff circle, Guy Lapointe gets numerous opportunities to unload his powerful slapshot on the Red Army goal. He will finish the game with six shots on net.[41] A confident Tretiak turns them all aside. "He has a quick [glove] hand, John," notes Gallivan after another unsuccessful Montreal shot on goal. "He certainly does, Danny," echoes Ferguson. "He's been super tonight for the Soviet Union. He's been the deciding factor as far as I'm concerned."[42] Aside from the icings the officials now seem content to put their whistles away and leave the game in the hands of the players.

In response, the checking only gets tighter. In one instance Kharlamov breaks into the Canadiens' zone only to be relieved of his puck possession by a back-checking Lafleur. In another, Alexander Maltsev and Vladimir Popov come down on a seemingly harmless two-on-two against the Canadiens defensive duo of Van Boxmeer and Savard. Receiving a pass from Maltsev, Vladimir Popov calmly gains the Canadiens' blue line, before quickly darting to the centre of the ice in an attempt to split the defence. In the process he loses control of the puck, batting at it in mid-air past a now paranoid Dryden, and ringing it off the goalpost. Bouncing off the post, the puck comes to a rest underneath the Canadiens goalie. Banging his stick on the ice, a disappointed Popov slowly makes his way off the ice.

"There's 19,000 people collectively holding their breath every time the Soviets get inside the Canadiens blue line," states Irvin.[43]

The crowd, now jolted by the closest of calls, resumes chanting, "Go Habs Go." The close call also seems to reinvigorate the Canadiens, who now make a late push for the winning goal. Tretiak faces down a Gainey slapshot from twenty feet out and he is forced to be alert when Lafleur beats out another potential icing. With Vasiliev draped all over him, Lafleur pivots around on the side boards and leaves the puck for an onrushing Mahovlich who gently slides it over to a wide-open Shutt five feet in front of Tretiak, with no Red Army skater in sight. His stick at the ready, Shutt positions himself perfectly for the one-timer that he envisions putting past Tretiak, to give the Canadiens a 4–3 lead with less than five minutes left. But just as he moves his stick, providence takes over, and the oncoming puck, which hadn't left the ice, hits a bump and hops over Shutt's stick. As the crowd falls out in disappointment, Shutt's knees buckle as the realization of what had been missed dawns on him.

"He fanned on it," yells Gallivan in the booth. "He was all alone in front of the net!"

"To give Shutt a break I think it hopped right over his stick," says Irvin. "John, I can't remember a recent game in the NHL where the Canadiens have had so many scoring chances."[44]

"If the opportunity had been earlier in the period I think I would have had it," Shutt lamented later in the post-game, "but the puck didn't come across right. It wasn't really rolling but it wasn't flat either. If it had been at the start of the period before the ice got chopped up, it would have been different."[45]

"In the third period that could have been the one, afterwards I looked at the play and realized that I could have stopped it and then taken the shot," Shutt says today. "The way I played, when I was in front of the net I got the puck away as quick as I could. On that play, the puck just jumped at that wrong time. Sometimes goaltenders get lucky."[46]

In the concluding minutes of the game, during breaks in the action, the broadcast team begins to attempt to put the game in perspective.

"This has been quite a hockey game," says Irvin, "everything everybody thought it would be. John, no matter what happens from here this game has lived up to its advance billing right to the hilt and I think it's a tribute to both hockey clubs."

"It certainly has, Dick," answers Ferguson, "and it's just been great hockey by both teams, good stickhandling by both teams, good goal-keeping by Tretiak, he's just been super."[47]

With less than ninety seconds remaining Serge Savard commences a rare end-to-end rush, starting at his own blue line, to behind the Soviet net, before he is stymied by the Russian defence. Bob Gainey pounces on the loose puck and goes to the corner of the Soviet end and unsuccessfully tries to centre it out front. Gainey's pass hits Alexander Gusev's stick but the Red Army defenceman inexplicably proceeds to overskate the puck, leaving a fortunate Jacques Lemaire five feet in front of Tretiak with the puck on his stick. Lemaire immediately takes a wrist shot that Tretiak coolly kicks aside with his right pad. After taking the shot, Lemaire turns in an effort to maintain his position, and the rebound finds the blade of his stick. Backhanding the puck along the ice, Tretiak steers the puck into the corner as Claude Mouton announces throughout the Forum that this will be the last minute of play. As soon as Mouton finishes an excited Gallivan lauds "the scintillating saves by Tretiak."[48]

"The New Year's Eve game was a big turnaround for Jacques Lemaire," remembers Dick Irvin. "He played a great game that night. That turned his season around; suddenly in that game he became a force. He was outstanding, a bit of an eye-opener."[49]

Over the next few days many in the media will point to Lemaire as being the best Canadien on the ice that night. Despite that, he will not be named one of the game's three stars.

Taking control of the puck is Kharlamov, who enters the Canadiens' zone, raising the tension of the crowd. He attempts to centre the puck to his linemate Mikhailov, but Savard thwarts him and sweeps the puck away. Petrov retrieves the puck in the corner and fires it to Mikhailov in front of the Canadiens' net. With his back to the goal, Mikhailov backhands the puck toward a slightly unnerved Dryden. The puck manages to squirt through the goaltender's body and arm and dribbles behind him before Lafleur spirits the puck out of danger and then clears it away.

The Forum crowd is breathless, caught between delirium and panic as a flabbergasted Gallivan yells from the booth, "Dryden looked behind him."[50] For Ken Dryden the game cannot come to an end fast enough. With thirty-four seconds remaining in the game Kharlamov makes one last attempt to split the Canadiens' defence. But he is unsuccessful and the siren wails.

"The game is over and the Soviets and the Canadiens tie at three," announces Gallivan.[51]

With both teams slowly streaming off their benches toward their goal-tenders, Tretiak triumphantly raises his arm in the air, while a somewhat pensive Dryden removes his mask and accepts the congratulations of his teammates.

"John, it's just amazing that the final score is 3–3," comments Irvin, becoming the first to say what many will repeat in the days, months, and years ahead. "The shots on goal were 16–6 in favour of the Canadiens in the final period, 38–13 overall. I don't think we're being anything but fair to say that the Soviets were completely outplayed tonight, but we've just seen one of the greatest displays of goaltending that you could ever see."

"Just tremendous," agrees Ferguson. "I watched them yesterday in practice work so very hard, even the pre-game warm-up tonight. He [Tretiak] has all the moves, watches the puck, very seldom does the rebound go out, just a great hockey game. We couldn't ask for anything better."

"It has been a fine hockey game," concludes Irvin. "There was nothing untoward happening in the way of anything physical on either side. The officials did a good job. The story of the game has to be Tretiak."[52]

"The Canadiens just overwhelmed them from start to finish," says Red Fisher today. "The difference in the game was goaltending. The Canadiens' forwards and defence were as near perfect as [they] could possibly be but Tretiak delivered as good a goaltending performance as you'll ever see. He was it."[53]

Skating off the ice, Wally Harris can't help but think that this is one of the top games he's worked in his decade-long career as a NHL referee.[54] The players from both teams line up at centre ice and in the grand post-game tradition move down the ice shaking hands with one another. There is a palpable sense of dejection among the Canadiens that is impossible to overlook. Overcome with the emotions of the moment and still thinking of the puck that hopped over his stick only minutes before, Steve Shutt, as hard as he might try, is unable to hold back the tears that streak down his face as he shakes hands with his Soviet opponents. As soon as he shakes the last Red Army hand, he makes a hasty retreat to the dressing room. While everyone else is still focused on what is happening on the ice, he will take the time in the shower to gather himself together before coming out to face the inevitable crush of reporters.[55]

Traditionally CBC would now go to a set of commercials, but Ralph Mellanby, still firmly planted in the producer's chair, decides to go against the accepted protocol and stays with the unfolding story at the Forum as Claude Mouton begins to announce the game's three stars.[56] It was a bold move by Mellanby, and one that surely wouldn't have happened had the show been in another's hands. Mellanby, however, wasn't the only one who couldn't walk away from what was happening. Inside the Montreal Forum, none of that night's crowd has left, setting the stage for one of the most singular moments in the history of the building.

Free of his mask, a fresh-faced Vladislav Tretiak sits alone by himself on the Red Army bench as countless cameramen stand on the ice in front of him, snapping a seemingly endless string of photographs. There is no doubt that this evening has been his. Named the game's first star, a humble Tretiak skates to centre ice, where he is treated to a prolonged, heartfelt standing ovation by the Forum faithful. The Cold War was still raging and perestroika is still over a decade away, but on this night in Montreal there is a brief respite; a fleeting moment where there are no boundaries and no competing ideologies. Tonight, a sold-out crowd of close to nineteen thousand Canadians salute a hockey player from the Soviet Union. No doubt that the millions watching on their televisions feel the same way. Sitting in the production truck, a satisfied Mellanby knows that he has captured an unforgettable moment. "The Canadiens fans at the Forum really took Tretiak to heart that night," he recalls today.[57]

Peter Mahovlich and Yvan Cournoyer are the last two players left on the Canadiens bench. Tonight has been an evening of personal vindication for both men. For Peter Mahovlich, it marks the greatest performance of what has been widely described as an uneven career. For Cournoyer, who has burnished his big-game reputation once again, he has proved to the naysayers that he is still capable of being a force on the ice. The past year and a half has been a difficult time for him professionally. The ascent of Guy Lafleur and his own nagging injuries have seen Cournoyer unwillingly relegated to a secondary role. Once the most popular and biggest goal-scorer on the team, he has had his role usurped by the younger Lafleur. As a result his offensive opportunities have started to shrink, as has his output. "Cournoyer has gone through the wrenching experience of seeing age rip the overdrive out of his legs and as a result, has been forced to change his whole playing style," wrote Tim Burke in the Montreal *Gazette*. "Always a gritty competitor, the little guy played the best two way game of his life Wednesday night."[58]

As the clamour begins to die down, Mouton announces the game's second star. Serenaded by the organist and the fans, Mahovlich skates out to centre ice. Waving to the crowd, he makes his way to Tretiak and reaches out his hand, which the Soviet goalie clasps. The playful Mahovlich throws his arm around a surprised, but delighted, Tretiak.

Proclaimed the game's third star, a downcast Yvan Cournoyer slowly skates toward centre ice. As he approaches the first two stars, his face begins to noticeably brighten and his trademark smile reappears. Surrounded by the photographers, Mahovlich insists on putting the shy, reticent Tretiak into the middle of the troika as all three men put their arms around each other. The picture of the three men runs on all of the front pages of the country's newspapers. In a time of the Cold War, it is a stunning statement of athletic solidarity.

On a normal night at the Forum, Roger Doucet was free to leave the Montreal Forum once he had performed his anthem-singing duties. But tonight, he had waited in the shadows as the game played out, preparing for what would have been an unprecedented, emotional encore. Dick Irvin later revealed the reason why. "If Montreal had won that night they were going to have Roger Doucet come back out and sing 'O Canada.' I remember my wife who was at the game saying, 'If they had done that, I'd have cried like a baby . . . I don't think she would have been the only one."[59]

Eventually the three players take their leave and begin to skate back to their respective dressing rooms. In the production truck, Mellanby finally cuts away to the commercials.

In a few minutes, the show goes back into the studio with Dave Reynolds and Howie Meeker. "Well, it finished tied at three, Howie," says a crestfallen Reynolds. "I'm a little disappointed; I'm a lot disappointed to be quite honest with you. I think the Canadiens had the run of the game pretty much, shots on goal were 38–13 as it finished. What do you think?"

In response, Meeker laughs as the two make light of his pre-game comments. "Just a great, great hockey game, you know what it proved, and the big fellow I think coming in here will agree," as Peter Mahovlich enters the studio for his interview.

What follows is one of the most memorable interview segments in the history of *Hockey Night in Canada*. After discussing strategy and the brilliant play of Tretiak, a clearly distraught Mahovlich lowers his head and shakes it back and forth while muttering to himself. The emotion plays out on his face. After wishing out loud to be included on the prospective Team Canada for the 1976 Canada Cup, a nomination seconded by Meeker and Reynolds, Mahovlich speaks from the heart.

"I just wish everyone a new year and we tried our best and a lot of Canadians depended on us, were with us in '72 and those that followed the '74 series . . . on behalf of the Montreal Canadiens I apologize, we didn't win [he laughs nervously], but we tried."

An amazed Reynolds steps in. "Peter, I don't think you have to apologize one bit. I think you played the finest game, the team has played the finest game I have seen it play in I don't know how many years . . . just excellent hockey." Meeker then chimes in to reiterate what Reynolds said, "You don't have to apologize for that effort, it was unbelievable." He then hits Mahovlich in the arm to further put his point across. "Look, it's the greatest entertainment in the world today, played by the greatest people, whether you're from Canada, the United States, Czechoslovakia, or Russia. This is just a true, skillful, exalting hockey game."

"It was definitely that," counters a sheepish Mahovlich.

"That's what it's all about," says Meeker.

"It certainly is," responds Mahovlich, "and the way they played, it brings back memories of the way we used to play it on the pond, really. You used to be able to take a puck and get your head up and not have to worry about a stick across your ears or whatever and to me that's the way I love to play and its great playing against competition like that."

After the television interview, a spent Peter Mahovlich stretches out in the dressing room on the team's rubbing table and continues to answer reporters' questions. Sam Pollock walks into the room to personally congratulate him on what has been a defining game for the twenty-nine-year-old. "Are they doing anything tomorrow night?" asks Mahovlich, hoping for another go at the Russians. Pollock silently replies with a pat on the big man's shoulder before taking his leave. Mahovlich springs up off the table and follows Pollock out of the room. "Sam, seriously, are they doing anything tomorrow night?"[60]

The twin pangs of regret and disappointment reverberate through the Montreal dressing room. "We made only four mistakes in the whole game," admitted Larry Robinson, "and they scored on three of them. On the fourth one, they hit the inside of the crossbar."[61]

"After the game I went to the Red Army dressing room first out of courtesy, and then I went to the Canadiens dressing room, speaking with Sam Pollock and Scotty Bowman, and the players," Alan Eagleson recalls. "They were a little bit down, because they felt they could have won, but I told them that they had put on the best show. That game was as exciting and as emotional as it would have been for a Stanley Cup finals game, not only for the players and the management, but for the fans. There was a unique feeling in the building that night. In fairness, it probably took a year or two for the players to come to the realization that the game had been an historic event, and as each year goes by it only increases in stature."[62]

"There was some disappointment in the tie," says Jim Roberts today. "But it was such a great game. After it was over you thought to yourself, maybe that's the way it should have ended. We wanted to win that game, but it was such a thrill to play in that game."[63]

The largest crowd of reporters gathered around the dressing-room stall of Ken Dryden. Many would point to him after the game and beyond as being the sole reason the Canadiens didn't emerge victorious, and Dryden himself would later label it the most disappointing game of his distinguished career. Amid the media crush surrounding the Montreal goaltender, Red Fisher decided to take a different, more patient approach.

"I remember going into the dressing room that night and Dryden was, of course, surrounded as he always was after every game. I just stood off to one side. After my colleagues had left the room, I was alone with Dryden and I said to Ken, 'Happy New Year.' And then I said much to Dryden's dismay, 'You screwed up,' and he thought about it for a few seconds and said, 'I guess I did,' and he had."[64]

"The criticism of Dryden was unfair," counters Scotty Bowman. "The Russians don't take a lot of shots, they were not a team that went for a lot of shots, they went for the perfect shot, the one you couldn't stop. It's not easy for goalies to play in twenty-shot games or less, because that one shot they're getting once in a while can be very difficult."[65]

In spite of the disappointment, there is also a feeling within the walls of the dressing room that the Canadiens have laid to rest the fears of Soviet hockey superiority and a Canadian deficit on the ice.

"I don't think our hockey is so bad," Scotty Bowman commented after the game. "I don't think we have to take a backseat to anybody. They were outclassed for 60 minutes except for the goaltending . . . We outplayed them and that's what important."[66]

Standing in the dressing room Guy Lapointe is multi-tasking: putting on his street clothes and calmly speaking about the game. "We've just proven that there are still excellent hockey players in Canada. I've always been proud to be a member of the Canadiens and I'm equally proud tonight. I don't want to take anything away from the Russian players. They played well, but it's not as though they are hockey gods. We outclassed them tonight. We were ready physically and mentally. We should have won the game, but what can you do? Tretiak was miraculous in net. It was really impressive to watch the likes of Mario Tremblay, Doug Jarvis, and Doug Risebrough, who really held their own. Every player worked hard. In my case, I felt just as strong at the end of the game as I did when it started. Curiously, I barely sweat a drop tonight. The fans were very supportive. In short, we'll enjoy New Year's Day."[67]

"Of one thing I'm sure. God was a Russian tonight," commented Serge Savard, half-seriously.[67] "If he's not, then how do you explain a tie when we outplayed them by so much?"[69]

Soon all the players are dressed. Joined by their families they will ring in the New Year with their traditional team party put on by the Canadiens ownership at Molson Breweries.

As has always been the custom, the Red Army locker room is closed to the media after the game. Only their coaches come out to speak to the assembled media. "We did not play our best game, but that is partly because of the good game played by the Canadiens," admitted Konstantin Loktev. "Still, a tie is a tie and it is better to have one dollar in your pocket than none."[70]

The hockey world will have to wait a couple of years to get the opinion of the player that they want to hear from most. "The game in Montreal left us with a very good impression," Tretiak writes in a book a few years later. "In my opinion, this was really super hockey, fast, filled with combination plays, tough – but not rough – with an interesting and dramatic script."[71]

"On a club level, it was probably the best game ever played, it was very skillfull, very intense," admitted Boris Mikhailov, years after the fact. And despite the time in between he can still rhyme off the names on the Montreal roster.[72]

After they finish dressing, the Red Army players are escorted to the Soviet consulate for a pre-planned New Year's Eve reception. "I think that everyone was satisfied with the outcome," Tretiak later writes. "A few minutes before midnight, highlights of the game were shown on television. When the color commentator returned to the screen, he dumped confetti over his head and exclaimed, 'Hurray it's a tie. Happy New Year!' And so ended an unforgettable evening."[73]

Now off the air, Ralph Mellanby gathers all of his talent, from both the English and the French broadcasts, and invites them to the restaurant above the Forum, La Mise au Jeu, where they all share a drink and discuss the game. By no means was this a regular get-together and in his entire career with *Hockey Night in Canada* it is the only time that Mellanby can recall such an event taking place. But for all of them this was truly a special night, one that they all wanted to savour.

Mellanby receives two phone calls the next day that only serve to reinforce how special and unique the New Year's Eve game had been. He finds out that according to the official broadcast numbers five million Canadians had watched the game. However, Mellanby to this day believes that the number should be higher. Extrapolating from studies of similar events and factoring in the many people watching at parties, bars, and so on, then it is more likely that *eight million* people watched the game, which among a population of twenty-three million (at the time) was pretty amazing.[74]

The second phone call is of a more surprising nature. "The day after the game I received a call from a friend of mine in Ottawa, who worked for the federal government," Mellanby says today. "He told me that during the time that the game was on, crime across the country dropped by fifty percent, compared to what it was the year before. It seems that everyone, including the criminals, stopped everything they were doing to watch that game."[75]

PART FOUR

THE AFTERMATH

"This is not only a victory for the Canadiens; it is a victory for hockey. I hope that this era of intimidation and violence that is hurting our national sport is coming to an end. Young people have seen that a team can play electrifying, fascinating hockey while still behaving like gentlemen."

SERGE SAVARD, 1976

19.

PHILADELPHIA

Montreal, Quebec, January 1, 1976. Sportswriter Jim Coleman launched the year by giving shape to the thoughts of those who had witnessed the remarkable Canadiens/Red Army encounter on New Year's Eve. His first column of 1976 spoke for many a Canadian.

"The performance of the Montreal Canadiens on Wednesday night was, without question, the finest which has been given by an individual hockey team within the limits of my memory," wrote the sixty-four-year-old in his syndicated column. "It was superbly exciting entertainment. Les Canadiens and Soviet Central Red Army demonstrated conclusively that ice hockey, at the very height of excellence, is a game of speed and skill and stamina. Just give us those end-to-end rushes and the rocketing shots on the net – and to hell with shoddy tactics such as intimidation, high-sticking, and brawling . . . The type of hockey on display New Year's Eve was the best that one could ever hope to see in this country. As pure hockey, it was even better than the memorable 1972 series between Team Canada and the Soviet national team."[1]

A reminder of what hockey could be, the game was a victory for those who preferred to see the game played with beauty and style.

"The Habitants regained a great deal of the NHL's sagging prestige with an extraordinary effort against a super team," wrote Frank Orr in the January 1 edition of the *Toronto Star*. "Come to think of it, the game of hockey really benefited last night."[2]

The buzz from the New Year's Eve game continued in the days that followed, with both the media and the public analyzing and dissecting it from all angles. With a week before the Red Army took to the ice again for their next game in the Super Series (against Boston on January 8), the media had time to digest all that had happened on New Year's Eve. The Canadiens too had time to absorb what had happened, though the game would stay with them for much longer.

"That game was so good I had flashbacks," Larry Robinson later wrote. "I'd be in the middle of a league game a couple of weeks or a month later, and I'd suddenly tune out, clearly visualizing specific things that had happened on New Year's Eve."[3]

After years of debate, hand-wringing, public inquiries, and police investigations, here was the most persuasive argument yet against the violence that had infiltrated the game at all levels, from youth and amateur all the way up to the professional ranks. The Canadiens and the Red Army in the course of sixty minutes had showcased the sport at its most elegant, in an exhibition contested with finesse and grace, which highlighted skill, sportsmanship and, above all, the beauty of the game.

Ever since the Russians had arrived in Montreal, Frank Orr, like many of his newspaper colleagues, had eagerly sought out an interview with one of the members of the Central Red Army team. The veteran newsman from the *Toronto Star* had been keen to set up an interview with Valeri Vasiliev, the defensive strongman on loan to the Red Army from his regular team back home, the Moscow Dynamo. However, Victor Khotochkin, the interpreter travelling with the team, had kept Orr at arm's length.

Finally, on a day when the Red Army was taking some rare time off, Orr got his opportunity. Walking into the Queen Elizabeth Hotel on New Year's Day, Orr unexpectedly bumped into the touring Russians, who were having their lunch in the Saint-Laurent dining suite. Vladislav Tretiak, disappointed that he couldn't find a newspaper that published on New Year's Day, wasn't even bothering with lunch, and had instead bought three chocolate bars from the hotel's gift shop and retreated to his room. Valeri Kharlamov, his most famous teammate, was a little more raucous, entering the hotel's dining room carrying a large portable stereo with the volume cranked up so loud that, in the words of Orr, it "placed whitecaps on the teacups."[4] Playing the part of court jester, the comedic Kharlamov was the life of the party, keeping up a steady stream of talk and leaving laughter in his wake.

The other Russian players boasted a wide assortment of fashion styles. Some were clad in their Soviet-issued tracksuits, while others were in brand-new blue jeans (status symbols back home), with Alexander Maltsev's still sporting the tags, and Boris Aleksandrov's too-long pair cuffed up five inches from his ankles. Coming from a country where everyday items like food were strictly rationed, the Russians couldn't believe how readily available certain items were, such as soft drinks and chocolate bars and potato chips, which they ate to the fullest.

"The players ate their lunch quickly," observed Orr, "most taking their selections from the dessert tray, washed down with soft drinks. Every player took at least three bottles with him when he left. Centre Vladimir Petrov had six 7-ups and only slightly less than a bushel of grapes."[5]

After closely studying the players, Orr returned to his main mission, persuading Khotochkin the interpreter to get him an interview with Vasiliev. Finally, after much pleading from Orr, a timid Khotochkin walked over to the imposing Russian blue-liner. Having just finished his lunch, Vasiliev seemed amiable, and he and Orr sat down for what would be a twenty-minute interview. After speaking about his life in and out of hockey, Vasiliev elaborated on the Soviets' main purpose for participating in the Super Series, stating that the Olympics and World Championships were their top priority and that this series of games represented "an opportunity to test candidates for the national side against top competition."[6] When Orr asked him about the game the night before, Vasiliev responded, "The Montreal Canadiens were an excellent team. I'm sure we learned something from them and they from us. That's the best product of these international friendly matches."[7]

Vasiliev's gracious comments did not extend, however, to the subject of Orr's next question. When Orr mentioned the Philadelphia Flyers, Vasiliev slowly raised his hand high over his head, his palm parallel to the floor to indicate a level and said, "Canadiens"; then he lowered his hand so that his palm fell below his waist and muttered, "Philadelphia."

"Canadiens are much the strongest team among the professionals," came the interpreter's translation of Vasiliev's words. "Philadelphia is a much lower-rated team."[8]

But before the Red Army's much anticipated showdown with the Stanley Cup champion Flyers, there was a game in between – in Boston against the Bruins.

Boston, Massachusetts, January 8, 1976. An intensely private man, Bobby Orr had grown accustomed to publicly masking his emotions.

But tonight as he watched the Central Red Army face his team, the Boston Bruins, in his building, the Boston Garden, he couldn't conceal his dismay. With his bad knee forcing him to observe the game from the stands, Orr, who had always shied away from attention, helplessly watched along with thousands of other spectators as the Red Army scored two goals in the third period to seal their 5–2 victory over the Bruins. As the last seconds ticked off the scoreboard, many in the disappointed, sold-out crowd at the Garden couldn't help but look his way and wonder what might have been.

"God, I'm disappointed," he admitted to the *Globe and Mail*. "I really wanted to play them. For godsakes, the last time I played them I was 16. It's really funny, everyone keeps asking me what they are like as a club, and I haven't played them since I was 16. All I've been doing is watching, and from that, I think they are a hell of a club. I missed them in '72. Last year when they were supposed to come over, I was ready and they didn't come. Now they are here, and I'm not."[9]

Bobby Orr was now twenty-seven years old. He was undoubtedly the greatest hockey player of his generation, and he inspired awe in those who shared the ice with him. These unabashed feelings of adoration even extended to the touring Soviets. Upon their arrival in Boston a few days before the game the Red Army was granted a tour of the Bruins' dressing room. The Russians were captivated by the luxury and decor of the room, which was starkly different from their own accommodations back home. Then they saw a hanger holding Orr's white jersey with its black number four.

The Red Army players approached it with a reverence usually reserved for a religious article. One by one the players touched Orr's jersey, as well as his sticks and the assemblage of his equipment lying on the floor in front of his vacated locker. Overseeing the eerie scene was Frank Torpey, the NHL's head of security. "They just kept touching everything that was his, stroking his sweater and stuff. It was really strange."[10]

Orr's hero status among the Russians was also displayed later. One of the Red Army players was dismayed to discover that three of his sticks had been mistakenly shipped back to the Soviet Union. This left him with only one stick for the remaining two games and the Bruins trainer was asked if he could find him a few spare sticks. The trainer returned with six sticks for the player. The other players noticed the name Orr stamped on their sides. Almost immediately, a pitched battle ensued for the Orr sticks, and at the end of the scuffle six players – none of them the player who actually needed the sticks – emerged with one each for his own personal collection.[11]

In the interval before this game, the Red Army had gone to a local movie theatre and watched *Jaws*, taken in a concert, and attended a Boston Celtics game, but more than anything they wanted to catch a glimpse of the great Bobby Orr. Every day the Russians would practise at ten in the morning; the Bruins would practise an hour later. Much to their delight one morning, the Russians discovered Orr on the ice by himself, practising before their own scheduled workout. Unfortunately, due to the lingering effects of surgery on his left knee, Orr quickly realized he would not be able to play against the Red Army. The touring Russians would get a brief chance, however, to meet the one North American player they idolized above all others. Through an interpreter he shared with them his frustration about not playing. Ironically, the visiting Russians attempted to console the wounded superstar by assuring him that there would be more chances in the future.[12]

What none of them knew at the time was that Bobby Orr would never again play in a Boston Bruins uniform.

Philadelphia, Pennsylvania, January 11, 1976. The Red Army's victory over the Bruins, along with the Soviet Wings' wins over the Chicago Black Hawks and the New York Islanders, had clinched the Super Series in the favour of the touring Russians. In seven games, the two Russian teams had won five, tied one, and lost one, a 12–6 drubbing administered to the Wings by the Buffalo Sabres on January 4.

On a Sunday afternoon they would wrap up the Super Series at the Philadelphia Spectrum by facing the two-time defending Stanley Cup champions. In both Montreal and Boston, the touring Russians had been greeted and treated in the spirit of friendship and goodwill. Arriving in Philadelphia they quickly found out that they entered hostile territory. "During the reception, held two days before the game, they made it perfectly clear that they had no intention of associating with the Soviet players," Vladislav Tretiak later recalled. "The Stanley Cup winners demonstrated their highly unfriendly, if not hostile attitude. Nobody came over to welcome us."[13] Unlike the previous stops on the Series, there would be no tours of the dressing room, sharing of sticks, or, as it turns out, post-game photos of the Red Army and their opponents arm in arm.

No one felt the stress of the Philadelphia game more keenly than Konstantin Loktev, the Red Army's head coach. With overall victory in the Super Series guaranteed, Loktev was facing incredible pressure from those in high positions within the Soviet hierarchy to bring home a healthy team because the Olympic Games were set to begin in less than a month. "I felt that, even if we won the game with Philadelphia but returned home with injuries, there would be some kind of punishment for me," Loktev later admitted.[14]

In an effort to avert any potential trouble, a nervous Loktev sought out Fred Shero, the Flyers' head coach, and stated his hope and desire that both teams, in the spirit of goodwill, could play their upcoming game honestly and cleanly. "Shero told me it was very difficult for him to work with his team because of two players – Bob Kelly and Dave Schultz . . . Shero said he never knew what these two were going to do at any given moment."[15]

Whether this was said by Shero with a straight face is unknown, but for him the game against the Red Army was a matchup for which he had waited his whole professional life. Amid all that was written and said about the Philadelphia Flyers of the mid-seventies – Bobby Clarke, Bernie Parent, the Broad Street Bullies, and so on – little notice had been taken of the fact that, unlike the vast majority of his North American hockey coaching brethren, Shero had quietly been a long-time student of the Russian game.

A little over a decade before, while coaching in St. Paul, Minnesota, Shero stumbled across a book written by Anatoli Tarasov. "That book became my bible," he later admitted. "I've read it at least 100 times."[16] From Tarasov he incorporated the idea of five-man units playing as one, and when this concept was paired with his belief in intimidating through aggression, Shero found the tonic that had been so successful in Philadelphia. And yet, despite the success, Shero wasn't satisfied, and that may help to explain why only three days after the Flyers' first Stanley Cup championship in 1974, he boarded a plane as one of one hundred Canadian hockey coaches invited to a clinic in the Soviet Union.

"Even now I still don't know all there is to coaching," he admitted to *Sports Illustrated* in the spring of 1975. "I'm still learning, which is why I went to Russia for a coaching clinic last summer. At least I realize I don't know everything. Trouble is, most coaches don't know – and certainly won't admit – that they don't know everything about coaching."[17] That may have helped to explain the fact that on the plane ride to Moscow, of the one hundred coaches who took up the Soviet invitation to the coaching clinic, Shero was the only one who coached an NHL team.

Shero's game plan for the Red Army was simple but effective. As opposed to Scotty Bowman and the Canadiens, who forced the Russians into making mistakes by using a tenacious forecheck and by dropping three players at the centre red line, Shero came up with the idea of not chasing the puck at all. Simply put, he would allow a single player (usually the centre) to forecheck up to the Soviet blue line and then circle back, while posting his other four players straight across his own blue line. In theory, this would take away from the Soviets two of the most lethal parts of their offensive game – the odd-man rush and the potential long "home run" pass. Furthermore, the Flyers, after watching the Canadiens and the Bruins wildly outshoot the Red Army, felt confident that they could control the puck, and since they wouldn't be challenged on the boards, that they would enjoy plenty of time to be judicious in their play selection. The other part of the strategy was well known to those who made up Philadelphia's opposition in the NHL. The Flyers were instructed to physically punish the Red Army at every opportunity, instill fear in them, and make them play the Flyers' style of game.

Right from the beginning it was clear that the atmosphere in Philadelphia was very different from the one in Montreal eleven days before. "Clarence Campbell and I walked into the Spectrum an hour before game time," remembers Alan Eagleson. "Aggie Kukulowicz came running over to us and said 'Al, the Russians aren't going to play.' I said why, he told me to take a look, and we walked into the Philadelphia Spectrum and there were, oh god, fifty banners of different sizes saying, 'Free Soviet Jews,' in Russian, I didn't know what the hell they were. I called Ed Snider, the Flyers' owner, over and I told him, you can't do this, they're our guests."

Snider informed Eagleson and Campbell that "the American Jewish Society were going to boycott the game and they convinced him to put up these posters." An agitated Eagleson told Snider that the protests were "'none of your bloody business and furthermore the Russian players aren't involved in politics.' I asked what he would have thought if the Flyers were playing in Russia and signs were up saying 'Free American Blacks.' Much to his credit, Ed gave the order to have the signs pulled down."[18]

The signs may have been pulled down inside the Spectrum, but outside the arena people coming to the game were confronted by an unfriendly air. When the Red Army players were introduced that day there would be no welcoming applause for the visitors, only boos and catcalls. For Fred Shero and his Flyers, this game was for nothing less than the unofficial World Championship of hockey.

"As far as the game is concerned I believe it's going to be the highlight of my life," claimed Shero in the pre-game interview broadcast live throughout North America. "If we win I'm going to be sky high and if we lose then I think it will be worse than dying. I'm ready. My team is ready and I believe we're going to win."[19]

The game had barely begun before Loktev's biggest fears were realized. The first ten minutes of action saw the Flyers not only physically impose their will on the Red Army but openly mug them. Boris Mikhailov had his face punched with Dave Schultz's glove one minute and André Dupont's stick waved under his nose the next. Both Alexander Maltsev and Boris Aleksandrov felt Ed Van Impe's stick in their stomachs while Bill Barber went headhunting, first with his stick and then with his elbow. And to top it off, Bobby Clarke gently tapped again and again at Kharlamov's ankle, as if the Russian needed to be reminded of what had happened the last time they met.[20]

Deeply imbedded within the Russian players' psyches were the memories of Clarke's vicious slash on Kharlamov in 1972, and Rick Ley's bloody beat down on Kharlamov in 1974. Loktev was determined not to allow a repeat occurrence. The final straw came at the 11:21 mark when Van Impe left the penalty box and made a beeline for an onrushing Kharlamov, belting him to the ice. It was clear to Loktev that his best players were being targeted by the Flyers.[21] Seeing Kharlamov, his best player, lying immobile on the ice and witnessing the inaction of Lloyd Gilmour, the referee, forced Loktev to take drastic action.

In a move reminiscent of his mentor Tarasov from his years earlier in Moscow, Loktev called his players to the bench in protest. When Gilmour assessed the Red Army a two-minute penalty for delay-of-game, an irate Loktev ordered his players back to their dressing room. "I decided to stop the game to show North Americans that this is not hockey," he later recalled. "I understood my decision to do this was a very serious one . . . But I didn't want to have the first line injured."[22]

Sitting in their dressing room, the players on the Red Army team presented a united front, in full support of their coach's decision. "No Red Army player wanted to play against the Philadelphia Flyers," Tretiak later wrote. "Each of us could have been hit from behind, cross-checked, kicked – what kind of sport was this? It had nothing at all in common with the sport of the hockey."[23]

After a sixteen-minute delay the Red Army, bolstered by assurances that the play would be cleaner, returned to the ice. The game was quickly resumed, and just sixteen seconds later the Flyers made good on the delay-of-game penalty when a Reggie Leach tip made the score 1–0. But in reality, the game's competitive phase was over; the Red Army, in Tretiak's words, "did not play, we merely skated."[24] Eager to let the clock run down and get off the ice, the Russians offered nothing more than token resistance in the Flyers' 4–1 victory.

In the eyes of the Flyers, and of some in the media, it had been a great triumph. "We are world champions," declared Shero in the victorious Flyers' locker room as his players celebrated.[25] The next day's front page of the Montreal *Gazette* opined that "the Philadelphia Flyers salvaged Canada's pride in her national sport with a near-perfect hockey master-piece here yesterday to beat Russia's best, the Central Red Army Team of Moscow, 4–1 . . . They accepted their victory with restraint and dig-nity and for that they are the most exemplary professional organization in all sports."[26]

There were others, however, who felt that the Flyers' win was a great deal less than a triumphant victory. "In their patriotic contribution to the Bicentennial celebration, the Broad Street Bullies, alias the Philadelphia Flyers, alias the Stanley Cup champions, dissected the touring Soviet Army hockey team Sunday, 4–1, and upheld the Spectrum's reputation as the cradle of licensed muggings," wrote the *New York Times*. "The triumph of terror over style could not have been more one-sided if Al Capone's mob had ambushed the Bolshoi Ballet dancers. Naturally, it warmed the hearts of the Flyers' followers, who would cheer for Frankenstein if he could skate."[27]

Serge Savard, like the vast majority of the hockey world, had watched the entire game from the comfort of his living room. Eleven days before he had played against the same Red Army team in a game that many believed showcased hockey at its most elegant. From his point of view, what he witnessed that Sunday afternoon on his television screen was the complete antithesis to that. Even now, after the passage of many years, he still bristles: "What happened in Philadelphia was a disgrace."[28]

20.

THE WHITE HATS VERSUS
THE BLACK HATS

The 1976 Stanley Cup Finals were about more than the trophy. A battle between the seamy and the stylish, this clash was a deeply personal one between two teams that not only disliked each other but played the game in sharply disparate ways. The Philadelphia Flyers and the Montreal Canadiens were battling each other, and the future direction of hockey was at stake.

"The Flyers thought they could win the game playing that way in the National Hockey League," Serge Savard says today. "The Montreal Canadiens didn't see it that way. We didn't think we could win with violence and we did everything we could to keep Philadelphia away from that. The sport did not need that."[1]

For the hungry Canadiens, the road to the finals and the dream encounter against the Flyers was the culmination of a season-long journey. "There was a great sense of quest that season," Ken Dryden later remembered. "We had not won the Stanley Cup for two years. The Flyers were champions, so we chased them – over the summer, in training camp, in every game we played. We left them behind in the standings; we chased what they had been, and still might be. We chased them until May; and caught them."[2]

Montreal, Quebec, September 20, 1975. The parameters of the Canadiens' mission had been set nine months before in a series of back-to-back exhibition games against the Flyers. Montreal was prepared to face a Philadelphia team composed of regulars, rookies, and those eventually destined to spend the upcoming season in the minors. The Flyers were prepared to send a message.

What transpired that evening was an intense game characterized by an unusual amount of talking, post-whistle scuffling, and sometimes downright nastiness. Dave Schultz, the lead enforcer of the Broad Street Bullies, targeted the Canadiens' newly announced captain, Yvan Cournoyer, who became the victim of a well-placed cross-check in the back. In his own unique way, Schultz was challenging the entire team, daring them to respond. For the past two seasons this type of behaviour had largely gone unchecked, allowing the rampaging Flyers to run roughshod over an intimidated league.

On this night, however, one person decided to take a stand. Despite being at a distinct height and weight disadvantage to his larger tormenter, a fearless Doug Risebrough immediately jumped on Schultz's back as the referees waded into the fray. It was a rough conclusion to the Flyers' 5–4 victory, and it set the stage for the all-out explosion that would take place in the game the next evening in Philadelphia.

The Montreal Canadiens team that showed up at the Spectrum was distinctly different from the one that had skated at the Forum the night before. Scouring through their training camp roster, Sam Pollock and Scotty Bowman had hand-picked a lineup every bit as imposing as the Flyers'. Players like Sean Shanahan, Glenn Goldup, Pierre Bouchard, and Rick Chartraw, each of them standing over six feet tall and weighing more than 200 pounds, were inserted.

"Our reasoning was simple," Larry Robinson later admitted. "If we could eliminate the Flyers' physical edge, or contain it, our superior hockey skills would allow us to beat them. If we could strip away Fred Shero's system, the flaws underneath would be exposed. As good as Clarke, MacLeish, Barber, and Leach were, Lafleur, Shutt, Mahovlich, Cournoyer, Lemaire, et al. were better. And it was time to prove it. The war came early. It couldn't even wait for the season to start."[3]

Simmering all night, the expected explosion came as the clock was winding down in the third period. With the game already over three hours' old, the score 6–2 in the Canadiens' favour, and the penalty minutes approaching the century mark, Doug Risebrough decided to respond to Schultz's challenge from the night before.

Skating back to their respective benches with ninety-five seconds left on the clock, Risebrough and Bobby Clarke heatedly exchanged insults.

There were few in the league as skilled at trash talking as Clarke, who was emboldened because of his backup. "Guys stay away from me because they know Dave Schultz or Bob Kelly or someone will beat them up," Clarke admitted to *Sports Illustrated*. "We've got to protect our leader at all times," added an unrepentant Schultz.[4] A highly skilled agitator, Clarke was not above informing his potential tormentors of what awaited them if they touched him, and many would frustratedly skate away. As a result, Clarke enjoyed a sort of immunity and was able to play and act accordingly.

In that moment, Risebrough did the unthinkable. In full view of the Flyers bench he dropped his gloves and began unmercifully pounding the Philadelphia captain.

Seeing their captain bloodied, the Flyers erupted. Led by an enraged Schultz they leapt over the bench, only to be greeted by a wave of red, white, and blue. Suddenly, the Spectrum ice was littered with gloves and sticks as fights broke out everywhere. The brawl lasted more than ten minutes, and before it was over that night's referee Bruce Hood had assessed a further 250 penalty minutes to the game's total, in addition to fifteen game misconducts. Rather than dropping the puck, an exasperated Hood decided to prematurely end the game.

The competitive dynamic between the Montreal Canadiens and the Philadelphia Flyers had forever been altered. "That preseason game did a lot for us [toward] winning the finals months later," Steve Shutt concludes today. "We'd established ourselves. They had a pack mentality and we proved we could match them."[5] Shutt had earlier remarked that "we won the Stanley Cup that night. It wasn't just official until next May. If you are going to beat the Stanley Cup champions, you have to beat them at their style because they dictate the game. Philadelphia was a tough team so we had to prove that we were tougher, to break them mentally. And even if we didn't win all the fights, which we did anyhow, they knew that fighting us was not going to help them."[6]

"It was too late for Philadelphia," Larry Robinson later remembered. "We had ended the Broad Street Bullies. Never again would they dictate their system or style of game to us, and eventually the rest of the league."[7]

It's hard to picture Larry Robinson ever being overlooked. Yet that was the case at the Queen Elizabeth Hotel in Montreal on June 10, 1971. In that day's draft, the Montreal Canadiens had already selected Guy

Lafleur with the first overall pick, and the team's brass was now going over their options for their next pick, their fourth in the draft, and the twentieth overall. Claude Ruel, part assistant coach, part assistant general manager, and part scout, had found a player he desperately wanted to take with the twentieth selection.[8] Impressed by Ruel's fervour, Sam Pollock allowed him to take the pick he wanted above all others. Hearing his name, Larry Robinson was initially less than enthused about his future destination. Newly married with a young family and needing money, he dreaded the thought of how long it might take him to crack the Montreal lineup, if he could make it at all.

Not surprisingly, the Canadiens sent Robinson to Nova Scotia, where they set about moulding him. Taking one look at the six-foot-four, 195-pound youngster, Voyageurs coach Al MacNeil took his charge aside and offered simple yet effective advice. "Larry, there are guys in the NHL who made it primarily on their aggressiveness. They didn't have a hell of a lot of skill. You have a lot of skill and you also have something else a lot of these guys don't have: Size. I want you to start using that size to your advantage. With aggressiveness and your size, plus your skills, you can be twice the player you are."[9]

In his year-and-a-half tenure with the Voyageurs, the eager and attentive Robinson learned to use his size as a form of intimidation. In addition, he refined his slapshot and built his strength. Already a quick skater, he sharpened his offensive instincts while honing his defensive knowledge. As a reward for his progress, Robinson was called up to Montreal in the first days of 1973, and despite being used sparingly he never looked back. Tutored relentlessly by Ruel, Robinson began to steadily improve and he was a regular by the 1973–74 season.

But it was in 1975–76 that Larry Robinson really began to blossom, and he and his defensive partners, Serge Savard and Guy Lapointe, became famously known as "the Big Three." No team, before or since, has had the luxury of having three elite defencemen on their blue line. Perched behind them was Ken Dryden, who had a first-hand look at Robinson's transformation into one of the most complete defencemen in the sport.

"In the next few years, more than just an outstanding player, Robinson became a presence. It had to do with being so big, so strong, so tough, so agile, that no one knew how good he was, and no one wanted to find out . . . anything you can do, he can do better . . . so what's the use. He had a numbing reputation, an imperial manner, and the goods to back them up, a game rooted in defense, opportunistic on offense, limited, economic, and dominant. He was the rare player whose effect on a game was far greater than any statistical or concrete contribution he might make. When he came onto the ice, the attitude of the play seemed to change. In 1976, Robinson discovered the big man's game."[10]

His discovery was not welcome news for the Philadelphia Flyers.

The first game of the 1976 Stanley Cup Finals did not follow the predicted script as the visiting Flyers jumped out to a surprising 2–0 first-period lead over a noticeably nervous Canadiens squad. However, as the second period began, Montreal began to assert themselves, taking the physical play to the Flyers and putting pressure on their goalie, Wayne Stephenson. With an injured and ineffective Bernie Parent watching the proceedings from the end of the bench, Stephenson found himself facing the awesome responsibility of trying to stop the Canadiens' potent offensive attack. Though the Canadiens were increasing the pressure, the lead remained at 4–3 with ten minutes to go. Unfortunately, the Flyers were unable to maintain it, as Jacques Lemaire, rapidly building his big-game reputation, tied the game when his backhand found its way past a screened Stephenson. The game appeared to be heading to overtime, with only eighty seconds remaining, when Guy Lapointe carried the puck on a two-on-one rush alongside Guy Lafleur, with the Flyers' Joe Watson the last line of defence. Everybody – Watson, Stephenson, and probably Lafleur – thought that Lapointe would pass the puck. Instead, the Montreal defenceman swung wide of Watson and from twenty-five feet out slapped the puck past Stephenson and into the far side of the net. The Flyers frantically tried to tie the score but were repeatedly repelled by a now confident Dryden.

With their physical advantage negated, the Flyers were at the mercy of their opponents. If the first game had been a showcase for the speed, mobility, and offensive skills of the Canadiens defence, the second game advertised the Montreal blue-liners' aggressiveness and physical advantage.

The Flyers' top line of Clarke, Barber, and Leach, holders of a league-record 141 combined goals in the regular season, were held to a measly three shots by the Canadiens' superb defence. "They've checked us so closely that you can tell what brand of deodorant they're using," declared a frustrated Gary Dornhoefer. "I'd like to take one stride, just one stride," complained another Flyer, "without some Canadien fighting me for the puck."[11] Montreal's dominance extended to the faceoff circle, where Clarke, widely considered the sport's finest, was being schooled by the upstart Jarvis. The result was that the Canadiens found themselves controlling the play while the Flyers chased them.

But it was two mistakes by the Flyers' own defence corps that would turn the tide of the finals' second game.

The first mistake occurred after thirty-five minutes of tightly played, scoreless hockey, when the Flyers were granted a power play. Gathering the puck to start an offensive rush was Philadephia defenceman Larry Goodenough. Carrying the puck out of his own end, he appeared to be in control. Looking up the ice, he suddenly felt the puck leaving his stick. Before he could react, Jacques Lemaire picked Goodenough's pocket, steamed in all alone on Stephenson, and broke the scoreless deadlock.

At the start of the third period, a similar Flyers' mistake led to the winning goal, when Tom Bladon got his skates and the puck tangled, allowing Guy Lafleur to break in on the Flyers' end. Using defenceman Joe Watson as a screen, Lafleur niftily placed the puck in the top corner of the Flyers' net. With the Canadiens in full control, up by two goals and threatening to take a two-game lead in the series, Larry Robinson stepped to the fore. What followed was the watershed moment in the series.

Over the course of the first two games, Robinson had been a force, using his offensive talent, defensive acumen, and physical skills in equal measure. Now he would put his own personal exclamation point on the Canadiens' supremacy over the Flyers. "I never have trouble getting up for games against Philadelphia," Robinson later admitted. "When you play the Flyers, there are more opportunities to hit people."[12]

With the third period just having passed the eleven-minute mark, Gary Dornhoefer, desperate to get his Flyers back in the game, lugged the puck along the near boards. From his left defence position, Robinson began to angle toward him, hoping to get a hip into him, while at the same time carefully playing possum. He wanted Dornhoefer to believe that he could make it past him. At the precise moment that the Flyer forward took that fateful stride, Robinson rapidly accelerated, driving his immense body into him just inside the Montreal blue line. The force of the blow was staggering, as both men after colliding with each other and then the boards tumbled to the ice. Almost immediately, play was halted by the referee. The crowd and the players gasped. Robinson's hit had left an indent of a full inch in the boards.

For the next few minutes the game ground to a halt as a group of Forum workmen used hammers and crowbars to fix what Robinson had broken. .Eventually, they succeeded in banging the board back into its old place but the memory and a slight indentation remained.

"He had done it with crushing ease," Ken Dryden later wrote, "no cross-ice leaping, elbowing, high sticking charge; just simple 'aw shucks' destruction, the kind that leaves behind the shuddering hint of something more to come. He had delivered a message – to the Flyers, to the rest of the league, to himself. A series that had been moving our way found its irrevocable direction . . . The Flyers held him in such awe, treating him with an embarrassing, almost fawning respect, that they seemed even to abandon their style of play when he was around, and with it any hope of winning."[13] A late goal would make the game appear closer than it had been, but the 2–1 final allowed the Canadiens to take a commanding two-games-to-none lead in the series.

"In the two games here," wrote the *Toronto Star*, "the Canadiens' superior speed, quickness and depth was their advantage when integrated into a sound tactical approach."[14] The intimidators had become the intimidated.

Now, on the eve of the third game, the upstart Canadiens appeared to hold all the advantages, offensive, defensive, and physical. "Going into Philly we knew that game three was going to be the game," remembers Steve Shutt. "We just had some great playoff players that were fearless, we had more talent than Philadelphia, and we didn't back down."[15]

Setting up shop five miles outside of Philadelphia, the Canadiens chose to stay across the Delaware River at the Cherry Hill Inn in New Jersey. The team was so keyed up that many of them played countless games of pool at night as opposed to sleeping. The tension and anxiety only increased as the team made their way to the hostile Philadelphia Spectrum for the third game. Before most games the Canadiens' dressing room was a casual place, with each player engaging in his own private rituals and much joking and socializing as the players gradually put their equipment on. This game was different.

"A half hour before the warmups, the whole team was fully dressed in our road reds, impatiently waiting for the buzzer to signal the warmup," Larry Robinson later recalled. "We were pacing up and down, chomping at the bit, and raring to go. Even after we came back from the warmups, most of the guys had trouble settling down."[16]

But the Flyers still had two aces up their sleeve: the Philadelphia

Spectrum and Kate Smith, their good-luck charm. Rarely in sports has there ever been a more unlikely combination than the wartime radio star and the Broad Street Bullies.

Six and a half years earlier when the Flyers were still a young franchise and America was a country in turmoil, instead of playing the traditional "Star-Spangled Banner," the team's vice-president, Lou Schienfield, made the decision to play a patriotic song, hoping that it might spark a sparse, otherwise uninspired crowd. Testing various songs in an empty Spectrum, Schienfield finally decided on Kate Smith's "God Bless America," for no other reason than it sounded the best in the arena. First played before a December 11, 1969, win against the Maple Leafs, the song developed a reputation as something of a good-luck charm for the Flyers. The decision to play Kate was in the hands of Schienfield, who decided on a game-to-game basis.

Game three of the 1976 Stanley Cup Finals would be the 52nd time that the song had been used, either by recording or in person. The Flyers resulting record was an astounding 47 wins, against 3 losses, and 1 tie. With both teams lined up at their respective blue lines, the recording was cued.

The Flyers drew comfort from the inspiration the song provided. Meanwhile, standing on their own blue line, the Canadiens were a nervous and excited bunch, unable to keep their skates still. The slow pace of the pre-game festivities only increased their anxiety. Larry Robinson later remarked that the public address announcer had sped through the Canadiens' introductions but had taken twenty minutes to leisurely introduce the Flyers.[17] Usually, the players stood at attention for the anthem, then skated a circuit or two in their own end, lightly tapping the pads of the goaltender as they skated by, before assuming their positions for the opening faceoff. Tonight, however, as the lights dimmed and the voice of Kate Smith began warbling over the loudspeaker, the hyped Canadiens one by one took off from the blue line. With the song playing, the defiant Canadiens began skating circuits, but at top speed, and not at the usual relaxed pace. Also, instead of fereling a light tap on his goalie pads as his teammates went by, Ken Dryden later recalled that his pads had acted as a form of protection against the hard sting of his teammates' sticks.

In an effort to shift the momentum of the series and to capitalize on the frenzy created in the pre-game, Fred Shero, the Flyers coach, employed a starting line of Don Saleski, Dave Schultz, and Bob Kelly, the three most infamous Broad Street Bullies. Aiming to intimidate the Canadiens, Shero was immediately forced to retract the line from the ice when Scotty Bowman countered with his top offensive line of Peter Mahovlich centring Steve Shutt and Guy Lafleur. A complete mismatch, the message from Bowman and his team was clear – the time to intimidate had passed.[18]

The Flyers had been noticeably tepid in the series' first two games, purposely steering clear of their usual aggressive tactics. But tonight, with their backs to the wall and emboldened by the emotion of being at home, their natural aggressiveness returned. Less than two minutes into the game Bill Barber took an elbowing penalty. On the Canadiens' subsequent power play, Steve Shutt, nearing the end of his shift, shot the puck from mid-ice and headed toward the Montreal bench when suddenly he heard the cheers of his teammates.

"I was the last guy in the place to know I'd scored," Shutt confirmed in the Canadiens dressing room after the game. "I fired it on the net to make the line change, saw it dip but figured he stopped it."[19] Instead, the puck, shot from eighty feet away, dipped and deflected off of Stephenson's glove into the net. It was a devastating goal and took the wind out of the Philly crowd's sails.

Yet the Flyers, showing the championship heart that had served them well through their title reign, refused to buckle under. In the series' first two games Bob Gainey had thrown a cloak around Reggie Leach, and with the exception of his goal in the first twenty-one seconds of game one, Gainey had proven to be startlingly effective. But with eight and a half minutes passed in the first period of the third game, Leach found some space on a Flyer power play and tied the score after a feed by Clarke. And then, ten minutes later on a rare Montreal giveaway, Leach once again struck, giving the Flyers a 2–1 advantage. Leach was a pure scorer, gifted with an unbelievably quick release, and he was riding an unbelievable hot streak now, having scored 18 goals in fifteen playoff games. "Leach can score while you blink," admitted Gainey. "He's hard to cover because once he touches the puck he shoots it on the net."[20]

Holding a tenuous lead, the Flyers unwisely took another ill-timed elbowing penalty, this time by Dornhoefer. And, once again, Steve Shutt exploited the resulting man advantage, stuffing the puck behind Stephenson to tie the score at two. The impact of Shutt's second goal, however, went beyond the scoreboard. In the first two games of the series the Broad Street Bullies had toned down their aggression to avoid penalties. Increasingly desperate, the Flyers reverted to what had always served them best. But their strategy backfired, as the Canadiens had taken advantage of their two power-play opportunities by depositing the puck in the back of the Philadelphia net.

With the score now tied at two apiece and the second period rolling around, the Philadelphia Flyers were caught in an untenable position. If they played their style of game they were bound to be whistled by the referees for any infraction and that would open the door for the Canadiens' strong power play. So the Flyers abandoned their rough-housing style, which allowed the Canadiens to impose their style of offensive pressure combined with defensive suffocation. In a straight matchup of hockey acumen the Canadiens enjoyed a wide advantage over the neutered Flyers.

As the second period continued, the score remained tied at two, but the tide began to turn as the Canadiens began to take control of the game. A besieged Stephenson was barely holding on, stopping successive breakaways by Murray Wilson and Yvan Cournoyer. It had been widely thought that Scotty Bowman would be unable to maintain his line matchups against the Flyers' top guns like he had in Montreal. Possessing the last change, Shero had hoped to free up Clarke and company, but the Canadiens coach was able to switch his personnel on the fly to get the matchups he wanted, frustrating Shero to no end.

With the score tied, it was amazing that the third period was played without a single penalty being whistled, a fact that clearly favoured the Canadiens. Halfway through the third period, the inevitable finally happened, although it came from a very unlikely source. With Dave Schultz jostling with Montreal's Rick Chartraw, the seldom-used Pierre Bouchard received a pass from Murray Wilson and threw the puck at the net from forty feet away. Screened by the two bodies in front of him, Stephenson never saw the puck that went past him and gave the Canadiens an imposing three-games-to-none series lead.

A sense of unavoidable dread now enveloped the Flyers as defeat loomed large. Even Bobby Clarke, a man who had accomplished so much in his career through sheer will and determination, was forced to admit that those two qualities wouldn't be enough. "Canadiens are just the best hockey club I've seen since I came to the NHL [in 1969]. Their work in their end of the rink has been exceptional. It's one hell of an advantage when a team has three of the best six or seven defensemen in the world. Our best game is fore-checking and sustaining pressure in their attacking zone. But their defensemen are so fast that we just can't seem to pin them in,[21] we can't sustain any pressure on them at all."[22]

In the background at the Spectrum, Sam Pollock was able to witness first-hand his greatest creation come to fruition. He had built this team from the ground up, a squad that could win playing any type of style, against any type of opponent. At the end of game three there was a sense that the Canadiens were not only on the verge of winning the Stanley Cup but also on the brink of another dynasty.

"During the past few National Hockey League seasons there's been little argument with the claim that the Montreal Canadiens possessed the most pure talent in the league," opined the *Toronto Star* the day after game three. "Now they've added muscle, experience and discipline and are one game away from what could be a lengthy hold on the Stanley Cup. In short: another Habitant dynasty has fallen into place this season."[23]

After their third straight victory, the Canadiens were anything but complacent. "We still had a mission after game three in Philadelphia," remembers Murray Wilson today. "We actually closed the dressing room for ten minutes after the game and had a team meeting. Serge Savard and Jacques Lemaire, who didn't say much, reiterated to us, 'We're one game away from accomplishing something we want to accomplish.'"[24]

The past few months had transformed thirty-year-old Jacques Lemaire. Seen by many as a talented player who had never lived up to expectations, Lemaire had finally found his niche, both within the team and within his sport. Lemaire was a revelation. Often critiqued in the years before for shying away from the physical aspects of the game, he was now regularly named as one of the team's hardest workers and one of the sport's pre-eminent two-way players. In addition, he had assumed a leadership role with the team. Yvan Cournoyer may have carried the captaincy but the Canadiens team was blessed with a strong assemblage of leaders who always ensured that the team kept its focus.

Immediately after the third game the Canadiens flew home on an overnight flight to Montreal. Sam Pollock wanted to avoid the usual hi-jinks associated with being a visitor in a hostile city, such as fire alarms, late-night phone calls, and other attempts to keep his players awake. He even went so far as to unsuccessfully petition the league to have the Canadiens fly back into Philadelphia on the morning of the next game. However, after practising at the Forum, the Canadiens flew into Philadelphia the day before, as per league policy.

Theirs was not the only flight arriving in Philadelphia. A desperate Ed Snider had decided to play his last trump card. In game three the Canadiens had overwhelmed the good-luck charm that was Kate Smith and "God Bless America." But her presence had only been through an audio recording. With his team facing elimination, the Flyers owner parted with ten thousand dollars of his own money and brought the good-luck charm straight to Philadelphia.

This would be the fourth time that Kate Smith had personally performed "God Bless America" in front of a rabid Philadelphia Spectrum audience. In each of her three previous appearances the Flyers had left the ice victorious. With the two teams lined up on the blue line for the fourth game, the Philadelphia Spectrum went dark, a single spotlight focused on the red carpet that was being rolled out. With the crowd reaching the edge of pandemonium, Kate Smith entered on the carpet and began belting the song that the world associated with her. And with the lights out, the Canadiens began doing what they had done a few nights before: swiftly skating in their own end of the rink and swinging their sticks at Ken Dryden's pads with great force. As Miss Smith finished and the lights came up, the crowd wildly applauded, only to discover that the visiting Canadiens were boldly circling in their own end.

At first, the good-luck charm appeared to work for the Flyers. After only thirty-one seconds, Reggie Leach unleashed a forty-five-foot shot past Dryden. Leach's nineteenth playoff goal gave Philadelphia a quick 1–0 lead. With their continuing reign at stake, the Flyers then played their best two periods of the final, leading by a score of 3–2 as the second period slowly drew to its conclusion. But as time wound down, Gary Dornhoefer took an unfortunately timed hooking penalty. Sitting in the box, he watched the clock intently, hoping that it would reach zero with the Flyers still ahead.

As the clock ticked down – 20 seconds, 19, 18 – Larry Robinson took the puck and charged up the ice before feeding the puck to a waiting Guy Lafleur, who promptly fired the puck toward a waiting Stephenson – 15, 14, 13 – Stephenson made the stop but, stretched out on the ice horizontally, he was in no position to block the rebound, which bounced toward the stick of Yvan Cournoyer. The Canadiens captain calmly shovelled the loose puck over the helpless Flyers goalie, tying the game at three apiece with eleven seconds left on the scoreboard clock.

Not only did Cournoyer's goal provide the equalizer but it also appeared to deflate the hopes of the Flyers. The stress and pressure of their third consecutive trip to the finals, the intense media and political attention, and the supremacy of the Canadiens seemed to finally wear them down. While the champions noticeably waned in the final period, the surging Canadiens seemed to gather strength. "Their injuries were catching up with them," Peter Mahovlich later observed. "They were really dragging, I was sure we'd get the break eventually."[25]

The sold-out crowd at the Philadelphia Spectrum and a North American television audience were witness to a gradual yet inevitable changing of the guard as the reluctant Flyers slowly and grudgingly relinquished their throne. All that remained was for the Canadiens to reach out and grab the championship. The series had been dominated by Montreal's defence, with their offensive superstars operating quietly in the background. Now, as the clock wound down in the third period, the Canadiens' top line would apply the killing stroke.

With less than six minutes remaining in the game and the Canadiens on the offensive, a blocked shot created a state of confusion within the Philadelphia zone, and Pete Mahovlich, spotting a wide-open Lafleur, took full advantage, passing the loose puck from the blue line toward the league's top scorer. Perched all alone at the side of the net, Lafleur made no mistake and calmly deposited the puck into the back of the net. Less than a minute later, the two reversed roles, with Mahovlich sweeping around the Flyers' net and backhanding a Lafleur setup into the goal, making the final score 5–3 for the conquering Canadiens.

The last minutes of the game played out against a silent backdrop at the Spectrum. Accepting the Stanley Cup from NHL president Clarence Campbell, Yvan Cournoyer held the Cup aloft and led his teammates in a skate around the rink as the vanquished Flyers quietly left the ice.

The Montreal Canadiens had successfully completed their year-long crusade. They had swept aside the infamous Broad Street Bullies and in the process launched a new era, in which speed overwhelmed brawn, skill overcame brutality, and, above all, the sport of hockey triumphed.

Moments later, in the crush of humanity between the two teams' dressing rooms a thirteen-year-old boy was attempting to squeeze his way into the victorious Canadiens' dressing room. After much wrangling, the teenager was able to amble up to Scotty Bowman and get the head coach's attention before handing him an envelope. Opening the envelope, Bowman read its contents.

"Congratulations on such a fantastic season. You're truly champions – not only of the league, but of the world."

The letter was signed Fred.

Inserting the letter back into its envelope, a humbled Bowman looked down at Raymond Shero, the son of the Flyers' head coach, and thanked him.[26]

All of the predictions and discussion of the Canadiens being a potential dynasty were not only fulfilled in the years ahead, they were arguably exceeded.

The 1975–76 season saw the Canadiens set new records for wins and points, win twelve out of a possible thirteen playoff games, and culminated in a convincing sweep of the two-time defending Stanley Cup champions. Many teams would have been content to rest on these achievements. But for the Montreal Canadiens of the mid- to late 1970s the sweep of the Flyers represented not an ending but a new beginning.

The conquest of the Flyers would be the first of an eventual four consecutive Stanley Cup championships. Yet that impressive record only hints at the scope of their dominance. Over the course of those years they would play in 378 regular season and playoff games, and emerge with a record of 277 wins, against only 56 losses and 45 ties. Individually, the Montreal players would win a total of sixteen NHL awards and sixteen All-Star selections, during their four-year reign at the summit of their sport. In addition to Sam Pollock, their general manager, and Scotty Bowman, their head coach, nine players on that team would one day be enshrined in the Hockey Hall of Fame.

For Scotty Bowman, all of it began with the game against the Central Red Army on December 31, 1975. "The New Year's Eve game was a stepping stone to our team starting to really gel, once we saw how confident we were after that game, I always felt that the game had a real positive impact on our team, we had a young team and that game made us realize that we were in elite company."[27]

The Canadiens' victory and the Flyers' defeat sounded the death knell to an era that had been defined by mayhem and violence. From now on the most talented and skilled teams would battle for the Stanley Cup as teams based on the Flyers model slowly faded into obscurity. That summer the NHL Players' Association would propose a complete ban on fighting, but the owners would only agree to a new rule calling for a major penalty and misconduct to the player who deliberately started a fight. A few months later, the Flyers would trade their lead enforcer, Dave Schultz, as they began the process of reshaping their team. Over time, the Flyers would remain the league's most aggressive team, and while they would revel in their roughhousing past they would never again fully embrace that style of play. Thirty-five years later, they are still seeking that elusive third Stanley Cup championship.

AFTERWORD

Montreal, Quebec, January 10, 1983. Instead of going to their jobs on a cold winter's day, thousands chose to spend their Monday morning making the trek to the Montreal Forum. That day the arena would throw its historic doors open, free of charge, allowing anyone to come and watch an open practice. Fifteen thousand fans filled the seats and warmly applauded as they watched their Canadiens go through a leisurely ninety-minute workout, which featured a skills competition at its conclusion.

Under normal circumstances, that workout would have been the end of the show, but after the Zamboni had resurfaced the ice the main attraction took to the ice. In the lead among the players was Vladislav Tretiak, greeted with a prolonged standing ovation. Then the touring Soviet National Team took to the ice and went through their own, rigorous ninety-minute workout.

"I was very surprised with the reception we received when we came on to the ice," Tretiak later admitted to the gathered media. "The response of the young fans was overwhelming for us. There were many young hockey players watching us train, and maybe they'll learn something and be better players."[1]

Much had changed in the seven years since the Red Army and the Montreal Canadiens had first clashed on December 31, 1975. With the dissolution of the WHA a few years before, the NHL was now made up of twenty-one different teams, and their rosters, which had once been almost exclusively Canadian, now contained the best players from all over the world – Sweden, Finland, Czechoslovakia, and the United

States. As a result the NHL was beginning to go global, with one major exception: the Soviet Union.

In the years since the historic New Year's Eve game, the public's appetite for best-on-best encounters among the world's hockey nations had grown. Less than four months after the Canadiens swept aside the Flyers, the inaugural Canada Cup was held. For the first time the best players represented their own countries in a round-robin tournament in which Canada, led by the gallant Bobby Orr, defeated Czechoslovakia in the finals. Another Canada Cup would follow five years later, with Tretiak backstopping the Soviet Union to the championship at the Montreal Forum. There was also the Challenge Cup, a three-game series held in 1979 between the Soviet National Team and the NHL All-Stars, and the continuing Super Series, which would become a semi-annual affair as touring Soviet teams faced off with various NHL teams in a series of exhibition games.

For the Russians, Tretiak had remained a constant in a period of instability. Vladimir Petrov and Boris Mikhailov had both retired. Their linemate, the spectacular Valeri Kharlamov, had died in a car accident in 1981. It was a time of transition in Soviet hockey and a new generation of stars had entered the scene, such as Slava Fetisov, Igor Larionov, and Sergei Makarov. But for the Montreal fans that morning in 1983, the sole focus of their rapt attention was Tretiak.

Vladislav Tretiak was thirty years old that day and recognized as one of the greatest goaltenders in the world, not to mention one of the most recognizable Russian citizens in the world. And he was surely the most beloved. As the Soviet practice ended, almost five hundred fans pushed their way through a police barricade and surrounded the great Russian goaltender. Children asked for his autograph, men to shake his hand, and women to embrace him.

"The Canadian people understand us," said a grateful Tretiak. "When we were in Minnesota and Philadelphia, I couldn't wait to get back to Canada. It's nice to be in a place where you have the feeling that people like you, respect you."[2]

Any political, cultural, and linguistic differences that years before may have divided Tretiak and the Montreal people were now long forgotten, bridged by the bond they shared in their love of the game of hockey.

—

Montreal, Quebec, June 8, 1983. The first wave of excitement in the annual entry draft had passed. The top prospects had already been taken. The Montreal Forum, crowded a few hours before, was now full of empty seats as Serge Savard, former star defenceman and current general manager of the Canadiens, debated who to select with the team's ninth selection, the 138th pick of the draft.

Savard shocked his colleagues and stunned those still in the building by selecting Vladislav Tretiak. Like many of his teammates, Tretiak had long dreamed of playing in the NHL, and in particular with the Montreal Canadiens. As more and more of his former European competition moved to ply their trade in the NHL, Tretiak's desire had only grown greater. He had shared his wish with Wayne Gretzky during the Great One's visit to Moscow in the summer of 1982. "He wanted to play for the Canadiens for two seasons when his USSR career was over," related Gretzky, "after the 1984 Olympics, a title the Soviets lost to the U.S. at Lake Placid in 1980 and very badly want[ed] back."[3]

"I still think he's the best goaltender in the world," Savard maintained after selecting Tretiak. "I'd like to have him playing here and I believe that's what he wants to do."[4] The Soviets, still waging the Cold War, would have never released Tretiak to an American-based team, but the Canadiens were a different matter. An eager Savard made four trips to Moscow in the winter months of 1983/84, and the Soviets, aware of Tretiak's retirement plans and advancing age, entertained his offers.

A hopeful Tretiak began preparing for the move in the spring of 1984, but then Soviet officials broke off talks with Savard and vetoed the transfer. Tretiak was a lieutenant-colonel in the Russian Army, and the official reason for the veto was that the country couldn't let a Soviet soldier, whose father had held the prestigious rank of major in the Soviet Union, emigrate to Canada and play professional hockey in the NHL. Upset with the rejection, a defiant Tretiak decided to retire from the sport at the age of thirty-two. Still at the peak of his powers he undoubtedly still could have continued his career. Years later he said that retirement was the only way he could register his protest with the authorities who denied him playing for the Canadiens.

"I'm mad about it because I would've liked to have played in the NHL," Tretiak reflected. "I would've liked to win the Stanley Cup. It was a joke. The Russian government said that my father was a big general, but it was not true. They said he was a very proud father and didn't like me to move. Nobody even asked me if I would like to go to Canada or not. I would've liked to go, but it wasn't possible a long time ago."[5]

Five years later, the Soviet government, crumbling under the weight of the Cold War, finally gave permission for one of its players to go to North America and play professionally in the NHL. But for Tretiak it was too late. Sergei Pryakin became the first Russian from the national team to play in the NHL, suiting up for the Calgary Flames on March 30, 1989. The following year saw the top players from the Red Army join the NHL, and after the dissolution of the Soviet Union in 1991 and the end of the Cold War, the floodgates opened, and all of the best Russian players joined the NHL.

Less than three months after Pryakin made his debut with the Flames, Vladislav Tretiak received the ultimate honour – induction into the Hockey Hall of Fame. He was the first player enshrined who had been born and trained in the Soviet Union.

Montreal, Quebec, January 29, 2007. Few retired players can claim to have had a post-hockey career as interesting, varied, and successful as Ken Dryden. A lawyer, a best-selling author, and a Member of Parliament, Dryden is, however, still in many Canadians' hearts and minds first and foremost a goalie. His stoic stance in front of the net, chin resting on hands calmly folded on the butt end of his goal stick, is a quintessentially Canadian image and has been reproduced in countless photos, on book and magazine covers, and on posters that hang on many a young boy's bedroom wall.

The sport had changed significantly in the twenty-eight years since Ken Dryden had stood guard in the Montreal Canadiens net. The Canadiens, long the dominant team in the sport, had only won two Stanley Cups since his departure, and none in the past fourteen years, a record drought for the proud franchise. The tradition may have endured, but on the ice the team was now just one of thirty franchises in an NHL growing ever more bloated, and the club struggled each year just to qualify for the playoffs. The days of expecting a parade each spring down Ste-Catherine Street were now a distant memory.

The Montreal Forum, the cathedral of hockey, had closed its doors for good in 1996, a victim of changing times and economics. Replaced by the Bell Centre, the new arena added four thousand extra seats and innumerable luxury suites, among other essential modern amenities.

Eventually the Forum was turned into a shopping and entertainment complex, part mall, part movie theatre. As the team counted down the years to its upcoming centennial in 2009, the organization looked to its proud past to find a sliver of hope for its uncertain future.

Honouring the team's history included the retiring of numbers of players who had contributed so much to the storied Canadiens past. In 2006, Serge Savard had watched his number 18 raised to the rafters. The year before, Yvan Cournoyer's 12 joined the numbers of the Richard brothers, Jean Béliveau, Jacques Plante, and other Canadiens immortals.

Tonight it was Ken Dryden's turn, and it would happen before a sold-out crowd at the Bell Centre of over twenty-one thousand people and a live nationwide television audience. For many the evening would bring back a host of cherished memories.

With the lights dimmed the ceremony commenced, with a video montage played on the Bell Centre's video scoreboard as Dryden's incredible statistical record was read out over the loud speaker. The video showed the evolution of his career, from his debut in the spring of 1971, to the Summit Series of 1972, the New Year's Eve game in 1975, the dethroning of the Flyers in 1976, and the subsequent Stanley Cup triumphs in 1977, 1978, and 1979. As the video came to an end, the feeling of nostalgia warming the arena, the scene on the screen shifted to a live image of the present-day Montreal Canadiens dressing room. There, clad in his familiar red, white, and blue number 29 jersey, with his back to the camera, stood Ken Dryden, now aged fifty-nine, older, wiser, but still imposing, his mask flipped up on top of his head, his hands resting on his goalstick.

The camera follows him as he makes his way out of the dressing room, now clutching his famous bull's-eye mask in his hand, pausing only to look at the faces on the wall, photographs of teammates, of friends, of players who fought the battles on the ice with him, and of men who celebrated championships together.

When he takes the ice in front of the sold-out Bell Centre crowd, he looks into the crowd, soaking in their adulation, and then embraces his family, who are waiting for him at centre ice. Then, standing alone under a spotlight, he waves to the admiring crowd as the cheers cascade over him. He eventually takes his seat on the ice alongside his family and the ceremony resumes.

Months earlier, when Dryden had been informed of the impending honour, Dryden sat down and built his own guest list. There was one person in particular he hoped could attend.

Now, stepping out onto the red carpet that leads to centre ice, clad in the jersey of the old Soviet National Team, Vladislav Tretiak is welcomed with a prolonged chorus of cheers that rival those for Dryden. His appearance electrifies the capacity crowd. In response he gently places his right hand over his heart. Then stepping to the podium, in a combination of halting French and English, Tretiak addresses the crowd and the guest of honour.

"I played against Team Canada in 1972 and in 1975 against the Montreal Canadiens – the best hockey I ever saw" – and then, glancing toward Dryden – "He was a fantastic goalie and a great man."[6]

Joining in the applause are the present-day Montreal Canadiens, all wearing number 29 jerseys in tribute to the guest of honour. Standing along their bench, they represent the new global face of the NHL. Their roster is sprinkled with players from Russia, Finland, Switzerland, Belarus, the Czech Republic, the United States, and Canada. The jerseys of the team's two most popular players, Saku Koivu and Alex Kovalev, from Finland and Russia respectively, are sported by many in the arena this evening. The days when a player is identified, first and foremost, by his nationality are forever gone. In today's world, the best hockey players test their skills and creativity against one another on a nightly basis, irrespective of their nationality. No longer are the best players barred from being in the NHL on the basis of political differences.

Finishing his short speech, Tretiak walks toward a waiting Dryden and the two men warmly embrace. They first competed against each other four decades before, when both were young men with their whole careers ahead of them. Now, as they share their mutual admiration and respect, they can look back on an unlikely, shared history, one that has changed the future course of the sport. Pulling apart, Tretiak spontaneously grabs his old adversary's right wrist with his left hand and pumps their arms in the air together, in a touching display of camaraderie that sets off a new round of applause throughout the arena.

On the night of December 31, 1975, the Montreal Canadiens and the Central Red Army engaged in a hockey game that reminded all those who watched how beautiful the sport could be when it is played in its purest form and at its highest level. Perhaps there was some justice in the game ending in a tie. Neither team won the "greatest game ever played." Instead, it was the sport of hockey that emerged as the true winner, both on that New Year's Eve and ever since.

ACKNOWLEDGEMENTS

In the life of an author, there are few things as daunting and discouraging as an empty sheet of paper (or in today's digital world, the blank computer screen). The long and often arduous process of taking an idea that has long gestated in your mind and putting it on the page can be, at the best of times, a lonely and often complicated journey. However, even at its most difficult it is not a trek that one undertakes alone. Along the way, one is advised, supported, and encouraged by a variety of people, each of whom in his or her own way makes a special contribution to the finished book.

And for that, I thank you all.

The idea for this particular book has long occupied a space in my mind. I would like to thank my agent, Arnold Gosewich, for believing in the idea and in my ability to transform it into a book. His resolve and expertise were crucial in getting the book done.

This book, like the one before it, could not have found a more ideal home. McClelland & Stewart, and more specifically Doug Pepper and Eric Jensen, have provided the ideal publishing environment for my work, and for that I am eternally grateful. In addition, I would like to thank my editor, Elizabeth Kribs, for bringing her unique perspective and her valuable insight to the manuscript; my copy editor, Lynn Schellenberg, for steering the manuscript to completion; and my publicist, Ruta Liormonas, for her unbridled enthusiasm and constant encouragement.

Once again, I was able to spend a few days at the Hockey Hall of Fame's resource centre, where I was able to wade through their large collection of archival materials. In particular, I would like to convey my gratitude to Miragh Addis for being extremely helpful and allowing me to do my research in the midst of their move, and to Craig Campbell for opening up the Hall's photo archives for use in the book.

I have been fortunate enough during my work on both books to have interviewed Frank Orr. Not only has Mr. Orr shared his memories and thoughts with me, but for this book, he also shared his original files from this time period. Without his valuable insights, both of my books would have been the poorer.

A researcher's work is only as good as the libraries he or she frequents. The library at Queen's University houses a treasure trove of archived newspapers and was invaluable in the creation of this book. The staff of the Cobourg Public Library and the Port Hope Public Library were also helpful in providing me with some of the books I consulted for this project. I would also like to thank Andrea Gordon at Canadian Press for supplying many of the photographs used in the book.

Paul Patskou possesses the finest private collection of hockey video that I'm aware of. I want to thank him for sharing his copy of the original broadcast of the New Year's Eve game along with his passion for the project. The chapter devoted to the game would have been radically different without his help and advice.

I wish to extend my heartfelt thanks to my fellow members in the Society for International Hockey Research, many of whom have been extremely generous and forthcoming with their suggestions and support. In particular, I would like to thank Lloyd Davis, Len Kotylo, Kevin van Steendelaar, and Eric Zweig.

When it comes to the history of Russian/Soviet hockey there is no person more knowledgeable than Denis Gibbons. As I researched this book, I was fortunate enough to have access to all of the information he had gathered over his long career spent investigating Russian hockey in this particular time period and the men who played for the Red Army, many of whom he has interviewed over the course of his journalistic career.

I am wholly indebted to the following people for going out of their way to help me along the way: Red Fisher, Dick Irvin, Pat Hickey, Mike Boone, Dave Stubbs, Jeff Pearlman, Jeff Marek, Scott Morrison, Robert Lefebvre, Joe Pelletier, Matt Gauthier, Mike Wyman, Mitch Melnick, Hank Schaffer, Philip Abbott, Glen Woodrow, and John Ovens.

On a personal note I would like to single out the following people for their unwavering support and enthusiasm during the course of writing this book:

Michael and Jane Thompson; Lloyd and Fran Jones; Derek and Sandra Eagleson; Nate and Jennifer Jones; Matt and Delta Jones; Nick and Mandy McKinley; Brett Mills; James Jones; Tim Horgan; Michele LaBossiere; Rob Davis; James Baxter; Terry Connors; and the entire gang at Kelly's Homelike Inn, especially Gord Kelly, Sr., Gord Kelly, Jr., and Kris Kelly.

Most of all I would like to thank those who accepted my request to be interviewed for the book. Without them this book would not have been possible. I personally would like to thank each of these men who took the time to share their memories with me and in particular, Jean Béliveau, Scotty Bowman, Alan Eagleson, Bob Gainey, Ralph Mellanby, Jim Roberts, Serge Savard, Steve Shutt, and Murray Wilson.

Last but not least, I would like to thank my family, whose love and encouragement have always been a source of inspiration and comfort for me. For my mother, father, and brother, none of this would have been remotely possible without the three of you.

NOTES

PROLOGUE
1. Mike Boone, "Cold Weather Can't Stop Die-Hard Hockey Fans," *Montreal Star,* December 19, 1975, p. C-7.
2. Mike Boone, interview by the author, December 19, 2009.
3. Mike Boone, interview by the author, December 19, 2009.

CHAPTER 1: A RUDE AWAKENING
1. Andrew Podnieks, *Canada's Olympic History, 1920–2010,* p. 10.
2. Lawrence Martin, *The Red Machine,* p. 46.
3. "Russia Defeats Canada 7–2 to Win World Hockey Title," *Globe and Mail,* March 8, 1954, p. 1.
4. Lawrence Martin, "Hockey's Red Dawn," *The Beaver,* December 2009–January 2010, p. 17.
5. "Russia Defeats Canada . . . ," p. 1.
6. Martin, *The Red Machine,* pp. 47–48.
7. Martin, "Hockey's Red Dawn . . . ," p. 17.
8. "Send Leafs Anywhere to Keep Flag Flying: Smythe," *Globe and Mail,* March 8, 1954, p. 17.

CHAPTER 2: THE FATHER OF RUSSIAN HOCKEY
1. Lawrence Martin, *The Red Machine,* p. 56.
2. Arch MacKenzie, "Hockey's Cold War Won by B.C. Team," *Globe and Mail,* March 7, 1955, p. 2.
3. MacKenzie, "Hockey's Cold War . . . ," p. 2.
4. Arch MacKenzie, "Canada Beats Russia," *Globe and Mail,* March 7, 1955, p. 1.
5. "V's Make Maple Leaf World's Top Hockey Emblem," *Globe and Mail,* March 7, 1955, p. 23
6. "Yevgeny Babich," Joe Pelletier's Greatest Hockey Legends Hockey History Blog, http://internationalhockeylegends.blogspot.com/2008/07/yevgeny-babich.html.

7. Roy MacSkimming, *Cold War: The Amazing Canada-Soviet Hockey Series of 1972*, p. 96.
8. Jeff Merron, "Russians Regroup on the Other Side of the Red Line," ESPN. com, February 14, 2002.
9. Martin, *The Red Machine*, p. 23.
10. Ken Dryden and Roy MacGregor, *Home Game*, p. 196.
11. Martin, *The Red Machine*, p. 33.
12. Wikipedia, "Vasily Dzhugashvili," http://en.wikipedia.org/wiki/Vasily_Dzhugashvili.
13. Dryden and MacGregor, *Home Game*, p. 197.
14. Frank Orr, *Great Goalies of Pro Hockey*, p. 135.
15. MacSkimming, *Cold War*, p. 100.
16. MacSkimming, *Cold War*, p. 99.
17. Martin, *The Red Machine*, p. 52.
18. Merron, "Russians Regroup . . ."
19. Wikipedia, "Lloyd Percival," http://en.wikipedia.org/wiki/Lloyd_Percival.
20. Martin, *The Red Machine*, p. 53.
21. Al Nickleson, "Fans Startled by Puckniks at Workout," *Globe and Mail*, November 21, 1957, p. 29.
22. Martin, *The Red Machine*, p. 58.
23. MacSkimming, *Cold War*, p. 99.
24. Martin, *The Red Machine*, p. 59.
25. Dryden and MacGregor, *Home Game*, p. 199.
26. Jim Proudfoot, "Rout of Habs Warning to Whitby," *Toronto Star*, December 7, 1957, p. 35.
27. Martin, *The Red Machine*, p. 61.
28. Dryden and MacGregor, *Home Game*, p. 199.
29. Martin, *The Red Machine*, p. 64.

CHAPTER 3: THE GODFATHER AND THE GOALTENDER
1. Jim Hunt, "Sam Pollock: New Boss of the Canadiens," *Canadian Weekly*, October 31, 1964, p. 8.
2. Red Fisher, "GM Built Habs Dynasties," Montreal *Gazette*, August 16, 2007.
3. Hunt, "Sam Pollock . . . ," p. 7.
4. Hunt, "Sam Pollock . . . ," p. 7.
5. Dave Stubbs, "Pollock's Keen Eye for Talent Made Him an NHL Legend," Montreal *Gazette*, August 15, 2007.
6. Eric Duhatschek, "Remembering Sam," *Globe and Mail*, August 20, 2007.
7. Louis Chantigny, "Un tyran? Un genie? Quelle sorte d'homme est Sam Pollock?" *La Patrie*, May 28, 1964, p. 36.
8. Red Burnett, "Sam Pollock Story Out of Horatio Alger," *Toronto Star*, May 15, 1964, p. 39.
9. D'Arcy Jenish, *The Montreal Canadiens: 100 Years of Glory*, p. 179.
10. Mark Mulvoy, "A Lot More Where They Came From," *Sports Illustrated*, April 2, 1973.
11. Pat Curran, "What If the Cheque Bounces?" Montreal *Gazette*, June 5, 1967, p. 37.

12. Red Fisher, "GM Built Habs Dynasties," Montreal *Gazette*, August 16, 2007.
13. Chrys Goyens and Allan Turowetz, *Lions in Winter*, p. 189.
14. Hal Bock, "How Hockey's Godfather Keeps the Canadiens on Top," *Hockey Sports Stars of 1974*, p. 19.
15. Bob Pennington, "Column of the Month – Ken Dryden," *Action Sports Hockey 1971/72*, p. 74.
16. Mark Mulvoy, "It's Dryden for the Defense," *Sports Illustrated*, February 14, 1972.
17. Hal Bock, *Save! Hockey's Brave Goalies*, p. 25.
18. Mulvoy, "It's Dryden for the Defense."
19. Mulvoy, "It's Dryden for the Defense."
20. Nick Seitz, "If Ken Dryden's So Smart, How Come He's a Goalie?" *Sport Magazine*, March 1973, p. 46.
21. Red Fisher, *Hockey, Heroes, and Me*, p. 63.
22. Mulvoy, "It's Dryden for the Defense."
23. Bock, *Save! Hockey's Brave Goalies*, p. 26.
24. Mulvoy, "It's Dryden for the Defense."
25. Ken Dryden, "Greatness Remembered," *Canadiens Magazine*, Vol. 22.1, p. 31.
26. Mulvoy, "It's Dryden for the Defense."
27. Frank Orr, "Dryden's Signing Climaxes Wild Week in Goalie Heaven," *Toronto Star*, July 16, 1969, p. 19.
28. Dryden, "Greatness Remembered," p. 33.
29. Milt Dunnell, "Travel, Education with Salary Attached," *Toronto Star*, July 16, 1969, p. 18.
30. Dryden, "Greatness Remembered," p. 33.

CHAPTER 4: A GIFT FROM GOD
1. Tom Watt, "Shazam – Super Nats!" *The Province* (Vancouver), p. 17.
2. Ken Dryden and Mark Mulvoy, *Face-Off at the Summit*, pp. 84–85.
3. Dryden and Mulvoy, *Face-Off at the Summit*, p. 84.
4. Dryden and Mulvoy, *Face-Off at the Summit*, p. 85.
5. Lawrence Martin, *The Red Machine*, p. 68.
6. "Russians Beat Smokies 4–2 to Win World Hockey Title," *Globe and Mail*, March 18, 1963, p. 17.
7. Martin, *The Red Machine*, p. 68.
8. Martin, *The Red Machine*, p. 70.
9. "Russians Beat Smokies . . . ," p. 17.
10. Rod Currie, "CAHA Head Agrees New Deal Is Needed After Smokies Wind Up in Fourth Spot," *Ottawa Citizen*, March 18, 1963, p. 15.
11. Jim Coleman, *Hockey Is Our Game*.
12. Martin, *The Red Machine*, p. 80.
13. Arthur R. Chidlovski, "The Summit in 72," http://www.chidlovski.com/personal/1972/speakers/bmayorov.htm.
14. Vladislav Tretiak, *Tretiak: The Legend*, p. 9.
15. Tretiak, *Tretiak: The Legend*, p. 18.
16. Tretiak, *Tretiak: The Legend*, p. 19.

17. Douglas Hunter, *A Breed Apart: An Illustrated History of Goaltending*, p. 159.
18. Martin, *The Red Machine*, p. 106.
19. Martin, *The Red Machine*, p. 107.
20. Tretiak, *Tretiak: The Legend*, p. 10.
21. Tretiak, *Tretiak: The Legend*, pp. 10–11.
22. Tretiak, *Tretiak: The Legend*, p. 21.
23. Tretiak, *Tretiak: The Legend*, pp. 11–12.
24. Tretiak, *Tretiak: The Legend*, p. 11.
25. Tretiak, *Tretiak: The Legend*, p. 14.
26. Martin, *The Red Machine*, p. 111.
27. Frank Orr, "Dryden's Signing Climaxes Wild Week in Goalie Heaven," *Toronto Star*, July 16, 1969, p. 19.
28. Frank Orr, "'Big Ned' Flattens the Nats," *Toronto Star*, January 2, 1970, p. 14.
29. Ken Dryden, "Greatness Remembered," *Canadiens Magazine*, Vol. 22.1, p. 31.

CHAPTER 5: YOU'VE GOT TO DIE TO BE BORN AGAIN
1. Maurice Richard and Stan Fischler, "The Flying Frenchmen: Hockey's Greatest Dynasty," p. 231.
2. Gord Walker, "Sam Pollock Has No Excuses for Canadiens Fifth-Place Finish," *Globe and Mail*, April 7, 1970, p. 37.
3. Richard and Fischler, "The Flying Frenchmen," p. 230.
4. "The Cup Runneth Over," *Time* magazine, May 25, 1970.
5. Pat Curran, "Nothing Like a Wake," Montreal *Gazette*, April 8, 1970, p. 19.
6. Ken Dryden, "Greatness Remembered," *Canadiens Magazine*, Vol. 22.1, p. 31.
7. Dryden, "Greatness Remembered," p. 42.
8. Ken Dryden, interview, *Legends of Hockey* television series, Network Entertainment.
9. Pat Hickey, "Dryden Shuns College Hockey, Eyes Berth With Voyageurs," *Montreal Star*, September 18, 1970, p. 10.
10. Pat Curran, "Habs' Kids Do Job Over Bruins," Montreal *Gazette*, October 5, 1970, p. 21.
11. Pat Curran, "Habs Look Good Now – Where Will They Be at Playoff Time," Montreal *Gazette*, October 7, 1970, p. 36.
12. George Hanson, "Canadiens Drop Dryden, Goalie to Emphasize Studies," *Montreal Star*, October 10, 1970, p. 49.
13. Hanson, "Canadiens Drop Dryden," p. 49.
14. Frank Orr, "Dryden's Skill Has Legal Repercussions," *Toronto Star*, April 13, 1971, p. 15.
15. Murray Dryden, with Jim Hunt. *Playing the Shots at Both Ends: The Story of Ken and Dave Dryden*, p. 11.
16. "64 Shots But No Goals in Hershey Tilt," *Gettysburg Times*, March 6, 1971, p. 5.
17. Geoffrey W. Kent, "Here Come the Vees," p. 29.
18. Ken Dryden, interview, *Legends of Hockey*.
19. Dick Irvin, *The Habs*, p. 239.
20. Pat Curran, "Backstrom Granted Wish – Trade to Warm L.A," by Montreal *Gazette*, January 27, 1971, p. 9.

21. Tom Murray, "Main Man in Montreal: Guy Lafleur," *Sport Magazine*, November 1975, p. 29.
22. Chrys Goyens and Allan Turowetz, *Lions in Winter*, p. 188.
23. Georges-Hébert Germaine, *Overtime: The Legend of Guy Lafleur*, p. 144.
24. Germaine, *Overtime*, p. 146.
25. Irvin, *The Habs*, pp. 239, 241.
26. Sam Pollock, interview, *Legends of Hockey* television series, Network Entertainment.
27. "Stanley Cup Playoffs to Open Tonight," *Gettysburg Times*, April 7, 1971, p. 11.
28. Murray Dryden, with Jim Hunt, p. 12.
29. Ken Dryden, interview, *Legends of Hockey*.
30. Irvin, *The Habs*, p. 243.
31. Murray Dryden, with Jim Hunt, p. 15.
32. Frank Orr, "No Mystery to It, Dryden Beat Bruins," *Toronto Star*, April 19, 1971, p. 10.
33. Milt Dunnell, "Maybe for MacNeil Belated Recognition," *Toronto Star*, April 19, 1971, p. 10.
34. Murray Dryden, with Jim Hunt, p. 15.
35. Orr, "Dryden's Skill Has Legal Repercussions," p. 15.
36. Douglas Hunter, *Scotty Bowman: A Life in Hockey*, p. 147.
37. Murray Dryden, with Jim Hunt, p. 18.
38. Dan Proudfoot, "Richard's Two Goals Spark Habs to Stanley Cup Victory," *Globe and Mail*, May 19, 1971, p. 34.
39. Milt Dunnell, "How Not to Run a Press Conference," *Toronto Star*, June 11, 1971, p. 18.
40. Hunter, *Scotty Bowman*, p. 149.
41. Red Fisher, "Bowman: Canadiens' Coach, MacNeil: Voyageurs' Boss," *Montreal Star*, June 10, 1971, p. 33.
42. Fisher, "Bowman: Canadiens' Coach, MacNeil: Voyageurs' Boss," p. 33.
43. George Hanson, "No Surprises – Montreal Picks Guy Lafleur," *Montreal Star*, June 10, 1971, p. 33.

CHAPTER 6: CHANGING OF THE GUARD

1. Lawrence Martin, *The Red Machine*, p. 98.
2. "'Distinguished Coach' Tarasov Under Fire from Soviet Fans, Press," *Globe and Mail*, May 14, 1969, p. 30.
3. Martin, *The Red Machine*, p. 99.
4. "'Distinguished Coach' Tarasov . . . ," p. 30.
5. "'Distinguished Coach' Tarasov . . . ," p. 30.
6. "'Distinguished Coach' Tarasov . . . ," p. 30.
7. "Tarasov Back," *Globe and Mail*, December 8, 1969, p. 19.
8. Martin, *The Red Machine*, p. 6.
9. Vladislav Tretiak, *Tretiak: The Legend*, pp. 13–14, 16.
10. Martin, *The Red Machine*, pp. 4–5.
11. Martin, *The Red Machine*, p. 76.
12. Tretiak, *Tretiak: The Legend*, p. 30.
13. Tretiak, *Tretiak: The Legend*, p. 44.

14. Louis Cauz, "Russian Challenge Fails to Excite Smythe, Molson," *Globe and Mail,* December 17, 1968, p. 30.
15. Anatoli Tarasov, "Russia's Tarasov Examines NHL Play," *Toronto Star,* December 30, 1969, p. 8.
16. "Russians Backed Down from NHL'ers Challenge," *Globe and Mail,* January 30, 1970, p. 26.
17. Martin, *The Red Machine,* p. 112.
18. Jim Coleman, *Toronto Sun,* February 25, 1972, p. 20.
19. Jim Coleman, *Toronto Sun,* February 29, 1972, p. 20.
20. "Russians Confirm Rumour by Firing Hockey Coaches," *Toronto Star,* February 25, 1972, p. 19.
21. "Ballard Sees Impending Hockey Series as 'Top Sports Event in Our History,'" *Globe and Mail,* April 20, 1972, p. 46.

CHAPTER 7: THE SUMMIT SERIES

1. Ken Dryden and Mark Mulvoy, *Face-Off at the Summit,* p. 3.
2. Dryden and Mulvoy, *Face-Off at the Summit,* p. 3.
3. "By Dick Beddoes," *Globe and Mail,* April 26, 1969, p. 35.
4. Louis Cauz, "Once Unwanted, Savard Touted for Smythe Trophy," *Globe and Mail,* May 3, 1969, p. 43.
5. Dave Stubbs, "Toughing Out a Great Career," Montreal *Gazette,* November 20, 2006.
6. Mark Mulvoy, "Mr. Band-Aid Pops Up Again For Montreal," *Sports Illustrated,* October 30, 1972, p.74
7. Stubbs, "Toughing Out a Great Career."
8. Mulvoy, "Mr. Band-Aid Pops Up Again . . ." p.75.
9. "Canadiens Heroes in Hotel Fire Rescue," *Globe and Mail,* March 11, 1972, p. 41.
10. Mulvoy, "Mr. Band-Aid Pops Up Again . . ." p.75.
11. Guy Lapointe, interview, *Legends of Hockey* television series, Network Entertainment.
12. Pat Curran, "Not Supermen Says Ruel About First Defeat," Montreal *Gazette,* October 29, 1968, p. 29.
13. Guy Lapointe, interview, *Legends of Hockey.*
14. Guy Lapointe, interview, *Legends of Hockey.*
15. Hockey Hall of Fame and Museum, "Legends of Hockey: One on One with Guy Lapointe," April 26, 2005, www.legendsofhockey.net/html/spot_one-ononep199301.htm.
16. Dick Irvin, interview, *Legends of Hockey* television series, Network Entertainment.
17. Roy MacSkimming, *Cold War: The Amazing Canada-Soviet Hockey Series of 1972,* p. 20.
18. "Guy Lapointe," Joe Pelletier's Greatest Hockey Legends Hockey History Blog, http://habslegends.blogspot.com/2006/05/guy-lapointe.html.
19. Red Fisher, "No. 14 Guy Lapointe: Blue-liner Had Big Shot," Montreal *Gazette,* October 16, 2009.
20. Scott Morrison, *The Days Canada Stood Still: Canada vs USSR 1972,* p. 108.

21. Mark Ruskie, "Montreal's Pete Mahovlich: Canadiens' Kid Brother," *1972 Hockey Yearbook Faceoff*, p. 58.

22. Jim Proudfoot, "Fergie Taught Me Says Little M," *Toronto Star*, May 1, 1971, p. 43.

23. Red Fisher, "Big Pete Was Perfect Fit," Montreal *Gazette*, October 12, 2007.

24. Milt Dunnell, "And the Hours Are Not Bad," *Toronto Star*, August 30, 1973, p. 16.

25. Dick Beddoes, "Hull 'Genuinely Gratified' With WHA-Winnipeg Contracts," *Globe and Mail*, June 28, 1972, p. 34.

26. MacSkimming, *Cold War*, p. 18.

27. Dick Beddoes, "Only a Game, But 15 Million Fans Want Fame, Not Shame," *Globe and Mail*, September 2, 1972, p. 37.

28. MacSkimming, *Cold War*, p. 26.

29. Dryden and Mulvoy, *Face-Off at the Summit*, p. 31.

CHAPTER 8: A LITTLE PIECE OF ALL OF US DIED TODAY

1. Vladislav Tretiak, *Tretiak: The Legend*, p. 51.

2. Scott Morrison, *The Days Canada Stood Still: Canada vs USSR 1972*, p. 45.

3. "Everybody Likes Canada," Montreal *Gazette*, September 1, 1972, p. 68.

4. Roy MacSkimming, *Cold War: The Amazing Canada-Soviet Hockey Series of 1972*, p. 29.

5. Morrison, *The Days Canada Stood Still*, p. 47.

6. Tretiak, *Tretiak: The Legend*, p. 52.

7. Tretiak, *Tretiak: The Legend*, p. 52.

8. Lawrence Martin, *The Red Machine*, p. 119.

9. Martin, *The Red Machine*, p. 119.

10. Morrison, *The Days Canada Stood Still*, pp. 51–52.

11. MacSkimming, *Cold War*, p. 50.

12. Martin, *The Red Machine*, p. 120.

13. Hockey Hall of Fame and Museum, "Legends of Hockey: One on One with Valeri Kharlamov," February 27, 2009, www.hhof.com/LegendsOfHockey/html/spot_oneononep200501.htm.

14. MacSkimming, *Cold War*, p. 54.

15. MacSkimming, *Cold War*, p. 55.

16. Ken Dryden and Mark Mulvoy, *Face-Off at the Summit*, p. 49.

17. Martin, *The Red Machine*, p. 120.

18. Martin, *The Red Machine*, p. 132.

19. "A Close Look at the Soviet Players," *Toronto Star*, September 1, 1972, p. A31.

20. Ron Ellis with Kevin Shea, *Over the Boards: The Ron Ellis Story*, p. 119.

21. "Ballard Says Kharlamov Worth $1 Million," *Globe and Mail*, September 4, 1972, p. S11.

22. Dryden and Mulvoy, *Face-Off at the Summit*, p. 55.

23. MacSkimming, *Cold War*, p. 56.

CHAPTER 9: THE TEAM WITHIN THE TEAM

1. Brian McFarlane, *Team Canada 1972: Where Are They Now?* p. 41.

2. Roy MacSkimming, *Cold War: The Amazing Canada-Soviet Hockey Series of 1972*, pp. 71, 163.

3. Louis Cauz, "Cournoyer Specializes in Embarrassing Leafs," *Globe and Mail*, April 22, 1967, p. 30.

4. Yvan Cournoyer, interview, *Legends of Hockey* television series, Network Entertainment.

5. Hockey Hall of Fame and Museum, "Legends of Hockey: One on One with Yvan Cournoyer," January 18, 2005, www.legendsofhockey.net/html/spot_oneononep198201.htm.

6. Milt Dunnell, "The Old Firm Was Broken Up," *Toronto Star*, November 2, 1967, p. 12.

7. MacSkimming, *Cold War*, p. 74.

8. MacSkimming, *Cold War*, p. 75.

9. McFarlane, *Team Canada 1972*, p. 140.

10. MacSkimming, *Cold War*, p. 131.

11. McFarlane, *Team Canada 1972*, p. 38.

12. Guy Lapointe, interview, *Legends of Hockey* television series, Network Entertainment.

13. Mark Mulvoy, "Mr. Band-Aid Pops Up Again for Montreal," *Sports Illustrated*, October 30, 1972, p.75.

14. "Hairline Ankle Fracture Puts Savard Out of Canada-USSR Series," *Globe and Mail*, September 9, 1972, p. 73.

15. McFarlane, *Team Canada 1972*, p. 172.

16. Ken Dryden and Mark Mulvoy, *Face-Off at the Summit*, p. 94.

17. Dryden and Mulvoy, *Face-Off at the Summit*, p. 125.

18. Dryden and Mulvoy, *Face-Off at the Summit*, p. 132.

19. Jim Proudfoot, "A Healthy Savard Is Difference," *Toronto Star*, September 27, 1972, p. B1.

20. Scott Morrison, *The Days Canada Stood Still: Canada vs USSR 1972*, p. 182.

21. Red Fisher, "Turned Summit Tide," Montreal *Gazette*, October 8, 2009.

21. McFarlane, *Team Canada 1972*, p. 40.

23. Morrison, *The Days Canada Stood Still*, p. 193.

24. McFarlane, *Team Canada 1972*, p. 49.

25. McFarlane, *Team Canada 1972*, p. 41.

26. Dryden and Mulvoy, *Face-Off at the Summit*, p. 185.

CHAPTER 10: A DYNASTY DELAYED

1. Tim Burke, "Long-Striding Murray Wilson Moves Like Big M," Montreal *Gazette*, October 2, 1972, p. 22.

2. Murray Wilson, interview by the author, January 15, 2010.

3. Murray Wilson, interview by the author, January 15, 2010.

4. Steve Shutt, interview by the author, December 18, 2009.

5. Red Fisher, "Canadiens Playoff Successes . . . ," *Hockey Illustrated*, April/May 1967, p. 34.

6. Murray Wilson, interview by the author, January 15, 2010.

7. Larry Robinson with Chrys Goyens, *Robinson for the Defence*, pp. 107, 110.

8. Mark Mulvoy, "A Lot More Where They Came From," *Sports Illustrated*, April 2, 1973.

9. Murray Wilson, interview by the author, January 15, 2010.

10. Steve Shutt, interview by the author, December 18, 2009.

11. Murray Wilson, interview by the author, January 15, 2010.

12. Jim Proudfoot, "Hawks Can't Cover the Roadrunner," *Toronto Star*, May 7, 1973, p. 29.

13. Al Rosenberg, "French Hero Yvan Cournoyer – Little Man, Big Deeds," *Sports Special Hockey,* December 1973, p. 7.

14. Ben Olan, "Yvan Cournoyer: The Canadiens' Big Gun," *Hockey Illustrated*, January 1974, p. 55.

15. Dick Irvin, *The Habs*, p. 259.

16. Tim Burke, "Cup for Richard the Lion-Hearted," Montreal *Gazette*, p. 88.

17. Burke, "Cup for Richard . . . ," p. 88.

18. "By Dick Beddoes," *Globe and Mail*, May 12, 1973, p. 47.

19. Mulvoy, "A Lot More Where They Came From."

20. "Tardif: Canadiens Didn't Try to Keep Me," Montreal *Gazette,* June 6, 1973, p. 18.

21. Chrys Goyens and Allan Turowetz, *Lions in Winter*, p. 179.

22. "Rejean Houle Signs with Les Nordiques," Montreal *Gazette,* July 21, 1973, p. 8.

23. Jim Proudfoot, "Dryden Says Exit Didn't Surprise Habs," *Toronto Star,* September 15, 1973, p. D2.

24. "Dryden Leaves Canadiens as 'Matter of Pride' – and Money," *Globe and Mail,* September 15, 1973, p. 41.

25. Red Fisher, "Dryden to the Rescue," Montreal *Gazette*, October 15, 2007.

26. "Dryden Leaves Canadiens . . . ," p. 41.

27. "Dick Beddoes," Globe and Mail, April 6, 1974, p. 45.

CHAPTER 11: THE WILD BUNCH

1. Chuck Gormley, *Orange, Black, and Blue: The Greatest Philadephia Flyers Stories Never Told*, p. 15.

2. Stan Fischler, *Bobby Clarke and the Ferocious Flyers*, p. 18.

3. Jay Greenberg, *Full Spectrum: The Complete History of the Philadelphia Flyers Hockey Club*, p. 42.

4. Gene Hart with Buzz Ringe, *Score: My Twenty-Five Years with the Broad Street Bullies*, p. 148.

5. Mark Mulvoy, *The Flyer from Flin Flon*, *Sports Illustrated*, October 22, 1973.

6. Mulvoy, *The Flyer from Flin Flon.*

7. Ray Kennedy, "Dr. Jekyll and Mr. Clarke," *Sports Illustrated*, February 23, 1976.

8. Kennedy, "Dr. Jekyll and Mr. Clarke."

9. Hockey Hall of Fame and Museum, "Legends of Hockey: One on One with Bobby Clarke," www.legendsofhockey.net/html/spot_oneononep198701.htm.

10. Gormley, *Orange, Black, and Blue*, p. 21.

11. Kennedy, "Dr. Jekyll and Mr. Clarke."

12. Kennedy, "Dr. Jekyll and Mr. Clarke."

13. Jim Jackson, *Walking Together Forever: The Broad Street Bullies, Then and Now*, p. 5.

14. Greenberg, *Full Spectrum*, p. 52.

15. Greenberg, *Full Spectrum*, p. 53.

16. Frank Orr, *Tough Guys of Pro Hockey*, p. 107.

17. Roy MacSkimming, *Cold War: The Amazing Canada-Soviet Hockey Series of 1972*, p. 21.

18. 1972 Summit Series.com, "Player Profile: Clarke Did What He Had to Do," www.1972summitseries.com/clarke.html.

19. Hockey Hall of Fame and Museum, "One on One with Bobby Clarke."

20. Scott Morrison, *The Days Canada Stood Still: Canada vs USSR 1972*, p. 166–67.

21. Morrison, *The Days Canada Stood Still*, p. 167.

22. Mark Mulvoy, "Hockey's Eclectic Wizard," *Sports Illustrated*, May 26, 1975.

23. Mark Mulvoy, "It's Sockey, the Way They Play It Here," *Sports Illustrated*, May 6, 1974.

24. Mark Mulvoy, "Bruisers and Bunny Hoppers," *Sports Illustrated*, December 23, 1974.

25. Stan Fischler, "The Philadelphia Flyers: Supermen of the Ice," p. 124.

26. Gormley, *Orange, Black, and Blue*, p. 23.

27. Greenberg, *Full Spectrum*, p. 66.

28. Orr, *Tough Guys of Pro Hockey*, p. 102.

29. Orr, *Tough Guys of Pro Hockey*, p. 107.

CHAPTER 12: THE LOST BOYS

1. Trent Frayne, "Ken Dryden Now Plays Defence – and He Pays for It," *Toronto Star*, November 17, 1973, p. A10.

2. Jim Page, "Ken Dryden: Montreal's Net Worth," *Hockey Illustrated*, April 1976, pp. 13, 15.

3. Marty Bell, "Sporting Life With Ken Dryden," *Sport Magazine*, April 1974, p. 14.

4. Bell, "Sporting Life With Ken Dryden," p. 14.

5. Page, "Ken Dryden: Montreal's Net Worth," p. 13.

6. Milt Dunnell, "Peddling Peter to Pay Paul?" *Toronto Star*, January 7, 1974, p. B01.

7. Red Fisher, *Hockey, Heroes, and Me*, p. 64.

8. Ken Dryden, "Greatness Remembered," *Canadiens Magazine*, Vol. 22.1, p. 38.

9. Mark Mulvoy, "Ken Dryden on Trial," *Sports Illustrated*, November 25, 1974.

10. Red Fisher, "Steve Shutt: A New Scoring Star Emerges for Montreal," *Hockey Digest*, April 1977, p. 32.

11. Red Fisher, "No. 13 Steve Shutt: Watch and Learn, Son," Montreal *Gazette*, October 10, 2009.

12. Fisher, "No. 13 Steve Shutt . . ."

13. Chris McDonell, *The Game I'll Never Forget: 100 Hockey Stars' Stories*, p. 182.

14. Mike Dennis, "Steve Shutt: Success Didn't Exactly Happen Overnight," *Hockey Pictorial-World*, April 1977, p. 26.

15. Dick Irvin, *The Habs*, p. 264.

16. Bob Gainey, interview, *Legends of Hockey* television series, Network Entertainment.

17. Dick Chapman, "Canadiens Optimistic and the Reason Is Ken Dryden," Montreal *Gazette*, September 16, 1974, p. 19.

18. Irvin, *The Habs*, p. 264.

19. Irvin, *The Habs*, p. 264.

20. Guy Lafleur, interview, *Legends of Hockey* television series, Network Entertainment.
21. D'Arcy Jenish, *The Montreal Canadiens: 100 Years of Glory*, p. 205.
22. Sam Pollock, interview, *Legends of Hockey* television series, Network Entertainment.
23. Chrys Goyens and Allan Turowetz, *Lions in Winter*, p. 184.
24. Ted Blackman, "Nordiques Rap Guy Lafleur Signing," Montreal *Gazette*, April 12, 1973, p. 27.
25. Chris Zelkovich, "Playing Like a Dream," *Hockey World*, February 1975, p. 9.
26. Claude Larochelle, *Guy Lafleur: Hockey's #1*, p. 194.
27. Larochelle, *Guy Lafleur*, p. 198.
28. Larochelle, *Guy Lafleur*, p. 199.
29. Lawrence Martin, "Lafleur Finally Blossoms into a Superstar," *Globe and Mail*, January 14, 1975, p. 32.
30. Ben Olan, "Guy Lafleur: Canadiens' Marked Man," *Argosy Hockey Yearbook 1978–79*, p. 12.
31. Guy Lafleur, interview, *Legends of Hockey*.
32. Tom Murray, "Main Man in Montreal: Guy Lafleur," *Sport Magazine*, November 1975, p. 91.
33. Bob Dunn, "Canadiens' Comet: Flashy Guy Lafleur," *Sporting News*, February 1, 1975, p. 3.
34. Murray, "Main Man in Montreal . . . ," p. 93.
35. Goyens and Turowetz, *Lions in Winter*, pp. 230–31.
36. Martin, "Lafleur Finally Blossoms . . . ," p. 32.
37. Martin, "Lafleur Finally Blossoms . . . ," p. 32.
38. Dunn, "Canadiens' Comet . . . ," p. 3.
39. Hockey Hall of Fame and Museum, "Legends of Hockey; Players: Guy Lafleur," www.legendsofhockey.net/LegendsOfHockey/jsp/LegendsMember.jsp?mem=p198802.

CHAPTER 13: WAR ON AND OFF THE ICE

1. "Courage and Fear in a Vortex of Violence," *Time* magazine, February 24, 1975.
2. Ray Kennedy, "Wanted: An End to Mayhem," *Sports Illustrated*, November 17, 1975.
3. Kennedy, "Wanted: An End to Mayhem."
4. Peter White, "Blues Born Amid Leisurely Talk," *Globe and Mail*, April 19, 1974, p. 35.
5. Christie Blatchford, "It's 'Matter of Life and Limb,' Bramalea Quits Hockey Series," *Globe and Mail*, April 18, 1974, p. 8.
6. James Golla, "Inquiry Told 'Foreign Object' Was Used in Fight During OHA Playoff Game," *Globe and Mail*, May 28, 1974, p. 35.
7. Blatchford, "It's 'Matter of Life and Limb' . . . " p. 8.
8. Blatchford, "It's 'Matter of Life and Limb' . . . " p. 8.
9. Blatchford, "It's 'Matter of Life and Limb' . . . " p. 8.
10. Norman Webster, "Violence Is Ruining Hockey, Official Says," *Globe and Mail*, April 24, 1974, p. 1.
11. Frank Orr, "Campbell Prepared for Villain's Role," *Toronto Star*, May 25, 1974, p. D01

12. Frank Orr, "Fighting Is Best Safety Valve: Campbell," *Toronto Star*, June 4, 1974, p. C01.
13. Frank Orr, "No 'Goons' for Team Canada '74," *Toronto Star*, June 5, 1974, p. C01.
14. Frank Orr, "Rough NHL Blamed for Amateur Hockey Violence," *Toronto Star*, August 21, 1974, p. A1.
15. Orr, "Rough NHL Blamed . . . ," p. A1.
16. "McMurtry Report Ignored as Governors Meet," *Globe and Mail*, August 23, 1974, p. 28.
17. "Sick Pro Hockey Sells Violence, McMurtry Says," *Globe and Mail*, June 27, 1974, p. 45.
18. "McMurtry Not Qualified to Criticize NHL: Shero," *Globe and Mail*, August 23, 1974, p. 28.
19. "Courage and Fear in a Vortex of Violence."
20. "NHL Has No Plans to Curb Violence Says League's Boss," *Toronto Star*, February 28, 1975, p. B01.
21. "NHL Has No Plans to Curb Violence . . . ," p. B01.
22. Kennedy, "Wanted: An End to Mayhem."
23. Sylvia Stead, "Hockey Tops TV Violence, Inquiry Told," *Globe and Mail*, October 25, 1975, p. 1.
24. Kennedy, "Wanted: An End to Mayhem."
25. Robert Williamson, "Police Ordered to Act on Hockey Violence," *Globe and Mail*, October 29, 1975, p. 1.
26. "Hockey Faces Off on Violence," *Toronto Star*, October 30, 1975, p. A1.
27. "McMurtry Vows He'll End Violence in Every Sport," *Toronto Star*, October 30, 1975, p. A3.
28. "Maloney First to Test McMurtry's Purge," *Ottawa Citizen*, November 7, 1975, p. 19.
29. Mary Trueman, "Maloney Is Charged with Assaulting Glennie During Game at Gardens," *Globe and Mail*, November 7, 1975, p. 1.
30. Kennedy, "Wanted: An End to Mayhem."

CHAPTER 14: THE RUSSIANS ARE COMING
1. Ken Dryden and Mark Mulvoy, *Face-Off at the Summit*, p. 180.
2. Dryden and Mulvoy, *Face-Off at the Summit*, p. 180.
3. "NHL, Soviet Teams Play 10-Game Set Next Season," *Globe and Mail*, November 15, 1972, p. 36.
4. "By Dick Beddoes," *Globe and Mail*, May 12, 1973, p. 47.
5. Lawrence Martin, *The Red Machine*, p. 143.
6. Frank Orr, "No 'Goons' for Team Canada '74," *Toronto Star*, June 5, 1974, p. C01.
7. Martin, *The Red Machine*, p. 148.
8. Martin, *The Red Machine*, p. 148.
9. Jim Proudfoot, "Team Canada's Goodwill Mission Ends as Soviet Coach Suggests Jail for Ley," *Toronto Star*, October 4, 1974, p. C1.
10. Dick Beddoes and Mary Trueman, "Jail Him, Russian Coach Says, as Ley Attacks Star Following 5–2 Loss," *Globe and Mail*, October 4, 1974, p. 2.

11. "'Disgrace to Canada,'" *Ottawa Citizen*, October 9, 1974, p. 1.
12. "NHL Begins Talks with Soviet Officials," *Globe and Mail*, June 10, 1975, p. 35.
13. "Negotiations Continue for Soviet-NHL Series," *Globe and Mail*, July 29, 1975, p. 30.
14. Alan Eagleson, interview by the author, January 12, 2010.
15. "Soviet-NHL Series Is All Set," *Toronto Star*, November 2, 1975, p. C03.
16. "Put Up or Shut Up, Russians are Coming!" Montreal *Gazette*, November 11, 1975, p. 18.

CHAPTER 15: THE NEW BREED
1. "'Desire Missing,' Richard Announces He'll Quit Habs," *Globe and Mail*, July 15, 1974, p. 30.
2. Al Strachan, "With Trembling Hands He Passes the Torch," Montreal *Gazette*, p. 17.
3. Jim Roberts, interview by the author, January 12, 2010.
4. Geoffrey Fisher, "Jim Roberts: He Turns on Blues For the Big Play," *Hockey Pictorial*, November 1968, p. 24.
5. Jim Roberts, interview by the author, January 12, 2010.
6. George Hanson, "Versatile Veteran Roberts Thinking of 20-Goal Season," *Montreal Star*, December 16, 1975, p. B-8.
7. "Jim Roberts Considers Habs Strongest Ever Behind Blue Line," *Globe and Mail*, April 28, 1973, p. 46.
8. Ian MacDonald, "Roberts Was Team Player," Montreal *Gazette*, May 14, 2007.
9. MacDonald, "Roberts Was Team Player."
10. Jim Devellano and Roger Lajoie, *The Road to Hockeytown: Jimmy Devellano's Forty Years in the NHL*, p. 25.
11. Chrys Goyens and Allan Turowetz, *Lions in Winter*, p. 190.
12. Red Fisher, "Gainey Stands Tall Among the Very Best," Montreal *Gazette*, February 24, 2008.
13. D'Arcy Jenish, *The Montreal Canadiens: 100 Years of Glory*, p. 218.
14. Doug Gilbert, "Sammy Continues Dealing but the Picks Get the Pot," by Montreal *Gazette*, May 16, 1973, p. 41.
15. Jenish, *The Montreal Canadiens*, p. 218.
16. Jenish, *The Montreal Canadiens*, p. 218.
17. Dick Chapman, "Canadiens Lose to the Bruins 5–3," Montreal *Gazette*, September 22, 1973, p. 10.
18. Red Fisher, "Fitting Honour for Hall of Famers," Montreal *Gazette*, September 6, 2007.
19. Michael Ulmer, *Canadiens Captains*, p. 171.
20. Dick Chapman, "Risebrough 'Muscle Act' Puts Canadiens on Spot in Boston," Montreal *Gazette*, September 26, 1974, p. 30.
21. Dick Chapman, "Bruins to 'Get' Risebrough After 4–0 Loss to the Canadiens," Montreal *Gazette*, September 23, 1974, p. 22.
22. Chapman, "Risebrough 'Muscle Act' . . . ," p. 30.
23. "Dryden in Top Form as Boston Bruised," Montreal *Gazette*, November 15, 1974, p. 25.

24. Dick Chapman, "Yvon Lambert's Arrived: 'Not Afraid of Mistakes,'" Montreal *Gazette*, October 15, 1974, p. 18.

25. "Dryden in Top Form as Boston Bruised," p. 25.

26. Tim Burke, "Lafleur Deals the Dramatics but Risebrough Lights Fires," Montreal *Gazette*, December 10, 1974, p. 13.

27. Dick Bacon, "Canadiens Special Practice Draws 13,000 Kids," Montreal *Gazette*, December 31, 1974, p. 17.

28. Al Strachan, "'Diamond in Rough' Jarvis Enriches a Trading Tradition," Montreal *Gazette*, October 1, 1975, p. 16.

29. Wayne Scanlon, *Roger's World: The Life and Unusual Times of Roger Neilson*, p. x.

30. Scotty Bowman, interview by the author, January 4, 2010.

31. Strachan, "'Diamond in Rough' Jarvis . . . ," p. 16.

32. Scotty Bowman, interview by the author, January 4, 2010.

33. Frank Orr, interview by the author, December 16, 2009.

34. Scotty Bowman, interview by the author, January 4, 2010.

CHAPTER 16: THE PREAMBLE

1. Vladislav Tretiak, *Tretiak: The Legend*, pp. 84–85.

2. Robin Herman, "N.H.L. Teams Not Taking Soviet Series Lightly," *New York Times*, December 28, 1975, p. 5-1.

3. "La 'grosse machine rouge' est arrivée!," *Le Soleil*, December 26, 1975, p. B1.

4. Bob Gainey, interview by the author, January 26, 2010.

5. Tretiak, *Tretiak: The Legend*, p. 86.

6. Michael Posner, "The Russians Are Coming and the Capitalists Can Hardly Wait," *Maclean's*, December 15, 1975, p. 53.

7. Parton Keese, "Hockey à la Russe Next on Program," *New York Times*, December 23, 1975, p. 21.

8. Tretiak, *Tretiak: The Legend*, p. 87.

9. Red Fisher, "Fat Rangers No Match For Slick Soviets," *Montreal Star*, December 29, 1975, p. C-1.

10. Peter White, "Soviet Army Is Overwhelming in 7–3 Victory Over Rangers," *Globe and Mail*, p. 19.

11. "Maybe Now Rangers Will Believe Espo," *Toronto Star*, December 29, 1975, p. B-1.

12. Fisher, "Fat Rangers No Match For Slick Soviets," , p. C-1.

13. Lawrence Martin, *The Red Machine*, p. 150.

14. Tretiak, *Tretiak: The Legend*, p. 86.

15. "Maybe Now Rangers Will Believe Espo," p. B-1.

16. Al Strachan, "Red Army Humbles Rangers 7–3," Montreal *Gazette*, December 29, 1975, p. 19.

17. John Robertson, "Les Canadiens vs. the Soviets: Here's One Root for the Home Team," Montreal *Gazette*, December 5, 1975, p. 82.

18. Jim Roberts, interview by the author, January 12, 2010.

19. Vladislav Tretiak, *The Hockey I Love*, p. 130.

20. Tretiak, *Tretiak: The Legend*, p. 88.

21. Montreal Canadiens vs. Central Red Army game, December 31, 1975, CBC Television. Rebroadcast December 31, 1995.

22. Al Strachan, "Pressure? Don Awrey Tells How It Really Is," Montreal *Gazette*, December 26, 1975, p. 15.
23. Tretiak, *The Hockey I Love*, p. 130.
24. Murray Wilson, interview by the author, January 15, 2010.
25. Bob Gainey, interview by the author, January 26, 2010.
26. "Summit on Ice," *Time* magazine, December 29, 1975.
27. Tim Burke, "'You're Carrying Country's Pride,'" Montreal *Gazette*, December 27, 1975, p. 11 and "Mahovlich Says Canadiens Ready, Won't Coast Against Russian Team," *Toronto Star*, December 25, 1975, p. 46.
28. "Russians No Longer in Awe of Canadians," *Globe and Mail*, December 31, 1975, p. 25.
29. Al Strachan, "Pete Eager for Showdown with Soviets," Montreal *Gazette*, December 31, 1975, p. 19.
30. Milt Dunnell, "A Hab Defeat Might Be Good," *Toronto Star*, December 31, 1975, p. B1.
31. Red Fisher, interview by the author, September 23, 2009.
32. D'Arcy Jenish, *The Montreal Canadiens: 100 Years of Glory*, p. 206.
33. Hockey Hall of Fame and Museum, "Legends of Hockey: One on One with Scotty Bowman," www.legendsofhockey.net/html/spot_oneononeb199101.htm.
34. Ken Dryden, interview, *Legends of Hockey* television series, Network Entertainment.
35. Jenish, *The Montreal Canadiens*, p. 208.
36. John Garrett, interview, *Legends of Hockey* television series, Network Entertainment.
37. Ken Dryden, *The Game*, p. 39.
38. Red Fisher, "No. 13 Steve Shutt: Watch and Learn, Son," Montreal *Gazette*, October 10, 2009.
39. Scotty Bowman, interview by the author, January 4, 2010.
40. Robin Herman, "Soviet Six Choice Over Canadiens," *New York Times*, December 31, 1975, p. 28.
41. Scotty Bowman, interview by the author, January 4, 2010.
42. Claude Larochelle, "Huit heures et c'en est fait du mythe Sovietique," *Le Soleil*, January 3, 1976, p. D7.
43. Steve Shutt, interview by the author, December 18, 2009.
44. Red Fisher, "Lemaire: Give 'Em No Room in Slot," *Montreal Star*, December 31, 1975, p. D1.

CHAPTER 17: THE CURTAIN RISES

1. Red Fisher, "Lemaire: Give 'Em No Room in Slot," *Montreal Star*, December 31, 1975, p. D1.
2. Fisher, "Lemaire: Give 'Em No Room in Slot," p. D1.
3. Jacques Beauchamp, "Un match memorable pour les Canadiens," *Journal de Montreal*, January 3, 1976, p. 50.
4. Bertrand Raymond, "'J'aimerais les embarquer dans la ligue' – Jacques Lemaire," *Journal de Montreal*, January 3, 1976, p. 53.
5. "'J'aimerais les embarquer dans la ligue' – Jacques Lemaire," p. 53.
6. Frank Orr, "Sabres' Key: Avoid Perreault vs. Lemaire," *Toronto Star*, May 6, 1975, p. C01.

7.   Steve Shutt, interview by the author, December 18, 2009.
8.   Larry Robinson and Chrys Goyens, *Robinson for the Defence*, p. 166.
9.   George Hanson, "Jacques Lemaire: The Consummate Canadien," *Hockey Illustrated*, January 1979, p. 10–11.
10. Robinson and Goyens, *Robinson for the Defence*, pp. 165–66.
11. Ralph Mellanby, interview by the author, December 18, 2009.
12. Ralph Mellanby with Mike Brophy, *Walking With Legends*, p. 54.
13. Ralph Mellanby, interview by the author, December 18, 2009.
14. Dick Irvin, *Now Back to You, Dick*, pp. 100–101.
15. Mellanby with Brophy, *Walking With Legends*, p. 54.
16. Robin Herman, "Canada's Gentle Hero Is a Willing Prisoner of His Nationwide Fame," *New York Times*, May 15, 1978, p. C1.
17. Jacques Beauchamp, "Jacques Beauchamp Notes," *Journal de Montreal*, January 3, 1976, p. 51.
18. Ralph Mellanby, interview by the author, December 18, 2009.
19. Ralph Mellanby, interview by the author, December 18, 2009.
20. Alan Eagleson, interview by the author, January 12, 2010.
21. Alan Eagleson, interview by the author, January 12, 2010.
22. Tim Burke, "'You're Carrying Country's Pride,'" Montreal *Gazette*, December 27, 1975, p. 11.
23. Peter White, "Canadiens Good, but Still Can't Beat Russians," *Globe and Mail*, January 1, 1976, p. 30.
24. Montreal Canadiens vs. Central Red Army game, December 31, 1975, CBC Television.
25. Murray Wilson, interview by the author, January 15, 2010.
26. Jim Roberts, interview by the author, January 12, 2010.
27. Montreal Canadiens vs. Central Red Army game, December 31, 1975, CBC Television. Rebroadcast December 31, 1995.
28. Montreal Canadiens vs. Central Red Army, December 31, 1975.
29. Dick Irvin, interview by the author, December 17, 2009.
30. Denis Gibbons, letter to author
31. Vladislav Tretiak, *The Hockey I Love*, p. 130.
32. Bertand Raymond, "Les Larmes de Steve Shutt: pas du chique," *Journal de Montreal*, January 3, 1976, p. 54.
33. Dick Irvin, *The Habs*, p. 272.
34. Ralph Mellanby, interview by the author, December 30, 2009.
35. Montreal Canadiens vs. Central Red Army, December 31, 1975.

CHAPTER 18: THE GAME
1.   Murray Wilson, interview by the author, January 15, 2010.
2.   Murray Wilson, interview by the author, January 15, 2010.
3.   Scotty Bowman, interview by the author, January 4, 2010.
4.   Steve Shutt, interview by the author, December 18, 2009.
5.   Montreal Canadiens vs. Central Red Army game, December 31, 1975, CBC Television.
6.   Montreal Canadiens vs. Central Red Army, December 31, 1975.

7. Steve Shutt, interview by the author, December 18, 2009.
8. Ken Dryden, *The Game*, p. 44.
9. Montreal Canadiens vs. Central Red Army, December 31, 1975.
10. Dick Irvin, *The Habs*, p. 274.
11. Montreal Canadiens vs. Central Red Army, December 31, 1975.
12. Ralph Mellanby, interview by the author, December 18, 2009.
13. Montreal Canadiens vs. Central Red Army, December 31, 1975.
14. Ralph Mellanby, interview by the author, December 18, 2009.
15. Montreal Canadiens vs. Central Red Army, December 31, 1975.
16. Montreal Canadiens vs. Central Red Army, December 31, 1975.
17. Vladislav Tretiak, *The Hockey I Love*, p. 131.
18. Steve Shutt, interview by the author, December 18, 2009.
19. Montreal Canadiens vs. Central Red Army, December 31, 1975.
20. Tretiak, *The Hockey I Love*, p. 131.
21. Montreal Canadiens vs. Central Red Army, December 31, 1975.
22. Montreal Canadiens vs. Central Red Army, December 31, 1975.
23. Montreal Canadiens vs. Central Red Army, December 31, 1975.
24. Irvin, *The Habs*, p. 274.
25. Scotty Bowman, interview by the author, January 4, 2010.
26. Tretiak, *The Hockey I Love*, p. 131.
27. Montreal Canadiens vs. Central Red Army, December 31, 1975.
28. Montreal Canadiens vs. Central Red Army, December 31, 1975.
29. Frank Orr, "Habs Deserved to Win but They Didn't," *Toronto Star*, January 1, 1976, p. B1.
30. Montreal Canadiens vs. Central Red Army, December 31, 1975.
31. Jacques Beauchamp, "Jacques Beauchamp Notes," *Journal de Montreal*, January 3, 1976, p. 51.
32. Montreal Canadiens vs. Central Red Army, December 31, 1975.
33. Montreal Canadiens vs. Central Red Army, December 31, 1975.
34. Montreal Canadiens vs. Central Red Army, December 31, 1975.
35. Montreal Canadiens vs. Central Red Army, December 31, 1975.
36. Tretiak, *The Hockey I Love*, pp. 131–32.
37. Montreal Canadiens vs. Central Red Army, December 31, 1975.
38. Jim Roberts, interview by the author, January 12, 2010.
39. Montreal Canadiens vs. Central Red Army, December 31, 1975.
40. Red Fisher, "Habs vs. Red Army, New Year's Eve '75," Montreal *Gazette*, December 31, 2004.
41. Bertand Raymond, "'God Must Be Russian' – Guy Lapointe," *Journal de Montreal*, January 3, 1976, p. 54.
42. Montreal Canadiens vs. Central Red Army, December 31, 1975.
43. Montreal Canadiens vs. Central Red Army, December 31, 1975.
44. Montreal Canadiens vs. Central Red Army, December 31, 1975.
45. Al Strachan, "Now That's How You Play Hockey, Comrade!" Montreal *Gazette*, January 2, 1976, p. 20.
46. Steve Shutt, interview by the author, December 18, 2009.
47. Montreal Canadiens vs. Central Red Army, December 31, 1975.

48. Montreal Canadiens vs. Central Red Army, December 31, 1975.
49. Dick Irvin, interview by the author, December 17, 2009.
50. Montreal Canadiens vs. Central Red Army, December 31, 1975.
51. Montreal Canadiens vs. Central Red Army, December 31, 1975.
52. Montreal Canadiens vs. Central Red Army, December 31, 1975.
53. Red Fisher, interview by the author, September 23, 2009.
54. Irvin, *The Habs*, p. 274.
55. Bertand Raymond, "Les Larmes de Steve Shutt: pas du chique," *Journal de Montreal,* January 3, 1976, p. 54.
56. Ralph Mellanby, interview by the author, December 18, 2009.
57. Ralph Mellanby, interview by the author, December 30, 2009.
58. Tim Burke, "A Night of Nights for Canadiens," Montreal *Gazette,* January 2, 1976, p. 19.
59. Montreal Canadiens vs. Central Red Army game, December 31, 1975, CBC Television. Rebroadcast December 31, 1995.
60. Christie Blatchford, "Habs Best Not Enough," *Globe and Mail,* January 1, 1976, p. 1.
61. Burke, "A Night of Nights for Canadiens," p. 19.
62. Alan Eagleson, interview by the author, January 12, 2010.
63. Jim Roberts, interview by the author, January 12, 2010.
64. Red Fisher, interview by the author, September 23, 2009.
65. Scotty Bowman, interview by the author, January 4, 2010.
66. Strachan, "Now That's How You Play Hockey, Comrade!" p. 20.
67. Jacques Beauchamp, "Un match memorable pour les Canadiens," *Journal de Montreal,* January 3, 1976, p. 50.
68. Burke, "A Night of Nights for Canadiens," p. 19.
69. Orr, "Habs Deserved to Win but They Didn't," p. B1.
70. Denis Gibbons, letter to author
71. Tretiak, *The Hockey I Love*, p. 132.
72. Denis Gibbons, letter to author
73. Tretiak, *The Hockey I Love*, p. 134.
74. Ralph Mellanby, interview by the author, December 18, 2009.
75. Ralph Mellanby, interview by the author, December 18, 2009.

CHAPTER 19: PHILADELPHIA

1. Jim Coleman, "The Night Time Stood Still in the Forum," *Ottawa Citizen,* January 2, 1976, p. 19.
2. Frank Orr, "Habs Deserved to Win but They Didn't," *Toronto Star,* January 1, 1976, p. B1.
3. Larry Robinson with Chrys Goyens, *Robinson for the Defence,* p. 180.
4. Frank Orr, "Kharlamov: Soviets' Eddie Shack," *Toronto Star,* January 3, 1976, p. D01.
5. Orr, "Kharlamov: Soviets' Eddie Shack," p. D01.
6. Orr, "Kharlamov: Soviets' Eddie Shack," p. D01.
7. Orr, "Kharlamov: Soviets' Eddie Shack," p. D01.
8. Orr, "Kharlamov: Soviets' Eddie Shack," p. D01.

9. "Christie Blatchford," *Globe and Mail,* January 9, 1976, p. 30
10. *Christie Blatchford,* p. 30.
11. *Christie Blatchford,* p. 30.
12. Vladislav Tretiak, *Tretiak: The Legend,* p. 96.
13. Tretiak, *Tretiak: The Legend,* pp. 97–98.
14. Lawrence Martin, *The Red Machine,* p. 152.
15. Martin, *The Red Machine,* p. 152.
16. Mark Mulvoy, "Hockey's Eclectic Wizard," *Sports Illustrated,* May 26, 1975.
17. Mulvoy, "Hockey's Eclectic Wizard."
18. Alan Eagleson, interview by the author, January 12, 2010.
19. Philadelphia Flyers vs. Central Red Army game, January 11, 1976, CBC Television.
20. Mark Mulvoy, "This Was Détente, Philly Style," *Sports Illustrated,* January 19, 1976.
21. Martin, *The Red Machine,* p. 153.
22. Martin, *The Red Machine,* p. 153.
23. Tretiak, *Tretiak: The Legend,* p. 98.
24. Tretiak, *Tretiak: The Legend,* p. 98.
25. Norm MacLean, "Flyers No. 1 Shero Claims World Championship by Routing Russians," *The Hockey News,* January 23, 1976, p. 3.
26. Tim Burke, "Flyers Salvage Canada's Pride," Montreal *Gazette,* January 12, 1976, p. 1.
27. Dave Anderson, "A Hockey Lesson for Dr. Kissinger; 'I Think I Hit Him, Anyway,'" *New York Times,* January 12, 1976, p. 47.
28. Serge Savard, interview by the author, December 21, 2009.

CHAPTER 20: THE WHITE HATS VS. THE BLACK HATS

1. Serge Savard, interview by the author, December 21, 2009.
2. Ken Dryden, *The Game,* p. 239.
3. Larry Robinson with Chrys Goyens, *Robinson for the Defence,* p. 55.
4. Mark Mulvoy, "The Flyer from Flin Flon," *Sports Illustrated,* October 22, 1973.
5. Steve Shutt, interview by the author, December 18, 2009.
6. Chrys Goyens and Allan Turowetz, *Lions in Winter,* p. 268.
7. Robinson with Goyens, *Robinson for the Defence,* p. 57.
8. Bertrand Raymond, "'God Sure Liked Me That Day' – Claude Ruel," *Le Journal de Montreal,* November 20, 2007.
9. Earl McRae, "It Is Larry Robinson's Fault the Canadiens Are Going for a Second Straight Cup," *Sport Magazine,* February 1977, p. 72.
10. Dryden, *The Game,* pp. 96, 99.
11. J.D. Reed, "But God Blessed the Canadiens," *Sports Illustrated,* May 24, 1976.
12. Reed, "But God Blessed the Canadiens."
13. Dryden, *The Game,* pp. 96–97.
14. Frank Orr, "Can Flyers Risk Rough Stuff?" *Toronto Star,* May 12, 1976, p. C1.
15. Steve Shutt, interview by the author, December 18, 2009.
16. Robinson with Goyens, *Robinson for the Defence,* p. 190.
17. Robinson with Goyens, *Robinson for the Defence,* p. 190.

18. Steve Shutt, interview by the author, December 18, 2009.
19. Frank Orr, "Habs Forming Another Dynasty," *Toronto Star,* May 14, 1976, p. C1.
20. Reed, "But God Blessed the Canadiens."
21. Orr, "Habs Forming Another Dynasty," p. C1.
22. Frank Orr, "Flyers Heap Praise on Canadiens," *Toronto Star,* May 14, 1976, p. C1.
23. Orr, "Habs Forming Another Dynasty," p. C1.
24. Murray Wilson, interview by the author, January 15, 2010.
25. Jay Greenberg, *Full Spectrum: The Complete History of the Philadelphia Flyers Hockey Club,* p. 108.
26. Frank Brown, "Montreal Nips Flyers,"Associated Press, May 17, 1976.
27. Scotty Bowman, interview by the author, January 4, 2010.

AFTERWORD
1. Glenn Cole, "Fans Give Tretiak Ovation in Open Forum Practice," *Globe and Mail,* January 10, 1983, p. S5.
2. David Johnston, "Montreal Love-In Ends Soviet Players' Tour," *Toronto Star,* January 10, 1983, p. A03.
3. Frank Orr, "Tretiak Misses His Family," *Toronto Star,* December 31, 1982, p. D1.
4. "Tretiak Drafted by Habs," *Toronto Star,* June 9, 1983, p. S01.
5. Jon A. Dolezar, "Sweeping Changes: Russian Hockey Looked Different After '72 Summit Series," CNN/Sports Illustrated, September 27, 2002, http://sportsillustrated.cnn.com/hockey/news/2002/09/27/soviet_legacy.
6. Bill Beacon, "Dryden Has No. 29 Jersey Raised to Bell Centre Rafters," *Toronto Star,* January 30, 2007, p. A1.

BIBLIOGRAPHY

BOOKS

Allen, Kevin, and Bob Duff. *Without Fear: Hockey's 50 Greatest Goaltenders*. Triumph Books, 2002.

Béliveau, Jean, with Chrys Goyens and Allan Turowetz. *My Life in Hockey*. McClelland & Stewart, 1994.

Benedict, Michael, and D'Arcy Jenish. *Canada on Ice: 50 Years of Great Hockey*. Penguin Books, 1999.

Bock, Hal. *Save! Hockey's Brave Goalies*. Avon Books, 1974.

Bortstein, Larry. *My Greatest Day in Hockey*. Grosset & Dunlap, 1974.

Bynum, Mike, and Celine Steinmetz, eds. *Montreal Canadiens' 25 Unforgettable Moments in Hockey*. Canada Hockey, 2005.

Campbell, Ken. *Habs Heroes: The Greatest Canadiens Ever from 1 to 100*. Transcontinental Books, 2008.

Cole, Stephen. *The Best of Hockey Night in Canada*. McArthur & Company, 2003.

Coleman, Jim. *Hockey Is Our Game*. Key Porter, 1987.

Devaney, John, and Burt Goldblatt. *The Stanley Cup: A Complete Pictorial History*. Rand McNally, 1975.

Devellano, Jim, and Roger Lajoie. *The Road to Hockeytown: Jimmy Devellano's Forty Years in the NHL*. Wiley, 2008.

Diamond, Dan, and Lew Stubbs. *Hockey: Twenty Years*. Doubleday Canada, 1987.

Diamond, Dan, James Duplacey, Ralph Dinger, Ernie Fitzsimmons, Igor Kuperman, and Eric Zweig, eds. *Total Hockey: The Official Encyclopedia of the National Hockey League*. 2nd edition. Total Sports, 2000.

Diamond, Dan, ed. *Total Stanley Cup: All the Games, All the Records, All the Stats; The Official Encyclopedia of the Stanley Cup*. Total Sports, 2000.

Dryden, Ken. *The Game*. Macmillan Canada, 1983.

Dryden, Ken, and Roy MacGregor. *Home Game: Hockey and Life in Canada*. McClelland & Stewart, 1990.

Dryden, Ken, and Mark Mulvoy. *Face-Off at the Summit*. Little, Brown, 1973.

Dryden, Murray, with Jim Hunt. *Playing the Shots at Both Ends: The Story of Ken and Dave Dryden*. McGraw-Hill Ryerson, 1972.

Dryden, Steve, and *The Hockey News*. *The Top 100 NHL Players of All-Time*. McClelland & Stewart, 1998.

Duplacey, James, and Charles Wilkins. *Forever Rivals*. Random House, 1996.

Eagleson, Alan, with Scott Young. *Power Play: The Memoirs of Hockey Czar Alan Eagleson*. McClelland & Stewart, 1991.

Ellis, Ron, with Kevin Shea. *Over the Boards: The Ron Ellis Story*. Fenn Publishing, 2002.

Ferguson, John, with Stan Fischler and Shirley Fischler. *Thunder and Lightning*. Prentice-Hall Canada, 1989.

Fischler, Stan. *Bobby Clarke and the Ferocious Flyers*. Warner Paperback Library, 1974.

———. *The Conquering Canadiens: Stanley Cup Champions*. Prentice-Hall of Canada, 1971.

———. *The Greatest Players and Moments of the Philadelphia Flyers*. Sports Publishing, 2002.

———. *The Philadelphia Flyers: Supermen of the Ice*. Prentice-Hall of Canada, 1974.

———. *The Rivalry: Canadiens vs. Leafs*. McGraw-Hill Ryerson, 1991.

———. *Speed and Style: The Montreal Canadiens*. Prentice-Hall of Canada, 1975.

Fisher, Red. *Hockey, Heroes, and Me*. McClelland & Stewart, 1994.

Germain, Georges-Hébert. *Overtime: The Legend of Guy Lafleur*. Viking Books, 1990.

Gormley, Chuck. *Orange, Black, and Blue: The Greatest Philadephia Flyers Stories Never Told*. Sports Challenge Network Publishing, 2009.

Goyens, Chrys, and Allan Turowetz. *Lions in Winter*. McGraw-Hill Ryerson, 1994.

Goyens, Chrys, with Allan Turrowetz and Jean-Luc Duguay. *The Montreal Forum: Forever Proud*. Les Editions Effix, 1996.

Greenberg, Jay. *Full Spectrum: The Complete History of the Philadelphia Flyers Hockey Club*. Dan Diamond and Associates, 1996.

Hart, Gene, with Buzz Ringe. *Score: My Twenty-Five Years with the Broad Street Bullies*. Bonus Books, 1990.

Hockey Hall of Fame. *Honoured Canadians*. HB Fenn, 2008.

The Hockey News. *60 Moments That Changed the Game*. Hockey News Collectors Edition, 2007.

Hunt, Jim. *The Men in the Nets*. McGraw-Hill Ryerson, 1972.

Hunter, Douglas. *A Breed Apart: An Illustrated History of Goaltending*. Viking Press, 1995.

———. *Champions: The Illustrated History of Hockey's Greatest Dynasties*. Triumph Books, 1997.

———. *Scotty Bowman: A Life in Hockey*. Viking Books, 1998.

Irvin, Dick. *Behind the Bench: Coaches Talk About Life in the NHL*. McClelland & Stewart, 1993.

———. *The Habs*, McClelland & Stewart, 1991.

———. *My 26 Stanley Cups: Memories of a Hockey Life*. McClelland & Stewart, 2001.

———. *Now Back to You, Dick: Two Lifetimes in Hockey*. McClelland & Stewart, 1989.

Jackson, Jim. *Walking Together Forever: The Broad Street Bullies, Then and Now*. Sports Publishing, 2003.

Jenish, D'Arcy. *The Montreal Canadiens: 100 Years of Glory*. Doubleday Books, 2008.

Kent, Geoffrey W. *Here Come the Vees: An Illustrated History of the Nova Scotia Voyageurs*. Nimbus, 1997.

Kidd, Bruce, and John MacFarlane. *The Death of Hockey*. New Press, 1972.

Kimelman, Adam. *The Good, the Bad, and the Ugly: Heart-Pounding, Jaw-Dropping, and Gut-Wrenching Moments From Philadelphia Flyers History*. Triumph Books, 2008.

Larochelle, Claude. *Guy Lafleur: Hockey's #1*. Lotographie, 1978.

Leonetti, Mike. *Canadiens Legends: Montreal's Hockey Heroes*. Raincoast Books, 2004.

———. *Hockey in the Seventies: The Game We Knew*. Raincoast Books, 1999.

Ludwig, Jack. *Hockey Night in Moscow*. McClelland & Stewart, 1972.

MacInnis, Craig, ed. *Remembering Guy Lafleur*. Raincoast Books, 2004.

MacSkimming, Roy. *Cold War: The Amazing Canada-Soviet Hockey Series of 1972*. Greystone Books, 1996.

Mahovlich, Ted. *The Big M: The Frank Mahovlich Story*. HarperCollins, 1999.

Martin, Lawrence. *The Red Machine: The Soviet Quest to Dominate Canada's Game*. Doubleday Books, 1990.

McDonell, Chris. *The Game I'll Never Forget: 100 Hockey Stars' Stories*. Firefly Books, 2002.

McFarlane, Brian. *The Habs*. Stoddart Publishing, 1996.

———. *Stanley Cup Fever*. Pagurian Press, 1978.

———. *Team Canada 1972: Where Are They Now?* Winding Stair Press, 2001.

McKinley, Michael. *Putting a Roof on Winter*. Greystone Books, 2002.

Mellanby, Ralph, with Mike Brophy. *Walking With Legends*. Fenn Publishing, 2007.

Morrison, Scott. *The Days Canada Stood Still: Canada vs USSR 1972*. McGraw-Hill Ryerson, 1989.

Mouton, Claude. *The Montreal Canadiens: A Hockey Dynasty*. Van Nostrand Reinhold, 1980.

———. *The Montreal Canadiens: An Illustrated History of a Hockey Dynasty*. Key Porter Books, 1988.

O'Brien, Andy. *Les Canadiens*. McGraw-Hill Ryerson, 1971.

Orr, Frank. *Great Goalies of Pro Hockey*. Random House, 1973.

———. *Tough Guys of Pro Hockey*. Random House, 1974.

Parent, Bernie, with Bill Fleischman and Sonny Schwartz. *Bernie! Bernie! Bernie!* Prentice-Hall, 1975.

Pedneault, Yvan. *Les Canadiens: Nos Glorieux Champions*. Les Editions de L'Homme, 1977.

———. *Guy Lafleur*. Les Editions de L'Homme, 1976.

Pincus, Arthur. *The Official Illustrated NHL History*. Triumph Books, 2001.

Podnieks, Andrew. *Canada's Olympic Hockey History, 1920–2010*. HB Fenn, 2009.

Richard, Maurice, and Stan Fischler. *The Flying Frenchmen: Hockey's Greatest Dynasty*. Hawthorn Books, 1971.

Robinson, Larry, with Chrys Goyens. *Robinson for the Defence*. McClelland & Stewart, 1989.

Robinson, Larry, with Brian McFarlane. *Robinson on Defence*. Collier Macmillan Canada, 1980.

Scanlan, Wayne. *Roger's World: The Life and Unusual Times of Roger Neilson*. McClelland & Stewart, 2004.

Schultz, Dave, with Stan Fischler. *The Hammer: Confessions of a Hockey Enforcer.* Collins Publishers, 1981.

Sherman, David, with Howard Jaffe. *The Philadelphia Flyers Encyclopedia.* Sports Publishing, 2003.

Shero, Fred, with Vijay S. Kothare. *Shero: The Man Behind the System.* Chilton/Haynes, 1975.

Sinden, Harry. *Hockey Showdown.* Doubleday Books, 1972.

Sports Illustrated. *The Canadiens Century: One Hundred Years.* Time Inc. Home Entertainment, 2009.

Tarasov, Anatoli. *Road to Olympus.* Griffin House, 1969.

———. *Tarasov: The Father of Russian Hockey.* Griffin Publishing, 1997.

Tretiak, Vladislav. *The Hockey I Love.* Lawrence & Co. 1983.

———. *Tretiak: The Legend.* Penguin Books, 1987.

Ulmer, Michael. *Canadiens Captains.* Macmillan Canada, 1996.

Willes, Ed. *The Rebel League: The Short and Unruly Life of the World Hockey Association.* McClelland & Stewart, 2005.

Young, Scott. *War on Ice: Canada in International Hockey.* McClelland & Stewart, 1976.

ARTICLES

"Beliveau Wants a Shot at the Russians." *Sport Canada,* October 1969.

Bell, Marty. "Sporting Life with Ken Dryden." *Sport Magazine,* April 1974.

Bellows, Keith. "How Great Is This Guy?" *Hockey,* October 1977.

"Between the Lines with . . . Ken Dryden." *Hockey Illustrated,* November 1971.

"Bob Gainey and Doug Jarvis: Check and Double Check!" *Action Sports Hockey,* March 1978.

Bock, Hal. "Hockey's Hottest Debate: Lafleur or Leach – Who's Better?" *Argosy Hockey Yearbook* 1976/77.

———. "How Hockey's Godfather Keeps the Canadiens on Top." *Hockey Sports Stars of 1974.*

———. "Is Lafleur the Greatest Canadien of All Time?" *Hockey Today,* 1978.

Boulton, Rick. "An In-Depth Interview with Goalie Ken Dryden." *Hockey Digest,* June 1976.

Bridgland, Ralph. "Canadiens Again Dominate NHL Amateur Draft." *The Hockey News,* June 1975.

———. "Canadiens Drop 'Mystery' Semi-Final Set." *The Hockey News,* May 23, 1975.

———. "Canadiens 'Kid Line' Stages Festive Reunion." *The Hockey News,* November 21, 1975.

———. "Canadiens' Name Magic at Playoff Time: Montreal's 16 Cup Wins Make Habs No. 1 in History of Post-Season Play." *The Hockey News,* May 2, 1975.

———. "Canadiens to Make Few Lineup Changes." *The Hockey News,* September 1975.

———. "Dryden NHL's Leading Goaler But Habs Fans Not So Sure." *The Hockey News,* December 12, 1975.

———. "Habs Fulfilling All Defensive Expectations." *The Hockey News,* November 7, 1975.

————. "Hard Work Got Canadiens Lambert to the Top." *The Hockey News*, December 5, 1975.

————. "Richard's Retirement Closes Out Hockey Era." *The Hockey News*, August 1975.

————. "Risebrough Wants to Play More Aggressively." *The Hockey News*, October 31, 1975.

————. "The Roadrunner: He Blazes the Way!" *The Hockey News*, November 28, 1975.

————. "Self Satisfaction Most Important to Shutt." *The Hockey News*, November 14, 1975.

————. "Training Camp Augers Well for Canadiens." *The Hockey News*, October 17, 1975.

Campbell, Ken. "Nyet, Vlad, Nyet." *The Hockey News: The Best of Everything in Hockey – Great Debates*, 2003.

"Courage and Fear in a Vortex of Violence." *Time* magazine, February 24, 1975.

"The Cup Runneth Over," *Time* magazine, May 25, 1970.

Dennis, Mike. "Hockey's Anonymous Superstar." *Hockey Pictorial*, October 1979.

————. "Steve Shutt: Success Didn't Exactly Happen Overnight." *Hockey Pictorial-World*, April 1977.

Dryden, Ken. "Greatness Remembered." *Canadiens Magazine*, Vol 22.1, 2007.

Dunn, Bob. "Canadiens' Comet: Flashy Guy Lafleur." *The Sporting News*, February 1, 1975.

————. "Flower Power Hypos Habs." *Hockey Digest*, June 1975.

Dunnell, Milt. "Larry Robinson: Clean, But Tough." *Action Sports Hockey*, February 1979.

————. "Montreal's Deadly Trio: Shutt, Lemaire and Lafleur." *Hockey Digest*, June 1978.

Eberson, Sharon. "Me and Guy!" *Action Sports Hockey*, November 1979.

Fischler, Shirley. "Hey! Hey! The American Way . . . Is Passé." *Action Sports Hockey*, May 1976.

Fischler, Stan. "The Canadiens Can't Win Without Bowman!" *Hockey Scene*, 1979/80 Giant Annual.

————. "Ken Dryden Is Overrated." *Hockey Today*, 1978.

————. "Why Ken Dryden Gets No Respect." *Action Sports Hockey*, February 1979.

Fisher, Geoffrey. "Jim Roberts: He Turns on Blues for the Big Play." *Hockey Pictorial*, November 1968.

Fisher, Red. "Canadiens' Playoff Successes . . ." *Hockey Illustrated*, April/May 1967.

————. "He Rests His Case." *Goal Magazine*, November 1978.

————. "How Good Are They?" *Montreal Canadiens Program*, December 31, 1975.

————. "Jacques Lemaire – Montreal's High Scoring Pacifist." *Ben Strong Series Hockey*, June 1973.

————. "Ken Dryden: Montreal's Scholarly Goalie." *Hockey Digest*, December 1972.

————. "Steve Shutt: A New Scoring Star Emerges For Montreal." *Hockey Digest*, April 1977.

————. "Why the Canadiens Will Win the Stanley Cup." *Ben Strong Series: Hockey*, June 1973.

Greer, Thom. "Les Canadiens: They Win With Class!" *Hockey Digest,* June 1978.

Halpin, Charlie. "The Russians Are Coming and 8 NHL Teams Are Ready for the Big Showdown." *The Hockey News,* December 28, 1975.

Hanson, George. "Is Yvan Cournoyer the Fastest Skater in Hockey History?" *Popular Sports Face-Off,* January 1974.

———. "Jacques Lemaire: The Consummate Canadien." *Hockey Illustrated,* January 1979.

———. "Ken Dryden: An Ivy Leaguer Makes It." *Hockey Yearbook Face-Off,* 1972.

"How Long Will Ken Dryden Stay in Hockey?" *Sports Review Series Hockey,* March 1972.

Hunt, Jim. "Sam Pollock: New Boss of the Canadiens." *Canadian Weekly,* October 31, 1964.

Johnston, Dick. "Dryden Brothers Stuck Together." *Hockey Pictorial,* November 1971.

Kennedy, Ray. "Dr. Jekyll and Mr. Clarke." *Sports Illustrated,* February 23, 1976.

———. "Wanted: An End to Mayhem," *Sports Illustrated,* November 17, 1975.

Kirshenbaum, Jerry. "On the Whole It's the Donut Line." *Sports Illustrated,* February 7, 1977.

———. "Would You Buy a Used Hockey Player from This Man." *Sports Illustrated,* April 18, 1977.

Lanken, Dane. "Le Phenomene." *The Canadian Magazine,* September 11, 1971.

Levinton, Jory. "Robinson Rates Respect." *Action Sports Hockey,* March 1978.

Lewis, Robert. "Outside the Net, Looking In." *Canadian Magazine,* April 13, 1974.

Litsky, Frank. "The Story Behind the Champion: Canadiens Do It by Firelight." *Inside Hockey* 1971/72.

Little, Lyndon. "Ken Dryden's Dilemma! What to Do for an Encore." *Hockey World,* October 1971.

Ludwig, Jack. "Ken Dryden, Hockey's Lonely Forerunner." *Maclean's,* February 1973.

MacGregor, Roy. "A Flower for All Seasons." *Maclean's,* October 16, 1978.

MacLean, Norman. "Close-Up Yvan Cournoyer." *Inside Hockey* 1973/74.

———. "Flyers No. 1 Shero Claims World Championship By Routing Russians," *The Hockey News,* January 23, 1976

———. "Shero, Esposito Feel One-Game Test Not Meaningful Against Disciplined Russians." *The Hockey News,* January 2, 1976.

———. "Will the NHL Turn to Europe and the Colleges for Talent?" *Hockey Pictorial,* April–March 1965.

———. "World Hockey Confrontation, Russia vs. NHL: Who Would Win?" *Hockey World,* April–May 1969.

Martin, Lawrence. "Hockey's Red Dawn." *The Beaver,* December 2009 – January 2010.

Martin, Ralph. "Guy Lafleur: Only One of Montreal's Weapons." *Hockey Illustrated,* May 1977.

McCarthy, Gary. "Cournoyer Turns Into Rocket in His Own Way." *The Sporting News,* April 3, 1971.

McRae, Earl. "It Is Larry Robinson's Fault the Canadiens are Going for a Second Straight Cup." *Sport Magazine,* February 1977.

Merron, Jeff. "Russians Regroup on the Other Side of the Red Line." ESPN.com, February 14, 2002.

Miller, Robert. "Newsy to Rocket to Guy." *Maclean's,* April 5, 1976.

Monahan, Leo. "Larry Robinson: Body Language." *Hockey Illustrated,* March 1977.

———. "NHL Scoring Whiz: Jacques Lemaire." *The Sporting News,* December 23, 1972.

———. "No One Will Beat Philly." *Hockey Illustrated,* May 1976.

Monahan, Leo, and Frank Orr. "Russia and the Stanley Cup." *Hockey Illustrated,* February 1976.

"Monsieur Roadrunner." *Hockey Guide 1974,* January 1974.

"Montreal, Philadelphia Again Teams to Beat." *The Hockey News,* October 24, 1975.

"The Montreal Mystique – Can It Hold the Torch High?" *Sports Special Hockey,* December 1971.

Moriarty, Tim. "The Canadiens Present 'Superfleur.'" *Hockey Illustrated Special,* 1976/77.

Mulvoy, Mark. "All Ablaze at Center." *Sports Illustrated,* February 26, 1973.

———. "Boris and His Boys Prepare For A Few Friendlies." *Sports Illustrated,* January 5, 1976.

———. "Brief Reign of the Lordly Bruins." *Sports Illustrated,* April 26, 1971.

———. "Bruisers and Bunny Hoppers." *Sports Illustrated,* December 23, 1974.

———. "A Bunch With Character." *Sports Illustrated,* June 9, 1975.

———. "A Dynasty Imperiled." *Sports Illustrated,* March 25, 1974.

———. "The Flyer from Flin Flon." *Sports Illustrated,* October 22, 1973.

———. "Flying Blades, Rising Ire." *Sports Illustrated,* April 30, 1973.

———. "Here Come the Big, Bad Bruins." *Sports Illustrated,* April 5, 1971.

———. "Hockey is Courting Disaster." *Sports Illustrated,* January 27, 1972.

———. "Hockey's Eclectic Wizard." *Sports Illustrated,* May 26, 1975.

———. "It's Dryden for the Defense." *Sports Illustrated,* February 14, 1972.

———. "It's Sockey, The Way They Play It Here," *Sports Illustrated,* May 6, 1974.

———. "Jubilation and a Cup in Philly." *Sports Illustrated,* May 27, 1974.

———. "Ken Dryden on Trial." *Sports Illustrated,* November 25, 1974.

———. "A Lot More Where They Came From." *Sports Illustrated,* April 2, 1973.

———. "Mr. Band-Aid Pops Up Again for Montreal." *Sports Illustrated,* October 30, 1972.

———. "An Old Custom at Customs, *Sports Illustrated,* May 31, 1971.

———. "Putting Some Cuffs on the Fists." *Sports Illustrated,* June 3, 1974.

———. "That Was Détente, Philly Style." *Sports Illustrated,* January 19, 1976.

———. "This Is Orr Country – Orr Is It?" *Sports Illustrated,* April 19, 1971.

———. "To Pick a Golden Flower." *Sports Illustrated,* March 1, 1971.

———. "Up Jumps a Sharpshooter." *Sports Illustrated,* January 8, 1973.

———. "Victory – and Reckoning." *Sports Illustrated,* May 21 1973.

Murray, Tom. "Main Man in Montreal: Guy Lafleur." *Sport Magazine,* November 1975.

"The Nagging Problems of Two Superstars." *Action Sports Hockey,* April 1975.

Namm, Steve. "Montreal's Serge Savard on Politics and Punishment." *Action Sports Hockey,* November 1977.

O'Brien, Andy. "The Team That Sam Built." *Weekend Magazine*, February 2, 1974.

Olan, Ben. "Guy Lafleur: Canadiens' Marked Man." *Argosy Hockey Yearbook*, 1978/79.

———. "Will Yvan Lead the Canadiens Back?" *Hockey Illustrated*, March 1971.

———. "Yvan Cournoyer: The Canadiens' Big Gun." *Hockey Illustrated*, January 1974.

Olsen, Jack. "Banned in Boston, Knighted in Montreal." *Sports Illustrated*, October 18, 1971.

Orr, Frank. "Bring the Cup Home." *Hockey Illustrated*, May 1976.

———. "Guy Lafleur: What It's Like Being the Very Best." *Action Sports Hockey*, March 1978.

Page, Jim. "Ken Dryden: Montreal's Net Worth." *Hockey Illustrated*, April 1976.

———. "Ken Dryden: Tried and Acquitted." *Hockey Illustrated*, February 1975.

Pennington, Bob. "Column of the Month – Ken Dryden." *Action Sports Hockey* 1971/72.

Philpott, Doug. "NHL's Newest Brother Act Stirs Some Ripples." *Hockey Pictorial*, May 1971.

Posner, Michael. "The Russians Are Coming and the Capitalists Can Hardly Wait." *Maclean's*, December 15, 1975.

Proudfoot, Jim. "Pete M May Be the Bigger M." *Hockey World*, January 1967.

Recht, Mike. "An In-Depth Study of Ken Dryden." *Inside Hockey* 1971/72.

Reed, J.D. "But God Blessed the Canadiens." *Sports Illustrated*, May 24, 1976.

———. "The Canadiens Say It with Flowers." *Sports Illustrated*, March 22, 1976.

Richman, Alan. "Ken Dryden: Age Is Relative." *Hockey Digest*, January 1977.

Rodriguez, Juan. "The Pete and Frank (Mahovlich) Show." *Action Sports Hockey*, April 1972.

———. "The Story behind Hockey's Biggest Upset." *Action Sports Hockey*, 1971/72 Yearbook.

Ronberg, Gary. "Philly Takes a Flyer on a Rookie With Heart." *Sports Illustrated*, November 17, 1969.

Rosenberg, Al. "French Hero Yvan Cournoyer – Little Man, Big Deeds." *Sports Special Hockey*, December 1973.

Rubenstein, Jules. "Ken Dryden – Intelligence in the Net." *Sports Extra Hockey*, February 1973.

Ruskie, Mark. "Montreal's Pete Mahovlich: Canadiens' Kid Brother." Hockey *Yearbook Face-Off*, 1972.

Scott, Margaret. "Serge Savard – Back on Track." *Hockey World*, March 1973.

Seitz, Nick. "If Ken Dryden's So Smart, How Come He's a Goalie?" *Sport Magazine*, March 1973.

"Shirley Fischler Votes for Ken Dryden." *Action Sports Hockey*, March 1977.

Smith, Gil. "Canada, Russia Series: Habs' Dryden Determined to Make It a Learning Experience." *Hockey World*, November 1972.

———. "Cournoyer! Montreal's Performance Has Been Off But You Can't Blame Yvan the Triggerman." *Hockey World*, March–April 1967.

———. "One Year, Cournoyer Could Break Through." *Hockey Pictorial*, February 1970.

———. "Will Lemaire Top 50 Goals?" *Hockey World*, February 1973.

"Sport: The Wild Bunch." *Time* magazine, May 20, 1974.

Strachan, Al. "Montreal Canadiens: Ken Dryden Sees Les Habitants' Teamwork the Key to Three Straight Cups." *Hockey Illustrated,* May 1978.

———. "Pierre Bouchard: Montreal's Most Reliable Defenseman." *Hockey Digest,* March 1976.

Telander, Rick. "'da Stadium.'" *Sports Illustrated,* June 1, 1992.

Tretiak, Vladislav. "Cowards Do Not Play Hockey." *Hockey,* October 1977.

Tuite, James. "Behind the Montreal Mystique." *Inside Hockey,* 1973/74.

Wilner, Barry. "Ken Dryden: The Puck Stops Here." *Hockey Illustrated,* February 1978.

———. "Larry Robinson: A Budding Star for Les Canadiens." *Hockey Digest,* June 1975.

"Yvan Cournoyer: Speed King of NHL Skaters." *Hockey World,* January 1973.

Zelkovich, Chris. "It Was Not A Very Good Year." *Hockey Pictorial,* May 1974.

———. "It's Fun Again." *Hockey Pictorial,* May 1975.

———. "Playing Like A Dream." *Hockey World,* February 1975.

Zurkowsky, Herb. "Hockey's Cannonading Voice." *The Hockey News: The Best of Everything in Hockey – Great Debates,* 2003.

INDEX

111, 140, 141, 209; hockey career, 83; on Soviet play in Super Series, 205

Smith, Kate, 279, 283

Smythe, Conn, 8

Smythe, Stafford, 78

Snider, Ed, 132-33, 269, 283

Solodukhin, Vyacheslav, 244

Soviet Air Force team, 12, 13

Soviet Elite League: 1969 final, 71-73; 1973 final, 179; 1974 final, 180; Kharlamov as top scorer, 102; Red Army dominance, 179-80, 207; top two coaches, 39, 76; Tretiak as top goaltender, 77; Western press pass issued, 72

Soviet National Team: 1954 World Championship gold, 6-8, 19, 38, 39; 1955 World Championship loss, 9-10; 1956 Olympic gold, 16, 19, 38, 39; 1963–1971 golds, 42; 1963 World Championship gold, 38-40, 42; 1969 games against Canada, 36-38, 49; 1969 Isvestia gold, 48, 74; 1970 World Championship gold, 76, 77; 1971 World Championship gold, 76, 78; 1972 Izvestia gold, 174; 1972 Olympic gold, 78-79, 102; 1972 Summit Series, preparation, 91-92; 1972 Summit Series, primary game, 93-103; 1972 Summit Series, rest of series, 104-16; 1973 Izvestia gold, 174; 1973 World Championship gold, 175; 1974 Summit Series, 174-77; 1974 World Championship gold, 175, 180; 1975 Izvestia gold, 202; 1981 Canada Cup win, 288; challenges Canadian teams, 78; competes against NHL All-Stars, 288; Tarasov's coaching, 15

Soviet Red Army see Central Red Army

Soviet Selects, 16-19

Soviet Union: closed to West, 72; Cold War development of hockey, 11-15, 18-20; Cold War rivalry with West, 6, 8, 11, 256; Cold War thaw, 80; cultural excellence, 11; dissolution, 290; emergence as superpower, 11; first hosting of World Championship, 19; hockey excellence, 38, 96, 100, 103, 175, 218-19; hockey popularity, 40, 71-74, 101; hockey style, 13-18, 175, 180, 258; hockey training techniques, 43-44, 75-76; invites Canadian coaches to Moscow symposium, 173

Soviet Wings: dominance in Soviet Union, 179; Super Series, announced, 171; Super Series, game against Black Hawks, 267; Super Series, game against Islanders, 267; Super Series, game against Penguins, 209; Super Series, game against Sabres, 267; Super Series, planning, 180-81; Super Series, Wings arrival in Canada, 202

Stalin, Joseph, 12, 13

Stalin, Vasily, 12, 13

Stanfield, Fred, 52

Stanley Cup: 1968 and 1969 Canadiens' wins, 28, 29, 35, 52; 1970 Bruins' win, 52; 1971 Canadiens' win, 62-69; 1973 Canadiens' win, 117, 123-24; 1974 and 1975 Flyers' wins, 145, 160; 1976 Canadiens' win, 285; Canadiens' success in, 51, 76, 122; St. Louis Blues' success in, 67; Tarasov's studies of, 13

Stapleton, Pat, 106, 174, 176

Starovoitov, Andrei, 79

Stemkowski, Pete, 205

Stephenson, Wayne, 48, 276, 277, 280-81, 283

St. Louis Blues: 1968 playoffs, 29, 133; 1969 playoffs, 133; 1971–1972 season, 85; 1973 draft, 187; acquire Roberts, 185; aggressive style, 144; hire Bowman, 67

St. Michael's Majors, 41

Storey, Red, 94

Stoughton, Blaine, 188

St. Paul Saints, 139

Summit Series (1972): planning and roster, 80-81, 82-92, 140-41; primary game, 93-103, 208-9; rest of series, 104-15, 141-42; triumph of final game, 115-16, 172

Summit Series (1974): games, 176-77; Ley's violence, and consequences, 177-78; planning and roster, 174

Super Series (1975–1976) (see also specific teams): announced, 171; negotiated, 180-81; Red Army–Bruins game, 264, 265-66; Red Army–Canadiens game see Super Series (1975–1976), NYE game; Red Army–Flyers game, 267-71; Red Army–Rangers game, 203-6; Soviet Wings–Black Hawks game, 267; Soviet Wings–Islanders game, 267; Soviet Wings–Penguins game, 209; Soviet Wings–Sabres game, 267

United States: Cold War, 6, 80; hockey excellence, 19, 38

Vachon, Rogatien: 1969–1970 season, 51, 84; 1971 playoffs, 62, 63, 65; protected in 1967 expansion draft, 28
Vadnais, Carol, 28, 204-5
Van Boxmeer, John, 241, 244, 248-49, 251
Vancouver Canucks, 160, 187
Van Impe, Ed, 139, 270
Vasiliev, Valeri: 1972 Summit Series, 114-15; NYE game, first period, 233-34, 236-37, 239; NYE game, introductions, 230; NYE game, second period, 243; NYE game, third period, 248, 252; Orr seeks and gets interview with, 264-65
Ververgaert, Dennis, 187
Vickers, Steve, 204
Vulcan Industrial Packaging Team, 145-48

Warwick, Bill, 9
Warwick, Dick, 9
Warwick, Grant, 9
Washington Capitals, 208
Watson, Jim, 139
Watson, Joe, 139, 276-77
WHA see World Hockey Association (WHA)
Whitby Dunlops, 17, 18, 19, 83
Wilson, Murray: 1972–1973 season and playoffs, 121; 1976 Stanley Cup finals, 281-82; hockey career, 118-21; mentored by Ruel, 122; NYE game, anticipation and preparation, 209, 227; NYE game, first period, 233-35; NYE game, second

period, 243, 246-47; NYE game, third period, 249, 250; with Voyageurs, 194
Winnipeg Falcons, 5
Winnipeg Jets, 90, 126, 168-69
Winter Olympic Games: 1920 Canadian gold, 5; 1956 Soviet gold, 16, 19, 38, 39; 1960 American gold, 19; 1964 Canadian loss, 42; 1968 Canadian bronze, 42; 1972 Soviet gold, 78-79, 102; hockey's importance in, 11
World Championships: 1920 Canadian gold, 5; 1930, becomes annual event, 5; 1947 and 1949 Czechoslovakian golds, 45; 1954 Soviet gold, 5-8, 19, 38, 39; 1955 Canadian gold, 9-10; 1957 Swedish gold, 19; 1958 and 1959 Canadian gold, 19, 83; 1960 American gold, 19; 1961 Canadian gold, 19, 38, 45; 1962 Swedish gold, 38, 41; 1963 Canada–Soviet game, 38-40; 1963–1971 Soviet golds, 38-40, 42, 76, 77, 78; 1966 and 1967 Canadian bronzes, 42; 1970 withdrawal of Canada, 49-50; 1973 and 1974 Soviet golds, 175, 180; Canada's early dominance, 5; Canadian tradition of sending Allan Cup winner, 41
World Hockey Association (WHA): and 1974 Summit Series, 174, 176, 177-78; created, 90, 161; dissolved, 287; and hockey violence, 165; instability, 156; player salaries, 125-26; rivalry with NHL, 125-26, 150, 191
Worsley, Gump, 26

Young, Scott, 69